D1571359

READINGS IN AMERICAN INDIAN LAW

RECALLING THE RHYTHM OF SURVIVAL

READINGS IN
AMERICAN INDIAN LAW

RECALLING THE RHYTHM OF SURVIVAL

EDITED BY

JO CARRILLO

TEMPLE UNIVERSITY PRESS PHILADELPHIA

Temple University Press, Philadelphia 19122

Copyright © 1998 by Temple University.

Published 1998

Printed in the United States of America

Interior design by Richard E. Rosenbaum

∞ The paper used in this publication meets the requirements
   of American National Standard for Information Sciences—
Permanence of Paper for Printed Library Materials, ANSI Z39.48–1984.

Library of Congress Cataloging-in-Publication Data

Readings in American Indian law : recalling the rhythm of survival /
   edited by Jo Carrillo.
      p.   cm.
      ISBN 1-56639-581-X (cl: alk. paper) / ISBN 1-56639-582-8 (pb: alk. paper)
      Includes bibliographical references and index.
      1. Indians of North America—Legal status, laws, etc.
   I. Carrillo, Juanita Jo, 1959– .
   KF8204.5.R424 1998
   342.73'0872—dc21   97-23754

For my family by birth, marriage, and friendship, but especially for my son Max, who was born into many traditions and hearts.

> it is possible for dreams
> to occur, the prayers full of the mystery
> of children, laughter, the dances,
> my own humanity, so it can last unto forever.
>
> This is what I want to teach my son.
>
> —Simon J. Ortiz
> *Juanita, Wife of Manuelito*

> While knowing what you hold most dear
> must eventually surrender to its own direction.
>
> —Ferron

CONTENTS

PREFACE AND ACKNOWLEDGMENTS

In some ways, this project began long ago when I met the grandson of a well-known, late-nineteenth century photographer who was one of the first photographers to travel through the southwestern United States. The photographer's grandson gave me a blanket woven in the Rio Grande weaver's style, circa 1910. His grandfather had collected the blanket on his travels through the place that I call home, and now he, the grandson, meant to return it—repatriate it, so to speak—even if it was a couple of generations late. I was the honored beneficiary of the collector's grandson's well-developed and kind sense of conscience.

The collector's grandson and I became fast, inseparable friends. We interacted in the present, but we were also knotted together in the past somewhere, somehow through the crossing of our ancestral paths, as represented by the blanket. We talked much about how the collector-photographer was known—the known point had a name—whereas my ancestral point was treated as unknown, unnamed, just a blanket woven by some anonymous person, a blanket whose value came from having been collected by a prominent white man.

I teach American Indian Law, and I teach it in San Francisco, California. The casebooks for American Indian Law, or Federal Indian Law as it is also called, assume the named position, leaving me, as a teacher, to communicate the unspoken, unnamed, excluded aspects of the field. To meet this daunting responsibility, I have supplemented the casebook with readings meant to inspire conversation, not doctrinal recitation. Over the years, that supplement took shape and form and became this book. I regard this book primarily as a teaching tool, both for my classes, but also (perhaps someday) for my young son. I grew up listening to my grandmothers and my mother and aunts tell stories, local histories really—

lots of them, all the time. My son was born into a different context, and so I am attempting to make do.

The subtitle, *Recalling the Rhythm of Survival*, is inspired by Sherman Alexie, who says in his story about death: "It happens this way: the body forgets the rhythm of survival." The academic trend today is to write histories about the middle ground. This marks a welcome recognition that imperial and colonial histories are problematic because they are only half-histories whose primary goal (whether conscious or not) is to erase indigenous presence in the Americas. It also marks historians' efforts to move away from "victim histories" or "cultural persistence" histories on the theory that those too are overly simplistic.

I like Alexie's phrase because it cuts across many theoretical lines. *It happens like this*—death certainly occurred here, in North America; in some places it rose to the level of genocide. Trying to understand what happened is not the same as indulging in the genres of indigenous-less colonial history or, alternatively, the game of "victim history." *The body forgets*—we embody (physicalize) much of our culture and ways of governing, hence recalling, remembering, feeling, and regenerating are all parts of the pattern of responding to and improving the conditions at hand. *The rhythm of survival*—personal, cultural, linguistic, spiritual, historical, environmental, narrative rhythms for and about survival exist as discourses. This book is very much in the movement and space-in-between tradition. At its broadest, it is about how Native Americans respond to postcolonial legal threats made by the surrounding U.S. society.

Recalling—

> there are waters hidden from us,
> in the maze we find them still
> We'll take you to them
> You take your young ones
> May they take their own in turn*

I am deeply grateful to the contributors, without whom there would be no book. The following contributors were especially kind and helpful: Vine Deloria, Jr., Robert A. Williams, Jr., Dr. Rennard Strickland, Jim Anaya, Gloria Valencia-Weber, Christine P. Zuni, Rayna Green, E. Richard Hart, Nell Jessup Newton, Francis G. Hutchins, William Kittredge, Jack F. Trope, Walter Echo-Hawk, Kenn Harper, Wilcomb E. Washburn (who passed away as this book was in process), Wendy Espeland, Robert E. Bieder, Nancy Oestreich Lurie, Melanie McCoy, Charlotte Black Elk, Hank Meshorer, Jo Ann Woodsum, Silvester J. Brito, Dorothea Theodoratus, Catharine MacKinnon, and Rowena Pattee Kryder, the artist whose work appears on the cover. All gave generously of their time, their work, and their expertise. Jo Ann Woodsum deftly compiled an updated bibliographic essay on very short notice. Professor Eric Yamamoto was especially supportive throughout the process, as was Doris Braendel, Senior Acquisitions Editor at Temple University Press, and Professor Kelly D. Weisberg.

I would also like to thank Carl Stewart, Mrs. Omer Stewart, Jon Christenson, Steve Quesenberry of the California Indian Legal Services; Professor John Borrows

* Ferron, "Testimony," Nemesis Publishing, 1977.

of the University of Vancouver, British Columbia; Tom Jameson, Federal Public Defender, 10th Circuit; Leroy Morgan, beloved friend; Chrystos, the poet; Professor Brian Gray and his committee; John Berlinsky; and Keith Wingate.

Deans Mary Kay Kane and Leo Martinez generously supported this research with faculty development grants, as did the Hastings 1066 Foundation, whose award lent welcome financial support in the last year of this project. Thanks as well to Katherine Franke and the University of Arizona School of Law's Feminist and Critical Race Theory Workshop, which allowed me an opportunity to present Chapter 5 formally, in draft form.

The librarians at Hastings College of the Law were helpful in countless ways. Professor Jenni Parrish and her staff, particularly Charles (Chuck) Marcus and Linda Weir, made impossible tasks possible. Hastings Faculty Support, and especially, Stephen Lothrop, helped with scanning, typing, and other important, time-consuming tasks.

Thanks to my American Indian Law classes of 1995–1996 and 1996–1997. A special thanks to the American Indian Law class of Spring 1997, which I would like to thank by name, though in no particular order: Lynn Keslar; Scott Heard; Yvonne Cudney; Jenny Clark; Richard Du Blois; Tariq Khero; Jason Hammon; Jamie Tenero; Sue Churbeka; Heidi Hudson; Laura Dawson; and Jessica Stavnezer, who also served as research assistant. Heidi Gewertz was part of our class circle in spirit, at least as far as I was concerned. David Vershure first introduced me to the Kennewick Man controversy. Thanks also to Jeff Cluett, Katherine Davis, and Dana Young for their help.

Finally, I would like to thank my family, especially my parents and Laurence Ostrow, whose patience and good heart show in everything they do.

Jo Carrillo
San Francisco

INTRODUCTION

This book is about the legal issues that concern Native Americans, as seen from a broad, interdisciplinary perspective. It goes beyond doctrine—the usual concern of judges and lawyers—to focus on the cultural, historical, and social reasons why indigenous and settler groups are so often in conflict.

Many articles in the field of federal Indian law analyze doctrine, or rules; few, however, discuss how the rules affect Native American people. Indeed, many scholars and lawyers write about federal Indian law without ever having visited a tribal community. The premise of this book is that, while knowing the doctrine is important to understanding the field, it is not enough. Local and regional context is also important because *place* matters. From place one gets a better idea of the legal issues that tribal people face on a daily basis. While these issues are often far different for rural and urban tribal people, these groups share the status of comprising part of the growing number of persistently poor people in America.

Legal scholars could address place by incorporating more of a Native American perspective into doctrinal scholarship. There is disagreement, however, on the value of this effort. Some scholars consistently overlook or ignore the issue of place and perspective in their work, even though they may agree about its importance otherwise. Others, especially those who regard judges as their audience, see no clear benefit to incorporating Native American experience or narrative into their work. Instead, they point to the main risk of allowing this *subjective* evidence into the dis-

Throughout the book, numbered notes in the text refer to end-of-chapter notes, which appeared in the original texts; text marked with asterisks, daggers, or double daggers refer to the editor's footnotes at the bottom of the page where the symbols appear.

puting process: namely, the risk of undermining the consistency of the rules themselves. If judges are not interested in subjective information, or alternatively if judges treat Native American experience as largely irrelevant to the disputing process, they argue, then why should legal scholars concern themselves with such information? From this perspective, federal Indian law becomes a conceptual system, self-contained and only vaguely related to actual historical time, community, or geography. The field gets saturated by abstract discussions of doctrinal topics that minimize the steady resistance of Native Americans to U.S. land policy. This doctrine-bound approach presupposes that legal rules are a more powerful force than actual experience when it comes to shaping Native American identity, action, and consciousness.

In a sense, scholarship that does not or will not consider the Native American experience is a gateway to a realm where indigenous interests are sympathized with but not taken seriously in their own right, and indigenous actors are pitied for representing a "dying" way of life, but not listened to as people who may have solutions to contemporary problems. Scholarship from this quarter rarely recognizes or acknowledges what is innovative about Native American approaches to the law. If anything, it obscures the issue.

Yet much of what keeps indigenous communities alive stems from stamina and innovation, some of which, at least historically, was forced by lack of money and opportunity. If, as the old saying goes, necessity is the mother of invention, then Native Americans have led the way, for at least two centuries, in innovating conservationist, community-centered responses to a national land policy. Doctrinal work that overlooks Native American experience tends also to overlook the innovative quality and the spirit of the Native American contribution to American law.

In rural communities, the poverty Native Americans face can be crushing. Sherman Alexie's stories and novels, one of which is included in Chapter 2, and Mary Brave Bird's autobiographies, cited in Chapter 5, convey what it means to be excluded from even the most basic opportunities in one's own country. The urban Native American experience, for its part, has not been fully described, much less understood; hence, it cannot be represented in this format. Nevertheless, as more Native Americans enter the legal profession, as they are doing, then legal scholarship cannot help but be influenced by what Patricia Nelson Limerick calls work that takes where one comes from seriously.[1]

Existing Native American scholars already understand that what shapes Native American consciousness is the land. They are willing to explore the complexities of communities under colonialism, specifically how stamina and intelligence intertwine with the despair and hopelessness that undergird poverty. They value personal narrative, understanding that just because they are educated in a formal sense does not mean that they are the only ones in their community with something to say. This means, by corollary, that Native American lawyers are more likely than their nonnative counterparts to seek out tribal historians and leaders, and to qualify them as experts. Native American scholars and lawyers alike show a preference for revisionist work, understanding that it can reveal new sources of evidence. Like new Western historians generally, they focus on symbolic sites, as well as on empirical or practical sites, coupling questions of symbolic meaning with those of actual meaning.

This book contextualizes some of the most symbolically important, if not contested, areas of federal Indian law, raising selected topics in a way that makes them accessible to people who have little or no prior knowledge of the field. Many topics and issues are not explicitly covered because of a lack of space: hunting and fishing rights, jurisdiction, gaming, to name just a few. These topics are just as important as the topics included here; it is hoped that this book will encourage someone to present them in a similar format. Similarly, issues pertaining specifically to Alaskan Native and Native Hawaiian communities are not covered in this volume, primarily for space reasons. These areas are critically important to the field of Indian law because detailed postcolonial historical accounts and legal challenges are emerging from them. As small consolation, I cite several sources throughout the book that may lead one in the direction of more specialized treatments and bibliographies than I can give here.

The book's organizing focus goes beyond the usual doctrine-driven discussions to include history, anthropology, ethnohistory, biography, sociology, socio-legal studies, feminist studies, and fiction, on the theory that doctrine too often clouds what is really at stake. As a whole, excerpts in this book give a new look at a very old field: Each has explanatory power; each reveals either some aspect of Indian law or some underlying aspect of how Indian law is made, understood, and implemented. All excerpts are taken from an extensively footnoted original text. I urge those of you with a deeper interest in the area to read those original texts, both as source material and bibliography.

As a word of caution, the bibliographical sources I provide here are designed to introduce students to the field. Some of the best sources for this purpose are not necessarily the most recent sources. I make no claims to offer the most up-to-date bibliography in the field, nor do I offer a critical bibliography. If a source within my field of focus was not accessible to a general audience, I tended to omit it rather than to cite it with a critical annotation. Law review articles were the one exception to this practice. Law review articles as a genre are long, dense, and heavily footnoted; there are literally thousands of articles on federal Indian law, and several journals devote themselves exclusively to the subject. So though I can make no promises about the accessibility of the law review articles I chose to cite, I can say that they were selected with both content and style (accessibility) in mind.

Of general importance are works written by leading Native American intellectuals such as Vine Deloria Jr., Dr. Rennard Strickland, Robert A. Williams Jr., John Borrows, and Rayna Green. These writers have extensive, innovative bodies of work. Gloria Valencia-Weber, Christine Zuni, and S. James Anaya, to name just a few, have also made invaluable contributions to the field, and serious students of federal Indian law should follow their work as it appears. Robert Allen Warrior's books, *Tribal Secrets: Recovering American Indian Intellectual Traditions* (1994) and *Like a Hurricane: The Indian Movement from Alcatraz to Wounded Knee* (1996), which he coauthored with Paul Chaat Smith, are well worth reading. These American Indian scholars bring a perspective to federal Indian law that is shifting it away from its focus on doctrine, and its rule-bound reluctance (almost fear) to take seriously the Native American side of the story, to a new focus on Native American peoples, concerns, ideas, intellectual traditions, criticism, perspectives, hopes, contexts, and strategies for building community and bringing about change.

One trait that links these writers is that they understand, to paraphrase Vine Deloria, that leaving the Indians out of Indian law is a serious flaw in a system of justice, especially one that supposedly exists to recognize indigenous rights and help administer tribal property. Another shared trait is that these writers start from the premise that scholars who think Native American experience ought to shape itself to doctrine and bureaucratic decision making are wrong; it ought to be the other way around.

Although this book is not about doctrine, it refers to many doctrinal areas. There are several useful treatises and casebooks on doctrine, including the *F. Cohen, Handbook of Federal Indian Law* (1982 ed.)—a guide to U.S. legal doctrine and statutory law related to areas such as land title, jurisdictional issues (federal, tribal, and state), hunting and fishing rights, tribal governmental powers, and other legal questions that come up in federal Indian law. *American Indian Law In a Nutshell* (1981), by William C. Canby, Jr., a judge on the U.S. Ninth Circuit Court of Appeals, is an accessible West Nutshell series book well worth consulting. Two casebooks exist in the area: the widely adopted Wilkinson, Getches, and Williams, *Federal Indian Law* (3d ed., 1993), and Clinton, Newton, and Price, *American Indian Law* (3d ed.) (1991). In addition, *Indigenous Peoples in International Law* (1996), by S. James Anaya, provides an important starting point for placing federal Indian law within the broader context of international law.

As a final general note, there are a few classic texts about the legal relationship between Native Americans and the United States. *The American Indian in Western Legal Thought: Discourses of Conquest* (1990), by Robert A. Williams Jr., covers the entire period of conquest, paying particular attention to what Williams calls the "West's will to empire." Also on this topic is David E. Stannard's, *American Holocaust: The Conquest of the New World* (1992). *American Indians, Time, and the Law* (1987), by Charles F. Wilkinson, is about federal Indian law doctrine and the various historical forces that have shaped or scattered it over time. The more compelling *American Indians, American Justice* (1983), by Vine Deloria Jr. and Clifford M. Lytle, covers the same topic. *God Is Red: A Native View of Religion* (2d ed., 1992), by Vine Deloria Jr., takes up the challenge of explaining tribal senses of spirituality to nontribal readers; there is no better, more direct, more insightful book on this topic. The same is true of *Custer Died for Your Sins: An Indian Manifesto* (1988), also by Deloria. These works, especially if read together, are a good starting point for understanding contemporary conflicts between indigenous and nonindigenous settler groups in the United States.

This reader covers six important and far-reaching topics. The first is identity: Who is and who is not a Native American for federal law purposes? The second is reparations: How did the United States try to compensate the indigenous people of this country for the harms of conquest, and how successful was the attempt? The third is incommensurability, or the question of whether there are some points on which tribal interests and the broader U.S. interests may never easily converge. The fourth is cultural property: How was cultural property lost by Native Americans during the conquest, and how can that property be returned? The fifth chapter is about gender and its relationship to tribal governance. Finally, the sixth chapter discusses litigation strategies in religious freedom cases.

The book opens with excerpts about cultural identity, a hotly contested topic in which point of view is everything. In most instances, the colonization of Native American communities by local and state settler populations was brutal. Native Americans were repeatedly pushed aside to make way for nonnative development and expansion; both state and federal law facilitated this displacement, as did federal military might. In the eyes of the law, Native Americans were noncitizens who could be disregarded by those who made and administrated the rules. Indeed, Native Americans were not granted U.S. citizenship by status of birth until the Indian Citizenship Act of 1924, making them the last American-born ethnic/racial group to be formally incorporated into the body politic.[2]

Because of the utter disregard that U.S. custom and law often had for Native American persons and communities, it is no surprise that tribal groups in disputed areas were collectively and individually discreet about their tribal heritage; or, in some cases even ashamed of it. Things are changing. Some groups and individuals are reclaiming a tribal identity, and that effort is often controversial. This is especially true where emerging tribal groups are biologically multiracial, or religiously and educationally multicultural.

Chapter 1 analyzes tribal reclamation. It looks at a case involving the Mashpee Wampanoags, an eastern Native American group that decided to reassert its tribal identity in order to regain control of what had once been tribal land. Using Mashpee as an example, the chapter considers the ways in which identity, doctrine, and scholarship (particularly anthropology and history) facilitate or hinder discussions of the relationship between political status and cultural identity. While the Mashpee tribe, along with other tribes in the eastern United States, California, and other geographic areas where European/American colonization was especially fast paced, represent one aspect of the Native American experience, there is another facet, which Chapter 2 presents.

Chapter 2 gives an overview of the Indian Claims Commission Act and the Indian Claims Commission (ICC), which was the administrative body set up to implement the ICC Act.[3] Passed by Congress in 1946, the ICC Act opened the U.S. to lawsuits by Native American tribal groups for claims arising out of (1) law, (2) equity (which is to say law modified by standard legal notions of fairness), (3) fraudulent dealings, (4) compensation for lost property, and (5) moral claims. Before the ICC Act's passage, Native American tribes could not sue the United States without first getting permission from Congress in the form of a special jurisdictional statute. While it may have been difficult for citizens across the board to sue the United States, the exclusion of Native Americans from the federal courts was particularly repressive, given the United States' colonial and "frontier" history.

But would it have been possible for the U.S. legal system to deliver justice to Native Americans under the ICC Act? If the promise of the ICC Act had been fully realized, would justice have been served? *Could* it have been served? Chapter 3 raises these questions by introducing the idea of constitutive incommensurables, or symbolic property. Symbolic property is property that is not easily comparable with money. Land, friendship, parent-child relations are all examples of constitutive incommensurables in contemporary American society. For some groups, or in some instances, these things go to the heart of cultural identity and so courts predictably refrain from equating them with money. But because law can be obscuring, particularly across cultures, the idea of land as a constitutive incommensurable can better help us understand some Native American legal claims. Chapter 3 looks at land as a constitutive incommensurable. It also considers two specific Native American efforts to protect land and participate in land-use planning, despite the challenges of communicating tribal values about land to the dominant society's agents—bureaucrats, judges, lawyers, and the like.

Chapter 4 considers the topic of tribal cultural objects, specifically who owns them, who is legally entitled to them, and how Native Americans lost possession of them. It does this in the context of the Native American Graves Protection and Repatriation Act, or NAGPRA for short.[4] One result of the conquest was that there was a Native American diaspora; another was that Native Americans lost land, as well as the opportunity to get full return of their land. After the full force of military conquest had come to a close, although Native Americans had the formal opportunity to bring claims for return of land under the ICC Act, they were effectively barred under state property laws from suing for the return of lost or stolen cultural objects. In fact, one often-ignored result of conquest was that Native Americans lost, misplaced, or were dispossessed of vast quantities of personal property. Much of this property had special religious, cultural, tribal, and personal significance to its original tribal owners. Some of this "property" was not ethically categorizable as property at all, neither then nor now—for example, the human skeletons and remains that were routinely stolen by nonnatives for personal or scientific gain. Chapter 4 discusses the ways in which Native Americans were dispossessed of this tribal personal property, telling the considerably troubling account of how nonnative grave diggers, explorers, physicians, and anthropologists desecrated Native American graves, often in the name of science.

NAGPRA's intent is to redress the loss of tribal personal property. However, whether NAGPRA will be fully implemented will depend upon how tribal governments and courts rise to the challenge of defining and implementing key terms under the Act. Since the integrity and strength of tribal governments will be crucial to making NAGPRA work, Chapter 5 takes a look at tribal governance and specific issues related to gender that arise under the Indian Civil Rights Act, or ICRA.[5]

Chapter 5 begins with an overview of the scholarly literature about Native American women—an important perspective because too often, as discussed in earlier chapters, it is *this* literature that law takes as descriptive of Native American reality, and particularly of Native American *women's* reality. In contemporary American society, women do not easily assume national political roles except as helpers of their male partners. First ladies in the United States, for example, are increasingly qualified to serve in the presidential role, and yet—for many complicated reasons—they do not. In American tribal societies, by contrast, the evidence shows that women often assume the role of political leadership. Native American feminists explain this by noting that Native American women have a long history of holding the reins of leadership, whether "formally" or "informally," in tribal societies. Of course, this history is stronger in some tribes than in others, but it is empirically observable nevertheless.

Colonialism has touched every aspect of tribal life, hence Chapter 5 examines political and legal *tribal* regimes that Native American women find themselves living within today. Emphasis is on how particular doctrinal and tribal legislative changes have affected women's lives and access to resources, power, and avenues of participation in the Diné (Navajo) Nation, one of the largest Native American nations in the United States. Finally, the chapter links questions of perception, leadership, and law to tribal legislative strategies for addressing domestic violence.

The theme of Chapter 6, the final chapter, is the ongoing legal struggle for religious freedom that Native Americans have waged against both the federal and state governments. The chapter takes up two broad forms of contested religious expression: the sacramental use of peyote by Native American Church practitioners, and the use of sacred sites by more "traditionally traditional" religious groups. The American Indian Religious Freedom Act, or AIRFA, which passed in 1978, should have protected these expressions,[6] and while it did in principle, it offered no protection in fact. AIRFA's rejection by the U.S. Supreme Court is documented in two cases: *Lyng v. Northwest Indian Cemetery Protective Association*[7] and *Employment Division, Department of Human Resources of Oregon v. Smith*.[8] Chapter 6 briefly examines Native American litigation strategies in land/religion cases.

Despite losses in these cases, Native Americans continue to respond to the steady force of law that has been brought against them, especially in relation to the national land policy. Indeed, their responses over the past several hundred years show a consistent pattern of legal innovation that is nothing short of inspirationally astounding, especially when one considers the injustices, the obstacles, the change, the sorrows, the loss, the poverty, the emotional struggles, the anger, the lack of opportunity, and the racism they encountered along the way. Indigenous legal stories are core parts of American history. Much is lost when they are treated as a backwater, or dismissed as "too sad," "too ethnic," or "too remote." Indeed, Native Americans' legal relationship with the United States has not defined Native American identity so much as it has defined American identity, at its core.

Throughout the book, I primarily use the term "Native American" because it is the term I prefer, though I sometimes use the term "Indian" when referring to statutes, since that is the phrase legislative enactments typically use. Others prefer other terms, such as "American Indian" or "Indian," a preference I am comfortable with. Some say that anyone born in America is a "native" American.

Fine. But by my use of the word "native" in relation to the word "American," I mean any indigenous group, or *any* group with a long-standing history vis-à-vis a particular place in the Western hemisphere, any group that self-identifies as indigenous to the Western hemisphere, and any person who has a substantive (and not just blood) connection to such a cultural group. Blood may be thicker than water, but culture is pretty thick too.

Finally, this book is admittedly concerned with broad themes of justice and injustice, since it is, after all, a book about law. Lawyers administer the American system of government in various substantive ways and at all different systemic levels. Lawyers also make up a good percentage of the total pool of legislators, administrators, policy analysts, and the like. While other fields have the privilege of declaring that justice is an outmoded or overdiscussed topic, the field of law does not. In fact, one could argue that justice, and not just rule making and rule applying, ought to be at the heart of any legal endeavor, especially one such as federal Indian law where relative differences in legal power are so noticeable. If this is true, then one of the quandaries of federal Indian law is that so little justice for Native Americans has come from such a long history of treaty making, rule making, and litigating. Students, ironically, start out knowing that justice matters; lawyers and professors, perhaps because they are embroiled in the equities and doctrines of specific cases, too easily forget. Ultimately, the purpose of this book is to help you remember.

NOTES

1. Limerick, Patricia Nelson, Clyde A. Milner II, and Charles E. Rankin, eds. *Trails: Toward a New Western History.* Lawrence, Kan.: University of Kansas Press, 1991.

2. *Indian Citizenship Act of 1924, U.S. Statutes at Large* vol. 43 (1924): 253. This principle is currently codified at *U.S. Code* vol. 8, sec. 1401(b) (1994).

3. Former *U.S. Code* vol. 25, secs. 70–70(n). The Indian Claims Commission was terminated on Sept. 30, 1978, pursuant to *U.S. Code* vol. 25, sec. 70(v).

4. *U.S. Code* vol. 18, sec. 1170 (criminal provisions); and vol. 25, secs. 3001 et seq. (repatriation provisions) (1994).

5. *U.S. Code* vol. 25, secs. 1301 et seq. (1994).

6. *American Indian Religious Freedom Act of 1978, U.S. Statutes at Large* vol. 92 (1978): 469–470.

7. *Lyng v. Northwest Indian Cemetery Protective Association*, 485 U.S. 439 (1988).

8. *Employment Division, Department of Human Resources of Oregon v. Smith*, 494 U.S. 872 (1990).

CHAPTER 1

IDENTITY

The term "political minority" is used to describe the status of Native Americans in the United States, since federal Indian law is based on the political relationship between the United States and the Native American nations. But what is a political minority group? Does or should ethnic, cultural identity define political status? How should the legal system treat cases where cultural and political identity overlap? This chapter explores these questions by looking at the case of *Mashpee v. New Seabury Corp.*[1]

Mashpee presents a complicated question about history and law. From 1776 to 1789, between the Declaration of Independence and the convening of the first Congress, each of the thirteen original states managed their Indian affairs separately. In 1789, the original states delegated their exclusive power to deal with Indian tribes to the newly formed federal government via the United States Constitution. In particular, the Constitution granted Congress the authority to regulate Indian commerce, an area that included land sales and transfers. Congress acted on this authority by enacting the first federal Indian Trade and Intercourse Act in 1790.[2] There were six such acts between 1790 and 1834 for regulating trade between Indians and non-Indians. The first act is significant, however, because it voided transfers of land "from any Indian nation or tribe of Indians" that were not approved by the federal government. Under this void title provision, not even the span of 150 years or more could make bad title good, as the *Oneida*[3] and *Passamaquoddy*[4] cases decided. The 1834 act is the last and enduring one.

In 1832, the first Indian law case of *Johnson v. McIntosh* ratified the authority of the federal government as the source of all land title in the United States.[5]

Johnson held that title to all land within the United States originated with the federal government, not with the states or the Indian tribes. States or settlers could still buy land directly from Native American grantors, but they could no longer legally expect the United States to stand behind such title in case of a dispute. Moreover, since the United States had priority after *Johnson,* if the United States happened to convey the same land, later in time, to a different person, then the legal result would be that the *later* grantee—and not the Native American grantor's grantee—would take good title under a rule known as the "first in time, first in right." In order for states or settlers to secure their future right to possession and exclusivity then, they had to take from a chain of title that commenced with the United States. Land title that did not originate with the United States was void or voidable, and thus subject to the claims of bona fide purchasers who could trace their title back to a grant from the federal government.

Johnson v. McIntosh is one of the most widely read cases in federal Indian law. It catalogs the sources of legal authority that the federal government originally used to justify its control over Indian land and affairs. The line of authority starts with the Doctrine of Discovery, a doctrine that European discoverers first used among themselves to negotiate jurisdiction rights to the Western hemisphere, and then proceeds through the Constitution and the Trade and Intercourse Act. England's rights to jurisdiction passed to the original thirteen states upon independence and the states subsequently transferred their rights to the federal government through the U.S. Constitution. In later years, the federal government further defined its power over Indian tribes through specific statutes, executive orders, court decisions, and administrative regulations.

Federal authority over Indian land presumes a preliminary finding that the community in question is indeed a tribe. This finding required little analytical nuance at the land cession stage when the presence of a treaty or the setting aside of a reservation was enough to prove that a group was a tribe. But the issue of tribal identity predictably became more complicated at the annuity distribution stage, particularly on the issue of who was an Indian for trade purposes. Today, the issue remains complicated and is often contested. Sometimes the issue is litigated, as in *Mashpee,* but more often it is decided by the federal Bureau of Indian Affairs (BIA), which employs a staff of professional anthropologists, historians, and ethnologists to decide claims of tribal status. This change was made in direct response to the outcome in *Mashpee.*

The Mashpee Wampanoag, of what is now the state of Massachusetts, had early contact with English settlers and, like many other Native American groups, survived disease, decimation, and violence in this period. In the nineteenth century they voted to subject their tribal lands to Massachusetts state law, a vote that opened up their tribal land for private sale. By the turn of the twentieth century, what had once been tribal land was in the hands of non-Mashpee owners. Nevertheless, the Mashpee still controlled the local political process since the new absentee landowners were summer residents who were not registered to vote in the Town of Mashpee. As more and more permanent residents moved into the Mashpee area in the mid-twentieth century, the Mashpee lost political control of the Town of Mashpee. They responded to this political loss, in part, by making a Non-Intercourse Act claim in federal court. They argued that since they were an Indian tribe for purposes of the Non-Intercourse Act and their land had been conveyed without prior federal approval, the unapproved conveyances were void or voidable. If this were indeed so, then the proper remedy for the tribe's claim was forfeiture, which is to say return to the Mashpee of roughly 11,000 acres of land.

The Defendant Town of Mashpee countered the suit by arguing that the Mashpee were not an Indian tribe for purposes of the Non-Intercourse Act. This defense was sufficient to set aside the Non-Intercourse Act claim so that the merits of the tribal identity issue could be litigated. Because the United States had not formally recognized the tribe's status as a political minority, the Mashpee had either to get BIA recognition as a tribe or else to litigate the issue of their status *before* they could pursue their land claim under the Non-Intercourse Act.

The Non-Intercourse Act of 1790 contemplated clear political divisions between tribal groups and nontribal groups. Even though the Mashpee had accepted federal support for certain benefits, like education, there were no political divisions on record since the federal government had never entered into a treaty with the Mashpee or otherwise formally acknowledged the group's tribal status. Nor had the Mashpee ever acknowledged their own sovereignty in the standard way of reaching out as political entities to England or the United States. To the contrary, it became known at trial that the Mashpee Wampanoags had fought against another Wampanoag, Metacomet (a sachem known as King Philip), in King Philip's War, which was the largest Wampanoag uprising against the English colonizers. Metacomet and his followers were annihilated, a fate the Mashpee Wampanoags would have met too, had they followed Metacomet. Instead, the group survived and 300 years later found itself in a legal catch-22. Had the Mashpee Wampanoags fought with Metacomet they would not have lived to bring their lawsuit, but the evidence that they had not fought with their Wampanoag relations was used at trial to show that the Mashpee had thus taken the first step of what historian Francis G. Hutchins characterized as their slow march toward full participation in U.S. society.[6] With history against them, the Mashpee needed a judicially crafted definition to prove their political minority status. They chose one first articulated in the 1901 case of *Montoya v. United States.*[7]

The *Montoya* case involved Victorio's Chiricahua and Mescalero Apache band and took place in the nineteenth century. In this period, the United States had used considerable military force against Native Americans in general and the Apache in particular, since they were the last military challengers to settlement policies.[8] *Montoya* defined an Indian tribe as "a body of Indians of the same or a similar race, united in a community under one leadership or government, and inhabiting a particular though sometimes ill-defined territory." Over time other standards have also determined "Indianness." Many tribal enrollment standards, for example, turn on a federally initiated blood-quantum system, with the minimum quantum eventually set by the tribal government itself. But *Montoya* was a depredations rule, which means that it determined when tribes in amity with the United States were liable for the hostile acts of their members.

The *Montoya* standard fit *Mashpee* badly, to say the least. First, the Mashpee were suing for the return of aboriginal land that had been transferred from the Wampanoags to private Massachusetts citizens in contravention of the federal Non-Intercourse Act; they were not being sued by settlers for depredations. Second, the Mashpee were trying to enforce legal guarantees reserved to tribes under the Non-Intercourse Act, whereas *Montoya* involved Victorio's Band, a band that was systematically excluded from any legal benefits under the American system as further punishment for its military resistance against the United States. Third, the Mashpee were an eastern group, one of the first tribal groups to have contact with the English, whereas the Apache were a western group, one of the last to concede military defeat to the United States. On the surface, the Apache fit stereotypical images of Indianness produced by nineteenth-century Westward expansion. The Mashpee did not.

Indeed the Mashpee fit almost no stereotypical images of Indianness. They were not what historian Robert M. Utley calls "horse and buffalo Indians";[9] they did not wear their hair in braids; they did not live in tepees or wigwams; they did not engage in armed conflict against colonial forces, despite their disputed claim to having fought with Metacomet against the English. Ironically, *had* the Mashpee met these images, they probably would have prevailed before the jury. But because they didn't—in fact, some of the Mashpee plaintiffs had land development businesses, college degrees, investment strategies—their claim to tribal status was fiercely contested. The Mashpee had to prove they were a tribe under *Montoya*, a difficult task in part because the Mashpee did not clearly meet all elements of the four-part test articulated in *Montoya*.

Montoya turned on four elements of proof. The first element called for a group of the same or similar race. The Mashpee, for their part, had intermarried with other ethnic groups, most notably with African Americans, and as a group they had not retained the Wampanoag language, spiritual customs, or kinship patterns. Second, *Montoya* required a territorial land base. The Mashpee had no such base, since they had voted to assume formal township status under Massachusetts law in 1869 and thus open up their tribal land to sale. Part of this lost tribal land was the very land whose conveyance they now argued was voidable under the Non-Intercourse Act.

Third, *Montoya* required evidence of a political organization or formal leadership of some sort. From 1869 to roughly 1964, the Town of Mashpee had been governed by local officials who happened to be of Mashpee descent, but who had not governed *as an Indian tribe.* Instead, the Mashpee had loose associations that they presented as political institutions for purposes of *Montoya*. Whether these hearth-style associations were sufficient to meet the *Montoya* test was hotly debated at trial. The Mashpee argued that their identity was Wampanoag and hence all their political expressions were by definition tribal. The defendants countered that culture and politics were separate, and they pointed out that while historically Mashpee had been designated an "Indian town," in the twentieth century Mashpee functioned for all intents and purposes like any other Massachusetts town along Cape Cod.

While the Mashpee presented a long history of informally recognizing and following Wampanoag tradition, they also presented a twentieth-century record of adopting pan-Indian traditions. These traditions grew into events such as pow-wow festivities, and they were vaguely, unself-consciously recorded in local history as conscious points of cultural reinvention. So while the Mashpee could not prove their political status as Indians under *Montoya*, they could prove that they regarded themselves *culturally* as Wampanoags, and also as contemporary Native Americans following pan-Indian traditions.

The *Mashpee* case raises profound and lingering questions about identity, assimilation, American Indian nationhood, and the ethics of making indigenous people prove they are entitled to political minority status. Who is a Native American? What is a "tribe" for purposes of federal law? Who gets to ask these questions and who gets to answer them? If people of tribal ancestry must prove their political, institutional authenticity, what form should the proof take? Is polymorphous evidence of "culture" sufficient to show political status as an inherent tribal sovereign, or does federal law require more? Does it require, for example, proof of institutions that non-Indians can recognize? If so, is this another way of imposing cultural change on Native Americans, this time by requiring that indigenous political institutions take certain forms and follow certain processes?

The readings in this chapter offer illustrative answers to these questions. The first excerpt is from James Clifford's "Identity in *Mashpee*." Clifford's piece places the *Mashpee* litigation in a broad debate about epistemology, or how it is that practitioners of particular disciplines produce scholarship. Using information observed at trial, Clifford identifies the theoretical difficulties inherent in having courts scrutinize political status claims. He also catalogs and analyzes the expert testimonies that were offered at trial.

The next excerpt is by Francis G. Hutchins, a historian who testified on behalf of the defendants in *Mashpee*. For Hutchins, the Mashpee plaintiffs did not meet the *Montoya* standard and hence were not legally entitled to federal protection under the Non-Intercourse Act. Hutchins based his testimony on historical documents, not on fieldwork or other methods of information gathering. From these documents he concluded that the Mashpee had abandoned their tribal status. According to Hutchins's argument, the abandonment took place over several centuries, provable by documented moments reflecting the Mashpee's decision to move into the mainstream. Refusing to side with Metacomet was one such historical moment. Another occurred in 1869, when the Mashpee elected by a split vote to assume formal township status under Massachusetts law, and thus open up their tribal land to sale. Encouraging the mid–twentieth-century development of the Town of Mashpee was the third turning point. Hutchins regarded these incidents as proof that the Mashpee did not consider themselves a political minority or a political sovereignty, even though they did identify culturally as Mashpee Wampanoags.

As Hutchins saw it, the issue was not whether the Mashpee plaintiffs were an American Indian tribe in some vague cultural sense, but rather whether they were a tribal unit in a concrete historical sense. If they were, then they must have had to maintain a government-to-government relationship with the United States according to the terms of *Montoya*, and so would be entitled to Non-Intercourse Act protection. If they were not a tribal unit, then they were politically like any other citizens of the state of Massachusetts, despite their Native American heritage. Finally, Hutchins testified that abstract discussions of culture were irrelevant to the *Montoya* standard, which he thought required documentary proof of a measurable and observable political structure, or system, of self-government. Hutchins noted that documentary proof of this sort was exactly what the Mashpee were missing. He argued that what the historical record showed instead was that the Mashpee had volitionally and intentionally abandoned their tribal status.

Jack Campisi presented the Mashpee's side of the debate. He testified that the Mashpee made their choices—for example the 1869 vote to assume township status—to survive, not to assimilate into a white society that shunned them on ethnic and racial grounds. Based on roughly a month of fieldwork, Campisi concluded that the trial process was not fine tuned enough to assess how choices such as siding with Metacomet or voting for township status related to Mashpee political identity.

On a theoretical level, Campisi's excerpt discusses how anthropology and law parted ways at trial. Anthropologists begin with the methodological premise that categories should be found, not imposed. They regard classifications and categories as socially constructed, and hence "subjective." Lawyers, on the other hand, are trained to objectify problems using prefigured categories. From a legal vantage point, prefigured categories may be socially constructed, but they are still regarded as more "objective" than case-by-case assessments. In law, this reach for objectivity is regarded as fair in typical cases, which Indian law cases are not.

Campisi explains how the parting of ways between anthropology, history, and law played itself out in the *Mashpee* trial. He also describes how it left in its wake anxious, possibly unanswerable questions about the ways in which experts construct knowledge. For instance, was Hutchins's testimony, which came from interpreting documents, *really* more objective than Campisi's fieldwork-inspired testimony, or Clifford's courtroom-inspired essay? Did it matter that the documents Hutchins analyzed had consistently been prepared by non-Indians, for non-Indian institutions? Was the purpose of cross-examination to uncover the truth, or just cast doubt on nuanced, self-reflective testimony by making it seem vulnerable, weak, and inconclusive?

Two waves of legal scholarship about *Mashpee* appeared in the law review literature. The first focused on doctrine.[10] It took federal law as a given, and simply set out to discuss whether the Mashpee had or had not proven their case. The second wave, which appeared almost ten years later, was more concerned with understanding what happened in *Mashpee*.[11] It presented and analyzed how theories of identity, ethnicity, and race relate to doctrine. My excerpt—the last one in this chapter—summarizes the second wave of legal scholarship about *Mashpee*. It also points out the importance of using local evidence to help bridge the gap between methodologies that work by finding categories—like anthropology of the sort

Clifford and Campisi describe—and those, like law, that work by applying prefigured categories.

As long as the United States is in the business of using Native American status to distribute benefits and burdens, a new standard must be developed. One Australian writer has suggested that Aboriginal status, under Australian law, be granted to those who: (1) are a distinctive people, (2) have a long sense of history, whether it be their own history, their contact history, or the conflict history, (3) live in a process of changing culture that produces a sense of belonging, and (4) have a feeling of identity that becomes the basis for a philosophy, or an ideology, or a political stance in the world—a philosophy that allows the group to survive, exist, even flourish in the independent state in which it finds itself.[12]

Had this standard been applied in *Mashpee*, the Mashpee plaintiffs would have prevailed at trial. But since the court was both using *Montoya*, with its focus on race and political institutional maintenance, and valuing "contact history" over "conflict history," the *Mashpee* lost their case. In other words, had the rules for deciding tribal status been explained in slightly broader terms than they were, decisions such as siding against Metacomet in King Philip's War or voting for township status under Massachusetts law in 1869 could have been presented in fuller, more historically and psychologically contextualized ways, as strategies for survival in a colonial state. Evidence of informal, hearth-style consensus forms of governance might have been given more weight as well.

Identity and its relation to political status continues to be a pressing problem for Native Americans. The Indian Child Welfare Act, or ICWA,[13] provides one example at the opposite extreme of *Mashpee*. ICWA is not covered in this volume, but it is an important statute that gives tribes authority to prevent non–Native Americans from adopting Native American children; it does this by giving the tribe the option to intervene in proceedings that involve a Native American child and a non-Indian placement.

In its 1978 form, ICWA did not require that states notify tribes in *voluntary* adoption proceedings involving Native American children.[14] Some states— Washington, Minnesota, Oklahoma and Michigan, for example—supplemented ICWA with legislation requiring that tribes be notified in voluntary proceedings; other states—Utah, North Dakota—made it a standard practice to notify tribal authorities in such cases. But states could only disclose a child's tribal heritage if the parents did so first. In cases where parents failed to disclose their cultural affiliation, bitter conflicts often arose over whether a tribe could intervene late in the adoption process. *In Re Bridget R.* was one such case.[15]

In *In Re Bridget R.*, a birth father decided not to reveal his tribal heritage since disclosure would implicate ICWA and slow down the voluntary adoption of his twin daughters by a non-Indian family. The father and his lawyer apparently felt justified in not disclosing the father's tribal (Pomo) heritage because although the father was culturally recognized as a Pomo, he was not an officially enrolled member of the Pomo tribe. This fine distinction was exploited on the grounds that ICWA defines an "Indian" as "any person who is a *member* of an Indian tribe."[16]

When the father's tribal relatives learned of the adoption proceedings, they notified the tribe, which intervened in the case. By the time the *In re Bridget R.* opinion was issued, the twins were almost three years old. The adoptive parents argued that parent–child bonding had occurred in the twins' early infancy; the tribe just as forcefully argued that the twins were being deprived of a political right—a right secured by principles of tribal sovereignty and ratified by ICWA—to be brought up with tribal birth relatives who, had they received notice of the proceedings from the outset, would have provided the children a home.

This short example is just one of many that illustrate that federal law has not adequately dealt with the issue of Native American identity and how it relates to political status. It is built on the nineteenth-century model that views tribes and tribalism as anathema to the direction that any reasonable, rational person would want to take. Current federal law cannot adequately resolve twentieth-century cases like *Mashpee.* But, as the ICWA example shows, neither can the law simply flip-flop from assuming a tribal identity is something no one in their right mind would claim, to assuming it is something that all who can would openly proclaim, regardless of the consequences. This failure to conceptualize the importance of identity is a central unresolved problem in the field of federal Indian law.

RECOMMENDED READINGS

On the *Mashpee* case, Paul Brodeur's journalistic account of the Mashpee as well as of other eastern Indian land claims cases, *Restitution: The Land Claims of the Mashpee, Passamaquoddy, and Penobscot Indians of New England* (1985), is well worth reading. Rona Sue Mazer's Ph.D. dissertation, "Town and Tribe in Conflict: A Study of Local-Level Politics in Mashpee, Massachusetts" (1980), analyzes a wealth of local Mashpee documents. "The Massachusetts Indian Enfranchisement Act: Ethnic Contest in Historical Context, 1849–1869," by Ann Marie Plane and Gregory Button, in *Ethnohistory* 40:4 (Fall 1993), gives a historical analysis of Massachusetts Indians in the colonial period. The Plane and Button article makes the important point that in colonial Massachusetts, policy affecting ethnic boundaries was linked to perceptions of ethnic identity, which is to say that lawmakers dealt with political and ethnic identity in similar ways. Jonathon Harr's *A Civil Action* (1996) gives yet another glimpse of Mashpee judge Walter Jay Skinner in action in a historically complex case.

In the law review literature, two additional studies about *Mashpee* are of interest. They are Gerald Torres and Kathryn Milun's "Translating *Yonnondio* by Precedent and Evidence: The Mashpee Indian Case," *Duke Law Journal* 625 (1990), and Martha Minow, "Identities," 3 *Yale Journal of Law & Humanities* 97 (1991). For relevant works that cite or briefly discuss Torres and Milun's article, see Peggy C. Davis, *Contextual Legal Criticism: A Demonstration Exploring Hierarchy and "Feminine" Style,* 66 *New York University Law Review* 1635 (1991); Cheryl I. Harris, "Whiteness as Property," 106 *Harvard Law Review* 1707,

1761–66 (1993); and Jane S. Schacter, "Metademocracy: The Changing Structure of Legitimacy in Statutory Interpretation," 108 *Harvard Law Review* 593, 624–26 (1995). Finally, Martha Minow discusses *Mashpee* in a civil rights context in her book *Making All the Difference: Inclusion, Exclusion, and American Law* (1990).

For general-interest books and articles about Native American identity, see "Place, Race, and Names: Layered Identities in *United States v. Oregon, Confederated Tribes of the Colville Reservation, Plaintiff-Intervenor*," by Susan Staiger Gooding. Gooding's article appears in 28 *Law & Society Review* 1181 (1994), in a Symposium issue titled "Community and Identity in Sociolegal Studies." For a related article that discusses Hispanic/Native American identity, see Luis Angel Toro's " 'A People Distinct from Others': Race and Identity in Federal Indian Law and the Hispanic Classification in OMB Directive No. 15," in 26 *Texas Tech Law Review* 1219 (1995).

More and more Native American autobiographies are being published, and many explicitly discuss the issue of identity and mixed ancestry. The references that follow are just a starting point for these contemporary works. Mi'kmaq poet Rita Joe has published *Song of Rita Joe: Autobiography of a Mi'kmaq Poet* (1996). Vincent L. Mendoza has a book titled *Son of Two Bloods* (1996); it depicts Mendoza's experiences as a Mexican American/Creek. Fiction writer Janet Campbell Hale's autobiography is *Bloodlines: Odyssey of a Native Daughter* (1993). Janet Campbell Hale's *The Jailing of Cecelia Capture* (1985) is a novel about a Native American law student. Activist Russell Means has a biography titled *Where White Men Fear to Tread* (1995). For accounts from social science interviews see *Messengers of the Wind: Native American Women Tell Their Life Stories* (1995), and Ward Churchill's *From a Native Son: Selected Essays on Indigenism, 1985–1995* (1997).

For a discussion about the vagaries of assessing tribal identity in the nineteenth century, especially in relation to prohibited activities under the federal Indian Trade and Intercourse Acts, see William E. Unrau, *White Man's Wicked Water: The Alcohol Trade and Prohibition in Indian Country, 1802–1892* (1996). Unrau's analysis is important because it provides evidence counter to the sometimes expressed contention that tribal status designations have become difficult only in the twentieth century. Mary Louise Pratt's *Imperial Eyes: Travel Writing and Transculturation* (1992) is a strong compliment to Unrau's work. Pratt explores how travel writing gave rise to imperial stylistics that then themselves contributed to the colonial view of North and South America as vast unsettled places. These ways of seeing, says Pratt, gave way to an intellectual process whereby diverse life forms were drawn out of what to imperial eyes was the chaos of their American surroundings and rewoven into a European order, one that held as its central discourse the systematizing of nature in both name and practice.

Finally, *Indigenous Peoples in International Law*, by S. James Anaya (1996), discusses international standards for determining political minority status. *The American Indian in Western Legal Thought: Discourses of Conquest* (1990), by Robert A. Williams, covers the early colonial period, as does his most recent book, *Linking Arms Together: American Indian Treaty Visions of Law and Peace, 1600–1800* (1997).

NOTES

1. 592 F.2d 575 (1st Cir. 1979), cert. Denied 444 U.S. 866 (1979). See also *Mashpee Tribe v. Secretary of the Interior*, 820 F.2d 480 (1st Cir. 1987).

2. *Trade and Intercourse Act of 1790, U.S. Statutes at Large* 1 (1790) 137–138.

3. *County of Oneida v. Oneida Indian Nation*, 470 U.S. 226 (1985).

4. *Joint Tribal Council of Passamaquoddy Tribe v. Morton*, 528 F.2d 370 (1st Cir. 1975).

5. 21 U.S. (8 Wheat) 543 (1823).

6. Francis G. Hutchins, *Mashpee: The Story of Cape Cod's Indian Town*, West Franklin, N.H.: Amarta Press, 1979.

7. 180 U.S. 261 (1901).

8. See generally Larry C. Skogen, *Indian Depredation Claims, 1796–1920*, Norman, Okla.: University of Oklahoma Press, 1996; and Thomas E. Mails, *The People Called Apache*, New York, N.Y.: Prentice-Hall, 1974.

9. Robert M. Utley, *The Lance and the Shield: The Life and Times of Sitting Bull*, New York, N.Y.: Ballantine Books, a Division of Random House, 1993, p. 4.

10. See generally "Symposium on Eastern Land Claims," 31 *Maine Law Review* 1 (1979).

11. See, e.g., Gerald Torres and Kathryn Milun, "Translating *Yonnondio* by Precedent and Evidence: The Mashpee Indian Case," *Duke Law Journal* 625 (1990); Martha Minow, "Identities," 3 *Yale Journal of Law & Humanities* 97 (1991); Jo Carrillo, Identity as Idiom: *Mashpee* Reconsidered, 28 *Indiana Law Review* 511 (1995).

12. Colin Tatz, "Aboriginality as Civilisation," *The Australian Quarterly* 52:3, pp. 252–262 (1980).

13. *Indian Child Welfare Act of 1978, U.S. Statutes at Large* 92 (1978): 3069–3078. Currently codified at *Indian Child Welfare Act, U.S. Code*, vol. 25, secs. 1901–1963 (1995).

14. *Indian Child Welfare Act, U.S. Code*, vol. 25, sec. 1913 (1995).

15. *In re Bridget R.*, 41 Cal. App. 4th 1483 (1996), *review denied*.

16. *Indian Child Welfare Act, U.S. Code*, vol. 25, sec. 1903(3) (1995).

Identity in Mashpee

James Clifford

In August 1976 the Mashpee Wampanoag Tribal Council, Inc., sued in federal court for possession of about 16,000 acres of land constituting three-quarters of Mashpee, "Cape Cod's Indian Town." . . . An unprecedented trial ensued whose purpose was not to settle the question of land ownership but rather to determine whether the group calling itself the Mashpee Tribe was in fact an Indian tribe, and the same tribe that in the mid-nineteenth century had lost its lands through a series of contested legislative acts. . . .

Although the Mashpee claim was similar to the [other eastern land claims cases] there were crucial differences. The Passamaquoddy and Penobscot [for example] were generally recognized Indian tribes with distinct communities and clear aboriginal roots in the area.* The Mashpee plaintiffs represented most of the nonwhite inhabitants of what, for over three centuries, had been known as an "Indian town" on Cape Cod; but their institutions of tribal governance had long been elusive, especially during the century and a half preceding the suit. Moreover, since about 1800 the Massachusetts language had ceased to be commonly spoken in Mashpee. The town was at first largely Presbyterian [and] then Baptist in its public religion. Over the centuries inhabitants had intermarried with other Indian groups. . . .

The inhabitants of Mashpee were active in the economy and society of modern Massachusetts. They were businessmen, schoolteachers, fishermen, domestic workers, small contractors. Could these people of Indian ancestry file suit as the Mashpee Tribe that had, they claimed, been despoiled of collectively held lands during the mid-nineteenth century? This was the question a federal judge posed to a Boston jury. Only if they answered yes could the matter proceed to a land-claim trial.

Reprinted by permission of the publisher from *The Predicament of Culture: Twentieth-Century Ethnography, Literature and Art*, by James Clifford. Cambridge, Mass.: Harvard University Press. © 1988 by the President and Fellows of Harvard College.

*Joint Tribal Council of Passamaquoddy Tribe v. Morton, 528 F.2d 370 (1st Cir. 1975).

The forty-one days of testimony that unfolded in Federal District Court during the late fall of 1977 bore the name *Mashpee Tribe v. New Seabury Corp.*, shorthand for a complex, multipartied dispute. Mashpee Tribe referred to the plaintiffs, the Mashpee Wampanoag Tribal Council, Inc., described by its members as an arm of the Mashpee Tribe. A team of lawyers from the Native American Rights Fund, a nonprofit advocacy group, prepared their suit. . . . New Seabury et al. referred to the New Seabury Corporation (a large development company), the Town of Mashpee (representing over a hundred individual landowners), and various other classes of defendants (insurance companies, businesses, property owners). The case for the defense was argued by James St. Clair (Richard Nixon's Watergate attorney) of the large Boston firm Hale and Dorr, and Allan Van Gestel of Goodwin, Proctor, and Hoar. They were assisted by a team of eight other lawyers.

The presence of the Town of Mashpee among the defendants requires explanation. It was not until 1869 that the community living in Mashpee was accorded formal township status. From 1869 until 1964 the town government was overwhelmingly in the hands of Indians. During this period every selectman but one was an Indian or married to an Indian. Genealogical evidence presented at the trial showed that the families of town officers were closely interrelated. No one contested the fact that before the 1960s Mashpee was governed by Indians. The disagreement was over whether they governed as an "Indian tribe." . . .

"Cape Cod's Indian Town" had finally been discovered. For centuries a backwater and a curiosity, in the 1950s and 1960s Mashpee became desirable as a site for retirement, vacation homes, condominiums, and luxury developments. Fast roads now made it accessible as a bedroom and weekend suburb of Boston. The new influx of money and jobs was first welcomed by many of Mashpee's Indian residents, including some of the leaders of the land-claim suit. They took advantage of the new situation. The town government, still run by Indians, enjoyed a surge in tax revenues. But when local government passed out of Indian control, perhaps for good, and as the scale of development increased, many Indians began to feel qualms. What they had taken for granted—that this was their town—no longer held true. Large tracts of undeveloped land formerly open for hunting and fishing were suddenly ringed with "No Trespassing" signs. The New Seabury development, on a choice stretch of coastline, with its two golf courses and expansionist plans, seemed particularly egregious. Tensions between traditional residents and newcomers increased, finally leading to the suit, filed with the support of most, but not all, of the Indians in Mashpee. The land claim, while focusing on a loss of property in the nineteenth century, was actually an attempt to regain control of a town that had slipped from Indian hands very recently. . . .

IMAGES

At the end of the trial Federal Judge Walter J. Skinner posed a number of specific questions to the jurors concerning tribal status at certain dates in Mashpee history;

but throughout the proceedings broader questions of Indian identity and power permeated the courtroom. Although the land claim was formally not at issue, the lawyers for New Seabury et al. sometimes seemed to be playing on a new nightmare. At the door of your suburban house a stranger in a business suit appears. He says he is a Native American. Your land has been illegally acquired generations ago, and you must relinquish your home. The stranger refers you to his lawyer.*

Such fears, the threat of a "giveaway" of private lands, were much exploited by politicians and the press in the Penobscot-Passamaquoddy negotiations [in Maine]. Actually small holdings by private citizens were never in danger; only large tracts of undeveloped land held by timber companies and the state were in question. In Mashpee the plaintiffs reduced their claim to 11,000 acres, formally excluding all private homes and lots up to an acre in size. Large-scale development, not small ownership, was manifestly the target; but their opponents refused pretrial compromises and the kinds of negotiation that had led to settlement of the Maine dispute.

According to [the Mashpee Tribe's attorney] the sorts of land claims pursued in Maine, Mashpee, Gay Head, and Charlestown were always drastically circumscribed. At that historical moment the courts were relatively open to Native American claims, a situation unlikely to last. In a decision of 1985 permitting Oneida, Mohawk, and Cayuga Non-Intercourse Act suits the Supreme Court made it abundantly clear [to quote the Plaintiff's attorney], "that Indians are dealing with the magnanimity of a rich and powerful nation, one that is not about to divest itself or its non-Indian citizens of large acreage in the name of its own laws."† In short, the United States will permit Indians a measure of recompense through the law—indeed, it has done so to an extent far greater than any other nation in a comparable situation—but it ultimately makes the rules and arbitrates the game.[1]

Seen in this light, the Mashpee trial was simply a clarification of the rules in an ongoing struggle between parties of greatly unequal power. But beneath the explicit fear of white citizens losing their homes because of an obscure past injustice, a troubling uncertainty was finding its way into the dominant image of Indians in America. The plaintiffs in the Non–Intercourse Act suits had power. In Maine, politicians lost office over the issue, and the Mashpee case made national headlines for several months. Scandalously, it now paid to be Indian. Acting aggressively, tribal groups were doing sophisticated, "nontraditional" things. All over the country they were becoming involved in a variety of businesses, some claiming exemption from state regulation. To many whites it was comprehensible for Northwest Coast tribes to demand traditional salmon-fishing privileges; but for tribes to run high-stakes bingo games in violation of state laws was not.

Indians had long filled a pathetic imaginative space for the dominant culture; they were always survivors, noble or wretched. Their cultures had been steadily

*This theme is presented in full detail in Alan van Gestel, "When Fictions Take Hostages," in *The Invented Indian: Cultural Fictions and Government Policies* (James A. Clifton, ed., 1990). New Brunswick, N.J.: Transaction Publishers, 1990.

†See *County of Oneida v. Oneida Indian Nation*, 470 U.S. 226 (1985).

eroding, at best hanging on in museumlike reservations. Native American societies could not by definition be dynamic, inventive, or expansive. . . . In Boston Federal Court a jury of white citizens would be confronted by a collection of highly ambiguous images. Could a [jury] of four women and eight men (no minorities) be made to believe in the persistent "Indian" existence of the Mashpee plaintiffs without costumes and props? This question surrounded and infused the trial's technical focus on whether a particular form of political-cultural organization called a tribe had existed continuously in Mashpee since the sixteenth century.

The image of Mashpee Indians, like that of several other eastern groups such as the Lumbee and the Ramapough, was complicated by issues of race.[2] Significant intermarriage with blacks had occurred since the mid-eighteenth century, and the Mashpee were, at times, widely identified as "colored." In court the defense occasionally suggested that they were really blacks rather than Native Americans. Like the Lumbee (and, less successfully, the Ramapough) the Mashpee plaintiffs had struggled to distinguish themselves from other minorities and ethnic groups, asserting tribal status based on a distinctive political-cultural history. In court they were not helped by the fact that few of them looked strongly "Indian." Some could pass for black, others for white. . . .

BORDERLINES

Mashpee Indians suffered the fate of many small Native American groups who remained in the original thirteen states. They were not accorded the reservations and sovereign status (steadily eroded) of tribes west of the Mississippi. Certain of the eastern communities, such as the Seneca and the Seminoles, occupied generally recognized tribal lands. Others—the Lumbee, for example—possessed no collective lands but clustered in discrete regions, maintaining kinship ties, traditions, and sporadic tribal institutions. In all cases the boundaries of the community were permeable. There was intermarriage and routine migration in and out of the tribal center—sometimes seasonal, sometimes longer term. Aboriginal languages were much diminished, often entirely lost. Religious life was diverse—sometimes Christian (with a distinctive twist), sometimes a transformed tradition such as the Iroquois Longhouse Religion. Moral and spiritual values were often Native American amalgams compounded from both local traditions and pan-Indian sources. . . . Eastern Indians generally lived in closer proximity to white (or black) society and in smaller groups than their western reservation counterparts. In the face of intense pressure some eastern communities have managed to acquire official federal recognition as tribes, others not. During the past two decades the rate of applications has risen dramatically.

Within this diversity of local histories and institutional arrangements the long-term residents of Mashpee occupied a gray area, at least in the eyes of the surrounding society and the law. The Indian identity of the Penobscot and Passamaquoddy was never seriously challenged, even though they had not been federally recognized and had lost or adapted many of their traditions. The Mashpee were more problematic. . . .

Indians in Mashpee owned no tribal lands (other than fifty-five acres acquired just before the trial). They had no surviving language, no clearly distinct religion, no blatant political structure. Their kinship was much diluted. Yet they did have a place and a reputation. For centuries Mashpee had been recognized as an Indian town. Its boundaries had not changed since 1665, when the land was formally deeded to a group called the South Sea Indians by the neighboring leaders Tookonchasun and Weepquish. The Mashpee plaintiffs of 1977 could offer as evidence surviving pieces of Native American tradition and political structures that seemed to have come and gone. They could also point to a sporadic history of Indian revivals continuing into the present.

The Mashpee were a borderline case. . . . Looked at one way, they were Indian; seen another way, they were not. Powerful ways of looking thus became inescapably problematic. The trial was less a search for the facts of Mashpee Indian culture and history than it was an experiment in translation, part of a long historical conflict and negotiation of "Indian" and "American" identities. . . .

THE EXPERTS

Expert testimony by professional anthropologists and historians played a major role in the Mashpee trial. The defense rested much of its case on the historical testimony of a single scholar [Francis Hutchins], while the plaintiffs depended more on anthropologists [James Axtell and Jack Campisi]. Indeed the trial can be seen as a struggle between history and anthropology. . . .

The anthropologists on the stand were clearly more comfortable with a polymorphous notion of culture than with the political category of tribe. And given the court's unwillingness to establish a rigid initial definition, much, if not most, of the testimony at the trial concerned the status of Indian "culture," broadly conceived, in Mashpee. This cornerstone of the anthropological discipline proved to be vulnerable under cross-examination. Culture appeared to have no essential features. Neither language, religion, land, economics, nor any other key institution or custom was its sine qua non. It seemed to be a contingent mix of elements. At times the concept was purely differential: cultural integrity involved recognized boundaries; it required merely an acceptance by the group and its neighbors of a meaningful difference, a we–they distinction. But what if the difference were accepted at certain times and denied at others? And what if every element in the cultural melange were combined with or borrowed from external sources?

At times the experts seemed to suggest that culture was always acculturating. But then how much historical mix-and-match would be permissible before a certain organic unity were lost? Was the criterion a quantitative one? Or was there a reliable qualitative method for judging a culture's identity? Was it necessary to frequent the people in question? In anthropology coherent representations of a way of life are expected to be based on fieldwork. But would a year's fieldwork in Mashpee have produced a professional account significantly better than Campisi's "twenty-four days and nights"? Doubtless yes; but would a year be enough to gain the trust of all factions in the area, Indian and white?

Campisi's limited familiarity with life in Mashpee was far greater than that of the opposing anthropological expert. Jean Guillemin, a sociologist by training, did no credible fieldwork in Mashpee at all. She had little choice: only a few Indian people would speak with her. The bulk of her testimony was thus based on sworn depositions taken by order of the court before the trial from a random sample of fifty Mashpee residents. On this basis, along with the evidence of written documents, she had no hesitation in affirming that Mashpee Indians never had a distinct culture and never were a tribe. . . . In cross-examination Guillemin's research practice of "anthropology by deposition" was effectively attacked, while her definition of tribe was shown to be heavily weighted toward formal leadership and sovereignty, exactly the elements most lacking in Mashpee.

Guillemin defended the adversarial questions and answers of the pretrial depositions as a source of social scientific data. This led to rebuttals by experts on social science methodology, covering sampling techniques, investigator bias, the value of telephone surveys, and so on. She derived statistical tables based on the depositions showing a low level of familiarity with Indian myths and legends in the randomly sampled cross-section of Mashpee Indians. The plaintiffs challenged these as misleading pseudoscience. . . . Interpretive and quantitative approaches to the study of society did battle in the courtroom, and neither came out looking rigorous.

Guillemin's inability to talk with Indians in Mashpee seriously undermined her credibility as an anthropological expert; but the difficulties and resistance she encountered raised a general doubt. How could a balanced, neutral cultural account ever be produced in a politically divided situation? Could any expert speak without bias in such a situation? Campisi was very clearly "positioned" in Mashpee, primarily associated with one segment of the population. Unlike a historian, an anthropologist drawing on fieldwork cannot—even in theory—control all the available evidence. A community reckoning itself among *possible futures* is not a finite archive. Unlike a psychiatric expert, moreover, an anthropologist cannot claim to have met alone with his or her subject—a "culture."

THE RECORD

The defense's crucial positive testimony was that of its historian, Francis Hutchins, who stayed on the stand for nearly five full days. His long, meticulous recitation of historical particulars summed up the case against the Tribal Council. Hutchins' manner on the stand was unhurried and thorough. He moved from document to document: deeds, petitions, laws, missionary correspondence, town records, state papers. He led the court again through the plague, the arrival of the

Pilgrims, Richard Bourne's plantation scheme for the South Sea Indian remnant. He explained English proprietary law, described the early deeds drafted by Bourne, recounted the transformation of the Mashpee Indians into Christian patriots. He documented their long struggle against second-class status, culminating in the community's final emergence as a township in 1869.

Hutchins' recitation was exhaustive, frequently tedious. He avoided dramatic gestures. For long periods he seemed little more than a conduit for the historical record. Unlike James Axtell, who was occasionally ironic about his own expertise and who openly raised the question of scholarly bias, Hutchins stuck to the facts. After so many clashing oral testimonies one had the sense of being on solid documentary ground. Everything rested on specific written evidence.

It was easy to forget that this historical narration was not a matter of walking on continuous solid ground but was more like jumping from one stone to the next. The documents relevant to life in Mashpee were often few and far between, biased in complex ways. The stones Hutchins landed on were slippery. One had to balance on them in a certain way. For example a missionary's "factual" record of how Indians had fallen from their proud ancestral past could reflect primarily his own discomfort at recent community changes that he was unable to control. A deed might record white more than Indian notions of ownership.

Hutchins' testimony—and his book (1979) based on it—leave no room for deep ambiguity. In his discourse the facts simply tell a story; they are not made to speak. Nor does the historian weigh the massive silences of the archives— Mashpee life as seen and lived by the vast majority of participants who did not write.

Coming as it did at the end of the long trial, the weight and coherence of Hutchins' long history lesson could not be adequately countered. . . .

THE VERDICT

When Hutchins finished, the defense rested its case. The two principal attorneys, St. Clair [for the defense] and Shubow [for the plaintiff], then delivered their summations. Each was a review of the trial's evidence in the form of a compelling story. Life in Mashpee over the centuries was given two heroic shapes and outcomes. [The plaintiff's attorney] recounted "an epic of survival and continuity." [The defense] celebrated a "slow but steady progress" toward "full participation" in American society.*

Judge Skinner then gave his instructions [to the jury]. He reviewed the course of the trial, mentioning briefly each witness. He reminded the jurors that the burden of proof was with the plaintiffs; they must prove by preponderance of the evidence (but not, as in a criminal case, beyond a reasonable doubt) the existence of a tribe

*For a detailed description of the defendants' trial strategy, see James D. St. Clair and William F. Lee, "Defense of Non-Intercourse Act Claims: The Requirement of Tribal Existence," 31 Maine Law Review 91 (1979).

in Mashpee. In its decision the jury was free to rely on inference and circumstantial evidence. They should not be unduly swayed by the authority of experts but must trust their own common sense judgment of the witnesses' credibility, weighing how well their conclusions matched the evidence presented, observing their way of speaking, even their "body English." . . .

The jurors were sequestered, accompanied by a large pile of documents. After twenty-one hours of deliberation they emerged with a verdict [that essentially said that the plaintiff was not a tribe for federal Non-Intercourse Act purposes.]

The verdict was a clear setback for the Indians' suit. But as a statement about their tribal history it was far from clear. . . .

AFTERTHOUGHTS

. . . The testimony I heard convinced me that organized Indian life had been going on in Mashpee for the past 350 years. Moreover a significant revival and reinvention of tribal identity was clearly in process. I concluded that since the ability to act collectively as Indians is currently bound up with tribal status, the Indians living in Mashpee and those who return regularly should be recognized as a "tribe."

Whether land improperly alienated after 1869 should be transferred to them, how much, and by what means was a separate issue. I was, and am, less clear on this matter. A wholesale transfer of property would in any case be politically unthinkable. Some negotiation and repurchase arrangement—such as that in Maine involving local, state, and federal governments—could eventually establish a tribal land base in some portion of Mashpee. But that, for the moment, is speculation. In the short run the outcome of the trial was a setback for Wampanoag tribal dynamism. . . .

NOTES

1. Thomas Tureen, "Afterword," in Paul Brodeur, *Restitution*, Boston, Mass.: Northeastern University Press, 1985, p. 147. Russel Barsh and James Youngblood Henderson, *The Road: Indians Tribes and Political Liberty*, Berkeley, Calif.: University of California Press, 1980, pp. 289–293.

2. Karen Blu, *The Lumbee Problem: The Making of an American Indian People*, Cambridge, Mass.: Cambridge University Press, 1980.

Mashpee: The Story of Cape Cod's Indian Town

Francis G. Hutchins

"It is a pleasant place to live, and the people are friendly to strangers," commented the young Harvard-trained school-teacher Simeon Kinsley in 1932. "But you can't hope to know them unless you live here, and go fishing with them."

Mashpee in 1960 was still as Kinsley had described it in 1932. What happened in Mashpee after 1960 was from an outside point of view simply part of what was happening to the Cape as a whole. A building boom, coupled with a sharp rise in the number of persons who made the Cape their year-round voting residence, altered the seasonal character of the entire Cape's economy and society. Mashpee's growth was actually slower-paced than that of the adjoining towns of Falmouth, Barnstable, and Sandwich. In Mashpee, however, because of Mashpee's small initial size and nonwhite character, this influx of new white voters had a vastly more convulsive effect. In the space of a few years, Mashpee underwent something resembling a revolution. Between 1960 and 1971, new homes were constructed in Mashpee at the rate of almost one hundred a year; it was as if an entirely new town had been added every year.

The switch-over to a voting majority of whites occurred so fast that few were aware of what was happening until it was completed. The political implications of Mashpee's building boom were obscured by the fact that whites had owned summer houses in Mashpee for decades. It was not immediately apparent that this time many home-builders would make Mashpee their principal residence. Nor was it automatically assumed that the new white voters would upset the political applecart. The initial reaction of Mashpee's political establishment to sky-rocketing land values and rapid development of shorefront property was enthusiastic. More wealth in town meant a larger tax base, and this had been considered beneficial in previous years. Throughout the 1960s and early 1970s, the annual reports of Mashpee's Indian-majority Boards of Selectmen spoke almost lyrically of the soaring number and value of building permits issued during the past twelve

From *Mashpee: The Story of Cape Cod's Indian Town*, by Francis G. Hutchins. West Franklin, N.H.: Amarta Press. © 1979 by Francis G. Hutchins.

months, and expressed pride that so many new people were discovering that Mashpee was a pleasant place to live. . . .

[But] one early sign of trouble came in 1971 when Mashpee enacted new zoning laws, rescinding an earlier zoning ordinance of 1963 which had been devised to accommodate the New Seabury Corporation. Occupying 1,240 acres of prime waterfront property, the New Seabury Corporation had developed a comprehensively planned recreational and retirement condominium community of several hundred units, which made it larger than the entire former town of Mashpee. Clustered housing with open expanses utilized as golf courses and bridle paths made New Seabury a splendid sight to behold. Unfortunately, limited access roads and signs reading KEEP OUT made it difficult for Mashpee's oldtimers to behold New Seabury's sights, let alone enjoy New Seabury's amenities. The closing of "ancient and traveled ways" had cut older Mashpee residents off from fishing spots familiar since childhood. Resentment at being made to feel unwelcome in portions of their own town lay behind the voters' decision to adopt the new zoning ordinance of 1971, forbidding certain of New Seabury's practices. New Seabury protested and in 1974 won vindication in Barnstable's Superior Court. New Seabury had received a binding commitment from the town in 1963, the Court ruled, and had proceeded with its development in good faith. Second thoughts were out of place.

A classic confrontation had developed. Like many other small towns overwhelmed by change, Mashpee was split between newcomers and oldtimers, between advocates of intensive development and advocates of more rustic traditions, between rich outsiders and long-established residents alarmed at the prospect of being priced out of their own neighborhood. But what served to catapult Mashpee's troubles onto the national stage was the fact that in Mashpee the oldtimers were Indians. . . .

The suit filed in Boston's federal district court on August 26, 1976, was formally a complaint filed by the "Mashpee Tribe" requesting that the court declare them to have always been the legal owners of most of the land in Mashpee. Their complaint required very few words to state, but the Indians filing suit were aware that they were launching a legal battle which could last for years. . . . The Indians had sued in federal court because they claimed to be a group with a status independent of the laws of Massachusetts. . . . In other words, if Mashpee was indeed the home of a federal Indian tribe, Mashpee was not a jurisdictional sub-unit of the Commonwealth of Massachusetts.

Federal primacy in relations with the tribes, proclaimed by the Constitution of 1789, had been spelled out in 1790 in the Indian Trade and Intercourse Act. By this act, the federal Congress set up procedures regulating numerous aspects of tribal relations, including land sales. Federal control of tribal land sales had several purposes. There was, first of all, a need to establish a procedure governing the transfer of ownership from tribal to state jurisdiction which would avert clashes among subsequent purchasers. Before land could be bought and sold by individuals, it had first to be recorded as land over which ordinary United States courts had authority. When private individuals negotiated directly with tribal Indians for the purchase of tribal land, disputes frequently arose because tribal Indians could not be restrained by state courts from selling the same tract several times to different white buyers. Making the federal government the only authorized purchaser of tribal land ensured an orderly chain of enforceable title: from tribe to federal government, to state government, to private owner.

Federal control thus helped prevent tribal Indians from cheating whites. It also helped prevent whites from cheating tribal Indians. A tribe which had been cheated might well seek revenge. Indian nations in the republic's early days were well-armed and, sometimes singly and often by combining together, could mount massive military campaigns with forces outnumbering those of any single state. . . .

From the very beginning, federal policy was based on a theory of cultural transformation. Signing treaties with semi-sovereign tribes was only the starting point; the goal was the eradication of most or all of these semi-sovereign entities and hence of the various tribal exceptions to ordinary United States jurisdiction as found in the states. . . .

[Thus] Federal Indian policy . . . anticipated a progression from foreign nation to federal ward to ordinary state citizenship of individual Indians. The federal government's plan was to encourage every individual Indian who owed allegiance to a federal Indian tribe to abandon what were called "tribal relations" and become instead a citizen of one of the several states. Since this process was to be voluntary, it would have to be gradual. Tribes would presumably be disbanded one-by-one in a more or less steady geographic progression from east to west as the nation's white population advanced toward them. . . .

Before 1776, the British monarch had exercised ultimate control of Indian affairs in North America. Then, for more than a decade, between the Declaration of Independence in 1776 and the adoption of the Constitution in 1789, the thirteen former British colonies, now thirteen sovereign nations, had conducted their foreign and Indian affairs individually, and had signed a number of treaties with Indian tribes. In 1789, the new federal government created by the Constitution formally took control of foreign and tribal affairs. But since tribal affairs were so close to home, the once-sovereign states were particularly reluctant to relinquish their role in this area. In these early days, powerful state governments were often able to defy the relatively weak federal government with impunity. . . . This is why the U.S. First Circuit Court of Appeals decided in 1975 that the Penobscot and Passamaquoddy* Indians of Maine belonged to tribes which should have been under federal protection from the beginning, but which had instead been dealt with almost exclusively by the state governments of Massachusetts and Maine for two hundred years. What was still unclear in 1976 when the "Mashpee Tribe" brought suit was whether Maine's Penobscot and Passamaquoddy tribes were an exception, or whether in Mashpee and indeed many places in the original thirteen states previously unrecognized federal tribes would now be found.

In 1789, the designers of federal Indian policy had assumed that the number of federal tribes would dwindle, not swell. The elimination of tribes from the roster

*Joint Tribal Council of Passamaquoddy Tribe v. Morton, 528 F. 2d 370 (1st Cir. 1975).

was to be the norm, the occasional addition of a new Indian nation, the exception. It would have been hard for the founders of the American republic to understand why any sensible individual who had not always been a member of a tribe would choose to become one. The survival and regrouping of existing Indian nations was thus allowed for. But it was not possible under the Constitution for a new nation to be created by non-tribal Indians. New names might be added to the federal roster of tribes in special circumstances, but there has never been any way under federal law for non-tribal Indians already living as ordinary citizens of an American state to organize a federal tribe. In conformity with its obligation to uphold existing federal laws, the federal court therefore had to ask, not whether Mashpee Indians now wished to form a federal tribe, but whether they had in fact always been a federal tribe, even if not previously recognized as such, from at least 1789 to the present.

At first glance, the best approach might seem to have been a review of the cultural characteristics of Mashpee Indians, of their dress, diet, customs, folklore and so on. But the presence of Indian cultural characteristics could not in itself prove the existence of a federal tribe. Nor could the absence of Indian cultural characteristics prove tribal non-existence. The legal concept of a federal tribe posits a political jurisdictional entity, which is rooted in an Indian culture existing before the United States came into being, but which may have evolved culturally, like any other political entity. The key to federal recognition of a tribe is continuity of tribal organization and not the relative degree of retention of pre-white-contact cultural characteristics. Indian cultural characteristics were potentially relevant, but only if they pointed to something beyond, to structures of governmental authority. . . .

Both sides agreed that the Mashpee Indians had shifted in formal terms from traditional tribal to English-derived structures of government by 1670. Lawyers for the Plaintiff, however, argued that the Mashpee Indians had made this shift in order to preserve an intact tribal community, that, in other words, they had adopted English-derived forms as a minimal, defensive concession to the need to survive in a now-alien world. Lawyers for the Defense, on the other hand, argued that the Mashpee Indians, in undertaking the far from minimal changes required of converts to Puritan Christianity, had made a sincere decision to renounce their tribal ties to Metacomet's Wampanoags and that throughout the subsequent centuries they had pressed steadily for a greater share of English-derived rights and privileges. Full legal equality had not been attained until 1869, but this, Defense lawyers contended, was more attributable to white resistance than to Indian reluctance. . . .

The basic facts of Mashpee history had never before been systematically assembled by anyone, and some of the facts recounted at the trial were as new to Mashpee Indian spectators as they were to the judge and jury. Many Mashpee Indians, for example, were accustomed to referring to themselves as the political heirs of Metacomet's Wampanoags. It was a surprise to hear testimony from experts for both sides that Indians from Mashpee had fought alongside the English against Metacomet in the war of 1675–1676. . . . Metacomet's heroic martyrdom has a strong appeal for modern-day Mashpee Indians. But if the Mashpee Indians had sided with Metacomet in 1675, the Mashpee community would have been eradicated just as completely as was Metacomet's Wampanoag federation. Mashpee survived as an organized entity because of conversion and adaptation, and not because of armed resistance. Armed resistance to English expansion did play a part in the history of Metacomet's Wampanoags, but the particular course of Cape Cod's history had led the Mashpee Indians, whether regretfully or not, to decide to live under English law a decade before Metacomet took up arms.

Was there evidence that Mashpee had lived in a tribal way in the centuries following the military eradication of Metacomet's Wampanoag nation in 1676? Mashpee's eighteenth and early nineteenth century mode of landholding, based on joint proprietorship of common lands, had similarities to surviving tribal practices in other parts of the United States. Before 1869, sales of Indian-owned land in Mashpee, like the sales of the lands of federal tribes, had been supervised, but in Mashpee the supervision had been state, not federal, and had stemmed not from jurisdictional considerations but simply from the state's fear that landless Indians would become paupers and hence expensive charges on the state's welfare rolls.

The most crucial historical question the jury had to confront was whether the Proprietors of Mashpee were a federal tribe in 1869 when whites began buying Mashpee land from individual Indians. The Massachusetts General Court had authorized such land sales despite the opposition of a majority of Mashpee residents present at the legislative hearing of February 9, 1869, and without referring the question to the federal government. If the Mashpee Indians were a federal tribe in 1869, the Massachusetts General Court could not legally have swept away the special restrictions on Mashpee land sales which had existed continuously ever since 1665. On the other hand, if the Mashpee Indians in 1869 were simply a disadvantaged group of Massachusetts residents, their disapproving vote could only be considered advisory, and the General Court's right to act as it thought fit would be validated. . . .

Judge Skinner interpreted the jury's verdict to mean that an "abandonment of tribal relations" had occurred between 1842 and 1869. In speculating about the jury's reasoning, the judge laid great stress on the pivotal importance of the legislative hearing held in Mashpee on February 9, 1869, just before the General Court abolished Mashpee's special legal status. At this hearing, many Mashpee residents had spoken eloquently of Mashpee's past accomplishments and future hopes. Judge Skinner noted that despite the two-to-one opposition to immediate acceptance of the "general laws" voiced at the hearing, all speakers had looked forward with definite satisfaction to being under the "general laws" before long. In 1869, all Mashpee Proprietors had seemed disposed to relinquish eventually all the statutory protections which set them apart from other Massachusetts residents. And since federal law treats tribal existence as something which cannot be resumed once dropped, there could be no turning back today by persons critical of a stance taken by their great-grandparents.

The Mashpee Indians: Tribe on Trial

Jack Campisi

The trial began on October 17 with the selection of a jury. The process was very simple: prospective jurors were called and examined by the judge. If in the opinion of the judge, the juror could render an unbiased decision, he or she was seated. . . .

The judge conducted the voir dire hearing. The prospective jurors were asked their occupations, the occupations of spouses, and whether they owned land on the Cape. Could they believe a tribe of Indians, some of whom might look black or white, could still live on the Cape? Had they formed an opinion about the case, and would a long trial seriously inconvenience them? At one point in the impanelment Shubow [the plaintiff's attorney] asked the court to inquire about a prospective juror's education, but the judge refused, saying, "I think we might get into a very serious problem if the issue of education were raised, like an elitist jury."[1] In relatively short order, the first twelve jurors were selected. . . . After a brief discussion between the judge and the attorneys on how to handle individuals wearing "Indian regalia" in court (the judge agreed not to permit it because it might distract members of the jury and provide an undue influence in their deliberations), the jury was seated and given some preliminary instruction by the judge. . . .

It was clear that the plaintiff was using as its definition of tribe one first enunciated in *Montoya v. United States*. In that case, the Supreme Court defined a tribe as "a body of Indians of the same or a similar race, united in a community under one leadership or government, and inhabiting a particular, though sometimes ill-defined, territory."[2]

Shubow's four "facts" or criteria, though not stated as concisely, hewed closely to *Montoya* in an attempt to place the weight of precedent behind the plaintiff's claim. The first criterion, that a tribe consists of a group of Indians "of the same or a similar race," though seemingly self-evident, nonetheless made it possible for a group that could not demonstrate a common ancestry to be recognized as a single entity. This was important in the Mashpee case because, as a "praying town" (a Protestant religious community), Mashpee undoubtedly included individuals from a number of Algonquian-speaking communities. The courts had consistently held that an Indian is a person who meets two qualifications: (1) at least some of his or her ancestors lived on the continent before discovery, and (2) the individual is identified as an Indian in the community in which he or she lives.[3] From a practical standpoint, if this criterion were accepted, the Mashpees need only show that they were direct descendants of some group of people previously identified as Indians. Since state and federal censuses as well as birth and marriage records were available, this task was relatively easy.

The second and third criteria required that the Mashpees be "united in a community under one leadership or government." The Mashpees contended that community was amply demonstrated by the close kin ties and the patterns of association they exhibited. "Leadership or government" implied the existence of formal structures and some centralization of power. From the perspective of the Mashpees, there was an alternative, more realistic model, one that consisted of a weak, decentralized unit which functioned on the basis of consensus. Political decisions were the result of interactions within and among the families, communicated informally to the leaders, and a continuous process of exchanging information and opinions that occurred, for the most part, away from public view. Social control was maintained by the sinuous reins of gossip, ridicule, and verbal assault. Such a system virtually defied documentation. Added to the plaintiff's woes was the need to explain how the tribe continued in existence after its aboriginal antecedents had disappeared and its government structure had been repeatedly altered to fit the fancy and dictates of the commonwealth. In relying on the *Montoya* decision, the Mashpees were asserting that they should not be held to a standard of leadership or government which exceeded that present at or around the time of contract. . . .

The fourth criterion, that they occupied a particular territory, was a crucial aspect of the case because it was for the recovery of land that the case had been instituted in the first place. The Mashpees alleged that the loss of their land, which they had held in common, had been the direct result of the unilateral action of the commonwealth. Such loss could not be used as an argument to deny their existence and thus prohibit their legal action. Judge Skinner concurred with this view. . . .

With the completion of Shubow's opening remarks, James St. Clair [the defendant's attorney] presented an outline of the defendant's position. . . . He told the jurors, "If I may be permitted to state what I understand the issue to be, it is substantially not whether a group of people in Mashpee consider themselves to be a community, as my brother [Shubow] had mentioned several times. The question is: Are they a tribe? Does this community exercise essential governmental functions? Is it a separate government? The defendants will show, through evidence, that under no circumstances does the community of Mashpee perform any such function."[4]

St. Clair briefly described three factors that would support the defendants' claim. First, the federal government had never recognized the Mashpees as a tribe.

Second, there had never been any taking of land from the Mashpees. Third, the Mashpees had never signed a treaty with either the Massachusetts Bay Colony, the king of England, or the United States. "So we have none of the emoluments of a formal government or state or tribe," he told the jury, "and it's for that reason we have to look back in history to see what the evolution of this group of people is, racially, economically, socially and governmentally, if you will."[5] . . .

The first expert called by the plaintiff was the eminent ethnohistorian James Axtell . . . who described in detail the history of the Mashpees from the early 1600s up to 1900. Axtell traced the development of the earliest community, the changes that occurred or were imposed, and the role of various missionaries. An expert on New England colonial history, he placed the Mashpees in a broad historical perspective, comparing them with other New England Indian groups. Axtell, however, addressed the definition of tribes only in an oblique and inferential manner.[6]

This writer, called to present data on the contemporary social organization of the Mashpees, offered the first of several definitions of *tribe.* Staying well within the parameters set by *Montoya,* I defined a tribe as a group of Indian people whose membership is by ascription, who share or claim a common territory, have a "consciousness of kind," and represent a community with a recognized leadership.[7] Based on these elements, I asserted that the Mashpees were a tribe.

Having described the historical and ethnographic record of the Mashpee tribe, the plaintiff presented witnesses who could show that the Mashpees' experiences were similar to those of recognized tribes in the United States, that the recognition of tribes was largely fortuitous, and that no definition that included the concepts of sovereignty or relied on racial or cultural purity or the presence of self-sustaining political and economic organizations would suffice. The first such witness called was Vine Deloria, Jr., a political scientist and member of the Sioux tribe. Margolin [the plaintiff's attorney] examined Deloria, trying to establish a definition of *tribe* and develop a broad comparative base for its implementation among American Indians. After repeated objections by the defense counsel to the content of the questions, Judge Skinner stepped in:

THE COURT: Let me try a question.
MR. MARGOLIN: Yes, your honor.
THE COURT: Can you tell us what criteria you use to identify an Indian community as a tribe? . . .
THE WITNESS: As I use it and as I understand other Indian people using it, it means a group of people living pretty much in the same place who know who their relatives are. And I think that's the basic way we look at things. You can add or subtract all kinds of footnotes if you want, but I think that would be the generally acceptable way Indians would look at it.[8]

Margolin attempted to develop the definition by asking if there could be a tribe without a political organization. The defense objected and was overruled and Deloria was allowed to answer.

This is getting increasingly difficult to respond to, because we don't make the distinctions that you do in the Anglican [Anglo] world, religious, political, and everything else. What you are talking about is a group of people who know where they are. They may have to respond to outside pressures and adopt political structures, religious structures, or economic structures to deal with that outside society. There is no question I can answer where I have to begin to divide that community up and say we have these identifiable structures, the same way you do in the white men's world, because it's not the way I look at it.[9]

Margolin then asked if a group could be a tribe if it could not exercise political control over a territory. The defendant objected, and the judge called for a bench conference. Bench conferences are held out of earshot of the witness and jury, but they are instructive about the court's views and attitudes. This one was particularly so because it indicated that the judge either did not understand the argument made by Deloria or was opposed to it. . . .

[It] is clear from the conference that Judge Skinner had formed an opinion as to what constituted a tribe and that the broad definition preferred by Deloria was not the direction in which he was heading.

The plaintiff next called Jean Ludtke, an anthropologist who had completed a dissertation on the planned community of New Seabury (1977) and before that had written a master's thesis on Mashpee. She had become interested in the problems of ethnic boundary maintenance and concluded that Mashpee was an Indian community amenable to ethnic boundary research. She spent the summer of 1973 gathering data for her thesis and thus was familiar with the tribe's and the town's recent history.[10]

Ludtke defined *tribe* as a group of people who are biologically and culturally homogeneous, with strong kinship ties, who inhabit a contiguous territory with clearly defined social boundaries, and who recognize a leadership drawn from among their members.[11] Based on these criteria, she asserted that the Mashpees are a tribe.

St. Clair handled the cross-examination. He began by challenging Ludtke's conclusion that the Mashpees are a tribe by referring to a passage from her thesis in which she classified them as a band community. . . . On this basis, St. Clair asked, was it not true that the Mashpees were a band community and not a tribe as she contended? Ludtke answered yes, and St. Clair then asked whether she had changed her mind since 1973. Ludtke attempted to explain the discrepancy between her 1973 and 1977 opinions by saying that she had changed her mind as to the applicability of the term *tribe* to the Mashpees between the writing of the first and last chapters, but St. Clair would have none of that. He asked her to whom she communicated this shift, and she responded, to the attorneys for the plaintiff. . . .

Toward the end of its presentation of fact, the plaintiff called William C. Sturtevant, ethnologist at the Smithsonian Institution. Like others, Sturtevant was called upon to define the term *tribe* and provide a professional opinion as to whether he thought the Mashpees were a tribe. And, like others, he was to present a range of ethnological data to show that other groups recognized as tribes by the United States and the Mashpees possessed the same characteristics. . . .

The difficulties of eliciting what at first blush seems like relatively routine information are illustrated by an exchange between the counsels for the plaintiff and defense and the court. Margolin asked Sturtevant how he used the word *tribe*, and St. Clair objected. When Judge Skinner asked Margolin if he was asking for a definition, he answered, "No, your honor, not exactly," which confused the judge sufficiently to necessitate another bench conference.

> THE COURT: What do you expect his answer to be to that one?
>
> MR. MARGOLIN: That the term is a comparative [sic] term which requires a determination in this case whether the characteristics of the group being studied are comparable to those of groups who are undisputably [sic] tribes, as the term is used, and the like. And that . . . it is not strictly a question of definition but of methodology of figuring out whether somebody is a tribe. . . .
>
> THE COURT: I think, perhaps, it would be better to go right to that. What factors, what are the proper factors in the determination of whether a group is a tribe; is that what you are trying to get at?
>
> MR. MARGOLIN: That the factors that are significant varied, depending on the group being studied; that there is a group of basic relatively easy questions on which there is not any dispute in the field. Then there is a group of disputed questions around the edges. I am simply asking for a definition. . . .
>
> THE COURT: How is this going to help the jury?
>
> MR. MARGOLIN: The ultimate purpose of the testimony is to elicit those factors which Dr. Sturtevant believes are essential in determining whether the Mashpees constitute a tribe in the sense comparable to that of the characteristics of other tribes that are undisputably tribes, as recognized by scholars in the field.[12]

Judge Skinner was displeased with Margolin's line of questioning and suggested that he ask the witness how he would determine whether a group was a tribe. Margolin agreed to use that approach and the parties returned to their respective stations, but before they could resume testimony the defense asked for another conference. The defendant raised the issue of "bootstrapping," the practice of one expert basing an opinion on the opinion of another expert. . . .

The plaintiff's case had hit a serious snag, and the lawyers spent the lunch break trying to unravel it. Sturtevant's testimony was essential to the plaintiff's argument, yet it would not be admitted if it appeared to be based on opinions expressed by Axtell and Campisi. In forming his opinion, Sturtevant could rely on facts presented by other witnesses. The problem was, in the judge's view, that there were not many facts, just "a lot of opinion." . . .

After reviewing the information drawn from past testimony and used to form an opinion, Margolin asked if the Mashpees were a tribe. Before Sturtevant could answer, St. Clair again objected, was overruled, and then requested a bench conference.

Once again St. Clair raised the issue of the admissibility of Sturtevant's opinion, arguing that it was based on conclusions and not facts. At issue was a discrepancy between the way anthropologists work and rules of evidence. The dilemma is summed up in the following exchange.

MR. ST. CLAIR: It has always been the law and for sound reasons that you cannot bootstrap one opinion on another and that includes conclusions drawn from data. That's all Campisi did. Remember, you may recall, I asked, "where are your notes," and all that. And I asked that they be brought, and they never did bring them.

THE COURT: They weren't obliged to. . . .

MR. ST. CLAIR: No. But, your Honor, there is [sic] the data. People can look at the data and draw different conclusions from it [sic]. He [Sturtevant] is entitled to draw his conclusions from it. Campisi is entitled to draw his. But he can't draw his conclusions from Campisi's conclusions.

THE COURT: Campisi reported some findings which were not conclusions, but observations. Now they may be inaccurate. I don't know.

MR. ST. CLAIR: We are not talking about accuracy.

MR. MARGOLIN: Dr. Sturtevant has testified that those are the kind of ethnographic observations on which an ethnologist like himself continually relies as a scholar, and I will have him expand on that.

THE COURT: I think it all goes to the weight of it. I think, as I said, it is pretty frail stuff coming in this way, but I think under the rule it is admissible.[13] . . .

This and other exchanges throughout the trial serve to illustrate the difficulties of bringing anthropological and historical data to bear on the resolution of a legal problem. What is fact in anthropology is not necessarily an admissible fact in law, and what is acceptable methodology in the discipline may well be questionable as evidence. Both the content and its presentation are determined by rules that have other evidential matters in mind. This was made clear by the difficulty of, and controversy over, separating fact from conclusion and in Judge Skinner's characterizations of the material as frail and flimsy. The court and defense seemed to be looking for an experimental model with its implication of replicability. The rules of evidence are designed to ensure that the jury hears facts or opinions based on facts; however, facts in anthropology are sometimes the recorded observations of the fieldworker, who exercises no control over variables and who stresses the anonymity of the sources. With a researcher's field notes, another researcher should come to the same or at least a similar conclusion, assuming agreement on definitions, which certainly was not possible in this instance. . . .

St. Clair conducted the cross-examination of Sturtevant, covering a wide range of subjects but always directed toward demonstrating that the witness had no special knowledge of the Mashpees, had relied on insufficient information in forming his opinions, and had an inadequate or at least imprecise understanding of the word *tribe*. At times the exchanges were sharp and confrontational.

Q. Now, sir, when you have used the word "tribe" in this case, you have not used that word in any legal sense, have you?

A. I'm not a lawyer, I don't know the legal sense.

Q. The answer, then, I take it, is you have not purported to use the word "tribe" in any legal sense.

A. Purported, no, I have not purported.

Q. Now, I take it that the word "tribe" in the anthropological sense that you have used the word does not have a precise meaning, so far as you were concerned?

A. I believe I used it in several anthropological senses.

Q. Do you have, when you testify in this courtroom, a precise definition for the word "tribe," a single definition?

A. Yes.

Q. Would you tell us what that definition is, sir?

A. The easiest way would be to have read back what I said yesterday. I can try to reproduce it again.

It's a group that is descended from aboriginal Indian[s]; that is a bounded social group—that is summarizing what I said—has recognized identity as Indian, recognized by themselves and by their neighbors; has groupwide internal social and political organizations; does not have any subdivisions which are more like tribes elsewhere than that division itself; nor [is] it a part itself of a larger group which is more like tribes elsewhere than that group is.

Q. Now, in addition to that definition, as I understand it, you have used the word in the comparative [sic] sense?

A. In the theoretical sense. This definition itself is in part comparative [sic].

Q. I was going to ask you that.

When you say it is, let's say, a bounded social group, you mean, if I understand your testimony correctly, compared to other recognized tribes?

A. In part, but also compared to the social groups with which it shares boundaries.

Q. But it's a comparison. There is no absolute standard in your definition.

A. The meaning of the word depends on the other—the other cases to which it's been applied in effect.

Q. Most of the cases to which it's been applied are so-called recognized tribes, are they not?

A. Bounded social group?

Q. As tribes.

A. Excuse me?

Q. I'll withdraw the question if you don't understand.

A. Better try another one.[14]

. . . The burden of presenting the defendant's argument that the Mashpees were not a tribe fell to Jeanne Guillemin, a sociologist from Boston College. . . . Guillemin had the responsibility of defining for the defense the meaning of *tribe.* . . . For her definition Guillemin relied on the works of two noted American anthropologists, George Murdock and Julian Steward. The testimony, with St. Clair questioning, went as follows:

Q. Would you tell us in substance what first Dr. Murdock's definition of the tribe and then Dr. Stewart's [Steward's].

A. The basis for a definition of a tribe that George Murdock used emphasizes the sovereignty of a particular group; that is, a tribe is known by, and I quote here, "original and definitive jurisdiction over some sphere of social life in which the organization (tribe) has the legitimate right to make decisions having a significant effect on its members." It gives, as an example, the allocation of economic resources, punishments of legal infractions, control of labor, et cetera.

Q. Is Dr. Murdock's definition recognized by anthropologists as being an authoritative definition?

A. Yes, it is.

Q. Now will you outline for us Dr. Stewart's [Steward's] definition?

A. Dr. Stewart's [Steward's] definition deals more with cultural aspects of tribal organization. He relies on three characteristics. The first one is basically the sovereignty one, that is, that a tribal group is fairly simply organized and independent and self-contained and with that is the understanding that it's usually a fairly isolated group. The second aspect has to do with cultural uniformity.

Q. Cultural what?

A. Uniformity. Unity. Uniformity. The idea that most people in the community conform in terms of their values and behavior to a certain general standard. It's acceptable by everyone. The third characteristic is that the culture of the tribe is unique relative to other cultural traditions. Those are the three aspects.[15]

Using these criteria, Guillemin concluded that the Mashpees were not a tribe.

The cross-examination of Guillemin was extensive, detailed, and at times acrimonious. She was questioned on her knowledge of the Mashpees, her methodology, and her definition of *tribe*. Under cross-examination she acknowledged that neither of the writers upon whom she relied for her definition used the term *sovereignty* in his definition. Shubow, who handled the cross-examination for the plaintiff, returned repeatedly to the witness's definition. Finally, at the request of the court, Guillemin read the portion of Steward's work that she used to formulate her definition. Though admitting that the quote did not contain the troublesome word, she maintained that it was implied. . . .

Shubow finished by asking the witness if she had not made an effort, after agreeing to serve as a witness, to find a definition of *tribe* that included the word *sovereignty*, and, not finding one "you went and found a definition of the word 'sovereignty' and added the word tribe." The defense objection was overruled and the witness allowed to respond. She said, "No." With this Shubow moved to strike all portions of the testimony having to do with the "notion of tribe," but the judge denied the motion, saying it was for the jury to sort out.

The last expert witness for the defense was Francis Hutchins. His direct testimony covered three days and consisted of a detailed review of the historical records, from which he concluded that the Mashpees had not been a tribe at any time from 1666 through 1976.[16] He defined a tribe as "an entity composed of persons of American Indian descent, which entity possesses distinct political, legal, cultural attributes, which attributes have descended directly from aboriginal precursors."[17] By political, he told the court, he meant that there was present an acknowledged leadership and a structure for decision making accepted by the members of the group and based on an internal organization different from that "followed by the ordinary citizen of the United States."[18] . . .

By the time Hutchins left the witness stand, the trial had produced a bewildering variety of definitions of tribe, more than the judge could take or the jury could fathom. With but a few days left in the trial, Skinner called the lawyers to the side bar and announced:

> THE COURT: I am seriously considering striking all of the definitions given by all of the experts of a tribe and all of their opinions as to whether or not the inhabitants of Mashpee at any time could constitute a tribe. I let it all in on the theory that there was a professionally accepted definition of tribe within these various disciplines. It is becoming more and more apparent that each definition is highly subjective and idiosyncratic and generated for a particular purpose not necessarily having anything to do with the Non-Intercourse Act of 1790, and I am rather persuaded that [what] it is doing, rather than helping us, is simply making the issue more difficult. I certainly invite comments.[19]

[Defense attorney] Van Gestel spoke first, arguing that a number of definitions were used by the disciplines and about all that could be expected was that they be given a hearing. Skinner countered that not only was there no accepted definition in history or anthropology, but, worse, "You figure that whatever definition of tribe you want, you just go find the right anthropologist, and you can get it."[20] Shubow suggested that since the court was going to instruct the jury as to the meaning of *tribe*, it would be valuable for the jurors to keep in mind how closely the experts' definitions were to the judge's. But Skinner seemed not to be listening. "As long as they [experts] stay with their thing," he told the lawyers, "they are in pretty good shape. It is when we get into these grandiose definitions that they all seem to be in trouble."[21] The conversation meandered on a bit longer with the attorneys bickering over the quality of the ongoing testimony and the judge musing about the possibility of cutting "some new ground," presumably meaning establishing a new legal definition of *tribe*. Finally, after thirty-eight days of trial, the two sides rested.

The trial had begun to answer a deceptively simply question: Are the Mashpees a tribe within the meaning of the Non-Intercourse Act? This, in turn, required a definition of *tribe* and the ascertaining of facts. But without an agreed-upon definition either in law or in social science, the search became a matter of fielder's choice. The sides presented witnesses whose definitions were consonant with their legal arguments. This portion of the trial was geared to influence the judge in the formation of his definition; however, in the end the conflicting views led him to discount all the alternatives for one of his own creation, one founded on less substance than those he discarded.

The jury was charged with the determination of fact. But this was not simply a matter of determining which set of experts was telling the truth because the experts were testifying to more than the events. They were speaking of their significance as indicators of tribal identity. . . . Definition and analysis were inseparably linked. . . .

It was now time for Judge Skinner to "break new ground," to tell the jury his definition of *tribe*. Lecturing extemporaneously, he gave a cursory background on the legal history of the term and then stated the definition from the *Montoya* case: "a body of Indians of the same or a similar race united in a community under one leadership or government and inhabiting a particular though sometimes ill-defined territory."[22] The difficult task, according to the judge, was in applying the general rule to the evidence, and to that end, he offered a series of amplifications of the definition's component parts. . . .

The judge instructed the jury for over three hours. It took the attorneys another two hours to make known their objections, most of which Skinner rejected. . . .

The judge's charge presented something for everybody. It gave the plaintiff the basic definition it had sought but modified it enough at least minimally to satisfy the defendant. But the judge went well beyond the effort to satisfy the parties; he altered the definition sufficiently to affect the outcome. It seems clear from his comments that Skinner could not accept the possible consequences of the application of the Non-Intercourse Acts in this case and because he could not control the facts, he changed the rules by which the facts were to be judged. He made his views explicit when he told the attorneys:

> I think that you have got a constitutional question, really. You (Margolin) are saying that somebody who sells his land in 1842 full and freely and for fair consideration with full knowledge, and being otherwise an adult human and so on, can get it back just for the say so 150 years later, and that rather severely distinguishes that group from the rest of the population; and, if you are going to make that distinction as a constitutional question, you have to show that there is a real honest-to-God difference between that group and everybody else; *and, you know the remedy you are seeking is a very radical remedy. It seems to me quite proper to say that whoever seeks that remedy has got to show that they are in a radically different kind of status than other people.*[23]

Although it was reasonable to set standards that differentiated between Indian tribes and other groups in society, it was not reasonable to draw those standards in such a way as to make them unattainable even for federally recognized tribes, which is precisely what Judge Skinner proposed to do. While acknowledging that there was no single set of criteria all tribes could meet and that federal tribal status was serendipitous, the judge then proceeded to draw his own definition, which few could meet. The radical remedy for taking Indian land was imposed by the federal courts not to protect the Indians as much as to ensure federal preeminence in the field of Indian relations. Skinner was trapped by his own legal prejudices. He could do no less than define away the plaintiff.

NOTES

1. *Mashpee Tribe v. New Seabury Corp.*, 427 F. Supp. 899 (D. Mass. 1977), and *Mashpee Tribe v. Town of Mashpee*, 447 F. Supp. 940 (D. Mass. 1978).
2. *Montoya v. U.S.*, 180 U.S. 261 (1901).
3. Felix Cohen, *Handbook of Federal Indian Law.* Facsimile ed. Albuquerque, N.M.: University of New Mexico Press, 1942.
4. TT 2:45.
5. TT 2:47.
6. TT 5:2–85.
7. TT 11:60–72.
8. TT 17:125–26.
9. TT 17:127–28.
10. TT 18:113–22.
11. TT 18:147–48.
12. TT 21:84–87.
13. TT 21:104–6.
14. TT 21:43–45.
15. TT 31:110–11.
16. TT 36:141.
17. TT 36:124.
18. TT 36:126.
19. TT 36:189–90.
20. TT 36:190.
21. TT 36:193.
22. TT 40:36.
23. TT 38:190–91; emphasis added.

Identity as Idiom: *Mashpee* Reconsidered

Jo Carrillo

DIFFERENT OR NOT?: THE LITERATURE ABOUT MASHPEE

One often-cited theoretical [law review] article emerged about Mashpee: *Translating Yonnondio by Precedent and Evidence: The Mashpee Indian Case* by Gerald Torres and Kathryn Milun.[1] Torres and Milun argued that the legal system, its rules of evidence and its use of precedent, rendered it unable to suppress its anti-Indian bias, and hence unable to hear the call of the Mashpee story.[2] In Torres and Milun's theoretical construct, "hearing the call of the Mashpee story" was a call for a presumption that would operate in favor of acknowledging tribal status. While this suggestion corresponded with the plaintiff's argument on appeal, it was nonetheless considered novel in the scholarly literature because of what it posited about American Indian culture(s). According to Torres and Milun, American Indian cultures were by definition irreconcilably different from mainstream American culture; and given that this irreconcilability could not be proven . . . it ought to be presumed as a matter of law.[3]

Although Torres and Milun were right to say that Mashpee Indian culture was in many ways significantly different from mainstream culture, it was not, at least in this case, irreconcilably so. *Mashpee* was not an either-or case because Mashpee Indian life was not altogether that different from Mashpee non-Indian life. Persons comprising the Mashpee tribe were neither clearly "Indian" nor "non-Indian" insofar as they had adopted American material culture, and, in most daily respects, were much like their neighbors in terms of how they lived and what they owned. . . .

The call for a presumption in favor of irreconcilable difference was highly problematic. As noted above, Mashpee "tribespeople" were in many material ways indistinguishable from Mashpee "townspeople," and when they showed up in court claiming difference, they *looked* like "contemporary Americans." Unfortunately, this picture brought with it the weight of a thousand words, ultimately exposing the Mashpee plaintiff to charges like those Hutchins voiced: that the persons calling themselves the Mashpee tribe had reconstructed their Indian identity in line with contemporary pan-Indian principles, not authentic, traditional Mashpee ones, and that they had done so out of greed.[4] It also subjected the Mashpee to the criticism that their decision to sue for return of their aboriginal land was so impractical as to be chaotic. Thus a judgment in favor of the Mashpee Indians, the critics warned, would "overturn almost 200 years of real property law and transactions," thereby forcing the court to serve as a "transitional government," a move that would itself "instigate civil disobedience on a massive scale."[5]

In *Making All the Difference*, Martha Minow, another legal scholar, took a different theoretical approach in an effort to support the Mashpee claim for tribal status. While Torres and Milun argued that Native American cultures were irreconcilably different from the mainstream, Minow argued against forcing cases like *Mashpee* into rigid "either-or" frameworks.[7] . . . Despite their point of disagreement, Torres, Milun, and Minow all took the position that the legal process unjustly discounted the Mashpee plaintiff's perception of itself as a tribe, a perception that should have counted in the assessment of legal difference. One good way to count it, Minow wrote, was first to initiate the breakdown of the idea that a tribe and a non-tribe were mutually exclusive legal entities, and then to set aside definitional questions so as to make possible a direct inquiry into the "real" issue: whether the plaintiff, given its history, ought to receive protection from land sales under federal law.[8] This line of inquiry, Minow argued, would have countered the defendants' effort to persuade the court that the *Mashpee* dispute was ultimately about competing visions of the town's future, rather than about the violation of federally protected American Indian rights.[9] In subordinating the question of land use to the more abstract question of rights, Minow's argument rested itself on one of the most . . . problematic assumptions of American property law: the assumption that land use—the physical use of land (space)—is an acultural activity, and thus a phenomenon completely separable from culture and identity.

To close, both Torres, Milun, with their procedural suggestion for defending tribal rights, and Minow, with her rights-based one, illustrate what makes the *Mashpee* case so central. On one hand, a tribe is a distinct entity. Based on that distinctness, the federal government decides whether or not to offer its (high-priced) protection under acts like the Non-Intercourse Act to groups like the Mashpee. Yet on the other hand, a tribe is very much part of the community at large, an observation especially true for eastern tribes. In *Mashpee* there was no distinct, impermeable boundary between the tribe and the town, at least as far as culture was concerned, though there were rigid class boundaries. And yet both sides (not just the defendants, as Minow asserts) held a vision for the town's future. These visions were in sharp competition, and, more importantly, they were culturally constructed. From this relational set of competing views, the distinct Mashpee vision emerged, unexpressed, and unarticulated until well after the final stages of litigation.[10] Here, too, what was distinctly "Indian" (or tribal) about

Mashpee life came into focus, not as an essential trait, but as a political and economic commitment to a specific way of using a specific set of resources.

One point of cultural irreconcilability [thus] . . . emerges from the record,
rather than from stereotypes of who the Mashpees were or should have been as
"Indians." Though the Mashpee Indians believed in and practiced the dictates
of private property, they viewed various waterfront areas as a common resource.
In this respect they were indeed irreconcilably different from their affluent
neighbors who regarded the shore as highly marketable (and hence exclusive)
private property. So integral a part of Mashpee culture was this view of the
commons, that in the years during which the tribe controlled the town of
Mashpee without holding title to most of its land, this notion had not been
articulated, either as ideal or concern.

Campisi testified that the failure to articulate this norm of the waterfront as
commons resulted because shared use of the waterfront areas was in fact so fundamental a part of Mashpee life that it had not been questioned until the influx of
newcomers; hence it had not been articulated, only acted upon.[11] The right to use
the waterfront areas as a commons, regardless of who owned the adjacent land,
was not consciously expressed as a "right" in Mashpee culture—it was simply
assumed. But when the process whereby the Mashpee tribespeople lost local political control rendered them outsiders to power, what was only background became
visible. At this point, key symbols of identity, and ultimately of access to power
(like the symbolic word "tribe"), became so charged that their meaning was adjudicated. Meanwhile, the system of non-Indian dominance—a system that opposed
custom to law, superstition to reason, impracticality to common sense, and Indian
to "American"—was left not only unquestioned, but more deeply entrenched
than before, both at the federal and the local levels.[12] Ironically, it was not until
the legal process reached its end that the Mashpee came to articulate their ideal
of the shore as a common, inalienable resource, and in some ways, regrettably, to
even reconfigure this idea into stereotype.[13]

CONCLUSION

The Mashpee Wampanoag Tribe turned to federal law to validate what it regarded
as its superior rights to its ancestral land. What the Mashpee Tribe discovered was
that federal law served as both resource and constraint; that is, the law that was
applied to resolve the dispute ended up escalating it instead. . . . The law presumed Indian ways to be primitive, chaotic, timeless, simple. More troubling, it
assumed that any tribal adaptation to colonial society was in fact an assimilative
embrace of the mainstream. Even as late as 1977, lawyers who prided themselves
on defending "innocent" land purchasers from the Non-Intercourse Act claims of
"greedy" Indians interpreted this body of law to allow for the unwitting and
unconscious assimilation of Indian tribes into the American mainstream.
According to this view, if tribespeople conformed to the broader culture, they

were said to be choosing to assimilate, even if only constructively so. This presumption, the lawyers argued, was rebuttable, but *only if* the tribe could prove that it had been coerced by the broader society into abandoning the "old" and embracing the "new."

The commentary that surfaced to explain and counter what happened in *Mashpee*, though sympathetic to the Mashpee Tribe's position, based itself on similarly general discussions about whether the Mashpee were or were not culturally different from the mainstream. But while the commentary noted that identity is negotiated and dependent on circumstance, it nevertheless conceptualized identity as something separate and apart from social life. Hence this commentary ignored a significant body of local evidence about land use patterns in Mashpee in favor of wrestling with time-weary stereotypes about Indians generally. The implication of the local data that rested directly beneath the surface of these various layers and articulations of stereotype linked the Mashpee Wampanoag Indians to other Indian nations across the country. In other words, while the Mashpee may have had a unique and on-the-surface "non-Indian" history, the way in which they lost control of their land linked them to other tribes who have also been forced to contend with the flow of a new, late-twentieth century wave of "settlers." These settlers moved to Indian Country and found themselves subject to tribal jurisdiction; this in turn fueled their bitter resentment about the fact that Indian nations have a legitimate governmental interest in those areas. In Indian Country, this particular kind of disappointment has given rise to rhetoric that Indian governments, because they represent "irreconcilably different" cultures, do not know how to use land in ways that maintain or increase property values, and that Indian people, because they have treaty rights, lead lives of luxury bankrolled by the federal government. These sorts of stereotypes carried persuasive weight in *Mashpee*, even though it was the Mashpee Wampanoag Indians' use of the shore as a common area that helped maintain its undeveloped and wild quality, a quality that contributed to making the lots along the shore some of the highest-priced real estate in Mashpee. But despite this irony, the non-Indians in Mashpee complained that their property rights ought to trump any rights that the Indians might have, and that it would be an injustice for federal law to validate Indian rights over what they considered the more fundamental property rights of non-Indians. From this position it was but a short leap to their next argument, which was that the Mashpee were not an Indian tribe and hence had no rights under federal law. All of this rhetoric found its way into the legal process, where it in turn found support in the existing doctrine. . . .

NOTES

1. Gerald Torres and Kathryn Milun, "Translating *Yonnondio* by Precedent and Evidence: The Mashpee Indian Case," 1990 *Duke Law Journal* 625 (1990). See also Peggy C. Davis, "Contextual Legal Criticism: A Demonstration Exploring Hierarchy and 'Feminine' Style," 66 *New York University Law Review* 1635 (1991); Cheryl I. Harris, "Whiteness as Property," 106 *Harvard Law Review* 1707, 1761–66 (1993) (discussing "the violence done to

the Mashpee and other oppressed groups [resulting] from the law's refusal to acknowledge the negotiated quality of identity"); Jane S. Schacter, "Metademocracy: The Changing Structure of Legitimacy in Statutory Interpretation," 108 *Harvard Law Review* 593, 624–626 (1995) (analyzing *Mashpee* in terms of applying postmodern theory to statutory interpretation).

Minow also dealt with *Mashpee*, and like Torres and Milun, Minow relied on James Clifford's work for her analysis. Martha Minow, *Making All the Difference: Inclusion, Exclusion and American Law*, Ithaca, N.Y.: Cornell University Press, 1990). at 351–356. See also Martha Minow, "Identities," 3 *Yale Journal of Law & Humanities* 97 (1991) (discussing the negotiated quality of identity).

2. Although Torres & Milun do not rely on Robert Coles, *The Call of Stories: Teaching and the Moral Imagination* Boston, Mass.: Houghton Mifflin Company, 1989, their article parallels Dr. Coles's book. In "Stories and Theories," for example, Coles describes the difference in approach between his two residency supervisors, Dr. Binger and Dr. Ludwig. Dr. Binger was regarded by his students as intensely theoretical; Dr. Ludwig as somewhat of an antitheorist. One day Dr. Ludwig suggested the following to Coles:

> "The people who come to see us bring us their stories. They hope they tell them well enough so that we understand the truth of their lives. They hope we know how to interpret their stories correctly. We have to remember that what we hear is *their story.*
> "Remember, what you are hearing [from the patient] is to some considerable extent a function of *you* hearing. . . .
> "In a manner of speaking," Dr. Ludwig added, "we physicians bring *our* stories to the consultation room—even as," he pointedly added, "the teachers of physicians carry *their* stories into the consulting rooms where 'supervisory interaction' takes place.

Sometimes our knowledge and our theories (the two are not to be confused with each other!) interfere with or interrupt a patient's momentum; hence the need for caution as we listen and get ready to ask our questions. The same was true for the 'case presentations' I was making to my supervisors: I formulated my account of a patient to a particular supervisor in keeping with the way I presumed that doctor was inclined to think with respect to psychological matters. The story I told would be affected by his mind's habits and predilection, *his* story." Coles, supra, at 7, 15, 24.

3. Torres & Milun, supra note 1, at 631–632, 658 (considering orality as one of the aspects of Native American culture responsible for the irreconcilable difference). The suggestion of a presumption in favor of tribal status has been made before. See, e.g., Terry Anderson, "Federal Recognition: The Vicious Myth," 4 *American Indian Journal*, May 1978, at 7, 19. *Cf.* William W. Quinn, Jr., "Federal Acknowledgment of American Indian Tribes: Authority, Judicial Interposition, and 25 C.F.R. §83," 17 *American Indian Law Review* 37 (1992). at 54–55 n.63 (arguing that under the new BIA process, petitions for tribal acknowledgment are apparently regularly opposed by other tribes, and noting that the Tulalip tribe opposed the Samish and Snohomish petition and the Navajo Tribe opposed the San Juan Southern Paiute claim for federal recognition).

4. For variations on this theme, see, e.g., Francis G. Hutchins, *Mashpee: the Story of Cape Cod's Indian Town*, West Franklin, N.H.: Amarta Press, 1979. (Professor Hutchins, a Senior Research Fellow at the Newberry Library in Chicago, testified as a witness for the defense in Mashpee); van Gestel, "When Fictions Take Hostages," in *The Invented Indian: Cultural Fictions and Government Policies*, James Clifton, ed., New Brunswick, N.J.: Transaction Publishers, 1990. (at the time of trial, Mr. van Gestel was a partner in the Boston, Massachusetts firm of Goodwin, Procter and Hoar; he represented title insurance companies in Mashpee); James D. St. Clair and William F. Lee, "Defense of Non-Intercourse Act Claims," 31 *Maine Law Review* 91 (1979) (St. Clair, a partner at the Boston, Massachusetts firm of Hale and Dorr, and Lee, his associate, represented the Town of Mashpee at trial).

5. van Gestel, supra note 4, at 293–294.

The characterization of the Non-Intercourse Act as an obscure federal statute only recently revived by Indian land claims cases is inaccurate given that the principle of inalienability is central to federal Indian law. The Non-Intercourse Act has in fact been the basis for a steady stream of twentieth-century cases meant to ensure federal preeminence over states by protecting Indian title. Tim Vollmann, "A Survey of Eastern Indian Land Claims: 1970–1979," 31 *Maine Law Review* 5 (1979).

The claim that chaos would follow the cancellation of conveyances of Indian land has been proven unlikely. In Oklahoma, for example, over the course of a fifteen-month period, the United States filed 301 bills in equity against 16,000 defendants to cancel 30,000 conveyances of Indian allotted lands. *Heckman v. United States*, 224 U.S. 413 (1912) (on behalf of the Cherokee). For other twentieth-century cases resting on the Non-Intercourse Act or principles of inalienability, see *United States v. Santa Fe Pac. R.R.*, 314 U.S. 339 (1941) (on behalf of the Hualpai); *United States v. Minnesota*, 270 U.S. 181 (1926) (on behalf of the Chippewa); *Cramer v. United States*, 261 U.S. 219 (1923) (on behalf of three Indians living separately in Siskiyou County, Cal.); *Winters v. United States*, 207 U.S. 564 (1908) (on behalf of the Gros Ventre and Assiniboing [sic] Tribes of the Fort Belknap Indian Reservation); *United States v. Winans*, 198 U.S. 371 (1905) (on behalf of the Yakima); *United States v. Rickert*, 188 U.S. 432 (1903) (on behalf of the Sioux); *First Nat'l Bank of Decatur v. United States*, 59 F.2d 367 (8th Cir. 1932) (on behalf of the Omaha); *United States v. Boylan*, 265 F. 165 (2d Cir. 1920) (on behalf of the Oneidas); *United States v. Abraham*, Civil No. 2256 (E.D. La., filed May 28, 1952) (on behalf of the Chitimachas); *United States v. Franklin County*, 50 F. Supp. 152 (N.D.N.Y. 1943) (on behalf of the St. Regis Mohawks); *United States v. Flournoy Live-Stock & Real Estate Co.*, 71 F. 576 (C.C.D. Neb. 1896) (on behalf of the Omaha and Winnebago); *United States v. Flournoy Live-Stock & Real Estate Co.*, 69 F. 886 (C.C.D. Neb. 1895) (on behalf of the Omaha and Winnebago).

Finally, in 1978 the American Land Title Association (ALTA) published a memorandum arguing (1) that Congress had the power and the duty to extinguish the eastern land claims cases; (2) that Congress could do so without fear of Fifth Amendment liability under *Tee-Hit-Ton Indians v. United States*, 348 U.S. 272 (1955); and (3) that Congress could also extinguish land claims cases founded on treaty rights by compensating tribes, via the Court of Claims process, for the market value of the lands at the date of the challenged transaction plus 5% simple interest per year to date (American Land Title Association, Indian Claims Under the Non-intercourse Act: The Constitutional Basis and Need for a Legislative Solution [1978]).

6. van Gestel, supra note 4, at 301–302. See also John M.R. Paterson and David Roseman, "A Reexamination of Passamaquoddy v. Morton," 31 *Maine Law Review* 115 (1979). Paterson and Roseman were then Attorneys General for the State of Maine who, to avoid conceding the issue of tribal identity, prefaced their article in this peculiar way:

> The two Indian groups are commonly known as the Passamaquoddy Tribe and the Penobscot Nation. While the article may hereafter use the terms "Passamaquoddy Tribe" and "Penobscot Nation," the use of the titles "Tribe" or "Nation" does not necessarily indicate that the authors believe those Indian groups constitute tribes in a legal sense. The legal status of the Maine Indians could presumably be an issue in any future litigation, as it was in *Mashpee Tribe v. New Seabury Corp.* . . . . However, because the Passamaquoddy and Penobscot are usually referred to as "Tribe" and "Nation," respectively, and for ease of reference, we have employed that nomenclature in this article.

Id. at 115 n.2.

7. Minow, *Making All the Difference*, supra note 1, at 351–356.

8. Ironically, it was federal law that required the splitting of these two issues. [Citations omitted.]

9. Minow, *Making All the Difference*, supra note 1, at 355–356.

10. Campisi, supra note 5, argues that there were aspects of Mashpee "Indian-ness" that were in fact so much a part of Mashpee culture as to be unarticulable until they were negotiated at trial. This makes sense if one keeps in mind that the Mashpee led an isolated existence at least until the construction of the freeway in the 1950s, which linked Cape Cod with Boston. Hence, before the conflict that led up to the lawsuit, the Mashpee had not had to define themselves in opposition to non-Indian groups in any essentialist way. See also Minow, "Identities," supra note 1.

11. See Jack Campisi, *The Mashpee Indians: Tribe on Trial.* Syracuse, N.Y.: Syracuse University Press, 1991.

12. See Barbara Yngvesson, "Inventing Law in Local Settings: Rethinking Popular Legal Culture," 98 *Yale Law Journal* 1689 (1989).

13. See, e.g., Campisi, supra note 11, at 142–144 (describing speeches given in Mashpee around the time of the litigation).

> In Mashpee, the Wampanoag tribe wails for their weakened home. Struggling to maintain the Earth's tender and tenuous balance, they hunt deer that dart across the landscape and bait lines to hook fat silvery fish. They harbor an unquestioning reverence for the land, for the trampled grasses, the ugly concrete and the towering trees with wind-rippled leaves just beginning to teeter toward gold.

Patricia Smith, "Gentle Bear was Warrior," *Boston Globe,* Sept. 16, 1994. at 33. Thus began the obituary for Lewis Gurwitz, who defended four members of the Mashpee tribe after they were arrested for taking shellfish without a permit and for exceeding the limits set by the state. Gurwitz argued that the Mashpee had an aboriginal right to take shellfish. The assistant district attorney countered that the Mashpee had no such right because they "are not a tribe, they are individuals who are assimilated into American society and culture." Campisi, supra note 11, at 157, citing *Cape Cod Times,* Sept. 15, 1984.

CHAPTER 2

LAND CLAIMS AND REPARATIONS

The names leave a trace not unlike that left by the Vietnam War Memorial. The Cherokee, the United Pottawatomi, the Fond du Lac, the Bois Forte, the Osage Nation, the Federated Indians of California—all these tribes, bands, or villages brought claims against the United States for the loss of property. The Pembina and White Earth Bands of Chippewa, the Yavapai-Apache, the Mescalero, the Chickasaw, the Chiricahua, the Hannahville Indian Community; the Unintah Utes, the Crow, the Choctaw, the Saginaw; the Sac and Fox, the Six Nations, the Navajo, the Quechan Tribe; the Duwamish, the Lummi, the S'Klallam. The Seminole, some of whom never surrendered to U.S. military forces in the nineteenth century and therefore refused to register for the draft during World War II, brought a claim. The Kickapoo, the Shoshone, the Yakima, the Pueblos of Zia, Jemez, and Santa Ana all brought claims for the loss of property due to conquest. The Joseph Band of the Nez Perce Tribe lost its aboriginal land, then its reservation, and finally its famous Nez Perce horse breeding stock—the breeding stock almost disappeared, though the Nez Perce are reviving it today.

The Yana of California lost everything; much of their material legacy ended up in the University of California Museum of Anthropology. The Tee-Hit-Ton lost land, timber, and fishing territory, as did the Red Lake Band of Chippewa, whose original 1951 claim is still ongoing and is still contested by the United States. The Creek Nation, the Tulalip, and the Tlingit and Haida brought claims against the United States for loss related to conquest, as did the Washoe, Skokomish, Ottawa, Ponca, Lemhi, and Tuscarora. The Shasta and Pit River, both California tribes, lost virtually everything in the California gold rush, as did many others. The Pueblos of San Ildefonso, Santo Domingo, Santa Clara, Taos, and Nambe brought claims against the United States. Perhaps the most widely written about claim was *Sioux Nation v. United States*, which eventually made its way to the Supreme Court.[1]

These tribes and many others lost lives, land, and personal property to conquest. All petitioned the Indian Claims Commission, an adjudicative body created by the Indian Claims Commission (ICC) Act of 1946, for claims against the United States arising from acts of conquest that occurred prior to August 13, 1946. A total of 370 claim dockets were reported by the Commission, though the Commission's official historian, Harvey D. Rosenthal, puts the number of total claims prosecuted to a finish at 549.[2]

Before the passage of the ICC Act, Native American tribes had to first petition Congress for a special jurisdictional statute under which to sue the U.S. government. Two hundred such statutes were passed between 1881 and 1946[3]; they authorized particular tribal claims before the U.S. Court of Claims. However, Court of Claims cases were different from Indian Claims Commission cases. The Court of Claims acquired its jurisdiction by virtue of the narrowly drafted, special statutes that only a few tribes were able to secure for themselves. The Indian Claims Commission, on the other hand, claimed its jurisdictional powers under the broadly stated ICC Act, which opened wide the federal courthouse doors to *any* Indian band, tribe, or nation that could claim a loss. ICC Act claims were initially heard by the Indian Claims Commission and reviewed through an appeals process by the Court of Claims (§20). A small number of these claims, like *Sioux Nation*, ultimately made their way to the U.S. Supreme Court by writ of *certiorari*.[4]

Five different causes of actions gave rise to jurisdiction under the ICC Act. They were for claims arising out of law, tort, fraudulent dealings on the part of the United States, uncompensated for lost property, and moral claims "not recognized by any existing rule of law or equity." The ICC Act also included a statute of limitations, under whose terms tribes had five years—from 1946 to 1951—either to file their claim or, at least theoretically, be forever barred. Claims arising after 1946 were returned to the Court of Claims, assuming proper jurisdiction.[5] Some tribal groups missed the deadline due to improper notice; in some cases they were allowed to intervene in already-filed cases.[6]

Although the ICC Act opened courthouse doors, it also served as a precursor to tribal termination legislation of the 1950s, this time by giving tribal nations their "day in court."

The Cherokee filed the first petition under the ICC Act, to which the United States asserted the defense of *res judicata*. To be sure, the ICC Act clearly deprived the United States of two defenses: laches and limitations. But it just as clearly allowed the United States to raise the defense of *res judicata*, a defense that precludes previously adjudicated claims from being raised in a later action. The United States argued that because the facts underlying the Cherokee petition had formed the basis of its earlier Court of Claims case, the petition before the Commission was barred as a matter of law.

The Commission held against the Cherokees in a decision that threatened to contradict radically Congress's purpose for passing the ICC Act.[7] But in *Osage Nation*, a case that came up on appeal from the Indian Claims Commission soon afterward, the Court of Claims reversed the Commission. It held instead that since the ICC Act set forth broader jurisdictional grounds than the special jurisdictional statutes, the Osage Nation's case before the Indian Claims Commission was by definition legally different from its prior case before the Court of Claims.[8] From *Osage Nation* on, *res judicata* remained available to the United States as a defense, but it did not automatically bar tribal claims previously heard by the Court of Claims on similar historical facts.

At the back end, the ICC Act relied on a statute of limitations to bar pre-1946 tribal claims not filed by the 1951 filing deadline (§12). These front- and back-end bars—*res judicata* and the ICC Act's own statute of limitations—bear pointing out because they illuminated Congress's proposed strategy to "get out of the Indian business" once and for all, this time by establishing a clear period during which tribal claims could be raised.[9]

The ICC Act was jurisdictionally broad, and its moral claims provision was so broad that it was controversial from the start. The phrase "moral claims" implied that Congress gave the Indian Claims Commission a wide grant of power to hear both typical and atypical cases. Indeed, the moral claims provision specifically stated that it applied in cases where there was no existing legal or equitable principle. But the phrase also suggested, at least to Native American claimants who were thirsty for justice, that the Commission had the authority to hear cases that could fundamentally, maybe even radically, challenge the many nefarious ways in which the United States (and its settlers) had dispossessed Native Americans. This suggestion was backed up by §13 of the ICC Act, which called for the creation of an Investigative Division whose purpose was to seek out *all* evidence [§13(b)], including the oral testimony of tribal members [§13(a)]. From the Native American claimants' point of view, the ICC Act as a whole seemed to invite a full and frank discussion of the economic, physical, and moral harms of conquest. But the discussion never happened. This chapter explains why.

Chapter 2 begins with an excerpt from *Fort Sill Apache Tribe of the State of Oklahoma v. United States*. In *Fort Sill*, the Chiricahua Tribe sued the United States for the harm to the tribe's governing structure that occurred when the tribe spent twenty-seven years as U.S. prisoners of war. The Chiricahua Tribe brought its claim under Section 2 (the tort provision) and Section 5 (the moral claims provision) of the ICC Act. Both claims were dismissed. Upon review, the Court of Claims upheld the dismissal on the ground that the ICC Act authorized only claims for harms to tribes, not to individuals. The court reasoned that since it was the individuals of the tribe who were incarcerated, not the tribe itself, the harm that occurred was to individuals, not to the Chiricahuas as an entity. As to the Tribe's Section 5 claim, the court held that since the Chiricahua were at war with the United States when they were interned, they were enemies of the state, and therefore the United States had no special duty to protect them. Neither did it have a duty to follow general standards of "fair and honorable dealings."

Fort Sill is just one example of the acrobatic reasoning that the Commission and its Court of Claims reviewers too often engaged in. It also serves as a counterpoint to the Felix Cohen excerpt that follows it. Felix Cohen is described by some as the most highly regarded and humanitarian scholar of federal Indian law. However, for some readers, Cohen's excerpt may provide a troubling new view of his position on Native American issues. Cohen wrote that the United States legitimately transacted to buy Indian land from Native American tribes, and pursuant to those negotiated deals, in most cases, paid the tribes what was due them. He articulated this argument before actual ICC Act claims started rolling in. I include his excerpt here because it lays the groundwork for what has become one of the myths of federal Indian law: the idea that the United States has met the many obligations to tribes that it voluntarily undertook in exchange for vast cessions of Indian land.

According to Cohen, land was by and large purchased by the United States from the Native Americans, making the United States "the one great nation in the world that has consistently sought to deal with an aboriginal population on fair and equitable terms." However, *seeking* to deal on equitable terms and *actually* dealing on such terms are two entirely distinct modes. Perhaps in some cases the U.S. did indeed seek to deal on equitable terms with the tribes, but those cases are few and far between. More often what happened was that the United States corrupted the negotiation process through force, manipulation, or as William E. Unrau has shown, alcohol.[10]

According to Unrau, the United States did indeed pay substantial sums of money to tribes in exchange for ceded lands, but this money made its way directly into the hands of non-Indian traders who charged exorbitant prices for staples and even higher prices for alcohol. Furthermore, Unrau's evidence shows that while the United States in the nineteenth century, in Indian country, officially prohibited the sale of alcohol to those classified as Indians under the Trade and Intercourse Acts, its own agents—reservation agents, military officers, and the like—actively involved themselves in the liquor trade. Some made substantial fortunes distributing annuity payments with one hand and then taking the cash away from Native American annuitants as payment for food and alcohol with the other. Unrau's thesis, in part, is that the annuity system was so intimately tied to the illicit alcohol trade that in actuality it was an *annuity-alcohol* system that allowed the United States to fund non-Indian expansion into Indian country. The United States paid Native American annuitants, as Cohen suggests, but, as Unrau argues, it did so knowing that within a short time the money would make its way into the pockets of non-Indian traders and settlers.

Unrau's work contradicts Cohen's implied thesis, especially Cohen's ignoring external market pressures that influenced annuitants to spend their cash immediately. Unrau also makes an important point about why any annuity/cash payment system might be unsatisfactory from the annuitants' point of view: Cash reparations are controversial, but they are temporary in nature, which makes them not nearly as controversial as land reparations. In other words, in the nineteenth-century context the lesson is clear: Annuities and cash went to and then *through* Native American communities, eventually to fund settler communities; only land reparations held or now hold the promise of restitution.

As problematic as Cohen's essay is, it represents the liberal strand of logic that led to the passage of the ICC Act. The United States has consistently balked at the extent of its liability to Native American tribes, typically by invoking what is known as the actual-state-of-things argument. Indeed, the United States has successfully used the actual-state-of-things argument to defend against Native American claims for reparations from the start. The basis for the argument is this: Though the United States may be liable to the tribes, honoring this liability would be more detrimental to the society as a whole than would ignoring it, especially since the tribes are a small, poor minority whose claims are extraordinary in the life of a settler group busy with nation building.

Anticipating this argument, Cohen subtly encouraged decision makers to reject the actual-state-of-things rationale. He argued that since most non-Indian land titles are founded on legitimate transfers (the exaggeration), recognizing Indian land claims would not upset the validity of non-Indian title (the reality). He also asserted that since most Native Americans had received a fair price from the United States for their land, the United States could afford to compensate those few who had not. This logic transformed the ICC Act from frightening "reparations legislation" to something more familiar. As Cohen put it, since the U.S. was an honorable nation generally, most of its dealings were by implication honorable; therefore, reparations, if they were to be had, would be the exception, not the rule.

Wilcomb Washburn's article later in this chapter challenges the idea that the U.S. paid for both purchases and transfers by government takings. On the issue of whether Native Americans can be compensated for aboriginal land confiscated by the U.S. government, Washburn points to Supreme Court cases. He argues that the U.S. Supreme Court, in *United States v. Alcea Band of Tillamooks*, may indeed have ordered the United States to compensate the Tillamooks for land the tribe were forced to surrender.[11] But that same Court later decided in *Tee-Hit-Ton Indians, v. United States* that *if* the United States compensated tribes for aboriginal title, it need only do so "as a matter of grace," not legal duty.[12] The corollary of this rule, as Washburn points out, is that the U.S. government not only had the power to extinguish Indian title, or occupancy, but it had the power to do so *without* compensating tribal owners. Thus, Washburn, like Unrau, uses historical data to counter the mythical dimensions of Cohen's legal premise that the United States took Native American land by legitimate transfer and cash exchange.

Nell Jessup Newton's excerpt later in this chapter shifts gears a bit by examining the particulars of the Indian Claims Commission, the body set up under the ICC Act to hear Indian claims. Newton describes three notable ICC Act cases: *Gila River Pima Maricopa Indian Community v. United States*,[13] the *Fort-Sill*[14] case that leads the Chapter, and *Aleut Community v. United States*.[15] She points out that the Commission's remedial arsenal was implicitly restricted by the terms of the ICC Act itself to money damages, a position most tribal claimants did not agree with since, as Nancy Oestreich Lurie explains in her excerpt, money simply could not address the harms of conquest.

Lurie's critique of the Indian Claims Commission is one of the best available. She puts the Commission's emergence and functioning in the context of the changing national scene; she also addresses difficult issues related to the mechanics of bringing ICC Act claims. Lurie accurately notes that Native American claimants became disappointed with the ICC Act because, while its legislative intent, in part, was to open up a substantive discussion about conquest, it was implemented as little more than a title-clearing mechanism. As such, the very idea, however wrong, that gave the Act life—the idea that the United States had legitimately bought its land from Native Americans, and thus that the issue of compensation could be readdressed in a few exceptional cases—was the same idea that lawyers used to change the Act from a potentially transformative piece of legislation into a title-clearing statute.

Lurie says that in the hands of busy, summary-hungry lawyers, the ICC Act was reduced to two questions: Did the tribal group have title to the land it claimed? and, if so, What were the group's monetary damages according to a formula that subtracted gratuitous transfers made by the United States (offsets) from total liability? Implemented like this, the ICC Act tucked neatly behind a post–World War II federal policy of tribal termination. Once a tribe accepted money, it forever relinquished any future claims to the land, for all future generations. So, while the ICC Act was important in at least raising the issue of reparations and in some cases securing some degree of reparations for the harms (particularly loss of land) related to conquest, the Act ultimately left a deeper wound. The promise of a full and frank discussion about colonialism and its effects on Native American communities was redirected into narrow legal inquiries about how to correct flawed land titles. Compensation came to mean only money, this time because of the still-palpable fear that Native Americans, with their claims, intended to take back all of the United States. Once again, the Native American side of the story got lost.

Promises and broken promises are inescapable themes in federal Indian law, and Vine Deloria's excerpt offers a look at the problems that plagued the ICC Commission. Deloria notes two lessons that were learned from the ICC Act and its history. The first was the importance of having a single judicial forum where Native Americans could file claims. This eliminated the need and complication of forum shopping, thereby ensuring that tribal claims would be heard by judges who were at least minimally familiar with U.S. and Native American history. The second lesson Deloria says the country learned (or should have learned) from the ICC Act was that deciding Indian cases involves more than a simple reading of case law. Indian cases do not allow for simple application of doctrine. They require a close attention to historical and socio-legal context, and indeed closer attention to such matters than most lawyers and judges are trained or inclined to give.

The last section in this chapter is an excerpt from Sherman Alexie's book of short stories, *The Lone Ranger and Tonto Fistfight in Heaven*. Alexie writes powerfully about the consequences of colonialism in individual Native American lives, often in individual *young* Native American lives. His work raises a series of encompassing questions. If the United States is as interested in reparations as it claims to be, then why hasn't justice been done? Why are Native Americans so often reduced to lives of utter poverty and lack of opportunity, especially on the reservation? Why do Native Americans continue to be among the persistently poor in America? What does it mean when a country—one that prides itself on being enlightened and humanitarian—allows such extreme contrasts in material comfort and opportunity between indigenous and settler groups?

RECOMMENDED READINGS

Two important novels present the lives of Native American characters who lived during the era in which the Indian Claims Commission Act was passed, an era that simultaneously was giving way to government tribal policies of relocation and termination. They are N. Scott Momaday's Pulitzer Prize–winning *House Made of Dawn* (1968), and Leslie Marmon Silko's novel *Ceremony* (1977). Sherman Alexie's work explores similar issues, but from a different generational perspective. His short stories in *The Lone Ranger and Tonto Fistfight in Heaven* (1993) and his recent novel *Reservation Blues* (1995) give one a sense of the extremes that can exist in reservation communities. In addition, Paula Allen Gunn has edited several anthologies of Native American literature, much of it about contemporary Native American life on or near reservation areas.

From Sand Creek (1981), by Acoma Pueblo poet Simon J. Ortiz, ought to be required reading for students of American Indian law despite student cries for "hard law," not poetry. So perhaps should Dee Brown's *Bury My Heart at Wounded Knee* (1970; reprint 1991). One simply cannot begin to understand what the deep hurts speak to unless one knows at least about the massacres at Sand Creek and Wounded Knee. These are just two incidents out of literally thousands in which Native American people were killed *en masse* by U.S. forces. Also covering this era is *The Lance and the Shield: The Life and Times of Sitting Bull* (1993), by Robert M. Utley.

Peter Nabokov's *Native American Testimony: A Chronicle of Indian-White Relations from Prophecy to the Present: 1492–1992* (1991) is an interesting collection of photographs and first-person accounts of the colonial process. *Documents of United States Indian Policy* (1990), collected and edited by Francis Paul Prucha, is an extensive and important collection of primary documents on the U.S. Indian policy over the last few centuries. *The Commissioners of Indian Affairs, 1824–1977* (1979), edited by Robert M. Kvasnicka and Herman J. Viola, is a necessary tool for understanding the backgrounds of individual BIA commissioners who implemented Indian policy over time—their beliefs, their prejudices, their limitations, their aspirations, their cruelties. Another important book by Francis Paul Prucha is *American Indian Treaties: The History of a Political Anomaly* (1994).

Now That the Buffalo's Gone: A Study of Today's American Indians (1982), by Alvin M. Josephy, Jr., is an important historical/social look at both contemporary Native American life and some of the broad issues that concern Native American people today. Sharon O'Brien's *American Indian Tribal Governments* (1989) is a useful survey of contemporary tribal governments, the challenges they have faced, and the structures they have assumed in the modern era. *The State of Native America: Genocide, Colonization, and Resistance* (1992), edited by M. Annette Jaimes, is a radical look at U.S. and Native American relations; whereas *The Invented Indian: Cultural Fictions and Government Policies* (1990), edited by James A. Clifton, takes the extreme opposite view, with its premise that people too often make up their Indianness to get government benefits.

Edward Lazarus wrote an account of the Sioux Nation case called *Black Hills/ White Justice: The Sioux Nations Versus the United States, 1775 to Present* (1991). Lazarus's account is riddled with substantive and methodological problems. It has not been well received by scholars, though it is a fast-paced and sometimes compelling account. In addition, Lazarus makes almost no effort to understand the Native American side of the story. His view of the long litigation, much of it involving the ICC Act and the ICC Commission, is that the Sioux were incapable of understanding the legal process (a process that Lazarus presumes was fair), and thus never came to accept the actual state of things. Ultimately, Lazarus's work, though a case history of the ICC Act and its implementation, is an example of how narrowly the legal mind comes to see Native American complaints. Lazarus's work ought to be read in the context of the critical reviews it received. One such review is Frank Pommersheim's "Making all the Difference: Native American Testimony and the Black Hills," which appears in 69 *North Dakota Law Review* 337 (1993). Frank Pommersheim's own book *Braid of Feathers: American Indian Law and Contemporary Tribal Life* (1996) is a good counterbalance to Lazarus's view of the reservation as a geographical, cultural, legal space.

In the same vein, *Tipi Rings: A Chronicle of the Jicarilla Apache Land Claim* (1995), by Robert J. Nordhaus, the attorney who represented the Jicarilla in their claim, is available from Bow Arrow Publishing Company, a Native American–owned press. Nordhaus represented the Jicarilla in its Indian Claims case. Unlike so many other claims attorneys, however, he was able to build a lasting relationship with his clients that continues today.

The Indian Claims Commission reports have been reproduced by Clearwater Publishing Co. in microfiche, and the Garland Publishing Co. in hard copy. See also Elbert B. Smith's two-volume compilation, *Indian Tribal Claims, Decided in the Court of Claims of the United States, Briefed and Compiled to June 30, 1947* (1976), and Imre Sutton's *Indian Land Tenure: Bibliographical Essays and a Guide to the Literature* (1975). In addition, *Irredeemable America: the Indians' Estate and Land Claims* (1985), the collection to which Nancy O. Lurie's essay serves as epilogue, provides a wealth of bibliographic information as well as an astonishingly broad range of essays on the Indian Claims Commission. The collection also includes a few case studies of Indian Claims Commission cases, written by experts from both petitioner (tribal) and defendant (U.S.) sides.

For an article about the difficulties faced by Native Hawaiians who want to use courts for culturally based claims, see Eric K. Yamamoto, "Courts and the Cultural Performance: Native Hawaiians' Uncertain Federal and State Court Rights to Sue," 16 *University of Hawaii Law Review* 1 (1994).

NOTES

1. *U.S. v. Sioux Nation of Indians*, 448 U.S. 371 (1980).
2. Harvey D. Rosenthal, *Their Day in Court: A History of the Indian Claims Commission*, New York, N.Y.: Garland Publishing, 1990, p. 256.

See also Harvey D. Rosenthal, "Indian Claims and the American Conscience," Imre Sutton et al., eds., *Irredeemable America: the Indians' Estate and Land Claims*, Albuquerque, N.M.: University of New Mexico Press, 1985, p. 46.

3. Harvey D. Rosenthal, *Their Day in Court: A History of the Indian Claims Commission*, New York, N.Y.: Garland Publishing, 1990, p. x.

4. See note 1. See also *U.S. v. Southern Ute Tribe or Band of Indians*, 402 U.S. 468 (1968); *Peoria Tribe of Indians of Oklahoma v. U.S.*, 390 U.S. 468 (1968).

5. *U.S. Code* vol. 28, sec. 1505.

6. See, e.g., *The Alabama-Coushatta Tribe of Texas v. The United States*, U.S. Court of Federal Claims, 1996 U.S. Claims LEXIS 128 (1996) (providing a history of the Alabama-Coushatta Tribe's efforts to overcome the 1951 limitations period).

7. *The Western (Old Settler) Cherokee Indians and the Eastern (Emigrant) Cherokee Indians v. The United States of America*, 1 Ind. Cl. Comm. 1 (Nov. 15, 1948).

8. *The Osage Nation of Indians v. United States*, 1. Ind. Cl. Comm. 43 (1948); 119 Ct. Cl. 592 cert. denied 342 U.S. 896 (1951).

9. See note 2.

10. William E. Unrau, *White Man's Wicked Water: The Alcohol Trade and Prohibition in Indian Country, 1802–1892*, Lawrence, Kan.: University Press of Kansas, 1996.

For additional analyses of Native American alcohol consumption, see Nancy Oesterich Lurie, "The World's Oldest On-Going Protest Demonstration: North American Indian Drinking Patterns," *Pacific Historical Review* 40 (August 1971): 311–321; and Philip A. May, "The Epidemiology of Alcohol Abuse Among American Indians: the Mythical and Real Properties," *American Indian Culture and Research Journal* 18 (1994): 121–144.

11. 329 U.S. 40 (1946).

12. 348 U.S. 272 (1955).

13. 427 F2d 1194 (Ct. Cl. 1970).

14. 477 F2d 1360 (Ct. Cl. 1973).

15. 480 F2d 831 (Ct. Cl. 1973).

Fort Sill Apache Tribe of State of Oklahoma v. United States

On appeal from the Indian claims commission, Bennett, Judge, Delivered the Opinion of the Court:

The case now before the court presents several novel problems which do not appear to have been resolved before. The issues all revolve around the extent to which an Indian tribe may claim compensation for wrongdoing to the tribe unrelated to property rights, when the actual victims of the wrongdoing were the individual members of the tribe. For reasons to be detailed, the court affirms the decision of the Indian Claims Commission,[1] in which it dismissed the claim without trial on the grounds of lack of jurisdiction over the subject matter, section 2, clause (2), and for failure to state a claim upon which relief could be granted under section 2, clause (5), of the Indian Claims Commission Act, 60 Stat. 1049, 1050, 25 U.S.C. § 70a(2), (5). . . .

In their petition before the Indian Claims Commission (ICC), the plaintiffs alleged that the 27 years of internment suffered by the members of the tribe gave rise to a cause of action under [the Act] for a cause sounding in tort [the clause (2) claim], and . . . for a claim based on the absence of "fair and honorable dealings" [the clause (5) claim]. It is important to note that the appellants in this case are now asserting only a tribal claim for injuries to the tribe's traditional power and structure resulting from the years of internment. The appellants are not seeking damages for false arrest and imprisonment of each member of the tribe, apparently recognizing that these would be little more than multiple individual claims and therefore outside the jurisdiction of the Indian Claims Commission.[2] In seeking tribal damages for this type of injury, appellants are presenting a novel argument. They allege that the wrongful imprisonment of the members of the Chiricahua Tribe, simply because they were members, constituted a compensable injury to the tribe as well as to the individual Indians involved. They argue that the internment of the tribe's members took from the tribe its power to hold territory, its power to gather and accumulate food, horses and other resources necessary to its

Fort Sill Apache Tribe of State of Oklahoma v. United States, 477 F.2d 1360 (1973).

communal existence, and its power to govern its people. The loss of these powers, the appellants contend, constitutes a separate and distinct compensable injury to the tribe, recoverable under both clause (2) and clause (5) and [the Act].

Any solution to the problem posed by the appellants requires the court to construe the pertinent sections of the Indian Claims Commission Act of August 13, 1946. . . .

The primary ground on which jurisdiction might rest is the language of clause (2) of [the Act].[3] The appellants have attempted to characterize a series of multiple torts committed on the individual members of this tribe as also constituting a tort against the tribe itself making clause (2) applicable. There is a separate cause of action resting with the tribe only if the Act can be read to recognize a distinct right in the tribe to foster and protect its own form and structure. The focal point here is whether clause (2) recognizes such a predictable right in the tribe. . . .

The court is faced with the resolution of this problem under circumstances in which the legislative history has a bearing on interpretation of the statute. For the following reasons, it finds that the ICC Act was not intended to cover, under clause (2), claims of the type now being pressed by the appellants. One of the problems the court has with the appellants' position is illustrated by the facts in *Gila River Pima-Maricopa Indian Community v. United States.*[4] A portion of the appellant's claim in *Gila River* was based on the allegation that "damage was caused by the Government when it 'undertook to, and did, subjugate petitioner under wardship to a stagnation of self-expression . . . . [and] bridled petitioner into cultural impotency.'"[5] For the purposes of that decision, the court assumed that this was a tribal claim and went on to dismiss the claim on other grounds. Both in *Gila River* and in the case now before the court, the tribes were seeking recovery for essentially the same type of injury. Each felt Government action caused damage to the power structure and viability of the tribal unit; that is, damage to Indian peoplehood in general. Opening the door to appellants in this case would leave it open for a multitude of other claims based on facts more closely akin to those in *Gila River.* While the court recognizes that a variety of injustices have been inflicted upon Indians both before and after they were relocated on the reservations, it nonetheless does not appear that Congress in 1946 thought this type of injury would come within the coverage of the Claims Commission Act. It has been noted that the Act "is a synthesis of those '. . . classes of cases . . . which have heretofore received congressional consideration in the form of special jurisdictional acts. . . .' "[6] The court has not been made aware of any of the special jurisdictional acts which were intended to cover tribal injuries of the type presented here. The apparent view of the Congress in 1946 was that these claims would be "for specific deprivations of land or property or rights protected by treaty, statute, or then-existing law. The instances cited in the Congressional history are of that kind."[7]

There can be no doubt that the Apache Tribe did not prosper from the injuries suffered by its constituent members. But, the injury to the tribe is subsumed by the multitude of individual claims. [Legal precedent dictates that] the measure of damages for any tribal injury arising out of the imprisonment of the Apaches would seem to be the cumulative damage to the individual victims of imprisonment who did not contest their imprisonment by seeking writs of habeas corpus.

We need not at this late date conjecture whether such efforts would have been successful, but the legal remedy was there. . . .

The jurisdiction of the Commission is only over claims by the tribes, bands, or other identifiable groups of American Indians which have group rights. There is no grant of jurisdiction to hear claims on behalf of individual Indians. The legislative history as well as the language of the Act makes this clear.[8]

Appellants also rely upon clause (5) of 25 U.S.C. § 70a, the "fair and honorable dealings" clause, as a basis for arguing that the ICC has jurisdiction over its claim. The claim presented by the appellants under clause (5) is identical to that presented and discussed with respect to clause (2), and suffers from many of the same weaknesses. The court has said that the reach of the "fair and honorable dealings" clause is limited to somewhat fewer situations than a literal reading would imply. More specifically, the United States is held liable under this "fair and honorable dealings" clause where "by its own acts, it has undertaken special duties which it has failed to fulfill."[9] The issue therefore, under the clause 5 portion of the appellants' claim, is whether the United States has undertaken a special duty to protect and foster the traditional power and structure of the tribal organization. We think it has not done so.

. . . The story of the wars between the United States and the Apache Indians is one of harsh treatment on both sides. . . . In 1886, when Geronimo surrendered, the organized hostilities came to an end. This court described the final surrender as involving "more prolonged negotiation than the army of Burgoyne at Saratoga or of Lee at Appomattox, and concluded by the granting of terms that the surrender be 'as prisoners of war to an army in the field'—terms which effectually removed the sagacious savage and his followers beyond the jurisdiction of the civil authorities." We see then that the decision to put the Apache Indians in confinement . . . was a military measure taken to prevent the possibility of a resumption of warfare. We do not consider the merits of that decision. The question now is not how mistreated the Indians were or how much provocation there was to explain the actions of the United States, but whether the Indian Claims Commission has jurisdiction of the claims.

With the perspective of history and the benefits of hindsight and ignorance of the temper, passions, and conditions of the times, it is easy to say that the actions of the United States were perhaps unwarranted and that reparations should be given to the Apache Indians for their suffering after surrender. The Congress knew all about the Apache wars and their aftermath when it enacted the Indian Claims Commission Act in 1946. This generous and remedial legislation did not, however, provide for claims by individual Indians, but only by tribes and identifiable bands and groups. We take the law as we find it. . . .

Affirmed.

NOTES

1. 26 Ind. Cl.Comm. 281 (1971).
2. See, 25 U.S.C. § 70a, § 70i. In a claim brought by the Ford Sill Apache Tribe for the false arrest and imprisonment of 450 members of the Warm Spring and Chiricahua Bands based on these same facts, the Indian Claims Commission dismissed the petition since it

concerned the rights of the individual Indians and not the rights of the Tribe. (Ind. Cl. Comm. Docket No. 30), 1-A Ind.Cl.Comm. 137, 141 (1949).

See, also, *Cherokee Freedmen v. United States*, 161 Ct.Cl. 787 (1963). *Minnesota Chippewa Tribe v. United States*, 315 F.2d 906, 161 Ct.Cl. 258 (1963).

3. . . . (2) all other claims in law or equality, including those sounding in tort, with respect to which the claimant would have been entitled to sue in a court of the United States if the United States was subject to suit. . . ."

4. 427 F.2d 1194, 190 Ct.Cl. 790, cert. denied, 400 U.S. 819, 91 S.Ct. 37, 27 L.Ed.2d 47 (1970)

5. 427 F.2d at 1195, 190 Ct.Cl. at 792.

6. *Gila River*, 427 F.2d at 1200, 190 Ct.Cl. at 801.

7. 427 F.2d at 1200-1201, 190 Ct.Cl. at 802. H.R.Rep. No. 1466, 79th Cong., 1st Sess. (1945).

8. On the legislative history, see the conversation between the Assistant Commissioner of the Bureau of Indian Affairs and Chairman Henry M. Jackson at the Hearings on H.R. 1198 and H.R. 1341 Before the House Committee on Indian Affairs, 79th Cong., 1st Sess., at 77 (March 28, 1945).

9. *Lipan Apache Tribe v. United States*, 180 Ct.Cl. 487, 502 (1967).

Original Indian Title

Felix S. Cohen

INDIAN CLOUDS IN LAND GRANT TITLES

Recent decisions of the Supreme Court recognizing the validity of original Indian Title[1] make the existence and extent of such aboriginal ownership a relevant issue in title examinations whenever a chain of title is traced back to a federal grant or patent. Grantees who have relied on the Great Seal of a federal department as assuring the validity of land grant titles have not infrequently discovered to their sorrow the truth of the old French saying, "Même le plus belle fille du monde ne peut donner que ce que l'à." Not even the Federal Government can grant what it does not have. The nature of Indian title and its extinguishment thus becomes, in those states that have been carved out of the Federal public domain, a matter of concern to real property lawyers generally. . . .

The fear that recognizing Indian title, or paying Indians for land, would unsettle land titles everywhere and threaten the Federal Government with bankruptcy would be well grounded if there were any factual basis for the current legend of how we acquired the United States from the Indians. If, as the cases hold, federal grants are normally subject to outstanding Indian titles, and if, over extensive areas where such grants have been made, Indian title has in fact never been lawfully extinguished, then a vast number of titles must today be subject to outstanding Indian possessory rights. The fact, however, is that except for a few tracts of land in the Southwest, practically all of the public domain of the continental United States (excluding Alaska) has been purchased from the Indians. . . .

Fortunately for the security of American real estate titles, the business of securing cessions of Indian titles has been, on the whole, conscientiously pursued by the Federal Government, as long as there has been a Federal Government. The notion that America was stolen from the Indians is one of the myths by which we Americans are prone to hide our real virtues and make our idealism look as hard-boiled as possible. We are probably the one great nation

From Felix S. Cohen, "Original Indian Title," *Minnesota Law Review* 32(1947):28. © 1948 by the Minnesota Law Review Foundation.

in the world that has consistently sought to deal with an aboriginal population on fair and equitable terms. We have not always succeeded in this effort but our deviations have not been typical.

It is, in fact, difficult to understand the decisions on Indian title or to appreciate their scope and their limitations if one views the history of American land settlement as a history of wholesale robbery. The basic historic facts are worth rehearsing before we attempt analysis of the cases dealing with the character and scope of original Indian title.

HOW WE BOUGHT THE UNITED STATES [2]

Every American schoolboy is taught to believe that the lands of the United States were acquired by purchase or treaty from Britain, Spain, France, Mexico, and Russia, and that for all the continental lands so purchased we paid about 50 million dollars out of the Federal Treasury. Most of us believe this story as unquestioningly as we believe in electricity or corporations. We have seen little maps of the United States in our history books and big maps in our geography books showing the vast area that Napoleon sold us in 1803 for 15 million dollars and the various other cessions that make up the story of our national expansion. As for the original Indian owners of the continent, the common impression is that we took the land from them by force and proceeded to lock them up in concentration camps called "reservations."

Notwithstanding this prevailing mythology, the historic fact is that practically all of the real estate acquired by the United States since 1776 was purchased not from Napoleon or any other emperor or czar but from its original Indian owners.[3] What we acquired from Napoleon in the Louisiana Purchase was not real estate, for practically all of the ceded territory that was not privately owned by Spanish and French settlers was still owned by the Indians, and the property rights of all the inhabitants were safeguarded by the terms of the treaty of cession.[4] What we did acquire from Napoleon was not the land, which was not his to sell, but simply the power to govern and to tax, the same sort of power that we gained with the acquisition of Puerto Rico or the Virgin Islands a century later.

It may help us to appreciate the distinction between a sale of land and the transfer of governmental power if we note that after paying Napoleon 15 million dollars for the cession of political authority over the Louisiana Territory we proceeded to pay the Indian tribes of the ceded territory more than twenty times this sum for such lands in their possession as they were willing to sell. And while Napoleon, when he took his 15 million dollars, was thoroughly and completely relieved of all connections with the territory, the Indian tribes were wise enough to reserve[5] from their cessions sufficient land to bring them a current income that exceeds each year the amount of our payment to Napoleon. One of these reservations, that of the Osages, has thus far brought its Indian owners 280 million dollars in oil royalties. Some other Indian tribes, less warlike, or less lucky, than the Osages, fared badly in their real estate transactions with the Great White Father. But in its totality the account of our land transactions with the Indians is not small potatoes. While nobody has ever calculated the total sum paid by the United States to Indian tribes as consideration for more than two million square miles of land purchased from them, and any such calculation would have to take account of the conjectural value of a myriad of commodities, special services, and tax exemptions, which commonly took the place of cash, a conservative estimate would put the total price of Indian lands sold to the United States at a figure somewhat in excess of 800 million dollars.

In some cases payment for ceded land has been long delayed. Most of the State of California falls within an area which various Indian tribes of that region had undertaken to cede to the United States in a series of treaties executed in the 1850's. The treaties called for a substantial payment in lands, goods, and services. The Federal Government took the land but the Senate refused to ratify the treaties, which were held in secret archives for more than half a century. Eventually Congress authorized the Indians to sue in the Court of Claims for the compensation promised under the unratified treaties,[6] and that Court found that the Indians were entitled to receive $17,053,941.98, from which, however, various past expenditures by the Federal Government for the benefit of the California Indians had to be deducted. The net recovery amounted to $5,024,842.34.

The settlement of the California land claims closes a chapter in our national history. Today we can say that from the Atlantic to the Pacific our national public domain consists, with rare exceptions,[7] of lands that we have bought from the Indians. Here and there we have probably missed a tract, or paid the wrong Indians for land they did not own and neglected the rightful owners. But the keynote of our land policy has been recognition of Indian property rights.[8] And this recognition of Indian property rights, far from hampering the development of our land, was of the greatest significance in such development. Where the Government had to pay Indians for land it could not afford to give the land away to favored retainers who could, in turn, afford to hold the land in idleness. Because land which the Government had paid for had to be sold to settlers for cash or equivalent services, our West has escaped the fate of areas of South America, Canada, and Australia, which, after being filched from native owners, were turned over, at the same price, to court favorites, Government bureaus, or other absentee owners incapable of, or uninterested in, developing the potential riches of the land.

Granted that the Federal Government bought the country from the Indians, the question may still be raised whether the Indians received anything like a fair price for what they sold. The only fair answer to that question is that except in a very few cases where military duress was present, the price paid for the land was one that satisfied the Indians. Whether the Indians should have been satisfied and what the land would be worth now if it had never been sold are questions that lead us to ethereal realms of speculation. The sale of Manhattan Island for $24 is commonly cited as a typical example of the white man's overreaching. But even if this were a typical example, which it is not, the matter of deciding whether a real estate deal was a fair bargain three hundred years after it took place is beset by many pitfalls. Hindsight is better than foresight, particularly in real estate deals. Whether the land the Dutch settlers bought would become a thriving metropolis or remain a wilderness, whether other Indian tribes or European powers would respect their title, and how long the land would remain in Dutch ownership were, in 1626, questions that were hid in the mists of the future. Many acres of land for which the United States later paid the Indians in the neighborhood of $1.25 an acre, less costs of surveying, still remain on the land books of the Federal Government, which has found no purchasers at that price and is now content to lease the lands for cattle grazing at a net return to the Federal Government of one or two cents per annum per acre.

Aside from the difference between hindsight and foresight, there is the question of the value of money that must be considered wherever we seek to appraise a 300-year-old transaction. There are many things other than Manhattan Island that might have been bought in 1626 for $24 that would be worth great fortunes today. Indeed if the Indians had put the $24 they received for Manhattan at interest at 6 per cent they could now, with the accrued interest, buy back Manhattan island at current realty valuations and still have four hundred million dollars or more left over. Besides which, they would have saved the billions of dollars that have been spent on streets, harbors, aqueducts, sewers, and other public improvements to bring the realty values of the island to their present level. . . .

These are factors which should caution against hasty conclusions as to the inadequacy of payments for land sales made hundreds of years ago, even when such sales were made between white men. But in the earliest of our Indian land sales we must consider that representatives of two entirely different civilizations were bargaining with things that had very different values to the different parties. It is much as if a representative of another planet should offer to buy sea water or nitrogen or some other commodity of which we think we have a surplus and in exchange offer us pocket television sets or other products of a technology higher than our own. We would make our bargains regardless of how valuable nitrogen or sea water might be on another planet and without considering whether it cost two cents or a thousand dollars to make a television set in some part of the stellar universe that we could not reach. In these cases we would be concerned only with the comparative value to us of what we surrendered and what we obtained.

So it was with the Indians. What they secured in the way of knives, axes, kettles and woven cloth, not to mention rum and firearms,[9] represented produce of a superior technology with a use value that had no relation to value in a competitive market three thousand miles across the ocean. And what is probably more important, the Indians secured, in these first land transactions, something of greater value than even the unimagined products of European technology, namely, a recognition of the just principle that free purchase and sale was to be the basis of dealings between the native inhabitants of the land and the white immigrants.

Three years after the sale of Manhattan island the principle that Indian lands should be acquired only with the consent of the Indians was written into the laws of the Colony of New Netherlands:

The Patroons of New Netherlands, shall be bound to purchase from the Lords Sachems in New Netherland, the soil where they propose to plant their colonies, and shall acquire such right thereunto as they will agree for with the said Sachems.[10]

Connecticut, New Jersey, and Rhode Island were quick to adopt similar laws and within a short time all of the colonies had adopted laws in the same vein. Only in Massachusetts and North Carolina were there significant departures from this just and honorable policy. In North Carolina generally anarchic conditions left individual settlers relatively free to deal with or dispose of Indians as they pleased, with the result that less than half of the State was actually purchased from the natives. In Massachusetts, although Plymouth Colony "adopted the just policy of purchasing from the natives the lands they desired to obtain" (Royce, *op. cit.* p. 601), Puritan Massachusetts, with much pious citation of Old Testament precedents, asserted the right to disregard Indian claims to unimproved and uncultivated lands. Despite this claim, the Puritans were prudent enough to purchase considerable areas of land from the native inhabitants. . . .

Perhaps it was only natural that the first settlers on these shores, who were for many decades outnumbered by the Indians and unable to defeat any of the more powerful Indian tribes in battle, should have adopted the prudent procedure of buying lands that the Indians were willing to sell instead of using the more direct methods of massacre and displacement that have commonly prevailed in other parts of the world. What is significant, however, is that at the end of the 18th Century when our population east of the Mississippi was at least 20 times as great as the Indian population in the same region and when our army of Revolutionary veterans might have been used to break down Indian claims to land ownership and reduce the Indians to serfdom or landlessness, we took seriously our national proclamation that all men are created equal and undertook to respect the property rights which Indians had enjoyed and maintained under their rude tribal governments. Our national policy was firmly established in the first great act of our Congress, the Northwest Ordinance of July 13, 1787, which declared:

> Art. 3. . . . The utmost good faith shall always be observed towards the Indians; their land and property shall never be taken from them without their consent; and in their property, rights and liberty, they never shall be invaded or disturbed, unless in just and lawful wars authorized by Congress; but laws founded in justice and humanity shall from time to time be made, for preventing wrongs being done to them, and for preserving peace and friendship with them. . . .

This is not to say that our Indian record is without its dark pages. We have fallen at times from the high national standards we set ourselves.

The purchase of more than two million square miles of land from the Indian tribes represents what is probably the largest real estate transaction in the history of the world. It would be miraculous if, across a period of 150 years, negotiations for the purchase and sale of these lands could be carried on without misunderstandings and inequities. We have been human, not angelic, in our real-estate transactions. We have driven hard Yankee bargains when we could;

we have often forgotten to make the payments that we promised, to respect the boundaries of lands that the Indians reserved for themselves, or to respect the privileges of tax exemption, or hunting and fishing, that were accorded to Indian tribes in exchange for the lands they granted us. But when Congress has been fairly apprised of any deviation from the plighted word of the United States, it has generally been willing to submit to court decision the claims of any injured Indian tribe.[11] And it has been willing to make whatever restitution the facts supported for wrongs committed by blundering or unfaithful public servants. There is no nation on the face of the earth which has set for itself so high a standard of dealing with a native aboriginal people as the United States and no nation on earth that has been more self-critical in seeking to rectify its deviations from those high standards. . . .

NOTES

1. *United States as Guardian of the Hualpai Indians v. Santa Fe Pacific R.R.*, (1941) 314 U.S. 339; *United States v. Alcea Band of Tillamooks*, (1946) 329 U.S. 40.

2. Some of the material in this section appears in "How We Bought the United States," *Collier's*, Jan. 19, 1946, pp. 23, 62, 77, and in an adaptation thereof in *This Month*, May, 1946, pp. 106–110.

3. This discrepancy between common opinion and historic fact was commented upon by Thomas Jefferson:

> That the lands of this country were taken from them by conquest, is not so general a truth as is supposed. I find in our historians and records, repeated proofs of purchase, which cover a considerable part of the lower country; and many more would doubtless be found on further search. The upper country, we know, has been acquired altogether by purchases made in the most unexceptional form." (Thomas Jefferson, "Notes on the State of Virginia, 1781–1785, reprinted in Padover, The Complete Jefferson, (1943) p. 632.)

4. The Treaty of April 30, 1803, for the cession of Louisiana, provided:

> Art. III. The inhabitants of the ceded territory shall be incorporated in the Union of the United States, and admitted as soon as possible, according to the principles of the Federal constitution, to the enjoyment of all the rights, advantages and immunities of citizens of the United States; and in the meantime they shall be maintained and protected in the free enjoyment of their liberty, property, and the religion which they profess."

> Art. VI. The United States promise to execute such treaties and articles as may have been agreed between Spain and the tribes and nations of Indians, until by mutual consent of the United States and the said tribes or nations, other suitable articles shall have been agreed upon.

5. "Indian reservations" acquired their name from the fact that when Indians ceded land they commonly made "reservations" of land to be retained in Indian ownership. This practice goes back at least to 1640, when Uncas, the Mohican chief, deeded a large area to the Colony of Connecticut, out of which he carved a reservation for himself and his tribe. See 1 Trumbull, History of Connecticut, (1818) p. 117.

6. Act of May 18, 1928, 45 Stat. 602.

7. The most significant exception is Alaska, where the Federal Government has not yet acquired any land from any of the native tribes. *Cf. Miller v. United States*, (C.C.A. 9th, 1947) 159 F. (2d) 997. Other areas for which no compensation appears to have been made are found in Southeastern California, Southern Nevada, Arizona, and New Mexico. See Frontispiece to 4th ed. of Felix S. Cohen, *Handbook of Federal Indian Law* Albuquerque, N.M.: University of New Mexico Press 1945.

8. The Report of the Commissioner of Indian Affairs for 1872 [is] illuminating [on this point].

9. In addition to the items listed above, items commonly listed in the earliest treaties are: flints, scissors, sugar, clothing, needles and hoes. Later treaties commonly mention horses, cattle, hogs, sheep, farm implements, looms, sawmills, flour mills, boats, and wagons.

10. New Project of Freedoms and Exemptions, Article 27, reprinted in Royce, Indian Land Cessions in the United States (18th Annual Report, U.S. Smithsonian Institute, 1900) p. 577.

11. For many decades such cases were tried under special jurisdictional acts. By the act of August 6, 1946, all existing tribal claims against the Government were referred to a special Indian Claims Commission, and jurisdiction was granted to the Court of Claims to hear and decide all future tribal claims. See 60 Stat. 1049, 25 U.S.C.A. (1946 Supp.) 70, 28 U.S.C.A. (1946 Supp.) 259a.

Original Indian Title [Revisited]

Wilcomb E. Washburn

It is the prevailing assumption among Americans that the bulk of the land of the United States was simply appropriated from the Indians without benefit of law or compensation. The assumption is persistent, but defective. . . .

The assumption prevalent in [Thomas] Jefferson's time has continued to this day. Felix Cohen, the great authority on Indian law and Associate Solicitor of the Department of the Interior, attributed the belief that America was stolen from the Indians to the desire of Americans to "make our idealism look as hard-boiled as possible."[1] Cohen, in 1947, noted that $800,000,000 of Federal funds had to that time been appropriated for the purchase of Indian lands. While the government had not always honored the principle of respect for Indian possessions, it had, Cohen pointed out, honored it to that degree. "To pay $800,000,000 for a principle is not a common occurrence in the world's history," he noted.[2]

Because educated persons as well as ignorant ones have assumed that most of the land of the United States was stolen from the Indians, there has usually been a frightened reaction by responsible officials to any legal decisions that seemed to uphold the right of the Indian to compensation for the taking of what is usually called "original Indian title": that is, land lived upon by the Indians without benefit of any formal recognition of that title by the United States. For example, in the case of *Cramer v. United States*, 1923 (261 U.S. 219), the Attorney General of Arizona filed a brief asserting that "Any suggestion by this Court that Indian tribes might have rights in property enforceable in a court of law by the mere fact of occupancy would at least cast a cloud upon the title to the major portion of Arizona."[3]

Despite this warning, the Supreme Court held in *Cramer*, and, in 1941, in *United States as Guardian of the Hualapai Indians v. Santa Fe Pacific Railway* (314 U.S. 339), that the Indian right of occupancy, even though not formally recognized, was not terminated by a subsequent statutory grant.[4]

From *Red Man's Land/White Man's Law: A Study of the Past and Present Status of the American Indian,* by Wilcomb E. Washburn. New York, N.Y.: Charles Scribner's Sons. © 1971 by Wilcomb E. Washburn.

These two cases served notice on purchasers of real property that Indian title could remain as an encumbrance upon grants made in ignorance of, or in defiance of that title. The fundamental constitutional issue of whether the taking by the United States of original unrecognized "Indian title" was compensable, and, if so, whether it was compensable under the strict provisions of the "due process" clause of the Fifth Amendment to the Constitution, was not faced until the case of the *United States v. Alcea Band of Tillamooks.* In this case, the Supreme Court, on November 25, 1946, affirmed the judgment of the Court of Claims that the Tillamooks were entitled to compensation for certain lands which they had been forced to surrender involuntarily and without compensation. . . . The government, fighting the case in the Court of Claims and in the Supreme Court, urged that in the absence of some form of official "recognition," original Indian title could be appropriated without liability on the part of the sovereign.[5] . . .

The *coup-de-grace* to claims for compensation under the Fifth Amendment was rendered in the case of the *Tee-Hit-Ton Indians, An Identifiable Group of Alaska Indians v. the United States,* decided by the Supreme Court on February 7, 1955. The Tee-Hit-Ton Indians, a small group of Tlingit Indians residing in Alaska, claimed compensation for a taking by the United States of certain timber from lands allegedly belonging to them. They established "original Indian title" or "Indian right of occupancy" to the lands in question. But, because of uncertainty concerning the compensable nature of this right, about which several court decisions disagreed, the Supreme Court agreed to hear the case.

In its majority decision, delivered by Mr. Justice Reed, the Court took a hard line, holding that Congress had never granted the Indians of Alaska permanent rights in the lands occupied by them, but, in the legislation dealing with Alaska, had deferred such a determination until a later time. The majority asserted that "No case in this Court has ever held that taking of Indian title or use by Congress required compensation," [and in so asserting] rejected the precedent of the . . . *Tillamook* case. . . . The Court was at pains to disallow a Fifth Amendment defense to the Tee-Hit-Ton Indians. "Generous provision has been willingly made to allow tribes to recover for wrongs," the Court noted, but "as a matter of grace, not because of legal liability."

In an opinion notable for its pejorative references to "tribal" ownership as opposed to individual ownership, to "savage tribes," "stages of civilization" and to "nomadic" patterns of land use among the Indians, the Court bolstered the "hard line" conclusion that "the line of cases adjudicating Indian rights on American soil leads to the conclusion that Indian occupancy, not specifically recognized as ownership by action authorized by Congress, may be extinguished by the Government without compensation." The majority, however, did not wish to be holding the monkey of responsibility for a harsh policy toward Indian claims. "Our conclusion . . . leaves with Congress, where it belongs, the policy of Indian gratuities for the termination of Indian occupancy of Government-owned land rather than making compensation for its value a rigid constitutional principle."[6] . . .

Recent decisions concerning Indian title have reflected a broadened understanding of the different Indian cultural patterns and a heightened awareness of the need to adjudicate Indian claims in terms of equity and morality rather than on the basis of narrow legality. For example, in *U.S. v. Seminole Indians of the State of Florida*, 1967 (180 Ct. Cl. 375), the Court noted that although proof of Indian title depends on a showing of actual, exclusive and continuous use and occupancy for a long time by the Indian tribe in question, it is also necessary to consider the nature of the use: whether primarily for agriculture, hunting, or trade, whether utilized seasonally or nomadically, and the like. Actual possession in the strict sense, the Court ruled, is not essential and Indian title may be established through the tribe's intermittent contacts in areas they control.

The Seminole decision was a rebuke to the government which had appealed the prior decision of the Indian Claims Commission on the grounds that it was not supported by the evidence. The peculiar insistence of the Lands Division of the Justice Department in stubbornly fighting and appealing even the weakest case reflects the bureaucratic ethos at its worst. The Lands Division has lost sight of the humane and benevolent purpose of the Indian Claims Commission Act and has acted as though it must fight, obstruct, extend, delay, and frustrate any effort on the Indians' part, or inclination on the government's part, to settle claims with generosity and good will. The attitude derives in part from professional pride, but it also reflects an irritation at the Indian claimants which seems to be a part of the mental equipment of those in government dealing with Indians.

In the Seminole case, the Court of Claims . . . upheld the Indian Claims Commission in its conclusion that the Seminole Indians justifiably had Indian title to most of Florida. To the government's objection that the Seminoles occupied only a handful of settlements before being joined by 2,500 Creeks (from whom the Seminoles had derived earlier) following American attacks in the period 1814–1819, the court pointed out that . . . use and occupancy essential to the recognition of Indian title "does not demand *actual* possession, [but rather] the key to Indian title lies in evaluating the manner of land-use over a period of time." . . .

The Court of Claims also laid down a liberal rule to determine the cultural identity of the Seminoles. It noted that the remnants of the original inhabitants of the Florida peninsula—some twenty-five groups with an estimated 50,000 population in 1512—were absorbed by the Seminoles who moved into the peninsula in the eighteenth century. "Cultural assimilation," stated the court, "extinguishes the identity, but not the people." "Therefore," the court went on, "whatever land rights were possessed by those absorbed may be recognized as inhering in the culture that emerges." . . .

NOTES

1. "Original Indian Title," *Minnesota Law Review*, XXXII (1947–48), 34.
2. *Ibid.*, 45–60.
3. Quoted in *ibid.*, 32.
4. *Ibid.*, 29.
5. 329 U.S. 40.

6. 348 U.S. 272. That fiscal considerations rather than moral or legal considerations have shaped the denial of a Fifth Amendment protection to Indian tribes suing for compensation for aboriginal title lands unjustly taken from them has been documented at considerable length by a young legal scholar, Howard M. Friedman, in an article entitled, "Interest on Indian Claims: Judicial Protection of the Fisc," published in the *Valparaiso Law Journal*, Vol. 5, No. 1 (Fall, 1970), 26–47. As Friedman puts it: "The allowance of interest on only small classes of claims eliminated politically unacceptable judgments while paying lip-service to the Fifth Amendment." Judicial fear of allowing any Fifth Amendment protection is evident in such recent rulings as that by the Court of Claims in *U.S. v. The Delaware Tribe of Indians* (Appeal No. 6-69, decided June 12, 1970), rejecting a procedural rule established by the Indian Claims Commission—the so-called "5% rule"—concerning gratuity offsets allowed the government in Indian claims cases.

Indian Claims in the Courts of the Conqueror

Nell Jessup Newton

THE INDIAN CLAIMS COMMISSION

A cardinal purpose of the Indian Claims Commission Act was to "grant" Indian tribes equal access to the Court of Claims.[1] In addition, the Indian Claims Commission Act was designed to grant tribes their long-deferred day in court by permitting them to sue for historic wrongs in order to settle Indian tribes' grievances against the Government permanently.[2] Despite these positive intentions, the Act's major goal was to settle tribes' ancient grievances in order to prepare them for the termination of their special status under United States law.[3]

The Indian Claims Commission Act created the Indian Claims Commission, which has jurisdiction over so-called "ancient claims," or those arising before the jurisdictional cut-off-date of 1951.[4] The statute created five broad classes of claims.

> (1) claims in law or equity arising under the Constitution, laws, treaties of the United States, and Executive orders of the President; (2) all other claims in law or equity, including those sounding in tort, . . . (3) claims which would result if the treaties, contracts, and agreements between the claimant and the United States were revised on the ground of fraud; (4) claims arising from the taking by the United States . . . of lands owned or occupied by the claimant without the payment for such lands of compensation . . . ; and (5) claims based upon fair and honorable dealings that are not recognized by any existing rule of law or equity.[5] . . .

Once the Commission became a court, it became a claims court. In other words, it viewed its remedial arsenal as restricted to money damages, a view that seems consistent with the legislative intent.[6] The Indian Claims Commission Act provided for review of Indian Claims Commission decisions to the Court of Claims, followed by certiorari review to the Supreme Court.[7] . . .

From "Indian Claims in the Courts of the Conqueror," *American University Law Review* 41 (1992): 753. © 1992 by Nell Jessup Newton.

When Congress finally dissolved the Indian Claims Commission in 1978, it transferred its 102 remaining cases to the Court of Claims.[8] When the Claims Court was created in 1982, the entire jurisdiction of the Court of Claims was transferred to the [regular federal] Court. As a result, the new court must resolve ancient claims that had never been tried in the Indian Claims Commission.[9] It also must hear claims on appeal from the Indian Claims Commission, modern claims arising from the Tucker Act, congressional reference claims,"[10] and claims from new jurisdictional statutes.[11] As a result, the judges, many of them coming from the patent bar or for other reasons having no knowledge of Indian law, must plunge immediately into the mysteries of the Indian Claims Commission Act's law.

Although the Claims Court is nearly finished with all ancient claims, it will never be completely finished, for Congress has referred to the claims in the Indian Claims Commission as bases for suit in at least one modern jurisdictional statute and may continue to do so in the future.[12] . . .

BREACH OF FAIR AND HONORABLE DEALING

. . . One might justifiably ask why it is necessary to focus on the law created in these ancient claims, if the Indian Claims Commission is no longer in existence. The answer is that the formalistic rules developed in Indian Claims Commission cases, especially those rules limiting liability and setting the boundaries of the permissible, continue to be cited and relied on today, even by the Supreme Court.[13] The widespread belief that tribes could not sue in federal district court before 1965 also resulted in an acceptance by tribal advocates and tribes of the basic premise of claims law: that payments of cash could and perhaps should be the only remedy for wrongs. As tribes perceived that they had alternatives to money damages claims, such as claims for equitable relief in federal courts of general jurisdiction, strategic options dramatically increased. Focusing on these early cases sets the stage to understand this development and demonstrates why tribes have begun to reject the equation of lost land and destruction of peoplehood with money.

Clause 5 of the Indian Claims Commission Act provides for "claims based upon fair and honorable dealings that are not recognized by any existing rule of law or equity."[14] Congress designed the fair and honorable dealings clause to allow the Commission to go beyond the confines of existing formal law. The deliberately open-ended language held out the promise that the Commission could apply moral principles to the entire course of dealings between the Government and Indian tribes. Only by this process could the old wounds be healed and Congress be freed from the necessity of continually revisiting them. . . .

Because the Commission gave priority to land claims, the remaining claims were left to the end. Thus, the Commission's first breach of fair and honorable dealings case did not reach the Court of Claims until 1970 in *Gila River Pima*

Maricopa Indian Community v. United States. The Gila River Pima-Maricopa Indians . . . clause 5 claim was truly sweeping. The tribe argued that the Government had reduced them to wardship with no concomitant benefits.[15] The Government had undertaken to provide them with educational and medical services, but the services actually provided were inadequate. Most seriously, the reduction to wardship, according to the tribe, resulted in "a stagnation of self-expression . . . [and] bridled petitioner into cultural impotency."[16]

Declining to give the fair and honorable dealings clause an expansive interpretation, the Court of Claims upheld the Commission's grant of summary judgment.[17] The court reasoned that . . . "While the remedial purpose and intent of [clause 5] should be effectuated, its scope should not be unduly extended." Because the Indian Claims Commission Act was designed to obviate the need for further special jurisdictional acts, the Court of Claims reasoned that Congress intended that clause 5 could only encompass the same kinds of claims brought earlier.[18]

In his concurrence, Judge Davis was a little more honest about the reasons for the crabbed interpretation of the statute. Given the "historic national policy of semi-apartheid," permitting the Gila River Pima-Maricopa Tribe to recover would subject the Government to far greater liability than legislators must have intended.[19] [Yet another judge on the panel,] Judge Nichols concurred in the result, noting that the Commission structure could not accommodate "every possible dispute that might have arisen between the United States and the Indians in 170 years of history."[20] . . .

The small hope of a tort suit [under clause 2] was dashed by the decision in *Fort Sill Apache Tribe v. United States* in 1973.[21] The Apache Tribe crafted a tort suit for loss of tribal identity caused by the tribe's unlawful incarceration for twenty-seven years. . . .

The imprisonment devastated the Chiricahua people and destroyed the tribe as an entity. During the first three and one-half years of confinement, 119 of the 498 tribespeople died.[22] One hundred twelve of the Apache children were dispatched to boarding school at Fort Carlisle, Pennsylvania,[23] where thirty died during the first year of instruction. The court carefully noted, however, that these deaths occurred "despite good sanitary conditions."[24]

In 1913, after twenty-seven years of what the court assumed to be "wrongful arrest, imprisonment, and excessive punishment of some individual Indians," the Government finally released the Apaches.[25] The remnants of the tribe stayed on the Fort Sill Reservation, although most of them moved to the Mescalero Apache Reservation in New Mexico.[26]

The tribe sued for the loss of its tribal identity, arguing that the destruction of the tribe's political structure was both a tort compensable under clause 2 and a breach of fair and honorable dealings under clause 5.[27] The Indian Claims Commission dismissed the claims.[28] Although the tort of wrongful imprisonment existed as a legal claim, the Commission held that the Indian Claims Commission waived sovereign immunity only for tribal claims, and not individual claims.[29] . . .

The Court of Claims affirmed.[30] The court held that the tribe could not bring a tort claim based on harm to a group right or interest because Congress had not intended to recognize a "distinct right in the tribe to foster and protect its own form and structure."[31] . . .

Although admitting that "the tribe did not prosper from the injuries suffered by its constituent members,"[32] the court stated that, at best, the claim was one for a multitude of individual claims for wrongful imprisonment, and thus outside the jurisdiction of the Indian Claims Commission Act.[33]

In discussing the scope of clause 5, the court [noted], apparently without irony, that the clause "is limited to somewhat fewer situations than a literal reading would imply."[34] To satisfy the requirements of [the legal precedent set by] *Gila River*, the tribe would have to demonstrate that the Government undertook a duty to protect the tribe's power structure.[35] Most assuredly, the Government had not undertaken such a duty in treaties or statutes.[36] The court recounted the history of the Apache wars, stressing the wars were long and hard-fought by both sides.[37] In this context, the imprisonment of the "sagacious savages"[38] was an act of war. Perhaps it was "unwarranted and reparations should be given to the Apache Indians for their suffering after surrender."[39] Nevertheless, while not condoning the Government's action, the majority concluded it had no jurisdiction: "We take the law as we find it."[40] . . .

Judge Nichols's dissent doubted the tribe's ability to recover, both because of the passage of time and because of the difficulty of measuring damages, but argued that the tribe should be given its chance to air its grievances in the public forum of a Commission proceeding.[41] Given the violence of that war, he noted that "justifying the imprisonment may well prove easier than condemning it; in any case, we should not fear to cast the light of day on this murky chapter of our nation's past, if Congress wished it."[42]

Judge Nichols criticized the majority's rejection of the aggregated claims of individuals drawing on analogies from international law in which the U.S. Government settled claims brought by foreign countries on behalf of their individual citizens.[43] In a particularly eloquent portion of his dissent, Judge Nichols criticized the Court of Claims and the Commission for taking an excessively narrow view of the Commission's role:

> [W]e must watch ourselves to avoid slipping into the excessive legalism we as lawyers, are normally prone to, wrongly limiting our task to . . . intellectual games . . . ; The Congress sought to put us on a broader plateau. It is error to pretend we face purely legal issues. Excessive legalism, a forgetting that the tribunal is called on not just for legal niceties, but statecraft too, produces . . . absurdities.[44] . . .

Fort Sill and Gila River reduced the fair and honorable dealings clause to nothing more than a statutory or treaty claim,[45] duplicating claims adjudicated under other provisions of the Indian Claims Commission Act. Consequently, clause 5 became practically a dead letter. Of the more than 600 claims adjudicated by the

Claims Commission, in only one did clause 5 provide the sole basis for relief. In *Aleut Community v. United States*,[46] the Court of Claims held that the Aleut people of St. Paul Island, who were kept in virtual slavery for seventy-six years, could recover damages, not because they were forbidden to leave the island, forbidden to marry anyone off the island, and forced to work in the seal trade at less than minimum wages for a lessee of the U.S. Government, but because two statutes authorizing leases of rights to trade in seal furs contained provisions specifically protecting the natives.[47] *Aleut Community* established the reach of the fair and honorable dealings clause as requiring the plaintiff to show (1) the United States undertook an obligation to a tribe by treaty, statute, or agreement; (2) the United States failed to meet the obligation; and (3) this failure resulted in damages.[48] Unfortunately, as of March 1983, this claim was still pending.[49]

NOTES

1. See 92 Cong. Rec. A4923 (1946) (statement of Rep. Mundt) ("This ought to be an example for all the world to follow in its treatment of minorities.").

2. See Indian Claims Commission Act of 1946, Pub. L No. 726. ch. 959. § 2, 60 Stat. 1049, 1050 (omitted from 25 U.S.C. § 70 upon termination of Commission on Sept. 30, 1978) (defining classes of complaints Commission shall hear against United States on behalf of Indians).

3. See Russell Lawrence Barsh, "Indian Land Claims Policy in the United States," 58 *North Dakota Law Review* 7, 37 (1982) (stating Indian claims settlement policy). Scholars wrote a thoughtful collection of essays assessing the Indian Claims Commission and faulting the process on many grounds. See *Irredeemable America: The Indians' Estate and Land Claims* (Imre Sutton ed.) Albuquerque, N.M.: University of New Mexico Press, 1985.; see Id at 6 ("[T]he litigation process—once perceived as their only recourse—has not fully met their expectations of an honorable resolution."). Even the Indian Claims Commission's own historian, Harvey D. Rosenthal, criticized the Commission. See Harvey D. Rosenthal, "Indian Claims and the American Conscience: A Brief History of the Indian Claims Commission," in *Irredeemable America,* supra, at 63 ("It became obvious that the commission broke no new ground and was really a government measure to enhance its own efficiency by disposing of the old claims and terminating the Indian tribes.").

4. Indian Claims Commission Act of 1946, Pub. L. No. 726, ch. 959, § 12, 60 Stat. 1049, 1052 (omitted from 25 U.S.C. § 70 upon termination of Commission on Sept. 30, 1978).

5. Id. § 2, 60 Stat. 1049, 1050 (omitted from 25 U.S.C. § 70 upon termination of Commission on Sept. 30, 1978).

6. The Act referred to the "amount" of liability, and appropriation of "sums as are necessary to pay the final determination of the Commission." Indian Claims Commission Act of 1946, Pub. L. No. 726, ch. 959, §§ 19, 22, 60 Stat. 1049, 1054–55 (omitted from 25 U.S.C. § 70 upon termination of Commission on Sept. 30, 1978).

7. Id. § 20(2)(c).

8. See United States Indian Claims Commission, Final Report 20 (1978).

9. In 1990, 12 cases remained of the Indian Claims Commission Act cases transferred to the Court Of Claims. See Reports of the Proceedings of the Judicial Conference of the United States, Annual Report of the Director of the Administrative Office of the United States Courts, Table G-3a, at 245 (1990) (reporting statistics from the Claims Court for year ending Sept. 30, 1990).

10. I am aware of only one congressional reference case involving an Indian claim. In that case, Congress requested the Claims Court to apply a "fair and honorable dealings" standard, to determine whether the United States had adequately protected the tribe's

aboriginal land in Texas. *Battise v. United States,* 12 Cl. Ct. 426, 433 (1987) (reporting to
Congress that tribe had not shown exclusive use and occupancy of aboriginal land and
that there was no basis for concluding Government had responsibility for loss of tribe's
land).

11. *Zuni Indian Tribe v. United States,* 16 Cl. Ct. 670, 675 (1989) (applying special jurisdiction conferred by Act of May 15, 1978, Pub. L. No. 95-280, 92 Stat. 244, to hold that
United States took aboriginal, but not recognized title).

12. See *Wichita Indian Tribe v. United States,* 696 F.2d 1378, 1386 (Fed. Cir. 1983)
(remanding to Claims Court to consider merits of case previously dismissed as beyond
scope of jurisdictional statute).

13. See, e.g., *United States v. Sioux Nation of Indians,* 448 U.S. 371, 386 (1986) (quoting *Three Affiliated Tribes of the Fort Berthold Reservation v. United States,* 390.F.2d
686, 609–94 (Ct. Cl. 1968) and adopting restrictive test devised by Claims Court in
review of Indian Claims Commission decision); *Battise v. United States,* 12 Cl. Ct. 426,
432–33 (1987) (applying concepts of aboriginal title and fair and honorable dealings to
congressional reference case).

14. Indian Claims Commission Act of 1946, Pub. L. No. 726, ch. 959, § 2(5), 60 Stat. 1049,
1054 (omitted from 25 U.S.C. § 70 upon termination of Commission on Sept. 30, 1978).

15. *Gila River,* 427 F.2d at 1195.

16. See id. (quoting petition of Gila River Pima-Maricopa Indian Community).

17. Id. at 1200.

18. Id.

19. Id. at 1201 (Davis, J., concurring).

20. Id. (Nichols, J., concurring).

21. See *Fort Sill Apache Tribe v. United States,* 477 F.2d 1360, 1361 (Ct. Cl. 1973)
(addressing Apache claim to recover compensation for wrongdoing to tribe as result of twenty-seven years of internment).

22. Id. at 1366.

23. Id.

24. Id.

25. Id. at 1361.

26. Id. at 1362.

27. *Fort Sill Apache Tribe v. United States,* 26 Indian Cl. Comm'n 281, 285 (1971).

28. Id. at 301 (dismissing Indian claim without trial on grounds of lack of subject matter
jurisdiction and failure to state claim).

29. Id. at 287.

30. *Fort Sill Apache Tribe,* 477 F.2d at 1368.

31. Id. at 1365. The court distinguished a successful nuisance claim brought by a church
on the ground that the church asserted property rights. Id. at 1363 (citing *Baltimore &
P.R.R. v. Fifth Baptist Church,* 108 U.S. 317, 329 (1883)).

32. Id. at 1365.

33. Id.

34. Id.

35. Id. at 1364.

36. Id.

37. Id. at 1361–62.

38. Id. at 1367 (quoting *Scott v. United States,* 33 Ct. Cl. 486, 488 (1898)).

39. Id.

40. Id.

41. Id. at 1368–69 (Nichols, J., dissenting). Judge Nichols took the same position in a
1981 case in which the majority refused to reopen a claim. Compare *Pueblo of Santo
Domingo v. United States,* 647 F.2d 1087, 1088–89 (Ct. Cl. 1981) (dismissing as untimely
motion to present new evidence that attorney's stipulation was unauthorized) with id. at
1089 (Nichols, J., dissenting) (urging remand and chiding court for refusing to take any testimony or set case for argument).

42. *Fort Sill Apache Tribe,* 477 F.2d at 1370 (Nichols J., dissenting).

43. See id. (analogizing to Alabama claims where privately owned ships and cargoes were destroyed by Confederate cruisers fitted for war by England in violation of country's duty to be neutral under international law).

44. Id. at 1375 (Nichols, J., dissenting). In 1955, Justice Jackson wrote a concurring opinion expressing belief that Indian concepts of property were so foreign to U.S. concepts that application of private property law to tribal property was artificial. *Northwestern Bands of Shoshone Indians v. United States,* 324 U.S. 335, 354 (1945) (Jackson, J., concurring). But see Nell Jessup Newton, "At the Whim of the Sovereign: Aboriginal Title Reconsidered," 31 *Hastings Law Journal* 1215, 1249–51 (1980) [hereinafter Newton, "At the Whim of the Sovereign] (criticizing Justice Jackson's concurring opinion in Northwestern Bands of Shoshone Indians).

45. See supra notes 125–138, 143–162 and accompanying text (explaining judicial reluctance to entertain broad moral claims under ICCA's fair and honorable dealings clause as unwillingness to subject Federal Government to seemingly unlimited liability).

46. 480 F.2d 831 (Ct. Cl. 1973).

47. See *Aleut Community v. United States,* 480 F.2d 831, 839–841 (Ct. Cl. 1973) (listing wide range of civil rights abuses endured by St. Paul Island Aleuts, but pointing to two federal seal-trade statutes as source of U.S. responsibility for protection of Aleuts). The first statute discussed is the Act of July 1, 1870, ch. 189, § 1, 16 Stat. 180, which states that the "natives of [St. Paul Island] shall have the privilege of killing such . . . seals as may be necessary for their own food and clothing . . . and for the manufacture of boats for their own use. . . ." Id. This provision explicitly recognizes the reliance placed by these Aleuts on seal hunting, and thus the Act acknowledges the impact government-sanctioned hunting will have on the Islanders by mandating that federal authorities "shall have due regard [for] the . . . comfort, maintenance, and education of the natives. . . ." Id § 4. The second statute discussed is the Act of April 21, 1910, ch. 183, § 3, 36 Stat. 326, which protects the Aleuts from exploitative fur traders by providing that they "shall receive for their labor fair compensation." The court in Aleut Community used this language to find that the U.S. Government was party to a "special relationship" with the Aleuts and was thus obliged to provide for the well-being of the natives. Aleut Community, 480 F.2d at 840.

48. *Aleut Community,* 480 F.2d at 839.

49. See *Aleut Tribe v. United States,* 702 F.2d 1015, 1016 (Fed. Cir. 1983) (relating that Government filed motion to dismiss fair and honorable dealings claim in Court of Claims in 1980 and dismissing interlocutory appeal with leave to seek another appeal in future).

Epilogue

Nancy Oestreich Lurie

My work as an expert witness before the Indian Claims Commission was entirely for tribal petitioners and covered the period from 1954 to 1964. . . . My last experience concerned the Potawatomis (Pottawatomies), where I collected some limited field data in Wisconsin and Michigan but served primarily as an ethnohistorical expert in the early hearings concerning the eastern bands, at which Commissioner Watkins presided. It is no coincidence that I dropped out of claims work after testifying before Commissioner Watkins.

In my experience, the original panel of commissioners—Witt, Holt, and O'Marr, and later Commissioner Scott—were sincerely dedicated to principles of fairness and impartiality. My criticism of their work really is directed to the fact that they were chosen because they had no experience in Indian matters, supposedly to assure objectivity and lack of preconceptions. The result was that they made simplistic, inadvertently biased interpretations owing to their lack of awareness of the historical and cultural complexities underlying Indian grievances, which the 1946 Act was designed to address. Later, when Commissioner Watkins was appointed, part of the justification was that he was informed on Indian affairs, having been the foremost promulgator of the termination policy (Watkins 1957). He had a lot of preconceptions, if no more cultural and historical understanding of the Indian scene than the earlier commissioners.

Also, if I appear critical of attorneys, I want to state clearly that all the attorneys I worked with were sincerely concerned for their clients and took great pains in preparing their cases. I learned a lot from them about Indian law and policy for which I will always be grateful. [However,] I [was] deeply distressed on one occasion to see a fellow anthropologist employed by the Justice Department cut to ribbons by one of "my" attorneys. On the other hand, I got some rough treatment myself on occasion in cross-examination. . . . What is hard for anthropologists to

From "Epilogue" by Nancy Oestreich Lurie, in *Irredeemable America: The Indians' Estate and Land Claims*, edited by Imre Sutton et al. Albuquerque, N.M.: University of New Mexico Press. © 1985 by Nancy Oestreich Lurie.

understand is that while lawyers and scientists both use the term "theory," lawyers really mean strategy—what succeeds under testing by trial, not necessarily what is thoroughly and objectively tested in an academic sense. . . .

THE CLAIMS COMMISSION AND ITS AFTERMATH

Despite the high promise of the Indian Claims Commission Act, with only a few exceptions, the benefits to the tribes were negligible. Money was appropriated, distributed, spent, and forgotten and did little if any thing to overcome the sense of Indian grievance. It is easy to attribute the failure of the Act to do much good to the familiar complaint that Indians are profligate and too "factional" to get together on plans to use their money wisely. The failure really must be attributed to the interpretation and implementation of the Act. . . . [T]he very creation of the commission speaks well for America as a nation, but like so many programs and policies based on benevolent motives, it fell short of its intent. . . .

THE COMMISSION AND THE CHANGING NATIONAL SCENE

A watershed in Indian policy had been reached by the time the Indian Claims Commission Act was passed. . . . [T]he Act was tied in some legislators' minds, at least, to termination, but the irony is that when judgments were finally handed down and settlements made, Congress was reluctant to grant per-capita payments, which most tribes desired, and encouraged using awards for community improvements and for starting tribal enterprises. One would have expected Congress to favor per-capitas, individualizing the tribal capital as a step toward assimilation, and that the Indians who opposed termination would have preferred to use their judgments for community development.

This seemingly curious turn of events is partly understandable in reference to the timetable of the hearings. Claims averaged about two decades between filing and settlement, which meant that significant numbers of requests for appropriations to pay claims did not begin to reach Congress until well into the 1960s, by which time the termination policy had slowed virtually to a halt. The American Indian Chicago Conference of 1961 signaled the beginning of Indian activism on a national scale, with Indians gaining increasing visibility before the general public over the next twenty years. Relocation, part of the 1950s termination package, backfired. Instead of promoting widespread assimilation of Indians into the general society as intended, relocation simply produced Indian people with urban savvy to argue and demonstrate for Indian rights before the general public. . . .

What is important in the scenario is that in the 1960s and 1970s as more claims cases were being settled, Congress realized that Indian communities were not about to disappear but were in dire financial straits and would continue to need massive federal assistance. As I see it, Congress looked to claims awards as a means of getting community improvements on the cheap. In 1973 it made a legislative attempt, which proved difficult to enforce, to require tribes to limit per-capita distributions to no more than 80 percent of their awards. If tribes could be convinced to put their own money into programs, Congress would have to appropriate less money to assist them. This was not an officially enunciated policy any more than termination was officially tied to claims awards in 1946, but the connection in both cases simply made sense at their particular times. I am sure that many people in Congress and in the Indian Bureau did not recognize the self-serving effect of their emphasis on using awards for community projects and only saw it as encouraging the tribes to derive the greatest benefit possible from their settlements.

The overwhelming Indian preference for per-capita distribution of all or a major portion of their awards actually was a predictable reaction against the tradition of governmental paternalism. From the Indian perspective, claims awards were to settle old grievances and not to get Congress off the hook in capitalizing programs which would address current, ongoing problems. There were, of course, many complicating factors involved in the preference for per-capita payments.

First, strong arguments for per-capita distributions were raised by many urban-based Indian people, even those who considered the reservation their real home, a place they visited frequently and where they hoped to retire. To them, investment of awards in community programs seemed unfair. The folks on the reservation have the benefits of tax-free land and various kinds of help from the Bureau of Indian Affairs and would receive the lion's share of benefits from claims awards put into community improvement projects or reservation-based industries. The Indian people in the cities who made the sacrifice of leaving home to seek better employment opportunities and were hanging in there for pension purposes while paying for their own housing would be penalized for their enterprise.

Second, there was and is pervasive and historically justified distrust of the Bureau of Indian Affairs and tribal governments in regard to money management for community improvements and starting up reservation businesses. This same distrust frustrated fiscally sophisticated Indian people who suggested investment and per-capita payments of interest which would benefit every one equally and in the long run provide more money, even for future generations, than dividing the actual award. Indian people understood such proposals insofar as awards increased through interest accrued from the time a claim was approved until the tribe agreed on a plan of use, often a matter of several years and substantial amounts of additional money. They simply feared that inevitably they would be bilked once their money got out of the federal treasury and the closely monitored investment program for claims awards[,] and into tribal management assisted by the Bureau and possibly by outside white financial advisors.

Finally, and perhaps most important, the awards were not perceived as one might expect of people so committed to the importance of their tribal identity and persistence. After all, the payments were for lands lost to the *entire* tribe; it was just chance that a particular generation was around to collect. The ancestors who were wronged directly could not benefit, but surely there should have been concern for future generations. My impression, based on direct experience with Wisconsin tribes and supported by Indian people and anthropologists I have talked to who are familiar with other areas of the country, is that generally only a handful of people in the various tribes that received awards really understood the basis of their claims. Those who did understand tended to be embittered at the low value put on their land. . . . Most people, however, only knew that as long as they could remember they had heard that the government owed them money, and they looked upon the claims awards as a kind of compensation for deprivations and other injustices they had suffered in general as Indians since being settled on reservations. Money, from the Indian perspective, cannot equal land as it does for whites [. . . Thus, some] tribes have tried to resist accepting awards, hoping for land restoration or land restoration in addition to monetary awards. Non-Indians familiar with the suits had factual understanding and philosophical perceptions of the awards not shared by many Indians. After the long, long wait for their money, Indian people were in no mood for history or philosophy lessons, which came across as just another white man's trick to get what was rightfully theirs. The problem was that the Commission dealt with Indian claims, not Indians' claims. That the claims were not husbanded for the general and ongoing good of the tribes in the vast majority of cases is due to the slow settlement of claims, the lack of an Investigation Division and of Indian input in preparing cases, and the narrowly construed grounds for suit. . . .

THE INVESTIGATION DIVISION

My opinion, shared by many anthropological colleagues involved in the claims cases, is that the greatest error of implementation of the 1946 act was the first Commissioners' failure to establish the Investigation Division provided for in Section 13(b) of the Act. No one can say at this time whether the Investigation Division would have made a difference but it certainly had enormous potential to make a difference, especially if it had been properly staffed. Commissioners Witt, Holt, and O'Marr's lack of knowledge of Indian affairs probably precluded their appreciating the need for the division in clarifying and expediting claims. The very idea of such a division in the Indian Claims Commission Act suggested procedures of continental European law, where experts serve the court, but the commissioners, and the attorneys who appeared before them, were schooled in American law, derived from British tradition, where experts are provided by the parties to a suit and often pitted against each other. This seems to work for Anglo-American litigation, but the important point is that these [Indian Claims] cases were based in large part on cultural considerations different from the culture on which Anglo-American law and legal procedures are based.

Although Section 13(b) [of the Indian Claims Commission Act] only makes reference to documentary evidence, Section 13(a), which provides for notification to identifiable tribes, bands, and groups of their right to bring suit, directs the Indian Bureau to contact federal tribes through its agencies and to prepare statements of tribal claims "together with the names of aged and invalid Indians from whom depositions should be taken immediately and a summary of their proposed testimonies." Considering that virtually all of the claims dealt with matters antedating living memory even in 1946, one can only wonder what kinds of claims and testimony the framers of the Act had in mind compared to the kinds of claims and testimony that dominated the hearings.

Section 18 refers to testimony, and the implication, at least, is that the framers of the 1946 Act had Indian deponents largely in mind because of references to going out into the country, including Alaska, to obtain testimony. It could be obtained in two ways. First, the Commission or its designated employees could administer oaths and question witnesses. Second, any designated individual competent to administer oaths could take testimony. Section 18 also provides for "cross-examination, under such regulations as the Commission may prescribe." The Investigation Division would have provided the Commission with a vehicle for obtaining its own testimony, but, lacking the division and apparently unable to spare or even see the need to spare its regular staff, the Commission fell back on the second provision and depended on attorneys to obtain witnesses and elicit testimony in hearings conducted according to conventional courtroom procedures. More important, the description of the division indicates it would help the Commission define claims, but in actual practice attorneys defined claims by a process of elimination, as shall be shown.

The act makes no explicit mention of anthropologists, historians, geographers, land assessors, and others whose testimony figured so importantly in the hearings. It is conceivable that such people could have staffed the Investigation Division, and certainly they should have. Indian testimony, when obtained at all, was taken by attorneys, who found the procedure so frustrating that they turned to anthropologists, particularly ethnologists, to act, in effect, as surrogate witnesses for the Indians. This was justifiable in some ways, because ethnologists, especially witnesses for tribal attorneys, had collected and published data independent of the commission cases, and their information often was based on "testimony" of people no longer alive to provide direct testimony. Anthropologists also had special skills in relating the documentary record, both governmental and other original and primary historical sources, to results of ethnographic or archaeological field research to round out and reinforce the substance of their testimony. Historians also used the ethnological literature in combination with their documentary expertise. The whole field of ethnohistory took on new life as a result of the Indian claims cases.

Even where there were Indian witnesses with a reliable grasp of tribal oral tradition, they tended to digress from matters directly related to their claims and wanted to talk about grievances not included in the claims petitions prepared by their attorneys. I am reminded of a claims attorney . . . who told of taking testimony from an aged Indian in the Southwest. The old man wanted to tell the entire tribal history from the time of creation and would respond through his interpreter to repeated interruptions to move his testimony along to points at issue, "But I ain't been born yet!" A few attorneys put Indian witnesses on the stand before the commission, but my observations of two such instances, the Rocky Boy Chippewa of Montana and the Eastern Potawatomi, suggested that their presence was mainly to give color to the suits, to remind the Commission that it was deciding cases of real people who had been concerned with the search for justice for a very long time.

Generally, rather than get testimony directly from the Indians, it was simpler and more persuasive to trot out white scholars with impressive credentials, degrees and publications, to speak about the evidence from the Indians. Although the Justice Department initially tried to get ethnological testimony dismissed as hearsay, it soon recognized the utility of such testimony for its own purposes and hired anthropologists as well as historians and the other kinds of experts used by Indians' attorneys to counter the Indians' attorneys' experts. It was a natural development because the cases were so readily reduced to the familiar two-phase formula . . . that is, establishing identity of petitioners and their lands, and establishing land values and offsets.

This became so routine that the commission was and is often referred to erroneously as the "Indian *Land* Claims Commission." It is worth noting that the two-phase formula is set forth nowhere in the Act but was an artifact of its implementation.

NARROW CONSTRUAL OF THE 1946 ACT

Since the Commissioners were expected to learn on the job, attorneys for both sides, for practical reasons, understandably tried to make the job as easy as possible. Attorneys experienced in Indian affairs bided their time to take the measure of the Commission. A bellwether case was that of the Fort Sill Apaches, whose grievance was based on the fact that while only a handful of the Chiricahuas had joined Geronimo in his depredations, the entire group had been rounded up and taken as prisoners to Florida, then to Alabama, and finally to Fort Sill, Oklahoma, where they were held for many years. The commission dismissed the case on a jurisdictional interpretation of the act, that the Fort Sill Apache claim was an aggregate of individual grievances rather than the collective grievance of a tribe, band or group (1 *Ind. Cl. Comm.* 137 [1969]).

This put a very fine point on the language of the act and moved the preparation of cases in the direction of simple, quantifiable issues. The Court of Claims proved more liberal than the Indian Claims Commission on appeals . . . and thus indicated to the Commission that in limiting grounds for suit to quantifiable acreage, a good deal of acreage could be considered compensable. In some instances, attorneys for the tribes and their experts, combing the historical sources, even found evidence of loss of lands once used and occupied by tribal petitioners that no longer figured in the petitioners' own traditional recollections of their original territory. . . . Certainly, the format the cases soon followed resulted in squeezing as much land as possible out of the documents, to the Indians' benefit, but this approach illustrated that the claims sometimes represented what attorneys felt Indians should be aggrieved about because what Indians really were aggrieved about did not stand a prayer in the Commissioners' narrow construal of grounds for suit. . . .

A small number of claims, about fifty, did not fall into the two-phase pattern of the hearings but concerned accounting, and many had to do with allotment, but only in terms of whether the Indians received fair compensation for reservation land thrown open to public sale after allotments were made. The commission did not address the legality, in light of treaties, of the opening up of reservation lands to white buyers. The proceeds of such sales were to go to the Indians for housing and other improvements relating to their allotments, whether they wanted them or not. The allotment system simply left the tribes worse off in the long run, and the money from sale of unallotted land was gone, along with the land itself. It was bitter experience of this kind—the government deciding for Indians how to spend what they were told was "their" money—which also helps to account for the desire for per-capita distributions of claims awards. . . .

Once attorneys were faced with the Commissioners' concept of aggregate grievances, allotment ceased to be a viable cause for suit if it had ever been considered at all. Grievances expressed by Indian people concerning allotment (and similar devices where they lost their land piecemeal, as in the case of the Wisconsin Winnebago homesteads) may have seemed hopeless or minor to attorneys. Reservation lands lost despite being promised in treaties were piddling acreages compared to the huge tracts the Indians gave up in treaties or that simply were taken from them before they were settled on reservations. I am not sure if many attorneys even understood the depth of Indian grievances about their treatment on the reservations in relation to allotment. In any event, it was understood that the Indians could only be compensated in money, not land, and attorneys, in their clients' and their own interests, naturally based claims on the largest areas they could demonstrate had been lost.

IF THERE HAD BEEN AN INVESTIGATION DIVISION

Possibly, an investigation division staffed with people who could go out and take testimony might have brought home to the Commission the need to address the allotment policy and perhaps other neglected grievances, in addition to the kind of land losses that dominated the hearings. Often during the actual course of the first stage of the hearings, and certainly in retrospect, people who served as expert witnesses on the two sides wished they could have worked together in an atmosphere of mutual and collegial concern for verifiable fact. The differences in their positions, often based on the same documentary sources and anthropological literature, were more apparent than real and were simply the result of which side was doing the direct examination and cross-examination of particular witnesses. . . .

Even if the division only had addressed the same kinds of questions that figured in the hearings, it could very well have saved time, money, and duplication of effort and could have assured equal access to expertise to the various tribal petitioners. The Indians' experts were paid ultimately from the awards. Some attorneys, unable or unwilling to assume a great deal of expense in preparing cases with the prospect of a long wait for settlement, did not provide sufficient expertise, or tried to ride the coattails of experts in related cases. The problem was ameliorated in 1963 when a revolving loan fund was established, administered through the Indian Bureau, to pay for expert assistance of a nonlegal nature. This, in itself, raises questions as to how many tribes were denied adequate expertise prior to 1963, expertise that might have been available to them if there had been an investigation division. The public funds, taxpayers' money, that paid for Justice Department witnesses could have gone directly to the Investigation Division, to which the Justice Department would also have had access, according to the language of Section 13(b).

If the first Commissioners had commanded any knowledge of Indian affairs at all before taking office, rather than getting their education through the hearings, there is no question in my mind that the Investigation Division soon would have included the kinds of experts employed by attorneys experienced in representing Indians. . . . But I do not believe the Investigation Division experts would have addressed the questions that were considered so routinely in the hearings or at least would not have concentrated exclusively on these questions. I like to think that *Fort Sill* would not have been so easily dismissed and that the hearings would have been more varied. In the best of all possible worlds, the division would have consisted of a small core of specialists drawing upon recognized experts in regard to specific claims and also would have included knowledgeable Indian people on the staff or as consultants. The latitude allowed the Commission in the 1946 Act regarding cross-examination procedures could have permitted a more comfortably ethnographic approach than a formidably legalistic one in eliciting data from Indian witnesses on the part of the division staff.

By way of substantiating this view, I recall the need for some genealogical evidence in preparing the eastern Potawatomi case. Although the knowledgeable but very deaf old man the attorneys and I visited was not sworn as a witness, one of the attorneys, to my dismay, began the questioning as if he were in a courtroom, bellowing questions, "Now, Mr. _____, to your certain knowledge, was the son of . . . ?" The attorney was sincerely concerned about the case, but his conventional approach to obtaining testimony first puzzled and then offended the elder, who refused to say anything. I asked the attorneys to leave and did what any trained anthropologist would do. I sketched out a kinship chart, pointing out the elder and his parents. With a knowing smile, he set to work, reciting names and adding a great many related data which served as internal checks on the accuracy of his recollections.

In addition to obtaining Indian testimony effectively, ethnologists working for the Investigation Division would have been in a position to discuss a wide range of grievances they knew about from their field work. They could have worked directly with Indian people to get their input and to keep them apprised of the status of their claims. . . .

The eastern seaboard claims [and the hunting and fishing rights cases] . . . as well as the potential for future litigation in Hawaii and Alaska . . . are indications that the Indian Claims Commission, instead of clearing the record of native peoples' grievances, dealt with a limited category of grievances but helped to inspire subsequent litigation. For all its deficiencies, the Commission served the Indian interest in a number of ways. The contingency payment provisions for attorneys meant that tribes all across the country could retain lawyers and . . . the tribes became educated in the use of the courts where previously their main recourse had been Congress and the Indian Bureau. There are now many lawyers familiar with Indian law and policy and a cadre of scholars experienced in ferreting out data relevant to litigation involving Indian issues. Young Indians are graduating from law schools that have courses and textbooks on Indian law, unheard of only a few years ago. There also are Indian legal organizations available to assist Indian groups.

The problem at this time, however, is that cases are brought before many levels of courts in a range of venues with inconsistent results because judges are differentially familiar with Indian issues. . . .

Deloria (1977:26–29) has suggested the creation of a federal court of Indian affairs. He recognizes the shortcomings of the Commission but also its potential as a model in its last years, when it included people informed about Indian affairs such as Margaret Hunter Pierce, who came to the Commission after many years of experience in the Indian section of the Court of Claims, and a Lumbee Indian, Brantley Blue. Deloria's court would have a panel of judges who would be expert in Indian history and policy and devoted only to Indian law, in contrast to other courts where judges must deal with a wide range of cases. The fact is, of course, that despite the proliferation of suits brought by Indians, individual judges might hear only one or two in the course of their terms, and the chances are that they would have no occasion to become as conversant in Indian matters as would be desirable to make informed decisions. A few bad precedents at this stage, like the Commission's ruling on *Fort Sill*, which set the pattern for all the litigation to follow, could seriously handicap the Indians' search for justice in the courts.

It would be unfortunate, however, if such a court were given a finite existence, like the Commission. Issues deriving from treaties and various aspects of the federal relationship will continue to occur and require solution, such as the controversies attendant on the discovery of minerals on Indian lands. I would see such a court served by an investigation division as it might have operated for the Commission, with access to competent, impartial experts in the various fields that might be called for in given kinds of litigation. . . .

The philosopher George Santayana's familiar phrase has it that "those who cannot remember the past are condemned to repeat it," but the catch is that individual judges or legislators can't remember something they never knew. What is needed is an institutional collective memory to refer to. The data are there . . . but the need is to activate brains to retrieve them and make them usable.

This discussion, of course, centers on the American legal and political system but by implication, at least, must go beyond Indian people to any native peoples under American jurisdiction such as Hawaiian, Inuit, Aleut, and others. . . . Indian people certainly can use all the support they can get, including pressures on our government to live up to a cherished national image as fair and humane.

The question arises as to how representative and knowledgeable, no matter how sincere, self selected Indian internationalists are. While I do not minimize the situation in the United States, the point is that our frontier period has passed and the Indian appeal to the international forums is significant for reasons beyond its own interests. It represents a painful legacy of a past which is just beginning in many parts of Latin America, Africa, Asia, and Oceania. When it is so difficult on the domestic scene to get those with power to remember the past—termination, for example, was the allotment policy in top gear but no one in Congress could remember allotment in the 1950s—it might be considered utterly futile to expect other nations to tune in our past. If we do not make our past retrievable and usable here, there is nothing for others to use either.

REFERENCES

American Indian Policy Review Commission, 1977. *Final Report*, 2 vols. Washington, D.C.: Government Printing Office.

Cahn, Edgar S., ed., 1969. *Our Brother's Keeper: The Indian in White America*. New York: New Community Press.

Deloria, Vine, Jr., 1969. *Custer Died For Your Sins*. New York, N.Y.: Macmillan.

———— 1977. *A Better Day for Indians*. New York, N.Y.: Field Foundation.

Kickingbird, Kirke, and Karen Ducheneaux, 1973. *One Hundred Million Acres*. New York, N.Y.: Macmillan.

Lurie, Nancy O., 1969. "Wisconsin Indians Lives and Land," *Wisconsin Magazine of History* 53(Autumn):2–20.

———— 1972. "Menominee Termination: from Reservation to Colony," *Human Organization* 31(3):257–269.

———— 1978. "The Indian Claims Commission," *Annals of the American Academy of Political and Social Science* 436(March):97–110.

Vance, John T., 1969. "The Congressional Mandate and the Indian Claims Commission," *North Dakota Law Review* 45(Spring):325–336.

Washburn, Wilcomb E., 1971. *Red Man's Land/White Man's Law: A Study of the Past and Present Status of the American Indian*. New York, N.Y.: Charles Scribner's Sons.

Watkins, Arthur V., 1957. "Termination of Federal Supervision: Removal of Restrictions over Indian Property and Person," *Annals of the American Academy of Political and Social Science* 311(May):47–55.

The Creation of a "Court of Indian Affairs"

Vine Deloria, Jr.

Most, if not all, of the legal concepts and doctrines that describe the rights and status of Indians and their tribes derive from the events and developments of American history. Forced migrations, the discovery of gold on tribal lands, the coalition of several tribes to share hunting grounds, the coming of the missionaries, and the drives for statehood in the West have all contributed to the formation of Indian legal rights. No doctrine of Indian law derives from the logical unfolding of a major legal concept. If we can identify any single concept that seems to describe the boundaries of the Indian legal situation, it might be the treaty; but even with respect to treaties, there is still sufficient latitude for state or federal courts to provide their own interpretations of historical facts and to articulate those conclusions which seem common sense or advantageous to them.

Tribes and their members seem to become embroiled in litigation which often has as its sole purpose the destruction of remaining treaty rights. In some cases, notably in the Pacific Northwest, tribes have taken the initiative in asserting the interpretation which must be given to treaty provisions. But it remains a fact of contemporary life that every year a variety of courts hear and decide cases involving not simply the rights of present tribal members, but the rights and property interests of future generations.

In order to reach a decision a court should properly consider all the evidence concerning an issue that it can adequately and conscientiously gather. When we apply this rule to Indian treaty cases we are talking about the massive documentation of the times and conditions under which treaties were signed and statutes passed. And treaties rarely receive adequate attention. Often state courts will rule in favor of state agencies without considering the treaty. Appeal to federal courts is often taken by Indians' lawyers on grounds other than the treaty, to preclude any discussion of it and its complicating history. In short, the very document that binds Indians to the United States is generally left out of efforts to define the relationship which it did much to create.

From *A Better Day for Indians.* New York, N.Y.: Field Foundation. © 1977 by Vine Deloria, Jr.

In 1946, Congress set up the Indian Claims Commission and this legislation allowed the tribes to file claims against the government that had accumulated during the previous century. Part of the authorizing legislation required that the Commission investigate the claims to determine if they were valid; the commission, for the most part, has not exercised this investigative function, avoiding the intent of Congress in establishing it. But two things can, nevertheless, be learned from its experience.

The first lesson is that one single commission was used to gather all the claims against the United States, thus eliminating the need for tribes to file in every court imaginable. The commissioners, because they had to deal with one subject matter—Indian law—have become more knowledgeable than most judges in the federal system about Indian history. Many of its decisions were just.

The second lesson is that the cases involved more than a simple reading of case law. They included reports from scholars who could present as fully as possible the circumstances surrounding each claim. The peculiarities of Indian history became an important factor in the determination of legal rights and responsibilities.

The present Indian Claims Commission should be changed into a permanent court for the settlement of all suits arising from or relating to the interpretation of treaties and statutes affecting Indian tribes. Tribes would have to file suit against government and government officials—local, state, and federal—in this court and this court only. The converse would also be true. The court should have commissioners whose job would be to resolve disputes between Indians and other political entities, using both arbitration techniques and the ordinary legal procedures and rules of evidence. The court should have continuing powers of supervision for monitoring its decisions. Particularly in the field of water rights and hunting and fishing rights, such continuing supervision would be necessary.

The federal court system already has several specialized courts and commissions. Establishment of this one would eliminate frivolous or malign law suits by states and local governments, in their own courts, and therefore they might have objections to its creation; but the power of Congress to regulate commerce with the Indian tribes is paramount. The power of this court to examine the legal problems of Indians in intelligible contexts that consider all factors ought not to be opposed by the state and local governments, if they were brought to see that such a court would also eliminate longstanding problems of jurisdiction which have plagued them for many decades. Indians, once they understood the role of such a court in protecting their rights, would probably support its creation. It could be initiated without . . . other reforms . . . though it naturally complements a larger transformation of Indian affairs.

Imagining the Reservation

Sherman Alexie

> We have to believe in the power of imagination because it's all we have, and ours is stronger than theirs
>
> —Lawrence Thornton

Imagine Crazy Horse invented the atom bomb in 1876 and detonated it over Washington, D.C. Would the urban Indians still be sprawled around the one-room apartment in the cable television reservation? Imagine a loaf of bread could feed the entire tribe. Didn't you know Jesus Christ was a Spokane Indian? Imagine Columbus landed in 1492 and some tribe or another drowned him in the ocean. Would Lester FallsApart still be shoplifting in the 7-11?

*   *   *

I am in the 7-11 of my dreams, surrounded by five hundred years of convenient lies. There are men here who take inventory, scan the aisles for minute changes, insist on small bills. Once, I worked the graveyard shift in a Seattle 7-11, until the night a man locked me in the cooler and stole all the money out of the cash register. But more than that, he took the dollar bill from my wallet, pulled the basketball shoes off my feet, and left me waiting for rescue between the expired milk and broken eggs. It was then I remembered the story of the hobo who hopped a train heading west, found himself locked in a refrigerator car, and froze to death. He was discovered when the train arrived at its final destination, his body ice cold, but the refrigerator car was never turned on, the temperature inside never dropped below fifty degrees. It happens that way: the body forgets the rhythm of survival.

> Survival = Anger $\times$ Imagination. Imagination is the only weapon on the reservation.

The reservation doesn't sing anymore but the songs still hang in the air. Every molecule waits for a drumbeat; every element dreams lyrics. Today I am walking between water, two parts hydrogen, one part oxygen, and the energy expelled is named *Forgiveness.*

The Indian child hears my voice on the telephone and he knows what color shirt I'm wearing. A few days or years ago, my brother and I took him to the bar and he read all of our futures by touching hands. He told me the twenty-dollar bill hidden in my shoe would change my life. *Imagine,* he said. But we all laughed, old Moses even spit his false teeth into the air, but the Indian child touched another hand, another, and another, until he touched every Skin. *Who do you think you are?* Seymour asked the Indian child. *You ain't some medicine man come back to change our lives.* But the Indian child told Seymour his missing daughter was in community college in San Francisco and his missing wedding ring was in a can of commodity beef high up in his kitchen. The Indian child told Lester his heart was buried at the base of a pine tree behind the Trading Post. The Indian child told me to break every mirror in my house and tape the pieces to my body. I followed his vision and the Indian child laughed and laughed when he saw me, reflecting every last word of the story.

What do you believe in? Does every Indian depend on Hollywood for a twentieth-century vision? Listen: when I was young, living on the reservation, eating potatoes every day of my life, I imagined the potatoes grew larger, filled my stomach, reversed the emptiness. My sisters saved up a few quarters and bought food coloring. For weeks we ate red potatoes, green potatoes, blue potatoes. In the dark, "The Tonight Show" on the television, my father and I telling stories about the food we wanted most. We imagined oranges, Pepsi-Cola, chocolate, deer jerky. We imagined the salt on our skin could change the world.

* * *

July 4th and all is hell. Adrian, I am waiting for someone to tell the truth. Today I am celebrating the Indian boy who blew his fingers off when an M80 exploded in his hand. But thank God for miracles, he has a thumb left to oppose his future. I am celebrating Tony Swaggard, sleeping in the basement with two thousand dollars' worth of fireworks when some spark of flame or history touched it all off. Driving home, I heard the explosion and thought it was a new story born. But, Adrian, it's the same old story, whispered past the same false teeth. How can we imagine a new language when the language of the enemy keeps our dismembered tongues tied to his belt? How can we imagine a new alphabet when the old jumps off billboards down into our stomachs? Adrian, what did you say? *I want to rasp into sober cryptology and say something dynamic but tonight is my laundry night.* How do we imagine a new life when a pocketful of quarters weighs our possibilities down?

There are so many possibilities in the reservation 7-11, so many methods of survival. Imagine every Skin on the reservation is the new lead guitarist for the Rolling Stones, on the cover of a rock-and-roll magazine. Imagine forgiveness is sold 2 for 1. Imagine every Indian is a video game with braids. Do you believe laughter can save us? All I know is that I count coyotes to help me sleep. Didn't you know? Imagination is the politics of dreams; imagination turns every word into a bottle rocket. Adrian, imagine every day is Independence Day and save us from traveling the river changed; save us from hitchhiking the long road home. Imagine an escape. Imagine that your own shadow on the wall is a perfect door. Imagine a song stronger than penicillin. Imagine a spring with water that mends broken bones. Imagine a drum which wraps itself around your heart. Imagine a story that puts wood in the fireplace.

CHAPTER 3

CONSTITUTIVE INCOMMENSURABLES: LAND, CULTURE, HISTORY

One of the first lawsuits brought in the Western hemisphere appears in pictographic form; that complaint is reproduced here. The complaint alleges that Cortés took lands to make a road to Mexico City. A pictograph plainly shows the road bisecting what may be a sugarcane field and an area where entheogens (sacred mushrooms) are gathered. The pictographic complaint was reportedly filed by the Indians of Tetla, in Morelos, in 1532, in an early colonial court.[1]

From 1532 to the present, whether in Mexico or what is now the United States, Native Americans have sued, with mixed results, to retain and regain land. Some groups "win" their lawsuits. The Lakota Nation, for example, won a $17.5 million judgment with interest, a figure that raised the judgment to approximately $106 million.[2] Since the Lakota would rather have the Black Hills than the money, interest continues to accrue on this unclaimed account. Other groups have successfully fought for return of ancestral land. Taos Pueblo, for example, used the political process to secure return of the sacred Blue Lake Lands in 1970.[3] The Indian Reorganization Act of 1934[4] returned to tribal owners land designated as "surplus land" under the earlier General Allotment Act of 1887.[5]

Despite these few successes, many, if not all, tribal groups have permanently lost land. Many lost it to the growing presence of settlers. Other tribes reserved land by treaty, only to have that land quickly opened up for nonnative settlement. The Yakima of what is now Washington state are an example. They signed a treaty in 1855. However, the land the treaty reserved for the tribe was opened up for nonnative settlement one month *after* the treaty was concluded, but *before* that same treaty was ratified by Congress.[6] Other primarily eastern groups, such as the Mashpee, watched their land disappear quickly at first, and then slowly, conveyance by conveyance.[7]

The Non-Intercourse Acts should have voided these *Mashpee*-type conveyances.[8] But lawyers for the settler groups argued that the "white settlement exception"—which appears in Section 19 of the 1802 version of the Non-Intercourse Act and has been referred to as the "remnant tribe" exception[9]—served to shield settlers from the reach of federal penalties for encroachment in cases where tribal areas were surrounded by settlers and under state, not federal, jurisdiction. If these lawyers were correct, however, then Congress's action in adding the white settlement exception to the Non-Intercourse Act was deeply counterproductive and contradictory to its carrying out of the United States' general trust responsibility to Native American peoples.[10] In other words, excusing settlers from encroaching on indigenous land just because the land was already surrounded by white settlement merely created an incentive for settler communities to further encroach on tribal communities. This incentive powerfully contradicted whatever federal penalties were otherwise threatened by the general Non-Intercourse Act scheme.

Section 19 of the 1802 Non-Intercourse Act figures prominently in the eastern land-claim cases. Lawyers representing the settlers contended that although the 1834 version of the Non-Intercourse Act dropped the white settlement exception, it did not *repeal* it. They reasoned that the white settlement exception continued to be implied in terms of the 1834 Non-Intercourse Act, either as a matter of law, or as a matter of "the actual state of things."[11]

The point is that both Eastern and Western tribal groups lost land to white settlement whether through treaty nullification, operation of the white settlement exception to the Non-Intercourse Act, removal, or outright theft. Land loss was a common element of the Native American experience, and understanding the importance of land to tribal claimants is critical to explaining how disputes arose and still continue to arise under federal law. Also critical is realizing the difficulties that Native American peoples face in relation to land-regulating agencies, especially those that are empowered or required to comply with laws such as the National Environmental Protection Act (NEPA)[12] or the Endangered Species Act (ESA),[13] to name just two of the Acts that are discussed in this chapter.

The duration and meaning of Native American land tenure is extremely difficult to convey cross-culturally. Arvol Looking Horse, whose interview opens this chapter, is a Lakota spiritual leader who tells of how his family has been the keeper of the Sacred Pipe for nineteen generations. Charlotte Black Elk describes her direct connection to Crazy Horse, a nineteenth-century Lakota leader who resisted the U.S. government in every respect. Most Americans with an immigrant experience have no concept of a nineteen-generation-long sense of history in relation to land, and certainly not in relation to U.S. land. And most lawyers have trouble communicating the significance, much less the experience, of such a long tenure to judicial or bureaucratic decision-making bodies. Thus, Looking Horse and Black Elk point to an emerging, perhaps preferable way to describe Native Americanness—a way that does not turn solely on race or on blood quantum.

They describe Native Americanness as a philosophical commitment that has cultural and political dimensions. Black Elk talks of her own sense of tribal identity and its relation to land in a way that perhaps the broader U.S. community can begin to understand. She speaks of herself as *philosophically,* as well as culturally, Lakota. From this point she articulates her tribal identity in a multidimensional fullness that takes into account culture, genealogy, politics, spirituality, philosophy, and the like.

Black Elk's interview is followed by an excerpt from William Kittredge's 1996 book *Who Owns the West?* Born into a homesteading family in southeastern Oregon, Kittredge farmed until he was thirty-five years old; today he is a professor at the University of Montana. Part of Kittredge's life as a white farmer involved changing the shape of the land, the course of the rivers, the content of the flora and fauna. Part of it involved digging up the old, as he puts it, to make way for the new. Kittredge provides a counterbalance to Looking Horse and Black Elk because while all three note the importance of philosophy to their identity, whether as Lakota or as a white agribusiness farmer tilling land once designated "Indian land," their philosophies take them to different places.

Kittredge openly discusses the troubling results that were wrought by his beliefs and actions. Kittredge was a farmer, a person within the dominant society who worked closely with the land. Yet, as he himself admits, he lacked a deep or enduring connection with the land. Kittredge raises the question (and the possibility) of whether those in dominant society *can* understand land any differently than they do now, absent some radical cultural shift. Thus, like Looking Horse and Black Elk, Kittredge implies that understanding one's relation to the land may indeed be primarily a cultural process, one driven by a multitude of similarly cultural choices, understandings, fears, and aspirations.

Kittredge's excerpt is followed by analyses of how two Native American groups—the Fort McDowell Yavapai and a group of Apache at San Carlos—negotiated two separate land disputes. Wendy Espeland, a sociologist, writes about the Yavapai; Robert A. Williams Jr., a legal scholar, writes about the Apache.

Both the Yavapai and the Apache disputes involved land. In the Yavapai case, the tribe fought against the flooding of their southern Arizona reservation by Orme Dam. In the Apache case, the fight was over Mt. Graham, a southern Arizona mountain that was sited for construction of a high-powered research telescope. In both cases the tribal groups faced different (and powerful) bureaucratic/corporate adversaries: The Yavapai were at odds with the U.S. Bureau of Reclamation; the Apache were at odds with their tribal government and with the University of Arizona. Both cases were framed in terms of how the proposed development intersected with, or was governed by, different federal environmental laws. In the Yavapai case, the National Environmental Protection Act was the implicated statute; in the Apache case, it was the National Environmental Protection Act and the Endangered Species Act. In both cases, the tribal groups were able to communicate their sense of the land as a constitutive incommensurable, which is to say as something so central to the group's cultural sense of self as to be beyond the reach of market forces or easy exchange.

The fact that the Yavapai and Apache senses of the story come through at all in either the Yavapai or the Mt. Graham disputes is a welcome turn in the field. The presence of their voices is possible, in part, because of the work of scholars such as Vine Deloria, Jr. Deloria reiterates the importance of research traditions that take seriously what constituents like Looking Horse, Black Elk, the Yavapai, and the Apache have to say. As Deloria explains, policy and history are not necessarily the same, though they are too often treated as such, particularly in law. Policy and history tell different stories. Policy histories operate on the premise that if a law is passed, people naturally follow it. Histories based on broader sources of data, like the Unrau work cited in Chapter 2, or the Washburn work excerpted in Chapter 2, complicate descriptions. They note the importance of law, but do not operate on the premise that people follow laws simply because those laws have been passed. Works based on broader sources of data challenge our understanding because they posit social reality as a multidimensional phenomenon—one not easily describable or understandable; one in which every rule is often met by a counter-rule or an exception; one in which established fact can and should be brought into question; one in which different perceptions can and do coexist, though one may be systemically subordinated to another. Deloria's analysis is important to the study of federal Indian law because it urges scholars and lawyers to look beneath the surface of what is now regarded as "established fact" for primary evidence that better articulates or presents Native American interests, hopes, and views, especially vis-à-vis their relation to ancestral lands.

RECOMMENDED READINGS

On the issue of incommensurability, while many authors try to articulate why land is incommensurable with money for many Native Americans as a general matter, only one comes close to doing so. That person is Vine Deloria Jr., whose book *God is Red: A Native View of Religion* (1992, 2d ed.) deals with the connection among people, land, and spiritual practice.

   Oral Traditions and the Verbal Arts: A Guide to Research Practices (1992), by Ruth Finnegan, gives one a sense of how extensive a field "oral history" is in itself. As Nancy O. Lurie suggested in the previous chapter, too many lawyers practicing in federal Indian law or related areas too often discount first-person interviews and the like for a variety of reasons, primarily having to do with "relevance" or "reliability." Students should try not to make the same mistake. Karl N. Llewellyn and E. Adamson Hoebel's *The Cheyenne Way: Conflict and Case Law in Primitive Jurisprudence* (1941), for example, is a classic study founded on reliable oral accounts and oral histories. In their book, Llewellyn and Hoebel illuminate "trouble cases," or disputes, among the Cheyenne, and they investigate how these cases were (or were not) resolved according to Cheyenne law.

   Also on the issue of history, historiography, and historicism, see other essays in *The American Indian and the Problem of History* (1987), edited by Calvin Martin, and *The New Historicism* (1989), edited by H. Aram Veeser. James Scott's *Domination and the Arts of Resistance: Hidden Transcripts* (1990) is an important analysis of how confrontations between elites and nonelites get recorded and historicized in relation to each other.

   Two accessible introductions to the very extensive field of colonial Mexico are Woodrow Borah's classic *Justice by Insurance: The General Indian Court of Mexico and the Legal Aides of the Half-Real* (1983), and Susan Kellogg's *Law and the Transformation of Aztec Culture, 1500–1700* (1995).

   Books such as Robert F. Heizer's The *Destruction of California Indians* (1993), or Wayne Moquin and Charles Van Doren's *Great Documents in American Indian History* (1995), are important collections that document the treatment of Native Americans in California, in Heizer's case, and the U.S. generally, in Moquin and

Van Doren's case. *The History of the Indians of Shasta County* (1995), edited by Dottie Smith, is a county-wide collection of documents, which I found hidden on a back shelf in an independent bookstore in Redding, California. I later learned that Smith, a local Shasta County historian, had made few, if any, friends among other local historians with the publication of her book. Smith frames her impressive collection in a way that bears witness to the innumerable massacres of Native Americans, particularly the Achomawi, the Atsugewi, the Okwanucho, the Wintu, and the Yana. In the end, she takes her local colleagues to task, noting that not one has adequately written about the genocide that fueled the development of Shasta County. "History, as it is taught now," she writes, "avoids the many injustices inflicted on Indians and does not address the reality, but instead deals with the 'safe' issues of culture, tribal boundaries, food, and ceremonies, to name a few." (p. vii) She also warns that her compilation "will not make you laugh. It will surely sadden your heart and cause you to shed tears. . . . you'll ask yourself if genocide really could have happened here. Happen it did." (p. vii).

Of particular interest in the Moquin and Van Doren collection is Luther Standing Bear's testimony to Congress in 1933, on what I am calling here the issue of incommensurability.

There Standing Bear explains:

> The white man does not understand the Indian for the reason that he does not understand America. He is too far removed from its formative processes. The roots of the tree of his life have not yet grasped the rock and soil. The white man is still troubled with primitive fears; he still has in his consciousness the perils of this frontier continent . . .
>
> But in the Indian the spirit of the land is still vested; it will be until other men are able to divine and meet its rhythm. Men must be born and reborn to belong. Their bodies must be formed of the dust of their forefathers' bones.[14]

NOTES

1. This lawsuit is identified and discussed at length in Gordon Wasson, *The Wonderous Mushroom: Mycolatry in Mesoamerica*, New York, N.Y.: McGraw-Hill, 1980, p. 110. It is cited there as having been found and discussed in Alfonso Caso, "El Paraíso Terrenal en Teotihuacán," *Cuadernos Americanos*, Nov.–Dec., 1942, México DF, pp. 127–136; and in Alfonso Caso, "Representaciones de Hongos en los Códices," Estudios de Cultura Nahuatl, vol. 4, pp. 27 ff, UNAM, México DF, 1963. See figure on p. 102.

2. *United States v. Sioux Nation of Indians*, 448 U.S. 371 (1980); *Oglala Sioux Tribe v. United States*, 650 F.2d 140 (8th. Cir. 1981).

3. *An Act to amend section 4 of the Act of May 31, 1933, (Return of Blue Lake Lands to Taos Pueblo)*, U.S. Statutes at Large vol. 84(1970):1437–1439.

4. *Wheeler-Howard Act (Indian Reorganization Act) of 1934*, U.S. Statutes at Large vol. 48 (1934):984–988.

5. *General Allotment Act (Dawes Act) of 1887*, U.S. Statutes at Large vol. 24 (1887):388–391.

6. For a full description of the Yakima treaty, see Sharon O'Brien, *American Indian Tribal Governments*, Norman, Okla.: University of Oklahoma Press, 1989, pp. 181–196.

7. See Chapter 1 supra.

8. *An Act to Regulate Trade and Intercourse with Indian Tribes*, U.S. Statutes at Large vol. 1 (1790):137; *An Act to Regulate Trade and Intercourse with Indian Tribes*, U.S. Statutes at Large vol. 1 (1793):329; *An Act to Regulate Trade and Intercourse with Indian Tribes and to Preserve Peace on the Frontiers*, U.S. Statutes at Large vol. 2 (1802):139–146; *An Act to Regulate Trade and Intercourse with Indian Tribes and to Preserve Peace on the Frontiers*, U.S. Statutes at Large vol. 4 (1834):729.

9. *An Act to Regulate Trade and Intercourse with Indian Tribes, U.S. Statutes at Large* vol. 2 (1802):139–146. Sec. 19 reads:

"[n]othing in this act shall be construed to prevent any trade or intercourse with Indians living on lands surrounded by settlements of the citizens of the United States, and being within the ordinary jurisdiction of any of the individual states."

10. See *Cherokee Nation v. Georgia,* 30 U.S. (5 Pet.) 1 (1831); *Worcester v. Georgia* 31 U.S. (6 Pet.) 515 (1832).

11. Johnson v. McIntosh, 21 U.S. (8 Wheat.) 543 (1823).

12. *National Environmental Policy Act of 1969, U.S. Statutes at Large* vol. 84 (1969):852–856.

13. *Endangered Species Act of 1973, U.S. Statutes at Large* 87 (1973):884–903.

14. *Great Documents in American Indian History,* Wayne Moquin and Charles Van Doren, eds., New York, N.Y.: Praeger Publishers; Da Capo Press Edition, 1973, p. 307.

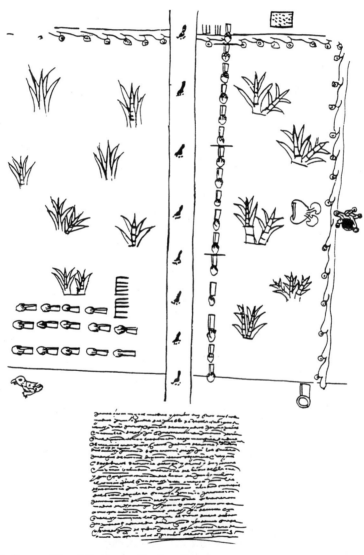

Codice Indigena No. 27. From R. Gordon Wasson, *The Wondrous Mushroom: Mycolatry in Mesoamerica,* New York: McGraw-Hill Book Company, 1980.

A Song from Sacred Mountain:
Lakota-Dakota and Cheyenne Interviews

Arvol Looking Horse

"It was brought down by a Buffalo woman and from there it was passed from generation to generation [for nineteen generations]—through a blood line. And this Pipe was given to me, it was given through a vision. All these happened through a Vision. It was my grandmother. Before she died, she had a Vision that I was supposed to take care of it until I die or until I have a Vision.

"When I got this Pipe, I was eleven years old, it was for the Sioux people and they can pray with this Pipe. And this sacred Pipe was the main part. And from there, they call it the roots, different families have Pipes. So this is the sacred Pipe and that is what I am taking care of now.

"There's a lot of things that go along with it. People come almost every day to our place and they pray with the Pipe, what we do is open our doors for them and let them all in. We just take care of it. There are certain things we have to do, but right now I can't mention those things because they are sacred.

"Long time ago, people go up there, a lot of people go up there they call it *hanbleceya*, they stand on the Hill and they have a Vision. So a lot of people go up there and it's probably, anyway, it's a powerful Hill. You can just feel it when you go there. It all happens, when you're in a situation and you go up there to pray, and you start seeing a lot of things. You can tell by—they call it *Kogara* and your attitude's different. All you think about is praying. Bear Butte is a sacred place and that's the place where everybody goes and there's a lot of stories that go behind it. What I mean by stories, everybody has their own. Everybody that goes up there the vision that they have, it belongs to them. When you have a vision, it belongs to them and the spirits work for *Tunkasila*, it means Great Spirit, Grandfather and Mother Earth. They go up on the Hill and they fast.

From *A Song From Sacred Mountain*, edited by the Oglala-Lakota Legal Rights Fund. Lakota Nation: Oglala Lakota Legal Rights Fund (1983). Archived at the Oglala-Lakota College as "Interviews Conducted by the Oglala Lakota Legal Rights Fund (SC34)."

"The Sioux believe that they originate from the Black Hills, and Bear Butte they view that as a most important spot because that's where they get their instructions, when they fast and have a Vision. So Bear Butte's always been very important.

"I try not to get involved in political [actions] but there's times when you have to do something. And I think this—about Bear Butte. We try to get everything off Bear Butte. Stop them from building housing and stuff up there. I think it's a pretty sacred place up there, and that's why I like to help out. Keep that place the way it is.

"It's important right now, cause everything is closing up. Even the Communities are getting bigger and the towns are getting closer together and we need some place—a place where we can feel free to be ourselves."

A Song from Sacred Mountain:
Lakota-Dakota and Cheyenne Interviews

Charlotte Black Elk

Our name for Bear Butte is *Paha Wakan*, sacred mountain. And when you look at everything sacred but having places where there's a centrality of power. Bear Butte was not only a religious place, it was also a meeting place. I'm *Oyuhpe*, I belong to the followers of Crazy Horse. And we have very strong ties to Bear Butte because that was one of our rallying places. In 1857, Crazy Horse was concerned about white encroachment on Indians and how it would affect our way of life. They met at Bear Butte to discuss that. And Crazy Horse telling the other Lakotas, I will not sell my mother. And Bear Butte being a part of the whole Black Hills area, our name for the Black Hills is the heart of the universe. Our full name for Bear Butte is *Sinte Ocunku Paha Wakan*, the sacred mountain at the edge of the trail. And so it sits at the edge of the Black Hills. When you look at the religious view that lands have—that all lands are sacred, but some areas are more sacred— you look at Bear Butte as a place for reflection. A place where no war party would attack someone who was there to pray. It was respected by all the Tribes. Other people came down—people who were our enemies came down to pray. We did not attack them. I think looking at that, the fact that it's remained a central part of the Lakota community, of people going back there continually, it shows that there has been a continuum in our religion—the ideas of everything being a part of the whole and at a place like Bear Butte, you would be at the center of the earth at the center of the Hoop.

The gathering at Bear Butte of the central government was a time of socializing, seeing relatives, courtships, marriages. It was an area that's not only central in terms of religion but also in terms of community. It was like going home. All of the family coming home. At this time, our governments sat down. The Lakota is a confederacy of seven nations. The seven nations would sit down and adopt new procedures, new words, new laws at that time. So it was a periodic coming home of a nomadic people. And at other times they would meet in areas—sometimes they would have a drought—sometimes they would meet closer to the river and other times they would meet at the Big Horn mountains, but when they came to Bear Butte, that was coming home. Our Creation legends are tied within that whole area—the Black Hills and Bear Butte. We were a nation that lived above the earth at one time. But because of some big disaster, we had to move underground in the caves and lived there for many years. At some point we came back on the surface and we started a long journey. Going to the south and to the east and coming back northward and coming back southward. Right at that time, in returning home we had white contact. And so again the name for Bear Butte—the sacred mountain at the end of the trail. Searching out the nation and coming back home, so Bear Butte has always been home for a nomadic people.

Throughout the reservation, if you know where to look, you'll find Sweat Lodges. You'll find a huge pit in the ground and you dig under the top dirt you find rocks where people had to hide their Sweat Lodges. The secret Sun Dances. The fact that *Yuwipi* and *Lowanpi* are done at night in a house where the windows are all covered up, that was a part of going underground. Of hiding the ceremonies. All those ceremonies were held out in the open until the repression.

One of my grandfathers being Black Elk, my other grandfather being Hollow Horn and because I'm *Oyuhpe* . . . if I am to be Lakota, it involves a number of things. One of these is the preservation of religious sites. I think I've always felt that my involvement in Bear Butte is that this is a vehicle that is available to us, it's not the best vehicle because we are [only] dealing with access. We're not dealing with that land being totally returned [to us] for religious purposes; I guess we're dealing with getting the best of a bad deal. Trying to balance religion with state-sponsored tourism at Bear Butte.

On one hand I would like not to be with that tremendous burden of saying, "I am Lakota" and doing what my grandfather did, saying, "I am Lakota, I will not live like a dog." What he did was fight for ceremonies to be out in the open for a level of respect to be had. For traditional customs and traditional religion, for sacred rights. I haven't reached the point for totally formulating what my role will be so that I will not live like a dog so that I will be Lakota. I will not be Sioux.

In terms of Bear Butte, I'm not Lakota because of Bear Butte but Bear Butte contributes to my being Lakota. Bear Butte contributes to my being Lakota because of the religious significance of that site, "the sacred mountain at the end of the trail." It has some philosophical principles that are central to my religion. And historically because it is a meeting place it has some historical relevance to my being Lakota. When we're looking at Bear Butte, we're talking about spiritual harmony. And when you're talking about Black Hills and other lands, then you're talking about harmony that goes beyond spirituality. You're talking about physical harmony.

But you can't divorce the two. Because they're all intertwined. It would be like taking a knitting and trying to drop out one loop. This is the loop and it would cause all of the garment to unravel. In knitting, because every knit is intertwined, and physical harmony is tied very much with the spiritual harmony. You may be able to isolate something that is specifically religious from community, but that doesn't diminish the physical harmony aspect. I think what I see happening now is people going through a period of reflection. What makes us Lakota. It's obviously not just Sun Dancing or fasting at Bear Butte or having Sun Dances or having powwows. It's something more than that. It's a whole philosophy. It's a state of mind that says, "I'm only a small part of this. And unless I live well, nothing else can live well and if something else doesn't live well, then I can't live well." And there's always this balancing and fine-tuning that has to go on. And you see a lot of activity going on as the crush for resources continues—whether it's sports resources like increasing revenue at Bear Butte or taking resources out of the land. "What are you putting back? Why are you having it? Do you need it?"

Someday, people will come to the realization that the earth lives. And if you abuse it to the point that you kill it, then nothing else will live. We're part of it. A small part. But a part of it. Philosophically Lakota.

I think accepting that responsibility has some secondary responsibility that causes that person to evolve into what we could call a respectable person. A person who walks softly. *Washwaca.* It's a person who moves softly.

But once you have the commitment of the people, then you can talk about building a structure. And so I don't think the cohesive force—the little stones that you gather and from which you build a house—is possible without the nation.

One of the things that's happening now, that my great grandfather saw in 1946, he said:

> My people now stand in suffering.
> But the people are growing again.
> They will start to live again.
> That I believe.
> The reason this will happen is that there
> Is a growing remembering of the Sacred Pipe.
> I am Lakota.
>   All of them.
>   The hardest suffering of men.
>   Stand strong in the face
> Of *Wakan Tanka.*"

Who Owns the West?

William Kittredge

But even as huge and open to anything as southeastern Oregon may have seemed in those old days, it was also inhabited by spooks. In autumn of the same year the Winnemucca-to-the-Sea highway came across our meadowlands, I had our heavy equipment, our Carry-All scrapers and D-7 bulldozers, at work on a great diversion canal we were cutting through three hundred yards of sage-covered sand hills at the south end of Warner, rerouting Twenty-Mile Creek.

Soon we were turning up bones—human bones, lots of them. I recall a clear October afternoon and all those white bones scattered in the gravel, and my catskinners standing there beside their great idling machines, perplexed and unwilling to continue. Ah, hell, never mind, I said. Crank 'em up.

There was nothing to do but keep rolling. Maybe bones from an ancient Indian burial ground were sacred, but so was our work, more so as I saw it. My catskinners threatened to quit. I told them I'd give them a ride to town, where I'd find plenty of men who would welcome the work. My catskinners didn't quit. I ducked my head so I couldn't see, and drove away.

If you are going to bake a cake, you must break some eggs. That was a theory we knew about. We thought we were doing God's work. We were cultivating, creating order and what we liked to think of as a version of Heaven on Earth.

What a pleasure that work was, like art, always there, always in need of improving, doing. It's reassuring, so long as the work is not boring, to wake up and find your work is still going on, your tools still in the tunnel. You can lose a life in the work. People do.

But we left, we quit, in a run of family trouble. I have been gone from farming and Warner for twenty-five years. People ask if I don't feel a great sense of loss, cut off from the valley and methods of my childhood. The answer is no.

Nothing much looks to have changed when I go back. The rimrock above the west side of the valley lies as black against the sunset light as it did when I was a child. The topography of my dreams, I like to think, is still intact.

But that's nonsense. We did great damage to the valley as we pursued our sweet impulse to create an agribusiness paradise. The rich peat ground began to go saline, the top layer just blew away. We drilled chemical fertilizers along with our barley seed, and sprayed with 2-4-D Ethyl and Parathion (which killed even the songbirds). Where did the waterbirds go?

But the waterbirds can be thought of as part of the *charismatic megafauna*. Everybody worries about the waterbirds. Forms of life we didn't even know about were equally threatened.

Catostomus warnerensis, the Warner sucker, is threatened. So are three other fish species in the region (three more are endangered, as are two plant species) and riparian tree communities of black cottonwood, red-osier dogwood, and willow.

As a child I loved to duck down and wander animal trails through dense brush by the creeksides, where ring-necked Manchurian pheasants and egg-eating raccoons and stalking lynx cats traveled. Maybe I was often among them, curled in the dry grass and sleeping in the sun, and didn't know it.

The way we built canals in our efforts to contain the wildness of the valley and regulate the ways of water to our own uses must have been close to absolutely destructive to the Warner sucker, a creature we would not have valued at all, slippery and useless, thus valueless. It's likely I sent my gang of four D-7 Caterpillar bulldozers to clean out the brush along stretches of creekside thick with red osier dogwood and black cottonwood.

Let in some light, let the grass grow, feed for the livestock, that was the theory. Maybe we didn't abandon those creatures in Warner, mostly we destroyed them before we left. We did enormous damage in the thirty years that we were there. Country like the Dordogne and Umbria and Tuscany, which has been farmed thousands of years, looks to be less damaged. But maybe that's because the serious kill-off there took place so long ago.

Legally Mediated Identity: The National Environmental Policy Act and the Bureaucratic Construction of Interests

Wendy Espeland

> If a rigid separation of form and content leads to error in the analysis of a work of art, how much more in the interpretation of human feelings.
>
> —Max Horkheimer

> It's true that we have to consider a piece of land as a tool to produce something useful with, but it's also true that we must recognize the love for a particular piece of land.
>
> —Bertolt Brecht

> The land is our mother. You don't sell your mother.
>
> —Yavapai teenager

"TRAIL OF TEARS" 1981

In 1981, during an unusually hot Arizona September, members of the Yavapai community at Fort McDowell began a 32-mile desert march from their reservation to the state capitol in Phoenix. This dramatic political event was designed to protest the proposed dam that would force them from their land. Launched with prayers and singing, the marchers, carrying signs protesting the proposed dam, walked alongside a busy highway for three days in temperatures reaching 110 degrees. Nearly 100 Yavapai (about a quarter of the reservation community) made the trek, including some frail but determined Yavapai elders and toddlers in wagons pulled by parents. Louisa Hood, a woman in her 60s with crippling arthritis, marched despite her doctor's admonitions. "The doctor said I should stay home," she said quietly. "But I wanted to march with the crowd" (Tulumello 1981). Those who were too sick or weak to march rode alongside in cars and pickup trucks, offering support and water for the marchers. John Williams, a quiet, serious man in his 70s, told one reporter he was marching for his grandmother. Each night, as the marchers camped, they held a small pow-wow to inspire and entertain themselves, with singing, drumming, dancing, and storytelling. The march culminated in a large political rally at the capitol, where tribal leaders delivered to the governor a hand-written bark scroll designed, they said, to make it hard for bureaucrats to file away and forget; the scroll proclaimed in simple, eloquent language their deep attachment to their land, the harm its loss would cause them, and their determination to retain it.

The march was a successful political protest, well-timed and garnering broad, sympathetic media coverage. It generated powerful images, the kind that television loves and that linger in your mind: a small group of women, all in their 70s, walking together in long camp dresses and new tennis shoes, a sensible accommodation of old to new, an old man marching with his walker, surrounded by chattering teenagers hoping to distract him from his slowness and pain; parents fanning the hot, sleepy babies they carried in their arms. These were some of the scenes that made the evening news. But this march was more than a well-executed protest. Named by participants "The Second Trail of Tears," it was explicitly cast as a reenactment of an earlier, brutal, and involuntary Trail of Tears that is a centerpiece of Yavapai history.

TRAIL OF TEARS 1875

Over a century earlier, in February 1875, about 1,400 Indians, most of them Yavapai, began a long, brutal resettlement march from the reservation at Camp Verde, Arizona, to the Apache reservation at San Carlos, Arizona, some 200 miles away (Mariella 1983:96–99; Espeland 1992:266–69). This march was instigated by a group of well-connected and corrupt contractors who sold reservation supplies to the government. These contractors, known as the Tucson Ring, were disturbed that the Yavapai at Camp Verde were becoming too self-sufficient, thus cutting into their profits (Mariella 1983:88–90; Bourke 1891:217–24; Bronson 1980:42). Through heroic efforts that included digging a 5-mile irrigation ditch with sharpened sticks, buckets, and even spoons, the Yavapai had managed to develop agriculture to the point that they could almost feed themselves (Corbusier 1971:17). They had worked so hard to do so because, after having been forced on the reservation in the first place, they were promised they could remain at Camp Verde forever. Now, just five years later, Ulysses Grant ordered their removal to the San Carlos reservation, the mountainous Apache reservation where poor land made farming difficult and where the Yavapai would be a small minority unable to even speak the language of most other inhabitants.

The march lasted nearly two weeks. Despite the protests of the Yavapai and their ally, William Corbusier, the camp doctor, Commissioner Alfred Dudley conducted it with deliberate cruelty. Instead of waiting for warmer weather, he initiated it during the cold winter months, when snow covered the mountains and when rivers and streams were full. Instead of using horses or donkeys, as the soldiers did, Dudley insisted: "They are Indians: let the beggars walk" (ibid., p. 267). . . .

The Trail of Tears is a pivotal event in Yavapai oral history. (Yavapai is not a written language.) A story all Yavapai know, it is often told as a reminder of the senseless brutality of white man, of the unreliability of promises government officials make, and of the pain of losing your land.

In casting their protest march in 1981 as a reenactment of this original Trail of Tears in 1875, the Yavapai were clearly emphasizing the parallels between their earlier forced resettlement and their impending one. They were trying to convey—to decision makers, politicians, and their neighbors—the deep cultural and psychological importance of their land. They were also trying to express their difference, their distinctiveness, in a dramatic, public way. But the second Trail of Tears was more than an example of clever political strategy, an astute manipulation of powerful images and symbols. This march was part of a complex process of the symbolic reappropriation and reinterpretation of their past, a process that was, in this case, stimulated and shaped by law, by the NEPA.

THE NATIONAL ENVIRONMENTAL POLICY ACT

. . .

[Signed into law in 1970], NEPA is perhaps best known as the law that requires federal agencies to prepare Environmental Impact Statements (EIS) in advance of any action that might "significantly affect the quality of the environment." An EIS is subject to unusually specific procedural guidelines; broadly, the impact statement requires federal agencies to show that a "rational" decision procedure was used to describe and evaluate the economic, social, and environmental impacts of proposed policy for a range of alternatives, including one plan to "do nothing." These alternatives then compete with one another as a solution to some specified problem or some set of goals. . . .

After NEPA was enacted, the bureau was forced to prepare an environmental impact statement analyzing the social and environmental consequences associated with the proposed dam. Orme Dam was part of a controversial and expensive plan to bring Colorado River water to central Arizona. This project, known as the Central Arizona Project and first proposed in 1944, consisted of an elaborate series of dams, pumps, and aqueducts. Since the bureau had been promoting, studying, and repackaging the Orme Dam for more than 40 years, it is possible to track, in the documentation, the changes that resulted from NEPA (Espeland 1993). One of NEPA's most obvious effects is that the law is directly responsible for forcing the bureau to even consider the consequences of the dam for the Yavapai. Before

NEPA, during the first 30 years of developing and promoting Orme Dam, the bureau never formally acknowledged that the Yavapai were even relevant to the decision. Although numerous reports and studies had been prepared on the project (which, after repeated attempts, was finally authorized by Congress in 1968), the Yavapai literally do not show up in any of these documents and are not acknowledged as relevant to the decision. Nor are the Yavapai mentioned in the first EIS prepared on the Central Arizona Project in 1972. It was only after the bureau learned that the EIS represented a new and potent weapon for environmental groups and, when the courts forced the agencies to hire new kinds of employees to prepare them, that NEPA was taken as something other than a minor legal loophole to be plugged. . . .

This realization of NEPA's significance was a gradual and contested process within the bureau. For example, the first EIS that dealt exclusively with Orme Dam was written in 1976—the first time the bureau included any analysis of the dam's consequences for the Yavapai. This analysis, conducted by external consultants, concluded that since the Yavapai had been subjected to forced relocations in the past, and since they had somehow survived, Yavapai culture possessed strong "survival elements" and that the tribe was likely to survive the threat posed by Orme Dam. Needless to say, this was a controversial interpretation of Yavapai history and culture. One consequence of this EIS was that it helped to galvanize organized opposition to the dam among members of the Yavapai community and their supporters.

RATIONAL DECISIONMAKING AS A RESPONSE TO NEPA

Partly because of the controversy generated by the 1976 EIS (which the bureau later rescinded), a new study was launched in 1978 to evaluate a series of plans for providing Phoenix [Arizona] with more flood protection and an improved water supply. This study was the largest, most expensive, and most complicated one the bureau had ever conducted. Hoping to buy time and provide a forum where political consensus might emerge, the bureau intended the study to be a test case for its new procedures for complying with NEPA and the new Principles and Standards issued by the Water Resources Council. The study would culminate in the requisite EIS and planning documents and in what most participants hoped would be a decision about Orme Dam that would finally stick.

Those in charge of designing and managing the formal investigation were a group of newer, nontraditional personnel the bureau had been forced to hire after NEPA—planners, sociologists, biologists, decision experts. The distinguishing feature of these employees was that they were not engineers in an organization that had been dominated by engineers since its founding in 1902. This group was in a difficult spot; its members were charged with resolving the seemingly intractable conflict over Orme Dam and with the arduous task of implementing NEPA in an agency that was, to put it mildly, hostile to the law; all this while simultaneously carving out for themselves some base of authority and autonomy within the organization. . . . They responded by invoking science and rationality in interpreting NEPA. . . .

The framework used in the investigation was partly dictated by federal regulations and partly by the desire of some groups within the bureau to adopt a formal rational decision model. Part of this framework's appeal was that it could document to a wide range of relevant audiences—to opponents, other federal agencies, and especially to the courts—that (1) certain kinds of information, among them public preferences, were included; (2) that alternatives were carefully considered; (3) and that the decision procedures were "rigorous," "objective," and "fair." While the details of the decision framework are too complex to be easily summarized, two characteristics are especially pertinent to how the interests and values of the Yavapai were portrayed: how different impacts were made commensurate and the consequentialist/causal logic underlying the framework.

Rational choice models are premised on the assumption that in order to make careful comparisons among alternative plans for accomplishing some goal, it is necessary to make the components of choice commensurate, to create a common metric that is the basis for displaying differences in magnitude among the relevant decision factors. Commensuration in rational decisionmaking requires that the separate dimensions of value be integrated via trade-offs, in a deliberate balancing of competing claims of values. Price and utility are two metrics that are often used; in policy decisions, cost-benefit analyses are a common form of value integration. Embedded in this logic is the assumption that all value is relative: that the value of something can only be expressed in terms of its relation to something else. This form of valuing denies the possibility of "intrinsic" value, "pricelessness" of any absolute category of value. Commensuration presupposes that in deciding something, transforming the relevant information into this form does not alter its meaning in ways that are detrimental to deciding. Rather, the parsimony conferred from commensuration improves clarity and rigor.

Various methods for commensuration were used in components of the analysis. For example, in the economic impacts of the proposed plans, impacts were expressed as prices in a cost-benefit analyses; in the public value assessment, people's preferences were expressed as a number derived from a multi-attribute trade-off scheme. The social analysis culminated in a "Social Well Being Account" where the cumulative social impact of each plan was expressed numerically. This required that all the social impacts, ranging from the forced relocation of the Yavapai to the reduction of floods to the forced relocation of a small portion of a non-Indian population, be made commensurate through a rating and weighting scheme. . . .

SELECTION, DISTORTION, SILENCE: THE POLITICS OF FRAMEWORK

Although the Yavapai did not use these terms, their land was to them an incommensurate value, and money or other land, regardless of the amount, could not capture its value or compensate for its loss. To the Yavapai, it was absurd and immoral to try to attach a price to land and to their culture, to, in effect, "sell their mother." Their land was an incommensurate value, and nothing else would represent its value or compensate for its loss. The decision models developed by the Bureau of Reclamation, however, could not accommodate incommensurable values and, as a result, subverted the symbolic boundaries that the Yavapai drew around their land and their heritage, boundaries that defined these as intrinsically valuable.

Another pattern imposed by the decision framework was that impacts were "measured" on the basis of the consequences of various alternatives. Information is organized according to a causal logic that tracks changes in future states of affairs. The consequentialist logic underlying the decision model makes it very hard to talk about issues that are not easily reduced to causal language. For example, the consequentialism underlying the bureau's rational choice procedures cannot accommodate history in any meaningful way. It is hard to incorporate the significance of history in spelling out its consequences in causal terms for future impacts or a future state of affairs. History cannot be used as a decision "factor" because it does not reflect impacts in a future condition. The significance of historical events does not "change" for each alternative in future states, regardless of how one feels about the indeterminacy of historical texts or the inevitability of reinterpretation. Events of the past cannot be used to measure or project the changes in future states of affairs that the proposed alternatives would cause. It is theoretically possible to incorporate the historical significance of the Yavapai by simply attaching a higher price to land or to assume that the factors used to represent the present condition somehow reflect the cumulative impacts of history. This is, however, an abstract, obscure, and almost uninterpretable representation of history. In practice, it does not communicate what most Yavapai believe is important to know about them.

For the Yavapai community, it was not simply their land or their lifestyle that was at stake but their ability to survive as "a people." The Yavapai understand themselves as a unique cultural group with a distinctive history. For them, the "cost" of losing their land extends back to the sacrifices of their ancestors and the legacy they fought to preserve and pass on. For the past 150 years, Yavapai history is largely a history of a people resisting forced relocation, of trying to stay with their land. While virtually all Native American peoples have been forced from their land, what is remarkable about the Yavapai is how persistently they have had to defend against resettlement and the extraordinary costs they have borne. The Yavapai are highly conscious of this heritage. Their bitter experience with actual and attempted forced resettlement, beginning when the U.S. Army tried to starve them onto reservations in the 1860s, to the Orme struggle in the 1980s, are central features of the oral tradition of the Yavapai. . . .

Losing the land that their ancestors fought so hard to preserve would mean betraying the ancestors' struggles and wishes. This sense of failure would be painful and profound. This "cost" would also extend to future generations who could not be Yavapai as a result of their contemporary defeat.

The exclusion of history does not affect all the interest groups equally in this decision. The ahistoricity of the decision procedure biases the presentation in ways that harmed the Yavapai more than other parties. The Yavapai believed that the exclusion of their history from the framework fundamentally misrepresented the stakes of the decision for them, since past injustices and broken promises were not explicitly part of the decision calculus. Ignoring Yavapai history meant excluding relevant information about which most white people knew little, or held wildly distorted views—the Hollywood version of the "Apache" wars; it was also information that was uncomfortable for white people to confront. Yavapai residents felt that the exclusion of their history made their relocation seem more comparable to relocation of white residents. . . .

The exclusion of Yavapai history from the decision also left a silence that others felt free to fill with their own distorted versions of the past. Some Orme supporters disputed the distinctiveness of the Yavapai and their special claim to the land at Fort McDowell [thus] trying to minimize the effects of the forced relocation. . . .

The framework's neglect of history also meant that the cumulative consequences of past government policies on the reservation were ignored. For nearly 80 years, the government refused to aid or even allow the Yavapai to develop the reservation in anticipation of their imminent resettlement. This meant that while white settlers and other reservations were receiving funds to develop water or agriculture, the Yavapai were prevented from developing their land and its resources. This relative lack of development was then used by Orme supporters to argue that reservation land was being wasted by Indians who were unwilling or unable to develop it. The overall effect of excluding history in the decision framework was to make it easier to justify the bureau's proposed project by minimizing the significance and distinctiveness of the Yavapai cultural heritage, the importance of understanding land as incommensurable, and the extent to which, in the past, white people's gains have been at the expense of indigenous people.

Another pattern stemming from the consequentialist logic informing the decision models was the exclusion of ethical concerns. It is difficult to capture moral dilemmas in consequentialist thinking since it is hard to ascertain how morality implicates future states in any direct, causal sequence. Yavapai leaders argued that the decision they confronted was ultimately a moral decision. One man described the taking of Indian land by force as "the white man's original sin." But "how many times can one commit original sin?" he asked. "You still come to take our land by force—over and over and over. And now, you come again" (Casserly 1981:10). The legacy of broken promises that had long characterized their relationships with the federal and local governments was a moral issue that many Yavapai believed could not be extricated from this particular decision. . . .

The Yavapai argued that it was wrong for the government to violate another promise to the Indians, but this type of concern is difficult to address in the rational choice framework, since this model emphasizes evaluating choice based on the consequences of specific, ojected action. It is difficult to discuss the implications of breaking yet another promise to the Indians in causal terms, in how this "wrongness" will alter future states. The resulting pattern is that the moral implications of the policy were not formally addressed in the decision documents. Some Yavapai leaders argued that the exclusion of these ethical issues distorted the stakes of the decision for them.

Fairness in the distribution of costs and benefits is another moral issue that was neglected within the rational procedures employed. There are usually clear winners and losers in public choice, since those who bear the costs often do not enjoy the benefits. Although fairness was a common theme in public discourse about the dam, within the context of the decision procedures there was no formal way to represent its distributive effects. Like broken promises, "fairness" is hard to capture in consequentialist terms.

The consequentialist logic of rational choice models is poorly equipped to incorporate symbolic values and systematically excludes these from the decision framework. Just as it is difficult to make causal connections based on moral principles, it is also hard to show how the symbolic significance of something implicates future states. The symbolic significance of the incommensurability of land, of the cultural boundary that the Yavapai draw around land and the other features of their culture they believe to be intrinsically valuable, cannot be captured in consequentialist terms. Incommensurable categories are a specific form of boundary, often signaling which classes of things or ideas have special symbolic value. Furthermore, the belief in the incommensurability of some categories may also provide people with signals about how to use or interact with those things, ideas, or people (Raz 1986:345–53).

Part of the stakes in making incommensurate qualities commensurate is that the symbolic logic of incommensurable boundaries is undermined. Although boundaries we define as incommensurable help constitute some of our most cherished categories, their symbolic significance largely depends on our capacity to "measure" their "empirical" impact. Often, what has symbolic significance is the very judgment that something is incommensurable. A belief in incommensurability may, itself, be a qualification for having certain kinds of relationships. For example, believing that friendship cannot be bought or that each child is unique is, in a way, a prerequisite for entering into relations as friends or parents as they are socially defined. The philosopher Joseph Raz (1986:345–53) calls such categories "constitutive incommensurables." They are beliefs attached to institutions or forms of life, and their symbolic significance derives from social conventions and contexts that sustain their meaning. For the Yavapai, land was a constitutive incommensurable, for it was a belief that was closely linked to one's capacity to be a Yavapai.

The distortions that emerge from the bureau's rational procedures stem not only from what it excluded but also from the kind of information that was included and the form it was given. For example, the discrete factors that were used to express the consequences of the proposed alternatives resulted in an artificial compartmentalization of Yavapai culture; the unity and the integrity of the impacts are not captured, and there is no mechanism other than simple quantified aggregation for expressing the interrelatedness of how the Yavapai experience their land and their culture. Carving up impacts into discrete, imposed categories or components is a forced fragmentation that minimizes the pervasiveness and cumulative experience of the impacts. Some Yavapai also believed that the often overwhelming complexity of the decisionmaking procedures distracted people from the real and relatively straightforward stakes of the decision. As one elder expressed it: "White men like to count things that aren't there. We have a way of life that will be destroyed if that dam comes through. Why don't they just say that?"

For the Yavapai, the inability of the rational choice framework to accommodate ultimate or incommensurate values made it an inaccurate, even a dangerous, representation of their interests. Since the models do not permit incommensurate values, they cannot capture the value of land and the value of a way of life. The Yavapai critique of this distortion was not couched in the often opaque language of rational choice theory but in vivid, practical terms. They argued that land and money were not, for them, comparable, and that money was an inappropriate expression of value. How could something that is sacred be given a monetary value? they would ask. As one of their leaders told a reporter, "We cannot compromise our principles, our birthright, our integrity. How do you negotiate honor? We will never negotiate." (Casserly 1981:5). The inappropriateness of doing so was something they were unable to explain to many other participants. Their refusal to negotiate on a price for their land was often misinterpreted by some bureaucrats and politicians as a bargaining strategy.

In transforming what is, for some groups, an incommensurate value into a price, as was done in the bureau's benefit-cost analysis, or into some weighted value summarizing the social impacts to the tribe, as was done in the social analysis, or as a component of a preference function, as was done in the public values assessment, the "cost" or "value" represented bore almost no relationship to the impact the tribe would experience. The very expression of value given the Yavapai land and culture was a contradiction of that value. Obviously, if participants view these procedures as distorting their values or interests, and if these distortions influence the outcome of decisions, they clearly matter. When the "costs" of a proposed policy are obscured or when they are expressed inappropriately, at the crudest level decisions are made with "bad" information; such distortions, however, may be important in other ways as well. They may influence how political debates are structured, who is allowed to participate in decisions, and who is granted authority to speak on behalf of affected parties.

The Yavapai were angered at how their history was misrepresented in the long struggle over Orme Dam. They were also weary of having to publicly defend the uniqueness and significance of their community against powerful interests who wanted their land. They understood, all too clearly, how politicized their difference had become. Their very understanding of themselves as a unique cultural group already presupposes a self-consciousness and scrutiny that reflects the challenges they have faced and the mediating structures that have shaped their encounters with the government and with other settlers. Culture that is not questioned, compromised, or compared does not require a label; it is taken for granted and does not demand the articulate description and defense that the Yavapai have been forced to provide. For the Yavapai, NEPA granted an unprecedented opportunity for inclusion; however, since they could not control the terms of their inclusion, NEPA also required them to provide yet another defense of their difference. This time, their defense was shaped in reaction to the conceptions of rationality, the limitations of consequentialism, and the partiality of science that financed the investigation.

One consequence of this defense of themselves and their land, however, was a heightened sensitivity, appreciation, and reinterpretation of what made them Yavapai. Being continually placed in the unusual position of having to define what makes them a unique people with ancestral rights to their property made them sensitive to attempts to make their concerns commensurate with that of other parties in the decision. Their repeated and protracted struggles with the government required them to construct a portrait of themselves in categories that made sense to them, that would privilege their experience and authority, and that were defensible and stable and sturdy enough to withstand intense scrutiny.

The Yavapai community, because of past experience, distrusted the government's ability or willingness to represent their interests in "neutral" terms. As the tribal president told me, "We know that government studies are always slanted in their favor." They also disagreed with the categories used to represent their interests, knowing that these were "white man's" categories, which would not serve them well. Many also suspected that even if the formal study supported their position, its findings would be ignored. This distrust and disapproval did not lead to them boycotting the formal study, however, since they recognized such a strategy as too risky. Most residents agreed to cooperate with the formal study, allowing themselves to be interviewed at length and letting strangers come to the reservation to participate in community events. But their distrust did, I think, greatly influence their response to the proposed plan. Instead of relying on the study to represent their views and interests, the Yavapai continually resorted to other, external political means of making their position known and trying to affect the outcome, and the strategies they adopted reflected their understanding of the political importance of defining and asserting their difference. In effect, the Yavapai reasserted the political nature of what experts, in implementing NEPA, had tried to make technical.

The community took great pains to publicize and explain their difference, their otherness, to other groups and to the media. While relying on well-known techniques of protest, they adapted these in ways that highlighted their distinctiveness. The reenactment of the Trail of Tears is one poignant example of this. This march was a dramatic reinsertion of their history back into the decision; it was a vivid public and symbolic expression of their cultural and historical distinctiveness, from the style of praying that launched the march to its culmination with a bark scroll designed to subvert normal bureaucratic practice. The genre, the protest march, was a familiar part of American politics and so was accessible and interpretable to white audiences. Cast as a reenactment, it was also the public assertion by the Yavapai of the continuity of both their oppression and their culture. It was a symbolic response (where symbolic value had been systematically

excluded) to the question of cultural continuity posed by powerful white opponents who assumed that continuity was the premise of cultural authority.

In the end, the Yavapai and their supporters prevailed. In 1981, Secretary of the
Interior James Watt made the final decision not to build Orme Dam. An alternative
policy was adopted under which, instead of a confluence structure, an existing dam
would be raised, another dam would be replaced, and a new dam would be built at
a different site. This decision surprised many people and was considered a huge victory for the Yavapai community. Each year, near the anniversary of Watt's decision,
the community celebrates with a joyous pow-wow commemorating their struggle
and their success in stopping the dam.

The long and painful history of Yavapai efforts to stay with the land has irrevo-
cably changed its meaning for them and their understanding of their relationship
to it. As one man told me: "What we have, who we are, is something we have
fought for, and in the fighting we have learned about ourselves, our heritage, and
what these mean to us." As a result of having to spend years explaining to others
their special claim to their land, of self-consciously taking stock among themselves
about the content and meaning of their culture and their collective identity, of
developing new and more elaborate explanations of their attachment to this place,
their appreciation has deepened and their explanations of their difference have
become more self-conscious, more articulate, and more institutionalized. . . .

The Yavapai struggle to stop the dam generated broad publicity for the community; as a result, Yavapai residents became adept at granting interviews and giving
speeches, and they generally became more experienced and sophisticated political
actors. Their political significance is now recognized beyond the reservation as
well; politics on the reservation is accorded a new significance and is now seen as
legitimate "regional news." Reservation events that in the past would never have
been mentioned in the news are now routinely covered. The accomplishments of
the Yavapai community have also inspired other native groups. Lawrence
Aschenbrenner, an attorney with the Native American Rights Fund, said of their
struggle (Blundell 1981:35):

> It's pretty amazing. All sorts of well-intentioned people told the Yavapai they
> were sticking their heads in the sand, that if they'd just negotiate, they could
> make a heck of a deal. The $33 million was a tentative bargaining offer, real-
> ly. What these people have done is an example to other tribes who can now
> say, "By God, if we get together and don't give up, we can win too."

CONCLUSION: POWER AND THE LEGAL AND BUREAUCRATIC
CONSTRUCTION OF A SUBJECT

. . .

[The Yavapai] case shows how the expression of interests is sometimes also the
expression or reconfiguration of the subject who is having an interest—in this
case, of what it meant to the Yavapai to be Yavapai. In treating universalistically

all those who were designated as having "a stake" in the outcome of this decision, the law, as it was implemented by the bureau, transformed all relationships to the proposed policy into some common standard: qualities became quantities, difference became magnitude. While the law was explicitly intended to empower new groups with an interest in preserving and improving the environment, the standing that it granted, and the procedural scrupulousness that it eventually fostered, carried with it assumptions about who and how someone could have an interest. Law was a means or a stimulus for imposing a particular kind of identity. What was presumed to be a neutral and fair way of categorizing and sorting information turned out to be a framework that many Yavapai felt misrepresented not only their interests, but them. Law also required that culture be transformed into a category called an "impact" and that culture be interpreted as an entity about which predictions can be made, sustained, and documented. Culture must be amenable to precise predictions about how the sometimes small variations in policy will differentially change the future, including future culture.

The Yavapai community accepted the standing that NEPA conferred but rejected the implicit identity that accompanied this standing. Their actual relationship to NEPA was remote. Most residents were largely unaware of the law and how it had motivated and shaped the investigation in which they were both subjects and reluctant participants. But in reacting to how the bureau was representing them and interpreting their interests in its attempt to implement and comply with the law, the Yavapai community was forced to grapple with fundamental questions of identity: Who are we? What unites us? What defines our culture? Why are we different? How do we represent our difference to others? In rejecting others' representations of their identity, they recognized the tacit form of power that a framework can impose. Participating in the formal EIS process was troubling to them because they knew that the debate's *forms* mattered, that these were nonnegotiable, and that these harmed them. They recognized that, in this decision, their ability to define themselves was at stake since the procedures used misrepresented them in ways that they believed diminished them and their claims. To counter this, they adopted political strategies based on representing themselves, on the reassertion of their cultural authority and their ability to describe themselves in their own terms. They used their distinctiveness, itself a consequence of past bitter struggles with the government, against the procedure; they reasserted their substantive values when bureaucrats were trying to translate these into the terms of instrumental rationality. In doing so, the Yavapai created a new interpretation and a renewed appreciation of their own "otherness." Knowing who they were was part of a complex process of knowing and reinterpreting who they weren't and why they were different; in this instance, this process was stimulated by law and shaped by legal and bureaucratic practice. . . .

[The] Yavapai criticism . . . [of] the NEPA-inspired framework did not subvert the framework or undermine the bureaucratic or legal legitimacy of these rational techniques, which are now more diffused than ever both within the bureau and outside it; Yavapai leaders correctly perceived their limited ability to shape bureaucratic procedure and that the framework of the investigation was nonnegotiable because, as they expressed it, "white men will do things their way." Despite their objections, in the formal investigation, a "fair market price" was attached to their land, their projected suffering was "quantified," and their culture was "measured."

The Yavapai criticisms were powerful, however, in other ways. Their critique did, I think, prompt them to rethink their difference, to articulate why what was important about them could not be captured in the terms imposed by the bureau and the courts, to redirect their political strategies, and to rethink their sense of themselves as effective political and cultural actors. In explaining why land could not be expressed as price, why their removal from land was different from the relocation of white people, and why the moral and historical dimensions of the decision should not be stripped away, they strengthened their resolve to use political means to represent themselves outside the strictures of the investigation. While they may not have convinced the bureaucrats of the narrowness of their framework's categories or the limitations of its logic, the Yavapai practical understanding of its failings informed their resistance. Their insistence on the political, moral, and historical dimensions of the decision was both empowering to them and persuasive to other publics. And in the process of trying to persuade others of these dimensions, they reinforced their importance for their own understanding of their identity, as Yavapai and as individuals. . . .

For the bureaucrats whose proffered solution to the plurality of values and interests confronting them was commensuration and formal rationality, identity entered into the debate primarily as ordered preferences. The formal disinterestedness that was the basis of their procedural authority stemmed from the transformation of individual preferences into something defensible as a "public" choice; it was only through an elaborate and largely invisible array of steps that the final decision could be linked back to the values of individuals. However crude or distorting commensuration may be, quantification permits an authoritative and defensible response to charges of bias. As Porter (1992a:20) has convincingly argued, objectivity in science is not synonymous with truth claims; rather, he contends: "The impersonality of numbers . . . is as least as crucial for their authority as is the plausibility of their claims to truth." In depersonalizing people's claims, rational decision procedures formed explicit identities into depersonalized, implicit subjects. Where Scheingold (1974) is persuaded that the role of legal ideology is to sustain the myth of the distinction between law and politics, in this instance, law was the vehicle for reasserting the distinction between politics and science, and between the public and the private.

Members of the Yavapai community did, and still are, responding to the categories of value, interest, and, implicitly, identity that were assumed within the bureau's rational decision framework. But rather than resulting in some neat commensurated closure, the effect of the imposition of the categories and assumptions of the rational decision framework was to deepen and make more evident, and perhaps even elicit, incommensurabilities among some groups and between arenas. . . .

While the economic and political sides of domination have been well analyzed by social scientists, less attention has been paid to the significance of cultural domination (Comaroffs 1988; 1991:309–14). Yet, as Jack Goody (1977:37), Stuart Hall (1992:252), and others have suggested, "modes of communication" and "relations of representation" are a distinct venue of power that demands explanation. Law, whether enacted by bureaucrats, judges, lawyers, or litigants, creates categories that become imposed on and practiced in the world. We should not be surprised that these categories have consequences: whether as basic as dictating causal logic, as implicit as defining which kind of person can have an interest, or as inclusive as controlling how to convey value, the potential of legally mediated categories to mark difference, shape consciousness, and inform the actions of those who confront them is a crucial form of power. . . .

REFERENCES

Anderson, Barry F., 1981. *Cascaded Trade-Offs: A Multi-Objective, Multi-Publics Method for Alternatives Evaluation in Water Resources Planning*. Washington, DC: U.S. Department of the Interior, Bureau of Reclamation.

Anderson, Frederick R., 1973. *NEPA in the Courts: A Legal Analysis of the National Environmental Policy Act*. Baltimore: Johns Hopkins Univ. Press.

Andrews, Richard N.L., 1976. *Environmental Analysis and Administrative Change*. Lexington, MA: Lexington Books.

Anonymous, 1988. "A Yavapai Woman Speaks," in S. Niederman, ed., *A Quilt of Words: Women's Diaries, Letters and Original Accounts of Life in the Southwest, 1860–1960*. Boulder, CO: Johnson Books.

Blundell, William E., 1981. "Arizona Indians Win Victory over U.S.: Refuse $33 Million," *Wall Street J.*, 17 Dec., sec. 1, p. 1.

Bourke, John G., 1891. *On the Border with Crook*. New York: Charles Scribner's Sons.

Bronson, Leisa, 1980. "The Long Walk of the Yavapai," 13 (1) *Wassaja/The Indian Historian* 36.

Caldwell, Lynton K., 1982. *Science and the National Environmental Policy Act: Redirecting Policy Through Procedural Reform*. University: Univ. of Alabama Press.

Cappelletti, Mauro, and Bryant Garth, 1978. *Access to Justice: A World Survey*. Milan: Sijthoff Giuffre.

Casserly, J.J., 1981. "Different Drummers: The Indians and Orme Dam," *Arizona Republic*, 22 May, sec. A. P. 5.

Comaroff, Jean, and John, 1988. "Through the Looking-Glass: Colonial Encounters of the First Kind," 1 *Journal of Historical Sociology* 6.

_____ 1991. *of Revelation and Revolution: Christianity, Colonialism, and Consciousness in South Africa*. Chicago: Univ. of Chicago Press.

Corbusier, William T., 1971. *Verde to San Carlos: Recollections of a Famous Army Surgeon and His Observant Family on the Western Frontier, 1869–1886*. Tucson, AZ: Dale Stuart King.

Culhane, Paul J., 1990. "Nepa's Impact on Federal Agencies, Anticipated and Unanticipated," 20 *Environmental Law* 681.

Curlin, James W., 1973. National Environmental Policy at of 1969: Environmental Indices. Prepared for Committee on Insular Affairs of the U.S. Senate. Washington, D.C. (Dec).

Cyert, Richard, and James G. March, 1963. *Behavioral Theory of the Firm*, Englewood Cliffs, N.J.: Prentice-Hall.

Espeland, Wendy N., 1992. "Contested Rationalities: Commensuration and the Representation of Value in Public Choice," Ph.D. diss., Dept. of Sociology, Univ. of Chicago.

_____ 1993. "Power, Policy and Paperwork: The Bureaucratic Representation of Interests," 16 *Qualitative Sociology* 297.

Finn, Terrence T., 1973. "Conflict and Compromise: Congress Makes a Law—The Passage of the National Environmental Policy Act," Ph.D. diss., Dept. of Political Science, Georgetown Univ.

Fitzsimmons, Stephen J., Lorrie I. Stuart, and Peter C. Wolff, 1977. *Social Assessment Manual: a Guide to the Preparation of the Social Well-being Account for Planning Water Resource Projects*, Boulder, Colo.: Westview Press.

Foucault, Michel, 1980. *Power/knowledge: Selected Interviews and Other Writings*, 1972–1977, ed. & trans. C. Gordon. Brighton, Sussex: Harvester Press.

———— 1982. "Afterword," in H. Dreyfus and P. Rabinow, eds., *Michel Foucault: Beyond Structuralism and Hermeneutics*. Brighton, Sussex: Harvester Press.

Friesema, H. Paul, and Paul J. Culhane, 1976. "Social Impacts, Politics, and the Environmental Impact Statement Process," 16 *Natural Resources J.* 339.

Goody, Jack, 1977. *The Domestication of the Savage Mind.* Cambridge, Mass.: Cambridge Univ. Press.

Granfield, Robert, 1992. *Making Elite Lawyers: Visions of Law at Harvard and Beyond.* New York, N.Y.: Routledge.

Hall, Stuart, 1992. "New Ethnicities," in J. Donald and A. Rattansi, eds., *"Race," Culture and Difference.* London: Sage.

Heinz, John P., and Edward O. Laumann, 1982. *Chicago Lawyers: The Social Structure of the Bar,* New York, N.Y.: Sage Foundation; Chicago, Ill.: American Bar Foundation.

Hunt, Alan, 1976. "Law, State and Class Struggle," 20 *Marxism Today* 178.

Khera, Sigrid, ed., 1978. *The Yavapai of Fort McDowell.* Foundation Hills, Ariz.: Fort McDowell Mohave-Apache Indian Community.

Lempert, Richard, and Joseph Sanders, 1986. *An Invitation of Law and Social Science.* Philadelphia, Pa.: Univ. of Pennsylvania Press.

Liroff, Richard A., 1976. *A National Policy for the Environment: NEPA and Its Aftermath.* Bloomington, Ind.: Indiana Univ. Press.

Mazmanian, Daniel A., and Jeanne Nienaber, 1979. *Can Organizations Change? Environmental Protection, Citizen Participation and the Corps of Engineers.* Washington, D.C.: Brookings Institution.

Mariella, Patricia, 1983. "The Political Economy of Federal Resettlement Communities: the Fort McDowell Yavapai Case," Ph.D. diss., Dept. of Anthropology, Arizona State Univ.

Miliband, Ralph, 1969. *The State in Capitalist Society.* New York, N.Y.: Basic Books.

Minow, Martha, 1990. *Making All the Difference: Inclusion, Exclusion and American Law,* Ithaca, N.Y.: Cornell Univ. Press.

Porter, Theodore, M., 1992a. "Objectivity as Standardization: the Rhetoric of Impersonality in Measurement, Statistics, and Cost-Benefit Analysis," 9 *Annals of Scholarship* 19.

———— 1992b. "Quantification and The Accounting Ideal in Science," 22 *Social Studies of Science* 633.

Poulantzas, Nicos, 1975. *Political Power and Social Classes.* London: NLB.

Raz, Joseph, 1986. *The Morality of Freedom.* New York, N.Y.: Oxford Univ. Press, Clarendon.

Rodgers, William H. Jr., 1990. "NEPA at Twenty: Mimicry and Recruitment in Environmental Law," 20 *Environmental Law* 485.

Scheingold, Stuart A., 1974. *The Politics of Rights: Lawyers, Public Policy and Political Change.* New Haven, Conn.: Yale Univ. Press.

Schnaiberg, Allan, 1986. *The Environment: From Surplus to Scarcity.* Oxford: Oxford Univ. Press.

Schroeder, Albert, 1974. *Yavapai Indians: A Study of Yavapai History.* New York, N.Y.: Garland Publications.

———— 1982. "Yavapai Land Tenure at Fort McDowell." U.S. Bureau of Reclamation Final Report Social Impacts and Effects, A-1, A-2.

Simmel, Georg, 1971. *On Individuality and Social Forms: Selected Writings,* ed. D. Levine, Chicago, Ill.: Univ. Of Chicago Press.

Taylor, Serge, 1984. *Making Bureaucracies Think: The Environmental Impact Strategy of Administrative Reform.* Stanford, Calif.: Stanford Univ. Press.

Thompson, Edward P., 1975. *Whigs and Hunters: The Origin of the Black Act*. New York, N.Y.: Pantheon.

Tulumello, Mike, 1981. "Indians Begin Hike to Capitol," *Mesa Tribune*, 24 Sept., p. 1.

Turner, Victor Witter, 1974. *Dramas, Fields, and Metaphors: Symbolic Action in Human Society*. Ithaca, N.Y.: Cornell Univ. Press.

U.S. Department of the Interior, 1873. *Annual Report of the Commissioner of Indian Affairs*. Washington, D.C.: U.S. Department of the Interior.

_____ 1874. *Annual Report of the Commissioner of Indian Affairs*. Washington DC: U.S. Department of the Interior.

U.S. Department of the Interior, Bureau of Reclamation, 1947. *Report on Central Arizona Project*. Project Planning Report No. 3-8b-4-2.

_____ 1963. *Pacific Southwest Water Plan: Supplemental Information on Central Arizona Project*.

_____ 1972. *Central Arizona Project Final Environmental Statement*.

_____ 1976a. *Socioeconomic Study of the Fort McDowell Indian Reservation and Community with and without the Development of Orme Dam and Reservoir*. Prepared by the Natelson Corp.

_____ 1976b. *Orme Dam Reservoir, Central Arizona Project, Arizona-New Mexico*. Draft Environmental Impact Statement.

_____ 1977. *Water and Land Resources Accomplishments*.

_____ 1981a. *Appendix A: Summary and Evaluation of Central Arizona Water Control Study Public Involvement Program*.

_____ 1981b. *Appendix B: Central Arizona Water Control Study Public Values Assessment*.

_____ 1981c. *Congressional Briefing on Central Arizona Project Status*.

_____ 1982a. *Field Draft, Environmental Impact Statement, Central Arizona Project Regulatory Storage Division, Central Arizona Water Control Study*.

_____ 1982b. *Summary and Evaluation of Central Arizona Water Control Study Public Involvement Program, 1979–1980*.

_____ 1982c. *Final Report: Social Impacts and Effects of Central Arizona Water Control Study Plans*.

U.S. Department of the Interior, Water and Power Resources Service [Bureau of Reclamation], 1979. *Commensuration in Federal Water Resources Planning: Problem Analysis and Research Appraisal*. Research Report 79-2 prepared by William Lord, Donald Deane, and Marvin Waterstone.

Walton, John, 1992. *Western Times and Water Wars: State, Culture, and Rebellion in California*. Berkeley, Calif.: Univ. of California Press.

Zelizer, Viviana A., 1989. "The Social Meaning of Money: 'Special Monies,'" 95 *American J. of Sociology* 342.

_____ 1994. *The Social Meaning of Money*. New York, N.Y.: Basic Books.

STATUTE

National Environmental Policy Act of 1969, 102 U.S.C. 4332, 1970.

Large Binocular Telescopes, Red Squirrel Piñatas, and Apache Sacred Mountains: Decolonizing Environmental Law in a Multicultural World

Robert A. Williams, Jr.

> The occupier, smarting from his failures, presents in a simplified and pejorative way the system of values by means of which the colonized person resists his innumerable offensives. What is in fact the assertion of a distinct identity, concern with keeping intact a few shreds of national existence, is attributed to religious, magical, fanatical behavior.
>
> —Frantz Fanon, A Dying Colonialism[1]

INTRODUCTION

For two years, as Director of the Office of Indian Programs at the University of Arizona, I was involved on a near-daily basis with what has come to be known throughout the southwestern United States, and in other parts of the country and world, as the Mt. Graham controversy.[2] The controversy centers around the efforts of the University of Arizona, together with a consortium of foreign astronomers from the Vatican, the Max Planck Institute in Germany, and Arcetri astrophysical observatory of Florence, Italy, to build an astronomical observatory on the peaks of Mt. Graham in southeastern Arizona. Because of my personal involvement, I cannot claim a detached neutrality in my recitation of the facts, or for my very tentative legal-cultural analysis of the controversy. But I do believe that as a minor bit-player in this multi-layered, multicultural drama involving large binocular telescopes, red squirrel piñatas, and Apache sacred mountains, I gained some valuable first-hand knowledge of how our environmental law has been colonized by a perverse system of values which is antithetical to achieving environmental justice for American Indian peoples.

From "Large Binocular Telescopes, Red Squirrel Piñatas, and Apache Sacred Mountains: Decolonizing Environmental Law in a Multicultural World," *West Virginia Law Review* 96(1994):1133. © 1996 by the West Virginia Law Review.

According to this system of values, the issue of protecting one of the most unique ecological and spiritual resources in North America can be decided by the vagaries and corrupting influences of the same interest-group dominated political processes which bid for marginal tax rates for millionaires and pork-barrel construction projects in our nation's capital. At the same time, this system of values guarantees a highly-select set of issues, such as those involving freedom of speech and expression or bodily integrity, from the sordid business of politics as usual in a democratic society. The perversity of this system, which privileges what it labels as "human values" over "environmental values," is its failure to recognize that both sets of values are intimately connected to who and what we are as human beings reliant on, and engaged with, the complete set of forces which give meaning and life to our world. The core human rights of freedom of speech and expression and bodily integrity are meaningless abstractions without the sustaining context provided by the interconnected physical, social, and spiritual worlds which we inhabit and which together comprise our environment. The perverse value system which has colonized our environmental law, however, fails to recognize or acknowledge that protecting environmental values is anterior to, and a prerequisite for, protecting all our other core human rights.

One point which I want to develop in this essay is that any efforts aimed at decolonizing our environmental law must first identify and confront this perverse value system. As I attempt to illustrate, American Indian peoples possess their own unique visions of environmental justice which are capable of inaugurating this decolonization process. The values animating these American Indian visions are typically reinforced throughout tribal culture by myths and narratives which seek to invoke our imaginative capacities to see the social, physical, and spiritual worlds we inhabit as connected and interdependent. Through such stories and their interrelated themes of harmony and humility, we are taught a system of values which induces a profound attitude of respect for the forces which give life to the complex world of which we are but a small part.[3]

As the Mt. Graham controversy demonstrates, however, the perverse system of values which has colonized our environmental law subjects these Indian visions of environmental justice to a political process, which presents these myths and narratives in a simplified and pejorative way. Indian resistance to the threats posed to our social, physical, and spiritual world by our environmental law are dismissed as attributable to "religious, magical, fanatical behavior."[4] If the stories and narratives of American Indian peoples are to serve as effective and viable paths of resistance against our currently colonized environmental law, then the environmental racism which has been institutionalized at the deepest levels of our society must also be identified and confronted, for it too is part of a dying colonialism.

MYTHOLOGIES

In the cultural symbology of colonialism, there comes that pivotal moment when the colonizer affirms the triumph over the colonized by an unspeakable act of religious defilement; the temple is ransacked, sacred artifacts are plundered, and heathen idols are destroyed. So too, with the Mt. Graham controversy. During the first stage of the University of Arizona's decade-long battle to site its large binocular telescope project on top of Mt. Graham, the Mt. Graham Red Squirrel (*Tamiasciurus hudsonicus grahamensis*), listed by the federal government as an endangered species, came to represent the primary obstacle to the university's desires to occupy the mountain.

After a million dollar legislative lobbying effort and several years of protracted litigation, a federal court decision was finally handed down, holding that Congress had exempted the telescope project from the Endangered Species Act [ESA] and other federal review processes normally required under our environmental law.[5] Officials at the university reportedly celebrated their triumph over the forces of resistance against their occupation of Mt. Graham by destroying a Red Squirrel piñata. . . .

All cultures develop their own myths and narratives of epic struggle.[6] The overly-insulated group of university scientists and administrators who had devoted the better parts of their professional lives for the past several years to the quest of conquering Mt. Graham was certainly capable of generating such a mythical narrative. Granted, the struggle for Mt. Graham was motivated in part by their strong desire to secure a nearby and accessible site to showcase and promote a new generation of honeycombed mirror telescopes being produced at the university's world-renowned Mirror Lab. Not only international prestige, but large sums of money would flow to the university by way of contracts and orders for large honeycombed mirror telescopes, just like the one on Mt. Graham. Hefty fees would also be paid by other astronomers who would travel from around the world to gaze out at the stars from the university's observatory on top of the mountain. Groups of local officials and civic leaders in Graham County, where Mt. Graham was located, had even formed a booster club to support and promote the telescope project and the economic development and tourism opportunities that the university promised would follow in its wake. . . .

But the money was only part of the reason for the waging of the epic struggle for Mt. Graham. From the beginning, there were quasireligious overtones to the university astronomers' unflagging devotion to their telescope project.[7] As I learned from the scientists I got to know on the project, conducting pure research in astronomical physics comes as close to a religious calling as secular humanism can provide its technological and scientific adherents. The fact that the university expected to receive a significant return on its sizable investment in the project, in terms of dollars and increased international prestige, was really beside the point. The astronomers were going to do "science" on that mountain, and that was a value in and of itself.

It was a value, as I quickly came to appreciate, so venerated by the institutional culture of a major research university that to question the wisdom of pursuing pure scientific research anywhere, even on a mountaintop sustaining several diverse ecosystems and endangered species, is regarded as near-blasphemy by the people who really matter at such places. At bottom, the scientists, at least the ones I got to know, were sincere in their belief that they were pursuing a higher calling in siting their telescopes on Mt. Graham.[8] [They saw] those environmen-

talists who had so vigorously opposed their occupation of the mountain were acting as irrational fanatics in their fetishistic idolatry of an inconsequential sub-
species of rodent. In the mythology generated by the Mt. Graham controversy, it
would be only fitting that when the large binocular telescope crusaders finally tri-
umphed over the tree-hugging New Age neo-luddites, the victory would be com-
memorated by the exquisite symbology represented by the (perhaps) mythical
story of the destruction of a Red Squirrel piñata.

A LAYER CAKE OF LIFEZONES

Aside from its asserted advantages as a telescope site, one can easily understand
why even quark-stalking astronomers would so ardently desire to possess Mt.
Graham for their own purposes. As environmentalists opposed to the telescopes
are quick to point out, the southernmost forest of spruce and fir in North America
grows on Mt. Graham's peaks, and the ecological diversity of the mountain marks
it as one of the truly unique environmental resources on the continent. It is reputed
as the only mountain range to stack five of the seven major ecosystems of North
America in one place, but it's in the seeing and experiencing, not the counting, that
Mt. Graham's uniqueness seizes you.[9] The hike up the mountain leads you from
the dry, harsh desert that most people think of when they conjure up their cactus-
laden images of Arizona, to a green, lush boreal forest at the summit. . . .

The entire mountain is a truly unique ecological space; "a layercake of life
zones," as the environmentalists like to call it.[10] But it is at Mt. Graham's summit, where you find a boreal zone of virgin spruce-fir forest standing yet
untouched by the Forest Service's devouring lessees, that it becomes clear what
makes this mountain worth fighting for. Wild nature still controls the desert sky-
island at the top of Mt. Graham. Mountain lions and black bears roam freely atop
the mountain's peaks. The Mexican Spotted Owl and goshawk, two gravely
threatened species in the southwest, are found here as well.

Mt. Graham can dispense many quiet types of blessings to the human visitor.
Sit down near one of the half-dozen or so perennial streams which flow from the
mountain's peaks, and you soon become totally absorbed in a world far removed
in space and time from that mundane, disconnected form of existence which most
of us call daily living. There is quiet here, but certainly no desperation. It is a wondrous and magical place, this mountain, as fit a site on earth as one can ever hope
to find to do science, or absolutely nothing. Each in its own way after all, can be
a form of worship, depending on your perspective.

THINKING LIKE AN ENVIRONMENTALIST

Perspective, of course, is everything when it comes to mountains. If humans
could learn to think like a mountain,[11] perhaps we could develop some truly

unique perspectives on the appropriateness of doing astronomical science on Mt. Graham. We have not quite yet developed that ability as a sentient species, and so we have surrogates who presume to do the mountain's thinking for it. Our society calls these self-appointed defenders of the natural places our Creator has entrusted to us, "environmentalists." . . .

On the whole, the environmentalists I dealt with spoke passionately about the need to protect Mt. Graham, but they never connected that passion to any particular vision or ethic of how we as human beings ought to relate to the mountain. Nor could they articulate any set of values not connected to some sterile form of economic calculus that made it clear to me why siting telescopes on Mt. Graham would be wrong.[12] From their perspective, what the university wanted to do on Mt. Graham was simply inappropriate, period. The telescopes had to be fought down from off that mountaintop. . . .

Besides their mystical devotion to trees and conspiracy theories, the environmentalists had a peculiar and most dulling habit of also resorting to cost/benefit analysis in defending the mountain from assault. They were never lacking for "studies" of what the appropriate use of the mountain should be. They found it particularly significant that a 1985 peer-review study of so-called "desirable" telescope sites in the United States and Northern Mexico ranked Mt. Graham thirty-seventh in terms of a place where telescopes ought to be put. In a poor marriage of the discourses of economic analysis and environmental extremism, they continually cited and relied on this and other "scientific," "objective," and "neutral" studies to attack "the efficacy and the necessity of the exploitation of Mt. Graham." Shouting a battle cry that they were certain would rally the masses to their cause, they asserted that the "ecological integrity" of the mountain had been challenged by the university.[13]

At least the astronomers could talk about seeing "larger meanings" in the universe with the aid of their large binocular telescopes, and the university administrators could tout the benefits of their $200 million capital investment in scientific and technological advancement in defending their position in the controversy. The problem for the environmentalists was that neither their mystical devotion to protecting wild nature from malevolent forces nor the sterile abstractions of their economic discourse were equal to the task of mobilizing public opinion and sentiment against a few telescopes on a mountain that nobody else seemed to be using. The beauty of a mountain rests in the eye of the beholder, and the conspiracy theories and cost/benefit studies of the environmentalists did little to evoke the imaginative capacity of the vast majority of the public, who had never seen Mt. Graham to envision the peaks of the mountain as something worth preserving in their pristine splendor. And so the environmentalists seized upon the Mt. Graham Red Squirrel in order to save Mt. Graham.

THE UNIVERSE IS EXPANDING CONSTANTLY

. . .

In the mid-1980s, an international consortium led by the University of Arizona had first proposed construction of 13 telescopes, support facilities, and an access road on Mt. Graham's peaks. The proposal drew protests from a number of environmental groups, forcing the Forest Service in 1985 to begin the Environmental Impact Statement (EIS) process under the National Environmental Protection Act (NEPA) for the project.[14]

The draft Environmental Impact Statement that the agency released the following year identified a "preferred alternative" in which only five telescopes would be constructed on High Peak, one of the various peaks of Mt. Graham. Meanwhile, in 1987, the U.S. Fish and Wildlife Service listed the Mt. Graham Red Squirrel as endangered.[15] This action, not wholly unexpected, required the Forest Service to initiate "formal consultation" with the Fish and Wildlife Service regarding the suitability of an astrophysical complex on Mt. Graham given the endangered status of the red squirrel. The Fish and Wildlife Service let it be known that it would likely agree to development on High Peak, but not to any development on Emerald Peak. The University of Arizona, however, notified the Forest Service that the High Peak alternative did "not provide for or allow a viable cost-effective research facility." At this point, the Forest Service suspended formal consultation with Fish and Wildlife and asked the university to present its own proposal for a "minimum viable observatory."[16]

In response to this invitation, the university, in late 1987, proposed the construction of three telescopes on High Peak and four telescopes on Emerald Peak, along with support facilities and access roads. Based on the university's proposal, the Forest Service prepared a new Biological Assessment. It also reinitiated formal consultation with the Fish and Wildlife Service. The Fish and Wildlife Service then issued a Biological Opinion in 1988, which found that "establishment of the seven telescope observatory on Emerald and High Peaks is likely to jeopardize the continued existence of the endangered red squirrel because this plan significantly increases the existing jeopardy status of this squirrel." Despite the seemingly inevitable conflict with the ESA that approval of the telescope project would appear to trigger two of the three "reasonable and prudent alternatives" contained in the opinion, the Fish and Wildlife Service allowed for the construction of an astrophysical complex on Mt. Graham. Surprisingly, one of these two alternatives, "Reasonable and Prudent Alternative Three," provided for construction on Emerald Peak per the university's stated desires, though clearly contrary to the Fish and Wildlife Service's earlier conclusion that development on Emerald Peak would be environmentally unsound.[17]

Given the language of Section 7 of the ESA, that forbids federal agencies from taking action "likely to jeopardize" or endanger species, and a federal agency's biological opinion that the university's telescopes would "likely jeopardize the continued existence" of the Mt. Graham Red Squirrel, the university recognized that its project could be interminably delayed by legal and political challenges from environmentalists, and perhaps even killed. But the cause of pure science was not so easily derailed by a furry red rodent. Like many public universities in the West, the University of Arizona possesses a delegation of United States senators and congressional representatives who see it as their privilege and responsibility to further the interests of the state's flagship institution of higher education in the pork-barrel politics of the nation's capital. Those same high-minded public servants also stand ready to take on the challenge of navigating the university through the regulatory shoals and barrier reefs maintained by the sirens of the bureaucracy in Washington, D.C., which controls so much of the public domain in the West. In short, the university lobbied the state's congressional delegation to lobby the rest of the Congress so that the university could get what it wanted to get: its large binocular telescopes on top of Mt. Graham.

A new strategy was developed to conquer Mt. Graham—simply exempt the entire project from NEPA and the Endangered Species Act. This stroke of brilliance was legislated into law in 1988, when Congress passed the Arizona-Idaho Conservation Act. In Section VI of the Act, Congress essentially assumed the role the Forest Service would ordinarily have played and made a selection among the three "reasonable and prudent" alternatives, choosing Alternative Three—the one that permitted construction on Emerald Peak, the most vital portion of the red squirrel's habitat.[18]

In April 1989, the Secretary of Agriculture issued the university a permit for the first phase of construction of the astrophysical complex. This permit allowed construction of the first three telescopes on Emerald Peak on a total of 8.6 acres of the 1,750 acres designated in the Biological Opinion as a refugium for the red squirrel. For all intents and purposes, Congress had granted the University of Arizona an exemption from all environmental laws and regulations that might delay construction of the first of three telescopes on Emerald Peak.[19] . . .

EXPANDING OUR HORIZONS

The environmentalists, of course, challenged all of this legislative legerdemain in the courts, and of course, the environmentalists lost.[20] Our environmental law allows for little in the way of mystical reverence for environmental values and dismisses out-of-hand conspiracy theories about management of the public domain as politics as usual in Washington. Under our environmental law, Congress can determine when various processes designed to protect environmental values are "deemed satisfied." . . .

Unlike the mystically-revered values of free speech, religious freedom, or bodily integrity, which are protected by the courts from the majoritarian, log-rolling political processes of day-to-day democratic government, the system of values which has colonized our environmental law concedes the last word on how to protect a place like Mt. Graham to the political process. As for that political process, the Mt. Graham Red Squirrel and all it was supposed to symbolize in carrying the fight for Mt. Graham was simply not enough to overcome a million dollar lobbying campaign by the university, and make Congress "stop, look, and listen" to what the red squirrel might be trying to tell us about Mt. Graham and about our environmental law as well.

BAROMETER FUNCTIONS

Even up to this point in the story, the symbology generated by the Mt. Graham controversy is irresistible to the cultural critic. Like the Northern Spotted Owl, which has pitted environmentalists against the logging industry of the Pacific Northwest,[21] endangered species like the Mt. Graham Red Squirrel perform a valuable "barometer function" in alerting humans to environmental threats.[22] Our modern environmental law, however, as is evidenced by the Mt. Graham controversy, has generally done a poor job of explaining the basic importance to us, as human beings connected to our ecosystems, of protecting endangered species. Using an endangered species such as the Mt. Graham Red Squirrel or the Northern Spotted Owl as a symbol of the need for preserving biological diversity and respecting its importance translates poorly in the public imagination. For the administrators at the University of Arizona, for astronomical scientists committed to advancing the knowledge base of their discipline, and even to the senators and congresspersons promoting the interests of the leading university in their state, the Mt. Graham Red Squirrel simply stood as an isolated symbol of the fetishistic excesses of fanatics in the environmental movement. In the press and even on the campus, the environmentalists involved in the Mt. Graham controversy were caricatured as groups of slightly unbalanced tree-huggers and wildly unbalanced eco-terrorists of the Earth First! variety, who preferred saving a sub-species of an otherwise ubiquitous rodent, as opposed to constructing a multi-million dollar astronomical observatory devoted to the highest causes of science. Given this symbology, the Mt. Graham Red Squirrel never had a chance of surviving unmolested in its mountain habitat. Nor could it even hope to carry the load of assisting the public and policymakers in imagining what makes preserving Mt. Graham important from our perspective as human beings. Given the terms of the debate and the symbols available in waging the war for Mt. Graham, the mountain was destined for colonization by the large binocular telescope crusaders.[23]

IMAGINATIVE CAPACITIES

As we have seen, the Mt. Graham Red Squirrel failed as a surrogate for depicting the constellation of values connected to protecting and preserving Mt. Graham. Similarly, neither the environmentalists' passion for trees and conspiracy theories, nor their abstract terminology combining economic analysis and extremist rhetoric similarly could halt the telescope project from proceeding.

One reason for this connected series of failures, I suggest, is that . . . some issues, like free speech, religious liberty, or bodily integrity, are regarded as too intimately connected to who and what we are as persons to submit them to the processes of politics as usual. But beyond this select set of highly valued core "human rights" which are declared off limits to majoritarian processes and popular prejudice, we allow various interest groups to fight it out. In other words, those things which, according to this system of values, are not regarded as fundamentally connected to who and what we are as human beings, like a mountain and the biological diversity which it sustains, are subject to a process where all values are up for grabs. . . . The perversity of this system is that . . . the political process to which we have subjected our environmental law is incapable of creating the imaginative capacity within us to see this absolutely vital connection [between environmental law and human values].

THE GAANS' EMERGENCE

The first stage of the Mt. Graham controversy came to a close in October of 1989, when the university was given the go-ahead by a federal district court to cut an access road to the proposed telescope site on the mountain.[24] Within a year, dozens of spruce and fir had been cut down to clear the site for two of the three telescopes to be built on Mt. Graham.

It was during this same period that the Mt. Graham controversy entered its second stage, with the appearance of a group called the Apache Survival Coalition. The Coalition claimed that Mt. Graham was sacred according to traditional Apache spiritual and ritual beliefs because it was the home of the Gaans. The Gaans, as members of the Coalition explained, represented the elemental forces of the Universe according to traditional Apache belief. The Gaans had emerged from Mt. Graham many ages ago to give the original medicine to an Apache medicine person. After performing this service for the Apaches, the Gaans had then gone back into Mt. Graham to rest. The university's telescopes, it was declared, would not only destroy the ability of traditional Apaches to worship on the mountain and give thanks to the Gaans, but if the Gaans were now disturbed by the university's digging and blasting on the top of the mountain, there would be a great cosmic disturbance in the universe.

University officials, to say the least, were skeptical about the Gaans resting on Mt. Graham. It was the first they had ever heard about any Apache religious interests in the mountain. They grew even more skeptical when it was discovered that the non-profit corporation calling itself the Apache Survival Coalition had on its board of directors several of the most prominent non-Indian environmentalists who had been fighting the telescope project since its inception.

It was at this point in the Mt. Graham controversy that university officials called on the office which I directed at the time, the Office of Indian Programs (OIP), for "advice." OIP had, as a primary function, liaison relations with all of Arizona's tribes, so it was not unusual for the university to look to OIP in this situation. While I was somewhat uncomfortable with my role as cultural mediator between the university and the Apaches, I took the time to talk with Apache members of the Coalition, whom I found to be sincere and entirely convincing in stating their belief that the university telescopes should not be built on Mt. Graham. I talked with the non-Indian members of the Coalition as well, all of them self-proclaimed environmentalists. I found them as a group to be quite cynical in their passionately professed concerns for Indian religious values that would be affected by the university's telescopes atop the mountain. I asked one of them what he would do if an Apache Gaan appeared to him in a dream and told him to ritually sacrifice all of the red squirrels that could be found on the mountain. All he could say was that he would not answer "trick questions."

In the course of OIP's efforts to gather information to gain a clearer under-standing of the Apache's religious claims, the anthropologist who had worked for the office for nearly two decades, Gordon Krutz, took a walk over to the Arizona State Museum, which is a part of the university and located on the campus. The OIP had been given a lead on some old field notes collected among the Apaches at San Carlos by Grenville Goodwin, a noted University of Arizona anthropologist during the 1920s and 30s.

Anthropologists are the brunt of many jokes and much criticism in Indian coun-try. There is an old joke one hears told among Indians in Arizona that captures the exasperated sense of exploitation Indian peoples have often felt at the hands of anthropologists—the traditional Indian family living in an Arizona reservation includes a grandmother, her daughters, their husbands, their children, and a University of Arizona anthropologist on research leave.

What goes around comes around, in a manner of speaking, and given that anthropologists collected reams and reams of information on Indians in the south-west, if any documentary evidence existed that would convince university offi-cials of the bona fide nature of the claims of the Apache members of the coalition, it would be found among the dusty notebooks of some long dead anthropologist.

Sure enough, right there in the Goodwin field notes recorded half a century ago, we found several Apaches retelling the story of the emergence of the Gaans from Mt. Graham. There were songs and chants about Mt. Graham as well; a wonder-ful story about a sacred white horse that lived on the mountain and much more about age-old Apache beliefs and connections to Mt. Graham.

The Goodwin field notes confirmed, virtually verbatim, what the Apache mem-bers of the Apache Survival Coalition were claiming about Mt. Graham—that the mountain was a sacred site for the Apaches, or at least some of the Apaches who remembered the old stories about the Mountain. Obviously, that part of the oral tradition identified in the Goodwin field notes as it related to Mt. Graham had survived among those Apache families whose members belonged to the Coalition. If the telescopes were built on Mt. Graham, the Gaans would be disturbed, and this would cause tremendous strife in the world according to their Apache vision of environmental justice.

A PRAYER TO MT. GRAHAM

It should come as little surprise to find out that Indian values and belief systems are not reflected in or accepted by our environmental law. The point that I have learned from working and talking with many Indian people is that this is precisely what is wrong with our environmental law.

In many Indian belief systems, you will find an intimate relation between the spiritual world, the physical world, and the social world. These three dimensions of human experience are all closely integrated in most Indian belief systems, an inte-gration which is totally alien to our environmental law. Indians have many ways to imagine and act upon this intimate relation between the spiritual, physical, and social worlds, but all of them basically boil down to a deep and abiding reverence for the land that sustains the interconnected worlds of the tribe. Without the land, in other words, there is no tribe. . . .

In the Goodwin field notes, I found an Apache song that was a prayer to Mt. Graham. It was sung before an Apache went to the mountain to hunt for deer so that the mountain's spirit and the Creator that controlled that spirit would give up its deer to the hunter. In the Apache belief system you pray to the mountain because it feeds you; or perhaps it would be more accurate to say that by your prayer to the mountain, you acknowledge your profound attitude of respect for the forces which give life to the complex world, where the human community is but a small part.

Thus, according to this Indian way of looking at Mt. Graham, you protect what a modern environmentalist might call the biodiversity of the mountain because it is that biodiversity which physically sustains you and the members of your tribe. It is a source of food and other forms of sustaining nourishment. It provides herbs and healing medicines. The Gaan story teaches that not only does Mt. Graham sustain you physically, but socially as well, because the sacred story of the Gaans connects the tribal community around a set of cohesive values which define tribal social life. The tribal society is sustained by the mountain's life-giving forces. Protecting Mt. Graham fulfills our obligations to the future generations which will constitute the tribal society. And the Gaan story also illuminates how the mountain sustains us spiritually, because those values represented by the story connect us to a transcendent vision of our place in the world. Mt. Graham is a powerful representation of the life-sustaining forces provided by the Creator. Trouble for the people will ensue if the mountain is not treated properly with respect and humility. The spiritual, the physical, and the social worlds are all integrated under this overarching vision of the Gaans emerging from Mt. Graham to give the medicine to the Apaches and returning to rest within the mountain, to be respectfully worshiped by the Apaches.

Our environmental law is simply incapable of reflecting the types of connection that the story of the Gaans on Mt. Graham can teach us. According to this Indian vision of environmental justice, if the mountain is threatened, the people are threatened, and the Gaans will emerge to wreak havoc on the world. The Gaans help the Apaches imagine their connection to the mountain and the importance of protecting that connection because Mt. Graham is a very special place. It is sacred because it sustains the Apaches spiritually, socially, and physically. . . .

"WHO PROTECTS THE LAW FROM HUMANS THEN?" THE GRANDFATHER ASKED

. . .

In Indian visions of environmental justice the idea that "the earth and its community of life should be 'untrammeled,'" thus disconnected from humans, is seen as an odd concept. There are sacred places, which should be approached with reverence, and in some instances, only by those properly trained in the rituals of respect for such places. Humans, however, are generally not viewed as mere visitors. . . . [H]umans are connected to the land, and a law that fails to recognize that connection will not likely be respected for long by humans.[25] I wonder, though, whether the best way to protect [the earth and its community of life] is to legislate their separateness from us into law. It is hard to respect what we do not feel connected to, whether it be a parent, our Creator, or a mountain wilderness.

I am not saying that we should not protect our wilderness. . . . I have already discussed Section 7 of the Endangered Species Act, which has played such a prominent note in the Mt. Graham controversy. Section 7 reads in pertinent part:

> "Each Federal agency shall . . . insure that any action authorized, funded, or carried out by such agency (hereinafter in this section referred to as an "agency action") is not likely to jeopardize the continued existence of any endangered species or threatened species or result in the destruction or adverse modification of habitat of such species which is determined . . . to be critical . . . ."[26]

Indian people have little problem with understanding why Section 7 is a good law—if the salmon aren't running, it threatens the social life of the tribe, and this is the punishment that is inflicted on the tribe for failing to act as a steward of the resource—a sacred duty. In Indian visions of environmental justice, there is a strong sense that protecting a resource which sustains the tribe physically, and around which so much of the social life of the tribe revolves, is a sacred duty. And these connections are reinforced by stories and myths which illuminate the spiritual relation between that resource and the human community. "Men and women," as seen according to Indian visions of environmental justice, "are members of a community that includes all beings . . . all beings have spirit . . . human-to-human relationships are similar to human-to-animal and human-to-plant relationships."[27] But what happens when our connection to that resource and its habitat have been severed, when we are no longer reliant on the resource for our sustenance and when maintaining species habitat appears as a luxury compared to other options. Our environmental law simply designates the species as endangered, in the hopes that the designation itself will suffice as a symbol for a set of larger meanings about the importance to us, as human beings, of preserving environmental values. The Mt. Graham controversy demonstrates, however, that this is not enough. If we as humans do not feel somehow connected to the red squirrel, we can simply change our environmental law.

THE FOREST SERVICE'S DRAFT ENVIRONMENTAL IMPACT STATEMENT

What I found most depressing about the Mt. Graham controversy is that the perverse system of values which has colonized our environmental law has so little difficulty in dismissing the relevance of Indian visions of environmental justice embodied in stories like the Gaans on Mt. Graham. It dismisses these visions through various mechanisms which have institutionalized environmental racism against Indian peoples at the deepest levels of our society.

In 1985, the Forest Service located what it termed three "shrines," consisting of various Indian artifacts on two of Mt. Graham's summits—Hawk Peak and High Peak. Because of the shrines' potential religious significance, the University of Arizona, working with the Forest Service, contacted nineteen local tribes concerning the find, including the San Carlos Apache. Two tribes, the Ak-Chin and Hopi, responded.

Subsequently, the University of Arizona prepared a report on the shrines and sent copies to the Forest Service and a number of tribes, including the San Carlos Apache, informed of the existence of the shrines. Although the Apache did not respond, representatives of the Zuni tribe of New Mexico requested permission to visit the site. After consultation with the Zuni, the Forest Service determined that the telescopes would have no adverse impact on the cultural sites it had identified. The Forest Service's Draft Environmental Impact Statement ("DEIS"), published in October 1986, was sent to the San Carlos Apache, and to other interest groups and tribes.

In May 1988, the Forest Service asked the San Carlos Apache and other tribes if they wished to receive a copy of the final EIS or to remain on the Forest Service's mailing list. The San Carlos Apache asked to be removed from the mailing list. The Forest Service kept the Tribe on the list anyway. The final EIS issued in the fall of 1988 stated that no further cultural resources had been discovered in the Mt. Graham area since the original discoveries. A copy of this final EIS was sent to the San Carlos Apache.

In late August 1990, some two years after the issuance of the final EIS, the San Carlos Apache Tribal Chairman informed the Forest Service of the religious importance of Mt. Graham to the Tribe. The chairman denied receipt of any prior correspondence and asked the Forest Service to halt construction immediately. The tribe failed to respond to a request by the Forest Service for information concerning specific sites that were of interest to the San Carlos Apache Tribe. Another letter was sent to the Service in June 1991, again demanding a halt to construction of the three telescopes. The tribe chose not to respond to the Service's request for a meeting to discuss their concerns. Instead, the tribe turned to the courts.

THE SAN CARLOS APACHE "COMMUNITY"

From the university's perspective, any rights—moral or legal—that the Apaches might have had to protest the telescope project on Mt. Graham had been waived by the San Carlos Apache Tribal governments' failure to formally respond in a timely fashion, or even at all, to the various Forest Service initiatives designed to inform the tribe about the project. The fact that the Tribal Government had not formally responded has been continually cited by university administrators to buttress their deeply-held convictions that the environmentalists had found some Indians to front for them. In reality, the process by which Indian peoples, be they Apaches or members of other tribes, were supposed to voice their visions on their connections to Mt. Graham had been, in effect, colonized by a system of values antithetical to achieving environmental justice for Indian peoples.

The San Carlos Apache Community is not a "community" at all, at least in the way that a non-Indian would normally understand that concept. The reservation is comprised of an amalgamation of Western Apache bands—Arivaipa, Tontos, Yavapais, Coyoteros, Chiricahuas, Mimbrenos—that were placed on the San Carlos reservation by the United States Army in the nineteenth century. Some of these bands included Apaches who were among the most recalcitrant and violent resisters to the United States' reservation policy. The Chiricahuas at San Carlos, for example, who recognized Geronimo as their leader, had been implacably hostile to invading whites. Other Apaches among these bands, however, had a long history of friendship and cooperation with the Army. Factionalism was further inbred from the start of the reservation's creation because many of these Apache groups had never been associated with each other. Even to this day, factionalism has never been eliminated as a dominant, defining fact of "community" life on the San Carlos reservation.[28]

Oftentimes, this factionalism expressed itself in a contest between various religious rivalries on the reservation. In the 1880s, at Cibecue on the reservation, an Apache shaman named Nocadelklinny led a messianic movement urging the destruction of all whites. The reservation failed to unite behind this movement, which was eventually crushed with the aid of army troops from New Mexico. In the 1920s, a split developed between the various Christian sects that had arisen on the reservation as a result of missionary activities. The "Holy Ground" movement, developed by an Apache spiritual leader named Silas John, and centered in the Bylas region of the reservation, was one by-product of this split. In the 1930s, a group of Apaches who had been members of the Lutheran church broke off and formed the Apache Independent Church. Religion, in other words, has always been a point of community factionalism, and not consensus, among the San Carlos Apaches.

These same propensities for factionalism were reflected in the reservation government in the 1920s and 30s. The BIA superintendents formed the government at San Carlos by gathering about themselves Apaches and Yavapais who could speak English fairly well, and who in the words of noted historian Edward Spicer, "were disposed to cooperate with the superintendent and his plans."[29]

The BIA's principal reason for forming the Tribal "Business Committee," as it came to be called, was so that the federal government could have some group to deal with in connection with the water rights and other issues that were arising at the time as a result of the Coolidge Dam Irrigation Project. To the BIA, it did not matter whether the Business Committee was a representative group; what mattered was that it fulfilled the legal requirements of signing agreements under the tribal name. Not surprisingly, the Committee became a focal point of opposition on the reservation and remains so to this day.

The fact is that the Apaches had never ruled themselves according to the type of "tribal government" that the BIA had provided for them, at least prior to their colonization by the United States. Apaches traditionally organize themselves at the band level, and to many Apaches, the idea that a BIA-created "tribal government" represents their interests generally, or particularly on issues of religious belief, is offensive and resisted in the extreme. The San Carlos Apache Community remains a reservation of many Apache communities, and depending upon where an individual Apache lives and what family he or she belongs to, an individual's views on tribal politics, where sovereignty resides in the tribe, and who is responsible for protecting the religious traditions of the tribe will differ dramatically.

INVASION OF THE LUTHERANIZERS

After learning about the claims of the Apache Survival Coalition, the university did try to immediately initiate contact with the San Carlos Apache tribal government. The tribal government was headed at that time by a chairman named Buck Kitcheyan, who told the university that the Apaches in the Coalition were a group of dissidents displeased with his administration and were allowing themselves to be manipulated by environmentalists, whom Kitcheyan called "outsiders." Chairman Kitcheyan told the university that none of the Apaches he had asked thought Mt. Graham was sacred. He said the members of the Coalition were just a group of malcontents determined to embarrass him in the upcoming tribal election by asserting that he, as tribal chairman, had failed to respond to the Forest Service inquiries about Mt. Graham, and therefore, had failed to protect Apache religious traditions.

Given the factionalized nature of the politics and religious life of the San Carlos reservation, it did not take a genius, or even much less, a cultural anthropologist, to figure that there must be another side to the story Kitcheyan was telling the university. The Apache members of the Apache Survival Coalition I spoke with, in fact, consistently spoke of the "tribal government people" as having been "Lutheranized." In other words, Lutheran missionaries had converted their families in the late nineteenth and early twentieth centuries, and those Apaches had subsequently forgotten or abandoned the Apache religious traditions. Such "Lutheranized" Apaches would not have known that Mt. Graham was sacred to some of the Apaches in a particular region of the reservation where traditional Apache beliefs had been maintained through oral tradition and stories. Trying to explain the complexities of Apache politics and the conflicting religious belief systems that intersected those politics to the scientists and to university administrations involved in Mt. Graham, of course, was not going to be an easy task. They simply wanted to build their telescopes and had no interest in political and religious factionalism on the San Carlos Apache Reservation, except to the extent that it might interfere with their plans.

Of course, our environmental law makes it so that they do not have to worry about such things. As has been seen with the process leading up to the Mt. Graham controversy, the various laws and regulatory procedures designed to incorporate Indians into the federal environmental and land use planning process need a point of access to identify tribal interests. Who do you contact if you are the University of Arizona or the United States Forest Service? Why, the tribal government, of course; but who is the tribal government, and where does tribal sovereignty reside? These are questions that our environmental law, colonized by the same system of values which colonized Indian tribes, does not bother to even ask.

The Mt. Graham controversy illustrates perfectly how the processes of our environmental law subtly perpetuate colonialism against Indian peoples. The history of treaties between tribes and the federal government teaches us how the United States would frequently designate a tribal "chief" to sell out the territorial interests of his people, or how the BIA would form a tribal government to facilitate surrender of tribal resources. From the perspective of the white man's law, these "chiefs" and these "governments" represented the Indians. In truth, these processes had little to do with how Indians actually governed themselves.

The history of the Apaches demonstrates the incommensurability of these processes, which have now been incorporated into our environmental laws, with tribal values and social life. And the Mt. Graham controversy demonstrates how our environmental law perpetuates the legacy of European colonialism and racism against American Indian peoples.[30] Historically, Indians have been required to conform to the dominant society's values, without any recognition of the values that might govern Indian social life. There are no alternatives by which the great diversity within Indian communities and across Indian country can be recognized and reflected in our environmental law. Thus, our environmental law tells Indians that they must run their governments the same way that the dominant society runs its governments. This means that when the tribal government in a factionalized Indian community fails to respond to a request from the Forest Service about the tribal community's religious interests in a mountain, our environmental law can treat the tribe as having no religious interests in that mountain at all. Indians can only engage in the federal land use and environmental regulatory process through cultural and political institutions determined by the dominant society.

Of course, the irony of all this concern over the method for incorporating Indians into the environmental regulatory process is that even if a way could be found so that tribal religious interests are adequately represented, our environmental law is not required to respect or protect those interests. This was the basic point that university counsel kept hammering away throughout this stage of the Mt. Graham controversy. The university, under our environmental law, does not have to worry about Apache religious claims to the mountain, because under the Supreme Court's *Lyng* case,[31] the telescope is on public land and there is no such thing as a religious easement for Indian tribes.

NEVER ASK THE CREATOR FOR ANYTHING

As was once explained to me by one of the Apaches, whenever an Apache prays to the Creator, he or she should only give thanks, because the Creator, through the Gaans, has given the Apache everything needed to live on this earth. An Apache, therefore, should never ask the Creator for anything. An Apache does have a responsibility, however, to protect the source from which these gifts flow. That is why the Apache members of the Coalition opposed construction of large binocular telescopes on Mt. Graham.

Now you can imagine how our scientists reacted to all of this: "Why aren't the Apaches like the Zuni?" they asked. "The Zunis wanted to look out of our telescopes once they were built." Well, the Apaches aren't like the Zunis in a number of ways. In fact, the Zunis have a very cohesive governing system that operates along traditional theocratic lines. It is no coincidence that the Zunis responded to the Forest Service letter and the Apaches did not. The Zuni government and their spiritual traditions remain integrated in a way that the Apaches have not been able yet to achieve, given their factionalized history. Our scientists would then ask, "How can Mt. Graham be sacred to the Apaches if the tribal government said it wasn't sacred?" As I tried to explain, the tribal government was not necessarily representative of the Apaches on religious matters (as are few non-Indian governments for that matter when it comes to their non-Indian constituents' religious beliefs.) Perhaps, the thing I found most depressing was that none of the scientists wanted to discuss what might happen if the Gaans were disturbed. Most just simply snickered when I explained what the Apaches believed about that mountain and dismissed Apache concerns out of hand. If these were legitimate religious claims they asked, then why didn't the tribal government take the necessary steps to assert these claims under our environmental law? All I could answer was that our environmental law was not their environmental law.

CONCLUSION: RELIGIOUS, MAGICAL, FANATICAL BEHAVIOR

Emerson once wrote that you can judge the nature and values of a society by the way it relates to its land. Under our existing laws, the relation between the spiritual world, the physical world, and the social world has been disintegrated. For Indians, stories and narratives like the Gaan creation myth invoke the imaginative capacity to visualize the connections between the physical environment, the social welfare of the community, and the spiritual values that create the consensus in Indian communities as to whether a particular use of the environment is beneficial or harmful to the human community. For non-Indians, there are no stories and myths which can help us imagine why preserving biodiversity is something deeply connected to who and what we are in the world—only science, economic analysis, vaguely stated appeals to aesthetic sensibility, and symbols generated by the Endangered Species Act such as the red squirrel. None of these has proven capable of generating consensus in our society about the importance of environmental values such as biodiversity to the human community.

Our technological society has lost its sense of reliance on nature for survival, and therefore, we have lost our sense of respect for the world we inhabit. We have thus lost those stories and myths which once must have helped us see our connections to our own world. And so our environmental law has been impoverished of such metaphors as the Gaans on Mt. Graham. Indian resistance to siting a telescope on Mt. Graham seems like "religious, magical, fanatical behavior." The price we pay for maintaining our dying colonialism is to dismiss the decolonizing potential of these Indian visions of environmental justice. And until we do decolonize our environmental law, we always risk the danger of the Gaans reemerging from Mt. Graham to wreak havoc upon our world.

NOTES

1. Frantz Fanon, *A Dying Colonialism*, Translated from French by Haakon Chevalier, 1st Evergreen ed. New York, N.Y.: Grove Press, 1967. c. 1965.

2. See *Mt. Graham Red Squirrel v. Madigan*, 954 F.2d 1441 (9th Cir. 1992); see also Jack Kitt, "Would You Baptize an Extraterrestrial?", *N.Y. Times*, May 29, 1994 (magazine), at 36–39.

3. See, e.g., "The Navajo Concept of Justice, Judicial Branch of the Navajo Nation," 1988 Annual Report 1–2, reprinted in David H. Getches et al., *Federal Indian Law: Cases and Materials* St. Paul, Minn.: West Publishing, 1993, pp. 531–532.

The basic theme of Navajo thought, is harmony. . . . Traditionally in our society, the idea of being superior to a fellow Navajo or nature is discouraged. There is an innate knowledge in each one of us that we are to treat with respect all persons and nature with whom we share this world. As long as we behave in a humble manner to all parts of the universe we are in harmony. To behave in a humble manner is to act without thoughts of power or control, without unnecessary action against others and against nature.

Id. at 532.

Ronald L. Trosper, Director of the National Indian Policy Center at the George Washington University in his paper, "Traditional American Indian Economic Policy" (on file with author) concludes from a review of recent literature on American Indian world views that generally speaking, "American Indian cultures share an attitude of respect toward the world around us." Id. at 2. Trosper identifies four basic components, or assumptions, in the American Indian definition of respect:

1. Community: Men and women are members of a community that includes all beings . . . all beings have spirit . . . human-to-human relationships are similar to human-to-animal and human-to-plant relationships.

2. Connectedness: Everything is connected. While the idea of community provides a source of obligation and a guide to proper behavior, the idea of connectedness is a description of how the world is.

3. Seventh Generation: . . . past generations left us a legacy, and we have a duty to our great-grandchildren and beyond, as far as to the seventh generation.

4. Humility: In taking action, humanity should be humble. The natural world is powerful and well able to cause trouble if not treated properly.

Id. at 23.

For an insightful and original analysis of the conflict between American Indian environmental values and European worldviews on nature during the colonial era, see Carolyn Merchant, *Ecological Revolutions: Nature, Gender, and Science in New England.* Chapel Hill, N.C.: University of North Carolina Press, 1989.

4. Fanon, supra note 1.

5. 954 F.2d at 1441, *supra* note 2.

6. As Professor Malinowski has explained, myths provide "for cohesion for local patriotism, for a feeling of union and kinship in a community." Bronislaw Malinowski, *Myth in*

Primitive Psychology, in Magic, Science and Religion and Other Essays 94 (Robert Redfield, ed.). Garden City, N.Y.: Doubleday, 1948.

7. See, e.g., Kitt, supra note 2, at 39.

8. Id.

9. See "Living Land, Sacred Land (The Case Against the Mt. Graham Observatory)," published by the Mt. Graham Coalition (on file with author). This rather slickly produced public relations packet provides a wealth of useful information on Mt. Graham's unique environmental values, including the fact that it is "the only mountain range to stack five of the seven major ecosystems of North America in one place." Id. The packet, of course, represents the perspective of environmental opponents to the telescope project, but at least with respect to Mt. Graham's unique environmental values, it contains some generally reliable information.

In any event, from my own perspective of legal culture critic, for anyone who has visited the mountain, it would be difficult to make the case against Mt. Graham's unique environmental values. The controversy over the Mt. Graham Observatory in fact is not about the mountain's environmental values; it's about the damage that might be inflicted on those values by the University of Arizona's telescope project.

10. Id.

11. The reference here to "thinking like a mountain," of course, is to Aldo Leopold, *A Sand County Almanac and Sketches Here and There.* New York, N.Y.: Oxford University Press, 1949. What Leopold said, at least from within the cultural tradition in which he wrote a generation ago, remains true today; "There is yet no ethic dealing with man's relation to land and to the animals and plants which grow upon it. The key-log which must be moved to release the evolutionary process for an ethic is simply this. Quit thinking about decent land-use as solely an economic problem." Id. at 224–225.

12. Id.

13. See "Living Land, Sacred Land," supra note 9.

14. See National Environmental Policy Act, 42 U.S.C. sections 4321–4370c (1988).

15. 52 Fed. Reg. 20,994 (1987).

16. 954 F.2d at 1444, *supra* note 2 (emphasis added).

17. Id. at 1445.

18. The Arizona-Idaho Conservation Act, Title VI, Mount Graham International Observatory, Pub. L. No. 100-696, 102 Stat. 4571, 4597 (1988), splits the construction of the university's astrophysical complex into two phases. It first states that:

> Subject to the terms and conditions of Reasonable and Prudent Alternative Three of the Biological Opinion, the requirements of section 7 of the Endangered Species Act shall be deemed satisfied as to the issuance of a Special Use Authorization for the first three telescopes and the Secretary shall immediately approve the construction of . . . (1) three telescopes to be located on Emerald Peak; (2) necessary support facilities; and (3) an access road to the Site.

Id. section 602(a). The Act further provides that (t)he Secretary shall, subject to the requirements of the Endangered Species Act and other applicable law, authorize the construction of four additional telescopes on Emerald Peak. Consultation under section 7(a)(2) of the Endangered Species Act with respect to the four additional telescopes . . . shall consider, among other things, all biological data obtained from monitoring the impact of construction of the first three telescopes upon the Mount Graham Red Squirrel.

Id. section 603. The Act requires·that the university, with the concurrence of the Secretary of Agriculture, develop and implement a Management Plan "consistent with the requirements of the Endangered Species Act and with the terms and conditions of Reasonable and Prudent Alternative Three of the Biological Opinion, for the Site." Id. section 604(a). Finally, the Act modifies the provisions of Reasonable and Prudent Alternative Three in that it delays the closure of the summer homes and Bible Camp currently located on Mount Graham. Id. section 605.

19. 954 F.2d at 1457 *supra* note 2.

20. Mt. Graham, 954 F.2d at 1441.

21. See Zygmunt J.B. Plater et al., *Environmental Law and Policy: A Casebook on Nature, Law and Society.* St. Paul, Minn.: West Publishing, 1992 at 682–683.

22. See *supra* text accompanying note 25.

23. See 954 F.2d at 1448 *supra* note 2.

24. See *supra* note 3.

25. See id.

26. 16 U.S.C. section 1536(a)(2) (1988).

27. Trosper, *supra* note 3.

28. Edward H. Spicer, *Cycles of Conquest: The Impact of Spain, Mexico, and the United States on the Indians of the South West, 1533–1960.* Tucson, Ariz.: University of Arizona Press, 1962.

29. Id. at 259.

30. Robert A. Williams, Jr., "Documents of Barbarism," 31 *Arizona Law Review* 237 (1989).

31. *Lyng v. Northwest Cemetery Protective Association,* 485 U.S. 439 (1988).

Revision and Reversion

Vine Deloria, Jr.

During the trial of Robert Butler and Dino Robideaux for the killing of two FBI agents on the Pine Ridge Reservation in South Dakota in June 1975, a confidential Justice Department memo came into the possession of the defense team at Cedar Rapids, Iowa. This document purported to explain why the Justice Department had lost so many cases involving Wounded Knee defendants. The memo argued that individual United States Attorneys were the victims of a "roving band" of liberal attorneys and two leftist, revisionist historians, Dee Brown and Vine Deloria Jr., who overpowered and outmanned district office attorneys. Not surprisingly, the memo did not discuss the misconduct of federal agencies which had produced a dismissal of the Means-Banks trial for government pollution of the waters of justice.

The only time that Dee Brown and I were together, with the "roving band" at any rate, was the Means-Banks trial in Minneapolis, where we gave testimony on the circumstances surrounding the signing of the Treaty of 1868. Our testimony can be obtained from the federal courthouse there and it will show no effort to revise what is already recorded in numerous government documents. Thus we were "revisionists" in the sense that we introduced into the record materials that had not previously been used to understand that period of history. By contrast it is worth noting that the government's witness in the Lincoln, Nebraska, hearings on the same treaty, Dr. Joseph Cash of the University of South Dakota, testified that he was an expert on several books, which were wholly fictional titles satirically devised at breakfast to see whether Cash was familiar with the subject area. When pressed by the defense Cash admitted that the Indian version of the circumstances of the treaty was essentially correct. Cash, to my knowledge, is not regarded as a revisionist historian.

The identification of scholars working in the field of Indian-white relations has this strange quality to it: proponents of the Indian version of things become "revisionists," while advocates of the traditional white interpretation of events retain a

From *The American Indian and the Problem of History*, edited by Calvin Martin. New York, N.Y.: Oxford University Press. © 1987 by Oxford University Press.

measure of prestige and reputation. Often the controversy revolves about beliefs held so tenaciously that questioning the orthodox point of view becomes a personal offense. Some years ago I was working with Elliot Arnold on a TV scenario for Marlon Brando. I favorably mentioned Thomas Marquis's fine book, *Keep the Last Bullet for Yourself* (1976), in which Marquis suggested that Custer's green troops, fearful they might fall into the hands of the Sioux and be tortured, fired a few shots and then killed themselves. When I began to talk about Marquis's evidence, Elliot's hands began to shake. He screamed that he would not discuss Marquis under any circumstances. The idea that American soldiers might consider this measure was beyond the scope of his emotional conception of Western history.

So Indian-white relations have many more pitfalls than we would suspect and most of these obstacles have little to do with historical facts or data. They are remnants of beliefs derived from other areas of experience—patriotism, the movies, older books advocating manifest destiny, personal preferences derived from participation in Westerner Clubs. Whether we can clean out the emotional swamp of white America and recount Indian-white relations more objectively or whether we must continue to struggle with old beliefs and shibboleths when we could be doing more important work remains to be seen. There are hardly any subjects we might mention that do not have this heavy investment of emotions on the part of white writers and historians.

"Revisionist" seems to be the label applied indiscriminately to people taking the Indian side of the story. This classification is merely an effort to influence the manner in which we consider historical fact, not a true statement of the writer's intent. In many respects the writing that most needs revision is that which seems to favor Indians. It is not inaccurate, it is simply too generalized and tends to mislead Indians into adopting liberal myths instead of conservative myths. A true revisionist would seek more precise interpretation of data regardless of the orientation of the writer, and there are very few of these people writing Indian-white history. Let me give some examples of generalizations that seem favorably inclined toward Indians but actually have negative implications when they are seen within the context of contemporary Indian life.

The General Allotment Act, passed in 1887, gave the President the authority to negotiate with Indian tribes for the cession of lands the government felt were "surplus" to the reservations. As a result of this statute, which was actually a detailed policy directive, United States Indian Inspectors were sent to the various tribes to negotiate allotments and reduced reservations. A number of special commissions were authorized by Congress also, for example, the Crook Commission to the Sioux, and the Dawes Commission to the Five Civilized Tribes, and these commissions forced these larger tribes to agree to allotments and reduced land holdings. The government finally stopped these negotiations in 1914, when the agreement with the Ute Mountain Utes of Colorado was made. Some tribes agreed to reduced reservations but not to allotments: the Red Lake Chippewa and the Hopi saved their reservations from allotment, the Sioux reservations adopted allotment in later agreements after they had agreed to a reduced number of smaller reservations in 1889.

When writers deal with this topic, they seem to neglect the history of Indians over the thirty-year period following the General Allotment Act and give to this statute a power and effect that it certainly did not have at the time it was passed. Nearly all Indian writers adopt the interpretation that the *act itself* allotted the reservations. All the white writers I have read have accepted this interpretation without a hint that it might be too general an interpretation to be valid. Within this general interpretation of the General Allotment Act we find two basic themes. Some writers take a very sympathetic view and recite the series of disasters that befell Indian culture following the act. Other writers sternly see in allotment an inevitable process which helped to settle and civilize the western states.

A good deal of important history is overlooked when this interpretation of allotment is uncritically accepted. Almost all of the tribes who made agreements with the United States secured some additional legal rights, generally unique to their own situation, in these negotiations. Contemporary Indians, bureaucrats, and attorneys pursuing remedies for federal intrusions against the tribe are prone to overlook or denigrate the agreements because they do not seem to be a part of the general historical flow that they find in books describing the treatment of Indians by the federal government. Thus interpretations of *policy* are mistaken for statements about *history*.

Breaking treaties is another subject that lends itself to misinterpretation when inadequately researched or understood. The general theme of writers dealing with Indian-white relations when dealing with treaties is to adopt the interpretation that the United States "broke" every treaty it signed with the Indians. So deeply entrenched is this belief that a writer hazards his reputation by suggesting otherwise. Yet this phrase has many unfortunate connotations which make it a difficult and misleading characterization of the situation. First, not all treaties that were made with the Indians were treaties that provided legal rights or demanded federal responsibilities toward Indians. A good many of the treaties were simple recitations of friendship and goodwill which each party agreed to display toward the other. Apart from a resolution by Congress stating that it did not want to remain friendly with a tribe, it is difficult to see how such a document could be breached.

There is a question whether a treaty can be legally breached apart from a straightforward abrogation by one of the parties. Federal courts have traditionally used a device called "severability" to interpret treaties. To find severability in a treaty one separates the article that is the subject of controversy from the remainder of the document and comments on its validity or relevance in law. Some articles of treaties have been abrogated, others have become void with the passage of time or the fulfillment of conditions, and still others have been included in subsequent amendments. Nullification of one article does not void a treaty as a legal document; the single article under consideration becomes void, the remainder of the treaty holds.

The belief that all treaties have been broken has many by-products. Conservatives find their mustaches bristling as if this idea had breached the wall of sensibility and patriotism, also. Indians harbor deep resentment against a society which so blithely breaks its word. Liberals wring their hands in anguish and find further evidence of a monstrous conspiracy to trample a helpless people. The simple fact is that the statement that all treaties have been broken is a moral rather than an historical judgment. Yet when it appears in historical writing without some explanatory comment it takes on wholly different connotations and triggers a set of responses, predictable to the last ounce of emotion, which are unwarranted. Tribes still enforce their treaty rights even though few people believe that the treaties have any efficacy at all.

People writing on the Indian Reorganization Act generally characterize this statute as the first opportunity Indians had for self-government in this century. Since the Indian Reorganization Act is the major policy shift that counteracts the effects of allotment, it is usually discussed as the reversal of allotment, and self-government is seen as an innovation devised by John Collier and Felix Cohen. Indians are generally described as greeting the opportunity to govern themselves with unrestrained enthusiasm. A great deal of this optimistic aura surrounding the Indian Reorganization Act comes from Collier's own writings, which describe in anecdotal form some of the successes that tribes enjoyed after operating under the provisions of the act for several years.

The fact is that tribes maintained some identifiable form of government long before the Indian Reorganization Act. The Five Civilized Tribes, for example, continued to hold meetings even though their governments had been reduced to presidentially appointed chiefs with little to do except appear at Fourth of July celebrations. The Sioux continued traditional forms of government in the Black Hills Treaty Council, the Chippewas continued to operate under traditional chiefs as did the Umatillas and other tribes. The Klamaths and Nooksacks had already adopted constitutions and by-laws decades before the Indian Reorganization Act. The effect of the act, when all is said and done, was to recognize the tribal governments as federal corporations and to require them to adopt new constitutions and by-laws approved by the Department of the Interior. Existing political powers of the tribes were clarified in law.

Indians and others reading descriptions of the Indian Reorganization Act come to believe that prior to its passage the people on the reservation had no institutions that could represent them, and did not know how to go about forming such groups. When traditional Indians raise complaints about the high-handed tactics of the Bureau of Indian Affairs in getting the tribes to adopt the IRA, or accuse the existing tribal government of being a white man's government, they have a great deal of historical fact behind their arguments, but these data are completely obscured by the mass of writing which suggests otherwise.

These examples could be multiplied many times with other specific topics. The cumulative weight of evidence would seem to suggest that when we speak of revisionists we are really speaking of people working with more data and seeking more precise articulations of the historical incidents and developments under consideration. If we return to Marquis's theory concerning the Little Big Horn, we would note painstakingly precise counts of the expended cartridges found at the sites where the soldiers' bodies were located and a comparison of these sites with other known battles in which no survivors were able to tell the white man's side of the story. Indications, according to Marquis, based on more precise use of evidence that had never before been considered, show that the soldiers fired a few times and then killed themselves. Where large piles of cartridges were found, there were also found the bodies of experienced Indian fighters and impressions where a number of Indians fell. This conclusion is simply more precise; emotional response to it calls it revisionist, as if Marquis were attempting to change history for his own purposes.

We should probably classify people who write on Indian-white relations as revisionists and reversionists: those who bring more data into their schemes of interpretation and thereby gain additional precision in describing the situation, and those who revert to older, more accepted ways of describing historical events without bothering to check the data to see if they really support the orthodox rendering of the situation. If this classification were accepted we would have a giant crowd of reversionists and a few isolated revisionists, and within the large crowd of reversionists we would have two camps, liberals and conservatives. Such a classification would cut across the whole spectrum of writing on Indian-white relations and include most Indian writers in the reversionist camp.

A great need exists, and will continue to exist, for more revisionist writers. When the cumulative impact of continuous misinterpretation of historical events is surveyed and appraised we will find that much of what passes for history dealing with Indians and whites is a mythological treatment of the development of policy disguised as history. We can grant that the General Allotment Act established an intellectual milieu within which a number of readily definable things happened to Indians and Indian properties, without negating the historical period that followed and the events of that era which have influenced the subsequent course of events, and continue to be influential today.

Political history is but one aspect of the much larger task of writing more precise treatments of developments, events, and personalities. The treatment of Indian religion begs to have a complete overhaul. Publications in that field today have such an aura of the exotic and mystical it is difficult to distinguish fact from fiction. Pre-Columbian history is another subject that begs further study. Orthodoxy insists on the preservation of certain themes and much evidence is collected to support those themes without a thought for alternative explanations.

The origin of our problem in writing more accurate and precise books and articles on Indian-white relations lies in the educational system itself. Throughout our academic careers we are fed summaries and generalizations which are acceptable because they require little imagination and less thought. By the time we recognize that the comfortable and uniform version of human experiences we have learned is not accurate, we have already taken much misinformation and misinterpretation into ourselves and have great difficulty in separating fact from mythology. Our academic institutions, from primary school through graduate study, all assume that at some later date we will adopt the posture of the cultivated, educated man, don our smoking jackets, and sit comfortably in our easy chairs filling in the gaps in our education. Unfortunately, the pace of modern life precludes almost all of us from even contemplating this luxury, and we know only that bit of history that we have managed to remember from what we have heard or have had the opportunity to read.

Bringing this confusion regarding Indian-white relations into some new and, one hopes, better orthodoxy by which we can become enlightened seems a forlorn hope at best. The qualifications for writing in the field of Indian-white relations now seem to be only sincerity and the confession that the writer has "always been interested in Indians." Exactly what that phrase means is never made clear. Presumably the attractiveness of the subject matter and the lack of clarity make it a field that appears to have many hidden and exotic secrets which need to be unfolded. The great mass of material in the field, much of which has not been brought into the arena of popular consumption, suggests that all of us could labor the remainder of our natural lives without acquiring a more precise knowledge of our subject.

We should, perhaps, popularize the idea of reversionism because it may act as a motivating force to encourage the next generation to undertake more precise renderings of this theme of Indian-white relations without lapsing into a recitation of the ideas that have been already articulated. Each generation should build on the accomplishments of its predecessors, yet writers in the area of Indian-white relations have not benefited from this expectation that knowledge eventually will be cumulative. Let us hope that more acquaintance with the source materials will produce some better writing in the future.

CHAPTER 4

THE REPATRIATION OF CULTURAL PROPERTY

To say the nineteenth century was one of destruction and diaspora for Native American peoples is an understatement. Great expanses of tribal lands made their way into nonnative hands during this period, and in the process, vast quantities of tribal cultural items were lost, stolen, or left behind as Native groups fled violence or were removed from their homes. Indigenous peoples were forced to leave their ancestral burial sites behind, unattended. The desecration of those sites became the foundation of physical anthropology in the U.S., as the excerpt by anthropologist Robert Bieder explains. Bieder presented his research to Congress, in conjunction with the Native American Rights Fund, during hearings on the Native American Graves Protection and Repatriation Act (NAGPRA), which was enacted in 1990.[1]

European Americans exhumed Native American grave sites, Bieder says, because those sites gave ready access to indigenous skeletal remains and grave artifacts. Ancestors and ceremonial items were taken from their final resting places, often so that anatomists and, later, phrenologists could conduct what they called scientific studies. Anatomists did this by mapping the gross anatomy of the brain and its influence on the skull; phrenologists, by positing a direct link between brain anatomy and particular human behaviors and characteristics. One methodology of these practices was to measure skulls of different races so as to draw comparisons about brain size. From this "data" the anatomists and phrenologists drew the racist conclusion that Caucasians were the most intelligent race on earth since they had the largest average skull measurement overall. Samuel George Morton, a professor of anatomy at the prestigious Philadelphia Medical College and the president of the Academy of Natural Science in Philadelphia, concluded in his

Catalogue of Skulls of Man and the Inferior Animals (1849), for example, that the Caucasian brain was the largest in the "Races and Families of Man." He decided this after measuring 623 crania.

Anatomy of this sort was eventually recognized as quackery; so was phrenology. But not before human remains, organs, brains, and mountains of skulls were stolen from tribal grave sites for the sake of measurement. Also stolen was the property that lay buried with the human remains. In this way artifacts, funerary objects, and the like made their way to museums, university collections, private studies, art markets, and antiquities markets, where eventually they began to circulate in nonnative communities.

Not surprisingly, the activity of phrenologists gave support to the Indian removal policies of the nineteenth century. The massive grab of Native American land was often justified on the racist theory that Native American peoples were inferior to Caucasians. Later policies mandating removal, allotment, suppression of religious expression, and the like were passed on similar grounds. For example, George Combs, a Scottish phrenologist who wrote *A System of Phrenology* (1843), provided an anatomical reason for why Native Americans could be moved from tribal lands without fear of mental distress on the part of the relocatees. Combs wrote:

> *Concentrativeness:* Observation proves that this is a distinct organ [of the brain which] . . . [i]s large in those animals and persons who are extremely attached to their country, while others are readily induced to migrate. Some tribes of American Indians and Tartars wander without fixed habitation.[2]

The implication of this finding was that Native Americans could be removed from their homelands without consequence, since phrenology proved that the area of "concentrativeness" in their brains was small and hence that their understanding of place was limited.

In addition, it was widely believed that though Native Americans may have been uncivilized, they were exempt from insanity, and thus, presumably, from whatever break in spirit might lead to it. The 1845 editor of the *American Journal of Insanity* wrote about "the exemption of Cherokee Indians and Africans from insanity."[3] The Army Medical Officer who oversaw the removal of the Cherokee from Georgia, a process that began in 1838 and resulted in the death of thousands of Cherokees, reported that he never saw or heard of a case of insanity among the relocatees.[4]

In one sense, phrenology gave settler societies permission to ignore the human suffering that removal policies begot. These policies assumed an Orwellian air to be sure, because while they menacingly *functioned* as methods for divesting Native Americans of massive amounts of property, they were *characterized* as policies through which (presumably genetically superior) Caucasians could "help" (presumably genetically inferior) Native Americans. The so-called help was to take two forms. First, removal, as authorized by the Removal Act of 1830,[5] would help preserve Native American political integrity by moving the tribes out of the

path of nonnative settlement. The two foundational cases of federal Indian law—
Cherokee Nation v. Georgia[6] and *Worcester v. Georgia*[7]—articulate this rationale.
Second, removal, allotment, suppression of ceremonial practices, and the extension of federal criminal jurisdiction into tribal territory were all rationalized as
policies that would help Native Americans along the evolutionary path posited by
social Darwinists.

In addition, the desecration of tribal graves, called a scientific endeavor by those
engaging in it, was done with little thought to excavation or identification. So,
although vast collections of tribal human remains and property were amassed in
the nineteenth century, they have little or no scientific value today. But even if
these collections had been acquired with careful attention to the science of it all,
ethical questions would still linger over the use of this material, just as ethical
questions lingered for so long over a related practice of housing Native persons in
museums as cultural exhibits.

Kenn Harper's account studies the human exhibit phenomenon. Harper's
excerpt is about Minik Wallace, one of the six Inuit persons whom Lieutenant
(later Admiral) Robert Peary brought from Greenland to the American Museum of
Natural History in New York as exhibits of study. The Inuit arrived in New York
on September 30, 1897; Minik was a child at the time, probably only seven or
eight years old.

Within two weeks of their arrival, the *New York Times* reported that the Inuit
had caught "cold," and that their efforts to ward off illness were "a source of
amusement to several scores of visitors . . ." Describing the Inuit exhibit in full
detail, the story concluded:

> "[O]ne of the most amusing forms of entertainment consisted in an illustra-
> tion of the manner in which the Eskimos attempt to conjure away illness.
> This in their opinion can only be accomplished by rubbing the sides of the
> body and singing a weird sort of lullaby that with all its peculiarities is not
> absolutely discordant."[8]

Harper analyzes this event differently. For Harper, the presence in the group of
the shaman, Atangana, made it more likely than not that this particular Inuit
healing ceremony was a serious matter, especially under the circumstances, since
two weeks later, by October 11, 1897 as the *New York Times* story notes, all six
Inuit were sick with colds and fever. By November 1, 1897, they were admitted to
Bellevue Hospital with tuberculosis. By February, Qisuk, Minik's father, was dead.
Atangana and two others died shortly thereafter. In the end, only two of the six
Inuit travelers survived: an adult, Uisaakassak, who later returned to Greenland,
and Minik, who was adopted by William Wallace, the building superintendent at
the American Museum of Natural History.

Harper's excerpt is additionally telling because it describes two points of history
that the American Museum of Natural History was less than open about until
recently. The first is how Minik was fooled by museum patricians into believing that
his father had been given a modified, but still proper, Inuit burial; and the second

was how, as a teenager, Minik discovered that his father's skeleton was on display in the American Museum of Natural History. Harper, an amateur historian, uses newspaper coverage of the Smith Sound Inuit as his primary source material, presenting it in a frame that, through its own language, gives a sense of the callousness the Inuit must have faced, even given the cultural context of the time. Based partly on Harper's efforts to tell the story of the Smith Sound Inuit, the American Museum of Natural History agreed to repatriate four Inuit skeletons to Qunaaq, Greenland for a proper Inuit burial. The remains were flown back in 1993. One of these skeletons was Qisuk, Minik's father. Minik, who died of the flu, lies buried in Pittsburg, New Hampshire.[9]

Other Native Americans have been housed as living museum exhibits. Perhaps the most famous was Ishi. Ishi—a Yahi word meaning *man*—was a survivor of the massacres and bounties put on Native Americans in Northern California during the gold rush. After months of hiding in the hills of northeastern California, Ishi found his way to a small mining town called Oroville, on the Feather River. Over time he was released into the custody of Dr. Alfred Kroeber, who was the director of the University of California Museum of Anthropology, then in San Francisco, today in Berkeley, California.

Ishi's story is heavily documented by scholars, journalists, and amateur historians. Theodora Kroeber's account, *Ishi: The Last of His Tribe* (1973), is perhaps the most widely read.[10] As a text, Kroeber's book has a quality similar to Harper's work. Indeed, one could place the two works in the same genre in terms of substance, style, and method. Originally titled *Ishi: the Last of the Wild Indians*, Kroeber's work assumes a social Darwinist frame, and so fails to grapple with the ethical questions that attend housing human beings as museum exhibits. Harper's work, on the other hand, because it does not take social Darwinism as a given, addresses these ethical issues directly. In addition, Kroeber assumed that the museum had done Ishi a great personal service against which all other ethical questions necessarily faded. For instance, Theodora Kroeber implies in the introduction to a later book about Ishi, *Ishi the Last Yahi: A Documentary History* (1979), that had Ishi not been released into the custody of Dr. Kroeber, he would have been sent to live with other Native Americans, a worse fate in Kroeber's estimation.[11] But while Ishi may indeed have benefitted from the museum as a place to live, the idea that his physical comfort minimized other discomforts cannot justify the disservice to Ishi or other Native Americans that the human exhibit phenomenon engendered. While Theodora Kroeber's popular book describes Ishi's isolation, as well as his shock and sadness at finding the material goods of his people in the museum's collection, Kroeber, like so many before and after her, never questioned or doubted the museum's right to possess and ultimately assert title to the indigenous human remains or tribal items included within its collections.

Ishi's language was Yahi, a dialect of Yana, which is a language that is itself part of the still-spoken Hokan language group. Therefore, Ishi is survived by tribes and persons with whom he shared a prehistoric relation; he is probably also survived by Yahi descendants of mixed parentage. Under NAGPRA, these persons have the right to request both return of Ishi's personal belongings and return of other Yahi objects from the museum's collection. However, this right can be asserted only if the requested objects are definable as items of cultural patrimony within the context of the claimant's own tribal culture.

Like the Indian Claims Commission Act discussed in Chapter 2, NAGPRA was passed to redress long-standing tribal claims. But whereas the Indian Claims Commission Act dealt primarily with land claims, NAGPRA itself applies exclusively to claims for human remains and cultural objects. Furthermore, since NAGPRA was passed as human rights legislation whose ultimate purpose is to ensure tribal cultural preservation, it carries within its legislative history a mandate for liberal interpretation. Just how effectively NAGPRA will work to repatriate cultural property to its rightful tribal owners is still uncertain.[12]

Specifically, NAGPRA works by suspending state law deadlines for bringing property claims, thus shielding tribal owners from the operation of state time bars. Time-bar statutes, or statutes of limitation, are implicated because federal courts often borrow state laws in property cases. Since state jurisdictions rely on statutes of limitation to bar stale claims, when federal courts borrow state statutes and apply them in a federal forum, the effect is to render tribal owners' claims stale. NAGPRA addresses this problem.

State statutes of limitation not only bar stale claims, they also vest title in the person or institution that has the current superior right to the property. As the saying goes, possession is nine-tenths of the law, so a "current superior right" is more often than not determined simply by mere possession. In a tribal property context, this mean that nonnative possessors are more likely than native owners to go into court, under state law, as the designated superior right holders. Because of state statutes of limitation, title to cultural items (or rights to human remains) are more likely to vest in museums, vendors, private collectors, scholars, and government agencies, depending on their status as possessors, not in tribal persons or entities. NAGPRA is key to changing this legal direction. But despite NAGPRA's power to extend the time in which a claim for cultural property can be made in federal court, NAGPRA is not an automatic return statute. NAGPRA simply lifts the time bar to reclaiming property; all other legal barriers to proving title remain.

The final three excerpts in this chapter address the legalities of passing human rights legislation that functionally circumvents state statutes, such as statutes of limitation, and policies, such as those barring stale claims. Jack Trope and Walter Echohawk discuss how, in the U.S., initiating the return of tribal property requires frank discussions about why and how state laws do not protect tribal interests, especially with respect to burial practices. In addition, they explain why federal action was and still is required in this area for a number of reasons, the most pressing of which are taken up in the Congressional testimony that follows Trope and Echohawk's excerpt.

Just as the Indian Claims Commission Act was important reparations legislation, so too is NAGPRA. The ICC Act was envisioned and implemented without the substantive participation of Native Americans. NAGPRA, on the other hand, was enacted at the insistence and direction of Native American constituents. Its very terms envision the substantive participation of tribal actors, and particularly of tribal governments, as Dr. Rennard Strickland points out. Dr. Strickland's excerpt underscores the power and corresponding responsibility that tribes have to define the words and concepts upon which NAGPRA claims are based, words such as "sacred," "cultural patrimony," and even "human remains."

As debated before Congress, NAGPRA had almost complete support from the national museum community. However, whether NAGPRA will work to return personal property to its tribal owners, or to ensure that Native American human remains are repatriated for proper burial, will also depend on the ground-level compliance of museums, scientists, ethnic art dealers, and the like, many of whom also work as or directly with international agents.

Not surprisingly, repatriation has received international attention.[13] The term "cultural property" was coined by the United Nations Educational, Scientific and Cultural Organization (UNESCO) Convention for the Protection of Cultural Property in the Event of Armed Conflict—known as the Hague Convention—in 1954. It was defined more fully in the 1970 UNESCO Convention on the Means of Prohibiting and Preventing the Illicit Import, Export and Transfer of Ownership of Cultural Property. The later Convention defined cultural property as "property which, on religious or secular grounds, is specifically designated by each State as being of importance for archaeology, prehistory, history, literature, art or science."

The Aymara, who are indigenous to what is now Bolivia, gained international support in 1988 under the 1970 UNESCO Convention for the return of sacred weavings that disappeared in 1978 during visits by North American ethnic art and antiquities dealers. The Kwakiotl, indigenous to what is now Canada, invoked the 1970 UNESCO Convention to repatriate items that were taken when a potlatch ceremony was disrupted by police in 1922, under laws that banned potlatching in Canada during the period from 1884 to 1951. Thus, NAGPRA's repatriation structure is a viable one that comports with international trends.

On its face, NAGPRA provides as follows. Ownership or control of any cultural items excavated or discovered on federal or tribal lands go first to lineal descendants of the original decedent, in the case of human remains and funerary objects, or to the lineal descendants of the original owner, in the case of cultural property. If no lineal descendants can be ascertained, then ownership or control goes to the tribe upon whose land the object was found, or, alternatively, to the tribe that has the closest cultural affiliation to the object. To qualify under these sections, tribes must show recognized title to the land upon which the remains or items were found, or, alternatively, aboriginal title recognized through the Indian Claims Commission process. Items found on federal land or land under federal control are also subject to NAGPRA's provisions.

Terms such as "Indian Tribe" and "Native American" are broadly defined by NAGPRA,[14] and the statute brings Native Hawaiian and Native Alaskan groups within its terms as well. Nevertheless, the tribal identity issues covered in Chapter 1 are implicated by NAGPRA, since once a tribe has been notified about the discovery of remains or cultural items, it must prove its cultural affiliation to the object. This proof is made through standard methods of status identification:

BIA recognition, recognized title boundaries, aboriginal title boundaries, definitions of terms like indigenous, and the like.

Post-NAGPRA excavation can only proceed if authorized by a valid federal permit. Hence should a scientist, for example, decide to conduct an archeological dig, she will need to first get a federal permit. Inadvertent finders of tribal human remains and cultural objects must report their discoveries to federal authorities. Discoveries made during a construction, logging, mining, or agricultural project theoretically bring the project to a halt until the developer can make a reasonable effort to protect the cultural items.

The first case on this issue was *Abenaki Nation of Mississquoi v. Hughes.*[15] The Abenaki Nation lacked formal status as a tribe. Nevertheless, they moved to stop the raising of a spillway elevation at a hydroelectric dam in Vermont, arguing that to raise the dam would destroy aboriginal burial sites containing remains, associated funerary objects, and other cultural artifacts. A federal court dismissed the Abenaki's claim, holding that NAGPRA applies only to remains and cultural items that have been actually excavated or discovered. In other words, the court reasoned that NAGPRA can protect remains only after they have been disturbed, not before. The Abenaki's evidence that the remains or objects almost certainly existed at the site for the spillway was rejected as irrelevant, since NAGPRA was interpreted to require 100% certainty in order to stop a construction project. Obviously, this holding was a blow to tribal interests.

To date, the most contentious NAGPRA disputes involve the status of ancient human remains. In 1994, an anthropologist allegedly working without a permit discovered a fossilized human hair on federal land near Dillon, Montana. The Kootenai-Salish and Shoshone Bannock Tribes moved to repatriate the hair under NAGPRA. The anthropologist moved to dismiss the tribal repatriation claim on the ground that the hair was "freely given or naturally shed," and thus outside the scope of NAGPRA's protection.[16] The distinction between prehistory and history also figured into this dispute because while the anthropologist claimed that the hair was an unaffiliated prehistoric object, the tribes claimed an affiliation traceable through a 10,000-year oral history.

A related NAGPRA conflict over ancient remains involves a 9,300-year-old skeleton found on July 28, 1996, in Kennewick, Washington, on the ancestral land of the Umatilla, a tribe now in northeastern Oregon. Scientists claim that the skeleton has "caucasoid features" rather than "Mongoloid features," and therefore that NAGPRA does not apply, since NAGPRA applies only to Native American remains. A five-tribe coalition led by the Umatilla made a formal claim for repatriation and reburial of the skeleton under NAGPRA. The scientists responded with a lawsuit of their own under the civil rights laws,[17] claiming that implementing NAGPRA to repatriate the skeleton would constitute a violation of their right not to be discriminated against on the basis of their race or national origin.[18]

These two recent conflicts resurrect the serious disagreement about who owns tribal cultural property that preceded the passage of NAGPRA. They also raise the possibility that science will proceed unrestrained and without regard to Native American sensibilities, as it did in the nineteenth century. If this happens, then

NAGPRA will likely go the way of the Indian Claims Commission Act (ICC). Under the ICC Act, Native American contributions, sensibilities, histories, and ways of knowing took second place in the process, falling far behind property rules and the rhetoric of efficiency. This understandably led many Native Americans to seriously question, if not reject, the ICC Act, which supposedly had been passed for their benefit. Similarly, if the archeologists and physical anthropologists are allowed to study contested human remains without limit, then NAGPRA will have incorporated a social Darwinist premise that regards Native American ethics, contributions, histories, and cultures as inferior to those of a dominant society that places its faith in science.

NAGPRA, as it was enacted, allows for limited scientific study,[19] but the current controversy over Kennewick Man is not about the scope of that phrase. It is about whether NAGPRA applies at all. The Umatilla claimants hold that their history accounts for Kennewick Man; the scientists reportedly disregard the tribal position as impossible to demonstrate—the working of religious fundamentalism, not reason. They claim that Kennewick Man's features, cranial measurements, and advanced stone culture mean that he could not have been an ancestor of current-day Native Americans. If a court holds that NAGPRA extends only to remains that are Mongoloid, on the theory that such remains are "indigenous" to the United States, whereas Caucasoid remains are "not indigenous," then NAGPRA will have been gutted. What was heralded as human rights legislation will pass into obscurity, causing more injustice to Native Americans than it alleviated.

As this book was going to press an article written by Douglas Preston appeared in the *New Yorker*.[20] What made Preston's article of note here was not that he declared "no human beings are indigenous to the New World; we are all immigrants."[21] Nor that he carefully articulated the position of the scientists at the expense of the tribal claimants. Nor that he positioned himself as one of the racially enlightened, educated, highbrow few who, from that position, was morally justified, unlike the "clearly racist," to ask questions such as: "If the original inhabitants of the New World were Europeans who were pushed out by Indians, would it change the Indians' position in the great moral landscape?"[22]

Rather, what made Preston's article of note here was that it recycled stereotypes from the nineteenth century in a way that made them palatable to educated late-twentieth century readers. Preston had clearly read, or at least heard of, NAGPRA's legislative history. Astonishingly, however, he concluded from it that (non-native) conservative Christians and liberals were behind NAGPRA's passage, not the Native American peoples themselves.[23] He characterized Kennewick as using advanced technology, citing technologic differences as the basis for his claim, thus implying that historic Native American cultures were inferior by comparison.[24] He scoffed at the idea that Native histories could hold truths comparable to that found from scientific methods, such as DNA testing, even though much of the early testing on Kennewick Man appears to support the Umatilla's position.[25] He characterized Native Americans as interested in NAGPRA primarily because the Act allowed them to engage in "emptying museums of bones and grave goods,"[26] and in gaining title to "priceless funerary objects."[27] Overall he presented those opposing the Umatilla as enlighted promoters of science, trying to teach us how we're all related, whereas he dismissed the Native Americans as beneficiaries of agency largess (this time the Army Corps of Engineers), in common cause with "less racially enlighted" whites who promote cultural divisions and frictions. Regrettably, Preston's article about NAGPRA is one of the first to reach a general audience.

Just as the controversy over NAGPRA is reminiscent of the controversy over the ICC Act, the conflict over Kennewick Man resonates with what happened in the *Mashpee* case covered in Chapter 1. In *Mashpee,* the conflict was over how to define the term "Indian Tribe." In the Kennewick Man case, the conflict will be over the meaning of the word "indigenous."

RECOMMENDED READINGS

The Arizona State Law Journal symposium in which Jack Trope and Walter Echo-Hawk's, and Dr. Rennard Strickland's articles appear is perhaps the best starting place for a sense of what NAGPRA provides for, as it was enacted. The NAGPRA symposium appears at *Arizona State Law Journal* (1992), Volume 24.

Robert E. Bieder, who is the Visiting Associate Professor at the School for Public and Environmental Affairs at Indiana University at Bloomington, Indiana, has written extensively on NAGPRA and repatriation. Two of Bieder's recent articles are "The Return of the Ancestors," which appears in *Zeitschrift für Ethnologie* 115 (1990) 229–240, and "The Collecting of Bones for Anthropological Narratives," which appears in *American Indian Culture and Research Journal* 16:2 (1992) 21–35. These works provide important background context to the repatriation issue. See also *American Indian Quarterly,* vol. 20:2, Spring 1996 for an entire issue devoted to repatriation.

The Spirit of Native America: Beauty and Mysticism in American Indian Art (1989) by Anna Lee Walters is a book of photographs from cowboy illustrator David T. Vernon's collection, which is on permanent display at the Colter Bay Visitor Center in Grand Teton National Park, Wyoming. Walters' book gives one a sense of the kinds of items that were (and still are) collected: medicine bags, medicine spoons, clothing, war shirts, and shields.

David Stannard's *American Holocaust* (1992) describes how General Leonard W. Colby took a child as a war curio after the Wounded Knee massacre in 1890. Reports of the time described "a baby of about a year old warmly wrapped and entirely unhurt" amidst the carnage. Her name was Zintka Lanuni, or Lost Bird. Colby displayed the child for personal profit, and then released her to the Buffalo Bill's Wild West Show. She died at the age of 29, in Los Angeles, where she was buried. In 1991, the Lakota repatriated Zintka Lanuni's remains. Stannard reports that today she lies buried, at Wounded Knee, "a hundred years after the massacre, next to the mass grave that still marks the killing field where the rest of her family lies buried." (Stannard, p. 127).

Whereas repatriation issues are discussed in the federal Indian law literature and in the Native American Studies Literature, in the field of property law, *The Deskbook of Art Law* (2d ed. 1993), by Leonard D. DuBoff contains only a short section on what the author classifies as "Indian Art."

On the history of physical anthropology, see *Bones, Bodies, Behavior: Essays on Biological Anthropology (Vol. 5* (1988), edited by George W. Stocking Jr. This work is part of a larger series called the *History of Anthropology* published by Wisconsin University Press. *Objects and Others: Essays on Museums and Material Culture (Vol. 3)* (1985), edited by George W. Stocking Jr. is relevant to the issue of repatriation as well.

Finally, "Science, Sovereignty, and the Sacred Text: Paleontological Resources and Native American Rights," 55 *Maryland Law Review* 84 (1996), by Allison M. Dussias discusses the issue of fossil collection and ownership, with emphasis on the Tyrannosaurous rex fossil ("Sue") found on the Cheyenne River Sioux Reservation.

NOTES

1. *Native American Graves Protection and Repatriation Act of 1990, U.S. Statutes at Large* 104 (1990):3048–3058. Currently at *U.S. Code* vol. 25, secs. 3061 et seq. (1997).

2. From a *System of Phrenology*, 5th ed., Edinburgh, 1843, p. 211; fig. 2.70, as cited in Lynn Gamwell and Nancy Tomes, *Madness in America: Cultural and Medical Perceptions of Mental Illness Before 1914*, Ithaca, N.Y.: Cornell University Press; Binghamton University Art Museum (1995).

3. See note 2.

4. See note 2.

5. *Indian Removal Act of 1830, U.S. Statutes at Large* 4 (1830):411–412.

6. 30 U.S. (5 Pet.) 1 (1831).

7. 31 U.S. (6 Pet.) 515 (1832).

8. New York Times, Oct. 1, 1897, cited in Michael T. Kaufman, *A Museum's Eskimo Skeletons and Its Own, New York Times*, Aug. 21, 1993, Sec. 1, p. 1, vol. 2.

9. See Kaufman note 8. See also Ben Mcintyre, *Off to the Land of Our Birth, New York Times*, Aug. 2, 1993, Features Section.

10. Kroeber, Theodora, *Ishi: The Last of His Tribe*, New York, N.Y.: Bantam Books, 1973.

11. *Ishi, the Last Yahi: A Documentary History* (Robert F. Heizer and Theodora Kroeber, eds.) Berkeley, Calif.: University of California Press, 1979, p. 1.

12. *Abenaki v. Hughes*, 805 F. Supp. 234 (D. Vermont 1992); *Na Iwi O Na Kupuna O Mokapu v. Dalton*, 894 F. Supp. 1397 (D. Hawaii 1995); *Sam Monet v. Lee Henderson & Wong*, 1995 U.S. Dist. LEXIS 17300; 76 A.F.T.R. 2d (P-H) 7366 (D. Hawaii, Dec. 30, 1995); *Sam Monet v. Lee Henderson & Wong*, 1995 U.S. Dist. LEXIS 12500 (D. Hawaii, Sept. 16, 1995); *U.S. v. Richard Nelson Corrow*, 941 F. Supp. 1553 (D. N.M. 1996); *Pueblo of San Ildefonso v. Daniel Ridlon and the Regents of the University of California*, 1996 U.S. App. LEXIS 33490 (10th Cir. Dec. 24, 1996).

13. For a brief overview of the topic, see generally, "Conserving Heritage: Cultural and Intellectual Property Rights," *UN Chronicle* (June 1993) 50–51.

14. *U.S. Code* vol. 25, sec. 3001(7) (defining "Indian Tribe" as "any tribe, band, nation, or other organized group or community of Indians, including any Alaska Native village which is recognized as eligible for the special programs and services provided by the United States to Indians because of their status as Indians"); and *U.S. Code* vol. 25, sec 3001(9) (defining "Native American" as "of, or relating to, a tribe, people, culture that is indigenous to the United States.").

15. See note 12.

16. *NAGPRA Regulations, Federal Regulations* 43 CFR 10.2(d)(1) (1995) (defining "human remains" as "the physical remains of a human body of a person of the Native American ancestry. The term does not include remains or portions of remains that may reasonably be determined to have been freely given or naturally shed by the individual from whose body they were obtained, such as hair made into ropes or nets.").

17. *Bonnichsen v. U.S.*, 969 F. Supp. 614 (1997), and *Bonnichsen v. U.S.*, 969 F. Supp. 628 (1977).

18. Ibid.

19. *U.S. Code* vol. 25, sec. 3005(b) (allowing scientific study when it is "indispensable for completion of a specific scientific study, the outcome of which would be a major benefit to the United States," but requiring that the cultural items be repatriated "90 days after the date on which the scientific study is completed.").

20. Douglas Preston, "The Lost Man: Why Are Scientists Suing the Government Over the Nine-Thousand-Year-Old Kennewick Man?" *The New Yorker*, vol. 73:16, June 16, 1997, p. 70.

21. Ibid., p. 74.

22. Ibid., p. 81.

23. Ibid., p. 74.

24. Ibid., p. 76.

25. Ibid., p. 74–76.

26. Ibid., p. 81.

27. Ibid., p. 81.

A Brief Historical Survey of the Expropriation of American Indian Remains

Robert E. Bieder

SAMUEL G. MORTON AND THE BEGINNING OF AMERICAN PHYSICAL ANTHROPOLOGY

Americans pursuing medical education in Europe in the late eighteenth and early nineteenth centuries, came under the influence of . . . ideas in craniology and phrenology. One who absorbed these theories in his studies at both Edinburgh and Paris was the Philadelphian physician, Samuel G. Morton, often referred to as the founder of physical anthropology in America. When Morton returned to Philadelphia in 1823, he assumed a teaching position at the Philadelphia Hospital and Pennsylvania College and discovered to his dismay that he had no skulls of different races for class use. His search for human skulls of all races and his subsequent investigations, led not only to the racial findings expressed in his *Crania Americana*, findings that would color racial thinking long after his death in 1851—but also laid the foundation for anthropological interest in the search for deceased Indians.[1] . . .

In an 1837 letter explaining what he wished to do, Morton wrote to his phrenologist-physician friend Dr. John Collins Warren in Boston, "my plan . . . is to give a preliminary view of the *Five Races** of men . . . and to illustrate each by genuine specimens. I shall then go on with the American series, in which, however, I am yet considerably deficient, but am promised assistance from so many different sources."[2] One of these sources to whom Morton sent a list of his crania needs was a Gerald Troost in Tennessee. Troost responded, "It seems from your list that you have no skull of the Cherokees[.] I am going to pay them a visit about the 1st of next month and I will try to get you one or more if I can, but those fellows do not like that anybody disturb the bones of their dead."[3] . . .

From *A Brief Historical Survey of the Expropriation of American Indian Remains*, by Robert E. Bieder. Bloomington, Ind.: Robert E. Bieder. © 1990 by the Native American Rights Fund and Robert E. Bieder.

*Morton is referring to Blumenbach's taxonomy, which divided humankind into five major racial groups.

When Morton's *Crania Americana*[4] came out in 1839, it was well received in both America and in Europe. His analysis of crania capacity [which he believed determined] intelligence buttressed popular racial prejudice. The crania were ranked in the [order of size, with "Caucasian" crania measuring largest and "African" crania smallest]. . . .

Morton's friend Combe stressed the point of size as indicative of intelligence. "The exact coincidence betwixt the development of these skulls and the character of this people [Indians] would lead us to suppose that they represent a national shape. The general size is greatly inferior to that of the average European head; indicating inferiority in natural mental power."[5] This same theme was echoed by a writer in the *American Phrenological Journal and Miscellany* in 1841. Claiming that since the "moral and religious organs are comparatively small, and the animal and semi-animal ones proportionably large," civilization for Indians was virtually impossible. Consequently, Indians faced inevitable extinction: "The experience of more than two centuries has abundantly evinced, that that 'family,' as a body, can be neither civilized nor actually conquered and enslaved; but that their ultimate extinction is an event which is approaching, and whose accomplishment nothing earthly can prevent."[6] . . .

But the needs of craniologist Morton did not provide the only stimulus that sent Americans digging for Indian human remains. Phrenology, or rather the rise of phrenological societies, the establishment of museums, and the romantic American interest in the mounds and search for ancient civilizations, often made collecting human remains profitable.

Phrenological societies arose during the 1830s and 1840s. The largest were in New York, Boston, and Philadelphia, but they also could be found in smaller places like Cincinnati. According to one report there were several skull collections in New York City.[7] Beginning as a "science" that many believed offered a window into the workings of the brain, phrenology soon degenerated into quackery and disrepute but not before it took root in American thought and contributed to American racial prejudice. By claiming to be able to determine personality by "reading" bumps or protrusions of the skull, phrenology was the poor man's psychology. Before slipping into disrepute, phrenological societies often included leading scientists and medical men in their membership lists. Most of the societies maintained rooms where a "library" of human and animal skulls and plaster casts of heads was available for study by its members. The plaster casts were usually those of famous or notable personages from both Europe and America and were compared with the skulls of criminals, the insane, the indigent, Indians and [African-Americans]. . . .

As late as 1856, books appeared on phrenology. One written by Orson S. Fowler, clergyman, architectural innovator, and phrenologist, was quite popular. Fowler, who owned a large phrenological (skull) library in New York City, never tired of promoting the "science." Concerning the Indian skulls in his collection, Fowler noted "[there is] a general feature common to them all." The skulls were large in areas that denoted destructiveness, secretiveness, and cautiousness, and combativeness. "This combination of organs indicates just such a character as the Indians generally possess."[8] . . . It is significant to note that those traits Fowler "discovered" in Native American crania coincided with the same negative traits which the public commonly identified with Indians.

Museums also manifested an interest in acquiring Indian remains. . . . Some museums were mere "show shops" where along with skulls, animal freaks and other natural oddities were displayed. . . . Other museums were very much devoted to science, such as the Museum of Comparative Zoology at Harvard, founded by the famous Swiss born zoologist Louis Agassiz.

Agassiz proved a brilliant scientist and organizer. With a network of influential friends—including Samuel G. Morton—Agassiz was able to amass funds to support his various projects; under his direction and influence, the Harvard museum grew. According to an Agassiz scholars, "Collectors sent in shipment after shipment of materials from all over the world ranging from turtle eggs of Australia to photographs of European racial types and 'one head of a North American Indian in alcohol.'"[9] At some point, Agassiz decided that the museum should increase its collection of Indian bodies for scientific study. Writing to Secretary of War, Edwin M. Stanton in January of 1865, Agassiz requested, "Now that the temperature is low enough . . . permit me to recall to your memory your promise to let me have the bodies of some Indians; if any should die at this time. . . . All that would be necessary . . . would be to forward the body express in a box. . . . In case the weather was not very cold . . . direct the surgeon in charge to inject through the carotids a solution of Arsenate of soda. I should like one or two handsome fellows entire and the heads of two or three more."[10]

By mid-century a noticeable shift had taken place in scientific views of the Indian and other non-whites. Changes . . . brought about by the industrial revolution—already in progress before the Civil War—foreshadowed even greater progress and further disruption in American society. Villages, cities, even landscapes, were being transformed. And as Americans looked around in bewilderment at the rapid pace of "progress," they saw in the Indian an unprogressive type. . . . [B]y mid-century many "scientists" drawing their conclusions from the study of bones, or from the investigations of others, held a negative view of non-whites and saw in them no possibility for progress. According to such thinking, they were innately inferior and their slavery or extinction could be attributed to biological circumstances. . . .

It is true that not all "scientists" held these views but many who did were extremely vocal in their assertions of non-white inferiority and inability to change. Politicians like Senator John C. Calhoun found Morton's work on crania especially useful in arguing the southern cause for slavery. Undoubtedly, others also found such arguments effective for the perpetuation of slavery and/or the expulsion of Indians from lands coveted by Euroamericans. . . .

MUSEUM COLLECTING IN THE LATE NINETEENTH CENTURY

. . .

The founding of museums, museum collecting and the competition between museums, contributed greatly to growing demand for artifacts and the digging of grave sites. European museums and their collections had long influenced European cultural and scientific life. In America, the founding of the Smithsonian Institution in 1846 and the Museum of Comparative Zoology at Harvard in 1859 were major events for American science. Spurred by the example that these institutions presented and the demands of local pride, Chicago and New York soon followed with their own museums of natural history. Among these institutions competition for artifacts and human remains grew. The collecting often proved intense and generally indiscriminate. In many instances those who collected for museums were untrained. Indeed, there was little training available at this time. "Although a few museums maintained loose connections with universities, archaeology was not a classroom topic." Many of the collectors were "self-styled adventurers, more interested in enjoying travel, romance, and pseudoscientific controversy than in attempting to establish archaeology as a science."[11] Partly the rather hasty and erratic collecting of American museums in 1880s and 1890s derived in part from a sense of injured nationalism and what they viewed as unfair competition from European museums absconding with American Indian artifacts and remains.[12]

Probably not the most notorious collector but certainly one who employed a rather cavalier approach to collecting artifacts and Indian bones was Warren K. Moorehead. . . . Educated at Denison University, he served for a while on the staff of the Smithsonian Institution and eventually became curator and later director of the department of archaeology at Phillips Academy in Andover, Massachusetts. "Largely self-taught, Moorehead sold antiquities to support his great passions, which were field work and collecting artifacts." Between 1891 and 1893, Frederic Ward Putnam of the Peabody Museum and Harvard University hired Moorehead to collect artifacts and Indian remains for Chicago World's Columbian Exposition.[13]

In his report of his expedition to southern Ohio, Moorehead seemed to flit with unusual speed from one burial mound site to another often hiring local help; "a force of men were employed to open graves and village sites along the banks of the Little Miami River, some three hundred feet below the level of Fort Ancient."[14] The funerary objects and occupants of these graves and many others were gathered for the Exposition. "From the river burials about thirty-five good crania were secured. Numbers of diseased bones . . . and other osteological peculiarities were observed."[15]

In other Indian burials Moorehead found "splendidly preserved skeletons" and from a large mound that took "some ten men . . . engaged for nearly three weeks" to excavate, he "took a total of seventy-nine skeletons."[16] Although Moorehead claimed that the "several hundred bones from all portions of the human body" would be of interest to anatomists, no anatomist seems to have looked at them.[17] Even human remains which were badly decayed were removed and sent to the Chicago exhibit. . . .[18] Some, like "grave number five" were "preserved with a view to reconstructing [them] in the Department Exhibit."[19] After exciting the morbid curiosity of the public at the World's Columbian Exposition, these Indian remains were deposited at the Field Museum of Natural History in Chicago which was founded after the close of the fair. . . .

* * * *

What value did Moorehead's collection serve to science? Very little. His "prizes" were poorly excavated and identified, the hundreds of skeletons collected were useless according to recent scholars who have examined them.[20]

There was, however, a more important goal in digging in the Ohio Valley and that was to assert one's institutional claim to an area. After the founding of the Field Museum, Moorehead wrote to George A. Dorsey, the curator of Anthropology at the Field Museum, warning him that the museum should not hesitate to assert its claims to the mounds and burial grounds of the Ohio Valley or other museums along with regional historical societies would. . . . The human remains and artifacts of the Ohio Valley were important not only to round out collections but also as "prizes" in regional and national competition.[21] . . .

PHYSICAL ANTHROPOLOGY AND THE ARMY MEDICAL MUSEUM: COLLECTING AS OFFICIAL POLICY

. . . While the Field Museum, the American Museum of Natural History, the Smithsonian Institution, and other smaller museums sought to collect all aspects of American Indian life and material culture, another Washington museum sought in the second half of the nineteenth century to collect only Indian osteological remains. The Army Medical Museum, founded in 1862, sought human remains of all races but from 1865 through the 1880s gathered primarily Indian remains. On September 1, 1868, the Assistant U.S. Surgeon General sent out the following official order to all Army medical officers:

> The Officers of the Medical Staff are informed that a craniological collection was commenced last year at the Army Medical Museum, and that it already includes 143 specimens of skulls. The chief purpose had in view [sic] in forming this collection is to aid in the progress of anthropological science by obtaining measurements of a large number of skulls of aboriginal races of North America. Medical officers stationed in the Indian country or in the vicinity of ancient mounds or cemeteries in the Mississippi Valley or the Atlantic region have peculiar facilities for promoting this undertaking. They have already enriched the Mortonian and other magnificent craniological cabinets by their contributions and it is hoped they will evince even greater zeal in collecting for their own Museum. A list of the crania now in the possession of the Museum will soon be published in the Catalogue of the Osteological Series of the Anatomical Section. . . .
>
> While exotic and normal and abnormal crania of all descriptions are valued at the Museum for purposes of comparison, it is chiefly desired to procure sufficiently large series of adult crania of the principal Indian tribes to furnish accurate average measurements. Medical Officers will enhance the value of their contributions by transmitting with the specimens the fullest attainable

memoranda, specifying the locality whence the skulls were derived, the presumed age and sex, and, in the case of 'Mound' skulls, or of those from cemeteries, describing the mode of sepulchre, and any traces of weapons, implements, utensils found with the specimens, or any other circumstance that may throw light on their ethnic character.

The subject is earnestly commended to the attention of the Medical Officers of the Army.

By order of the Surgeon General[22]

. . . The response was favorable. By 1873 Surgeon General J. K. Barnes could write,

The Medical Officers of the Army have collected a much larger series of American skulls than have ever before been available for study. . . .

Stationed at military posts in the West, and often near the scene of fighting, army medical personnel were in a good position to acquire Indian remains and to provide appropriate biographical and historical context. . . .

Army physicians also had the medical facilities to "prepare" the bones and the means to send them to Washington. . . . Referring to the head of a recently killed Kiowa Indian, [one contributor said] "his scalp and the soft parts of the face and neck were carefully dissected up from the skull, atlas and axis, and these were subsequently boiled and cleaned for the Army Medical Museum. The skull was carefully cleaned and then steeped in solution of lime for 36 hours. . . ."[23] And not just bones were prepared and preserved. "I have at last (today) secured a fresh Indian *brain* for the Museum. It is now being soaked in Erlick's fluid and will be ready for shipment in a week. . . . It comes from a fullblooded adult male Apache."[24] . . .

The official reason the Army Medical Museum gave for collecting osteological remains of American Indians was for comparative racial study. It sought to demonstrate racial characteristics. After his examination of "osteological peculiarities," Dr. George A. Otis of the Army Medical Museum announced in 1870 that data indicated that American Indians "must be assigned a lower position in the human scale than has been believed heretofore." . . . The rapid rise of physical anthropology after the Civil War was rooted in a national sense of human progress both culturally and biologically; it also grew out of the fascination with statistical methodology and its usefulness in anthropometric investigations. . . . Through the use of statistics scientists hoped to discover a way to redesign man. Measurements were made of body size and head size. To measure the Indian was to know the Indian; to know his capabilities and weaknesses; and to possibly reshape the Indian into a being able to survive in civilization as Americans defined it. Although voluminous measurements were indeed made of living Indians, Indian remains continued to be vital in research.[25]

This statistical preoccupation with physical characteristics was to underscore the work of the Bureau of American Ethnology. In a draft of a letter written by

Samuel P. Langley, Secretary of the Smithsonian Institution to William H. Holmes, Chief of the Bureau of American Ethnology, Langley was sharply critical of the Bureau's work and reminded Holmes that the Congress expected something more practical from the Bureau and suggested, among other things, the "application of methods of anthropometry and in general physical anthropology to the American Indian. This to include the study of the mixture of the Indian with white and other races and its results, as far as possible." Such osteological data, along with examples of Indian art and industry should be "secured, arranged and placed on display" and would not only illustrate the history of the American Indian but also aid the government in formulating [its] Indian policy [which was founded on the removal, genocide, and legal dispossession of Native American tribal groups]. . . .

GLOSSARY

APS   American Philosophical Society
MHS   Massachusetts Historical Society
LCP   Library Company of Philadelphia
MCZ   Museum of Comparative Zoology, Cambridge
NA   National Archives
BAE   Bureau of American Ethnology
AMM-NAA   Army Medical Museum-National Anthropological Archives
FM   Field Museum
NMHM   National Museum of Health and Medicine

NOTES

1. Bieder, 55–64.
2. S.G. Morton to John C. Warren, 2/27/1837, MHS.
3. Gerald Troost to S. G. Morton 3/4/1837, APS.
4. Samuel G. Morton, *Crania Americana; or A Comparative View of the Skulls of Various Aboriginal Nations of North and South America, to which is Prefixed an Essay on the Varieties of the Human Species.* (Philadelphia: n.p., 1839).
5. George C. Combe, *A System of Phrenology*, 3rd American ed., Boston, Mass.: Marsh, Capen and Lyon, 1835, p. 574.
6. *American Phrenological Journal and Miscellany*, 3 (1841):209.
7. Cooper to S.G. Morton, 2/5/37, APS.
8. Orson S. Fowler, *Practical Phrenology*. New York, N.Y.: Fowler and Wells, 1856, pp. 29–30.
9. Edward Lurie, *Louis Agassiz: A Life in Science*. Chicago, Ill.: University of Chicago Press, 1960, p. 304.
10. Ibid., 338.
11. C. William Clewlow, "Some Thoughts on the Background of Early Man, Hrdlicka, and Folsom," in Kroeber *Anthropological Society Papers*, 42–43 (1970): 26–46.
12. Douglas Cole, *Captured Heritage: The Scramble for Northwest Coast Artifacts.* Seattle, Wash.: University of Washington Press, 1985, chap. 3.

13. Tom D. Crouch, "Moorehead, Warren K. 1866–1939," in *History of Indian-White Relations: Handbook of North American Indians* 4, Washington, D.C.: Smithsonian Institution, 1988, p. 670; "Citadel or Coliseum? Past and Present Field Museum Explorations of a Major American Monument," *Field Museum Natural History Bulletin* 55 (June 1984): 20–21.

14. Warren K. Moorehead "Report to World's Columbian Exposition about Moorehead Expedition in Ohio," (1892):1 Ms., FM.

15. Ibid., p. 3.

16. Ibid., pp. 4–5.

17. Ibid.

18. Ibid., p. 8.

19. Ibid., pp. 6–10.

20. See Patricia Sue Essenpreise, "The Anderson Village Site: Redefining the Anderson Phase of the Fort Ancient Tradition of the Middle Ohio Valley." (Ph.D. diss., Harvard University, 1982); and Essenpreise and Moseley, 5–26.

21. "Extracts from Letter of W.K. Moorehead to Dr. Dorsey, dated June 2, 1898." Ms., and Moorehead to Dorsey June 25, 1909, FM. See also letters: Dorsey to Clinton Cowan, December 8, 1909; Clinton Cowan to C.L. Owen, Dec. 8, 1909; Charles L. Owen to G.A. Dorsey, September 29, 1910; Dorsey to F.J.V. Skiff, October 27, 1910; and May 7, 1911, FM.

22. "Memorandum for the Information of Medical Officers," September 1, 1858. Quoted in D. S. Lamb, "A History of the United States Army Medical Museum: 1662–1917," n.d., Ms. 56–56b, NMHM. See also D. S. Lamb, "The Army Medical Museum in American Anthropology," *Proceedings 19th International Congress of Americanists*. Washington, D.C., 1917: pp. 625–32.

23. S. M. Horton to _____ , n.d., Box 4, AMM-NAA.

24. W. Matthews to S. Millings, 6/16/91, Box 8., AMM-NAA, his emphasis.

25. John Haller, Jr., *Outcasts from Evolution: Scientific Attitudes of Racial Inferiority, 1859–1900.* Urbana, Ill.: University of Illinois Press, 1971, pp. 19–39.

Give Me My Father's Body

Kenn Harper

By 1907 New York had largely forgotten about Minik. . . . [I]n early January, when the *World*, a New York paper, carried a sensational full-page article in its magazine section. Amid pictures of Minik and an artist's sketch of the pleading boy, his arms outstretched toward the museum, the headline blared, "Give Me My Father's Body." The subtitle read "The Pathetic Story of Minik, the Esquimau Boy, Who is Growing Up in New York and . . . Who Now Wants Most the Bones of His Father from the Museum of Natural History."

The article shocked the *World*'s readership. It read in part:

> Minik, the Esquimau boy, longed for but one Christmas gift, but that one he couldn't have. He asked back his father's bones that he might put them in a quiet grave somewhere, where they could rest in peace forever. . . .
>
> And Minik wept just a little, stoic that he is, when he found that it couldn't be.
>
> . . . Minik . . . is the sole survivor of six Esquimaux whom Lieut. Robert E. Peary brought [to New York]. . . . Four died, including Qisuk, Minik's father, and one went back again to the frozen north, glad to escape from the death and disease of New York.
>
> The scientists who were delighted to study leisurely the Esquimaux here in New York have long since forgotten these simple folk from the bleak Arctic. True, four of them died here, all of tuberculosis, but not until these wise men had learned everything they cared to know.
>
> And then, were not the corpses turned over to the doctors for very interesting dissections which added much to our knowledge on ethnological subjects? But, best of all, the perfect skeletons were turned over to the American Museum of Natural History, up in Manhattan Square, where savants who wish to study Esquimau anatomy may do so quite comfortably.

From *Give Me My Father's Body: The Life of Minik, the New York Eskimo*, by Kenn Harper. (Igaluit) Frobisher Bay, NWT: Blacklead Books. © 1986 by Kenn Harper.

And that is where the bones of Minik's father, nicely articulated, are now.

There, too, is his precious kayak—his boat of skins—his gun and his knife and his Esquimau clothes, a most interesting exhibit. . . . Minik thinks that according to the American laws of inheritance these things ought to be his. He has heard at school, too, of fair play and the square deal, and he has in his mind an idea that he ought to be allowed to bury his father as the Christians do, in some quiet country churchyard.

But an upstairs room—at the museum—is his father's last resting place. His coffin is a showcase, his shroud a piece of plate glass. No quiet of the graveyard is there; the noise of shuffling feet and the tap, tap of the hammers as the workmen fix up other skeletons, is ever present. And when the sunlight fades they turn on the electric lights so that Minik's father may not have even the pall of darkness to hide his naked bones. . . .[1]

In February of 1898 when Minik's father, Qisuk, lay dying in Bellevue Hospital, that institution had written to Franz Boas at the museum, "I hardly believe Qisuk will survive the night. The body will I suppose belong to the Museum of Natural History or Mr. Peary and they can of course do anything they wish with it. . . ."[2] Minik was eight years of age. Had he been older and able to read, he might possibly have seen reports in the newspaper two days later, after his father's death, under the heading "The Esquimau's Body" and the prophetic title "Trouble Over the Dead Eskimo." The American Museum of Natural History and Bellevue Hospital were fighting over Qisuk's remains. By that evening the situation had been resolved. The paper reported, "The disposition of the body was adjusted last night. It was agreed that students at Bellevue should make such use of it as possible in the dissecting-room, and that the skeleton should then be mounted and preserved in the Museum of Natural History."[3] . . .

Even had Minik been older and able to read, it is unlikely he would have chanced to see a dry scientific report by the anthropologist, Alfred Kroeber, one of those who had studied the Eskimos while all six were yet alive. Kroeber had written a detailed paper on the Smith Sound Eskimos without ever leaving the comfort of New York[.] He had based it on the information he had gathered from the museum's six living specimens, under the direction of Boas and with . . . [an] interpreter. Kroeber continued to work with the Eskimos right through the time of their illnesses, their residence at Bellevue, and the deaths of Qisuk and Atangana. He had ample opportunity, therefore, to observe the Eskimos' manner of mourning their dead, and in the report he published in 1899, there is a startling admission implied in one small word in brackets in the section of the report dealing with the death of Qisuk. Kroeber reported that Nuktaq insisted, some time after Qisuk's death, that Minik "visit the (supposed) grave of his father, and instructed him how to act."[4]

The "supposed" in brackets is Kroeber's. For, incredible as it may seem, the scientists at the American Museum of Natural History had staged a phony funeral for the benefit of little Minik[.] . . .

The scientists at the American Museum of Natural History decided to duplicate [an Inuit] funeral as best they could on the museum grounds. Years later, William Wallace [the Museum Superintendent who took Minik in as a foster child] would recall the bizarre ceremony:

"That night some of us gathered on the museum grounds by order of the scientific staff, and got an old log about the length of a human corpse. This was wrapped in cloth, a mask attached to one end of it and all was in readiness.

"Dusk was the time chosen for the mock burial, as there was some fear of attracting too much attention from the street which might invite an investigation that would prove disastrous. Then, too, the boy would be less apt to discover the ruse. The funeral party knew the act must be accomplished quickly and quietly, so about the time the lights began to flare up Minik was taken out on the grounds, where the imitation body was placed on the ground and a mound of stones piled on top of it after the Eskimo fashion.

"While Minik stood sobbing by, the museum men lingered around watching the proceedings. The thing worked well. The boy never suspected, and when the grave was complete he made his mark on the north side of it. You see that is the Eskimo way. They think that the mark prevents the spirit of the dead coming back to haunt them, and the mark is always made between the home of the living and the resting place of the dead. . . .

"When he got back to the other Eskimos he told them he had seen his father buried. . . ."[5]

[T]here is verification of the bizarre event from another source . . . [anthropologist] Franz Boas. . . . In 1909 Boas, by then at the anthropology department of Columbia University, confirmed to a reporter that the burial had taken place much as William Wallace had described it. The purpose of the burial, Boas claimed, was "to appease the boy, and keep him from discovering that his father's body had been chopped up and the bones placed in the collection of the institution."[6] . . . [Boas] said that he saw "nothing particularly deserving severe criticism" in the act. "The other Eskimos who were still alive were not very well, and then there was Minik, and of course it was only reasonable to spare them any shock or uneasiness. The burial accomplished that purpose I suppose."[7]

The reporter questioned the right of the museum to claim the body of a man whose relatives were still alive, but Boas responded, "Oh, that was perfectly legitimate. There was no one to bury the body, and the museum had as good a right to it as any other institution authorised to claim bodies." But, protested the reporter, did not that body belong rightfully to Minik, the son of the deceased. "Well," was Boas' reply, "Minik was just a little boy, and he did not ask for the body. If he had, he might have got it."[8]

The same reporter questioned Dr. Huntington of the College of Physicians and Surgeons, who said that the brain of Qisuk was in preserving fluid at the college and that, following his death at Bellevue Hospital, his body had been shipped to the school where an autopsy was performed in accordance with the agreement reached with the museum. . . .

[P]reparation of the Eskimos' bodies for the museum . . . took place in what was known as the "bone house" on the Wallace farm in Lawyersville[, New York]. In 1909, looking back on the events, Wallace said, "We were only acting under instructions from the museum authorities. It had all been arranged that the bones should be prepared for exhibition and they had to be cleaned."[9]

Nuktaq[, one of the six Inuits brought by Peary to New York] was troubled at not being able to go to see the grave of Atangana[, his wife] . . . and it is fortunate for the museum's scientists that he was too sick himself to leave the little cottage at Highbridge, for the scientists had not arranged a mock burial for the dead lady, nor had they heeded any of the woman's other last requests. Immediately after her death, Atangana's body was spirited away to the College of Physicians and Surgeons, where her brain was removed for study and an autopsy performed. From there, she ultimately made her way, as had Qisuk, to the American Museum of Natural History.

Atangana, Nuktaq and Aviaq all followed Qisuk through the Wallace "bone house" and the College of Physicians and Surgeons to the Osteological Department of the American Museum of Natural History. The child, Aviaq, was the last to die. There were no more fake funerals to impress or appease any other members of the party. Nor did the press take any interest in the fate of these bodies.

IN THE INTEREST OF SCIENCE

Dr. Åles Hrdlicka [of the Smithsonian] was one of the scientists who studied Minik and the five other Polar Eskimos in New York. . . .

He was one of the first to examine the Polar Eskimos after their arrival in New York and he saw them often during their illnesses. Yet his interest in them cannot have been the same as that of Boas or Kroeber, folklorists and ethnologists, for to a physical anthropologist obsessed with the collecting of skeletons, one brief but final breath separates a human curiosity from a scientific specimen. In the spring of 1898 Hrdlicka got the opportunity he relished with the deaths, in a space of two months, of four of the Eskimos. Of them, he wrote, "These six individuals the writer was able to examine during life and, in one instance, immediately after death; he further secured and described the brain of one of the men and made a preliminary report on the others. . . . Finally, he was able to examine the skeletal remains of the four who died, as well as several additional skulls and skeletons collected in . . . the Smith Sound region by Mr. Peary."[10]

Perhaps the final indignity for Qisuk was the publication of Hrdlicka's article, "An Eskimo Brain," in 1901. The identity of specimens usually remains unknown, but this one was denied the dignity of anonymity; the article began, "The brain in question is that of Qisuk. . . . The article contains two photographs, which Minik mercifully never saw; they were labelled "Qisuk's Cerebrum (Dorsal Aspect)" and "Qisuk's Cerebrum (Basal Aspect)."[11]

★ ★ ★ ★

A number of years passed between the death and phony burial of Qisuk and Minik's discovery that the bones of his father were on display in the American Museum of Natural History. During those years, as Minik grew up a loved member of the Wallace family, William Wallace kept the terrible secret of Qisuk's fate from the boy. He regretted his involvement in the whole disgusting affair and he dreaded to think what opinion his foster son would form of him should he chance to become aware of the truth. Then, finally, Minik did learn the truth. Wallace tells the story:

> The newspapers had found out that the bones of his father were in the museum, and though they never knew of the fake burial or the bone cleaning in Cobleskill, they printed stories about the skeletons. At school Minik was thrown in contact with other children, and naturally they talked to him about the Eskimos. Eventually he learned that he had not witnessed the burial of his father's remains, but he kept it to himself for a long time. We noticed that there was a change coming over him, and then one day we learned its cause.
>
> He was coming home from school with my son Willie one snowy afternoon, when he suddenly began to cry. 'My father is not in his grave,' he said; 'his bones are in the museum.'
>
> We questioned him and found out how he had learned the truth. But after that he was never the same boy. He became morbid and restless. Often we would find him sitting crying, and sometimes he would not speak for days.
>
> We did our best to cheer him up, but it was no use. His heart was broken. He had lost faith in the new people he had come among." Minik's own version of his discovery of the fate of his father is more dramatic, if less truthful: "Unexpectedly one day I came face to face with it. I felt as though I must die then and there. I threw myself at the bottom of the glass case and prayed and wept. I went straight to the director and implored him to let me bury my father. He would not. I swore I never would rest until I had given my father burial.[12]

NOTES

1. "Minik, the Esquimau boy": *World*, January 6, 1907, p. 3.
2. "I hardly believed": AMNH [American Museum of Natural History], Department of Anthropology, File 1900-6, Memo, Robert W. Daley, Bellevue Hospital to Franz Boas, 17 February 1898.
3. "The disposition of the body": *New York Daily Tribune*, February 19, 1898, p. 10.
4. "visit the (supposed) grave": Kroeber, *"The Eskimo of Smith Sound,"* 1899, p. 316.
5. "That night some of us gathered": *Evening Mail*, April 21, 1909, p. 4.
6. "to appease the boy:" *Evening Mail*, April 24, 1909, p. 4.
7. "nothing particularly deserving severe criticism": ibid.
8. "Oh, that was perfectly legitimate": ibid.
9. "We were only acting": *Evening Mail*, April 21, 1909, p. 4.

10. "These six individuals": Hrdlicka, ["Contribution to the Anthropology of Central and Smith Sound Eskimo, Anthropological Papers of the American Museum of Natural History, vol. V,] 1910 p. 175 at 223.

11. "The brain in question": ibid.

12. "Unexpectedly one day": *San Francisco Examiner* (Magazine Supplement), May 9, 1909.

The Native American Graves Protection and Repatriation Act:
Background and Legislative History

Jack F. Trope and Walter R. Echohawk

THE ORIGINS, SCOPE, AND NATURE OF THE REPATRIATION ISSUE

. . .

A. Human Remains and Funerary Objects

[B]asic values [according respect to the dead] are strictly protected in all fifty states, and the District of Columbia, by statutes that comprehensively regulate cemeteries and protect graves from vandalism and desecration.[1] Criminal laws prohibit grave robbing and mutilation of the dead and ensure that human remains are not mistreated. Statutes in most states guarantee that all persons—including paupers, indigents, prisoners, strangers, and other unclaimed dead—are entitled to a decent burial.[2]

Disinterment of the dead is strongly disfavored under American common law except under the most compelling circumstances,[3] and then only under close judicial supervision or under carefully prescribed permit requirements, which may include judicial consent.[4] Common law goes to great lengths to protect the sanctity of the dead.[5]

Unfortunately, the above legal protections—which most citizens take for granted—have failed to protect the graves and the dead of Native people. Massive numbers of Indian dead have been dug up from their graves and carried away. National estimates are that between 100,000 and two million deceased Native people have been dug up from their graves for storage or display by government agencies, museums, universities and tourist attractions.[6] The practice is so widespread that virtually every Indian tribe or Native group in the country has been affected by non-Indian grave looting.[7] . . .

From "The Native American Graves Protection and Repatriation Act: Background and Legislative History," *Arizona State Law Journal* 24(1992):35. © 1992 by the Arizona State Law Journal.

The problem that the law seeks to remedy is one that has characterized Indian/ white relations since the Pilgrims landed at Plymouth Rock in 1620. The first Pilgrim exploring party returned to the Mayflower with corn taken from Indian storage pits and items removed from a grave: "We brought sundry of the prettiest things away with us, and covered up the corpse again."[8]

Early interest in systematically collecting Indian body parts began before the Civil War. Dr. Samuel Morton, the father of American physical anthropology, collected large numbers of Indian crania in the 1840s. . . . Morton's findings established the "Vanishing Red Man" theory, which was embraced by government policy-makers as "scientific justification" for relocating Indian tribes, taking tribal land, and conducting genocide—in certain instances—against American Indians.[9]

Later, the search for Indian body parts became official federal policy with the Surgeon General's Order of 1868. The policy directed army personnel to procure Indian crania and other body parts for the Army Medical Museum.[10] In ensuing decades, over 4,000 heads were taken from battlefields, burial grounds, POW camps, hospitals, fresh graves, and burial scaffolds across the country. Government headhunters decapitated Natives who had never been buried, such as slain Pawnee warriors from a western Kansas battleground,[11] Cheyenne and Arapaho victims of Colorado's Sand Creek Massacre,[12] and defeated Modoc leaders who were hanged and then shipped to the Army Medical Museum.[13] . . .

At the turn of the century, Congress continued its deplorable federal policy with the passage of the Antiquities Act of 1906.[14] That Act, which was intended to protect "archaeological resources" located on federal lands from looters, defined dead Indians interred on federal lands as "archaeological resources" and, contrary to long standing common-law principles, converted these dead persons into "federal property."[15] The Antiquities Act allowed these dead persons to be dug up pursuant to a federal permit "for the permanent preservation [of the remains] in public museums."[16] Since then, thousands of Indian dead have been classified as "archaeological resources" and exhumed as "federal property."[17]

In summary, American social policy has historically treated Indian dead differently than the dead of other races. Unfortunately, it has been commonplace for public agencies to treat Native American dead as archaeological resources, property, pathological material, data, specimens, or library books, but not as human beings. Many contemporary examples of mistreatment of Native graves and dead bodies occurred in recent years under this rubric, which shocked the Nation's conscience as social ethics have changed and society has become more sensitive to this Equal Protection problem.

B. Sacred Objects and Cultural Patrimony

One pattern that defines Indian-white relations in the United States is the one-way transfer of Indian property to non-Indian ownership. By the 1870s, after most tribes were placed on small reservations, the Government's acquisition of Indian lands had in large part been accomplished. Thereafter, the pattern shifted from real estate to personalty and continued until most of the material culture of Native people had been transferred to white hands. That massive property transfer invariably included some stolen or improperly acquired Native sacred objects and cultural patrimony. Native owners who sought the return of their property, as it turned up in museums, experienced inordinate difficulty in securing its return.[18]

One historian commented on the enormous transfer of cultural property that occurred in a short, fifty-year period:

> During the half-century or so after 1875, a staggering quantity of material, both secular and sacred—from spindle whorls to soul-catchers—left the hands of their native creators and users for the private and public collections of the European world. The scramble . . . was pursued sometimes with respect, occasionally with rapacity, often with avarice. By the time it ended there was more Kwakiutal material in Milwaukee than in Mamalillikulla, more Salish pieces in Cambridge than in Comox. The City of Washington contained more Northwest Coast material than the state of Washington and New York City probably housed more British Columbia material than British Columbia itself. . . .
>
> In retrospect it is clear that the goods flowed irrevocably from Native hands to Euro-American ones until little was left in possession of the people who had invented, made, and used them.[19]

Though some of that property transfer was through legitimate trade and intercourse, a significant amount of Native property was acquired through illegitimate means. This problem was brought to the attention of Congress by the Carter Administration in 1979 following a one-year study mandated by the American Indian Religious Freedom Act[.][20]

The adverse impacts that a refusal to return stolen or improperly acquired sacred material has upon First Amendment rights of tribal religious practitioners,[21] and upon basic property rights,[22] has . . . increasingly become of great concern among tribes and traditional religious practitioners. NAGPRA establishes a national standard and procedure for the return of this property to Native owners.

LEGAL RIGHTS TO REPATRIATE THE DEAD

A. The Failure of the Legal System to Protect Native Burial Sites

1. Common Law
The legal system also contributed to the disparate treatment of Native American human remains and funerary objects by failing to incorporate indigenous needs and values into the common law as it developed in the United States. . . . Unfortunately, during its development in this country, the com-

mon law failed to take into account unique . . . Native mortuary practices such as scaffold, canoe, or tree burials.[23] The law did not protect unmarked Native graves like it protected marked European graves. Nor did the law recognize that Native people maintain close religious connections with ancient dead; instead, the right to protect the dead was limited to the decedent's immediate next of kin. The law also failed to take into account relevant historical circumstances such as government removal of tribes away from their burial grounds, and the need to accord legal protection for the graves and cemeteries that were involuntarily left behind.

Native people were faced with highly ethnocentric decisions in some common-law cases. For example, in *Wana the Bear v. Community Construction, Inc.*,[24] the court held that a historic Indian cemetery was not a "cemetery" within the meaning of state cemetery-protection laws.[25] In *State v. Glass*,[26] the court held that older human skeletal remains are not considered "human" for purposes of an Ohio grave-robbing statute, which leaves only aboriginal remains in an unprotected status in that state.[27] The decision in *Carter v. City of Zanesville*[28] held that a cemetery may be considered "abandoned" if no further interments are done.[29] The abandonment doctrine might make sense if applied to European communities that voluntarily abandon local cemeteries, but it becomes highly ethnocentric when applied to cemeteries of relocated Indian tribes.

2. State Statutory Law

Loopholes in state statutory law, which universally supplement common law protections, contributed to the failure to protect Native graves.[30] State grave and cemetery protection statutes typically regulated and protected marked graves, but not unmarked graves. Because in many instances Indian graves are unmarked, they received no statutory protection. As such, many unmarked Indian graves were discovered, disturbed, or dug up through construction, natural causes, or pothunting—and the remains were never reburied. For example, Illinois, despite comprehensive grave-protection laws, allowed an entire Indian cemetery containing 234 men, women, and children to be uncovered for public display at the Dixon Mounds Museum.[31]

B. Legal Theories Supporting Protection and Repatriation of Native Dead

Despite the failure of law and social policy to protect Native American graves in the past, a proper non-discriminatory application of the law provides a strong legal basis for tribal grave protection and repatriation efforts. In addition to new statutory rights, five sources of law exist that can provide the underpinning for tribal grave protection efforts and repatriation claims: (1) the common law; (2) the Equal Protection Clauses of the Fifth and Fourteenth Amendments; (3) the First Amendment; (4) the sovereign right of Indian tribal governments to govern internal domestic affairs; and (5) Indian treaties.

1. Common Law

If applied equally, [case] law offers a variety of protections for Native Americans. Although the common law that protects the dead is voluminous and sometimes obscure, it dispels many popular myths and legal fictions that have been injurious to Native Americans. First, no "property interest" exists in a dead body in the eyes of the . . . law.[32] This rule makes it impossible to own the remains of a Native American; the dead of any race are simply not [items of personal property] to be bought or sold in the marketplace.

Second, the popular fiction that a landowner may own and sell the contents of Indian graves located on his land is legally erroneous. A landowner only has technical possession of graves located on his land and is required to hold them in trust for the relatives of the deceased.[33] Therefore, no institution may have title to dead Indians obtained from landowners because landowners have no title to convey.[34]

Another harmful myth that is popular among pothunters and private collectors is that objects found in Indian graves belong to the finder under a finders keepers, losers weepers rule. This myth runs afoul of the rule that personal possessions interred with the dead[35] are not abandoned property. To the contrary, whenever funerary objects are removed from graves, they belong to the person who furnished the grave or to his known descendants.[36] Thus, the title that pot hunters and collectors have to objects that were removed from Indian graves may be invalid under the common law. In summary, common law protections should apply to Indian graves and Indian dead with the same force that the courts have applied them to the dead of other races. In fact, some courts have applied the common law to protect Indian dead.[37]

2. Equal Protection

Disparate racial treatment in matters affecting Indian dead may run afoul of the Equal Protection Clauses of the Fifth and Fourteenth Amendments.[38] An Equal Protection claim may arise if government agencies treat Indian graves or remains differently than the dead of other races. Laws and policies that treat Indian dead as archaeological resources, property, or historic property are suspect when compared to laws that ordinarily protect the dead of other races. Overt discrimination, such as the 1868 Surgeon General's Order,* could not pass muster today under the Equal Protection Clause.

3. First Amendment

First Amendment Free Exercise rights are implicated if the government withholds Indian dead from next of kin or tribes of origin. Mankind has always buried the dead with religion, and Native Americans are no different. Therefore, it is not surprising that Native religious beliefs and practices may be infringed upon when tribal dead are desecrated, disturbed, or withheld from burial by the government. . . .

Indeed, Indian Tribes, Native Alaskans, and Native Hawaiians commonly believe that if the dead are disturbed or robbed, the spirit is disturbed and wan-

---

* See Beider, *supra* pp. 168–169.

ders—a spiritual trauma for the deceased that can also bring ill upon the living.[39] The adverse impacts of such interference on tribal religion was described by the Carter Administration to Congress in 1979 as follows:

> Native American religions, along with most other religions, provide standards for the care and treatment of cemeteries and human remains. Tribal customary laws generally include standards of conduct for the care and treatment of all cemeteries encountered and human remains uncovered, as well as for the burial sites and bodies of their own ancestors. Grounded in Native American religious beliefs, these laws may, for example, require the performance of certain types of rituals at the burial site, specify who may visit the site or prescribe the proper disposition of burial offerings.
>
> The prevalent view in the society of applicable disciplines is that Native American remains are public property and artifacts for study, display, and cultural investment. It is understandable that this view is in conflict with and repugnant to those Native people whose ancestors and near relatives are considered the property at issue. Most Native American religious beliefs dictate that burial sites once completed are not to be disturbed or displaced, except by natural occurrence.[40]

State interference with religious-based mortuary beliefs and practices has given rise to a Free Exercise cause of action when other citizens are concerned.[41] The continuing strength of First Amendment protection, however, must be reassessed in light of a recent United States Supreme Court decision. In *Employment Division of Oregon v. Smith*,[42] the Supreme Court seriously weakened religious liberty for all citizens.[43]

4. Sovereign Rights

Political rights of Indian Nations as sovereigns can provide another legal basis to repatriate dead tribal members and ancestors. One basic attribute of tribal sovereignty that has been repeatedly recognized by the Supreme Court is the right of Indian tribes to govern domestic internal affairs of their members.[44] In *United States v. Quiver*,[45] the Court said that "the relations of the Indians among themselves—the conduct of one toward another—is to be controlled by the customs and laws of the tribe, save when Congress expressly or clearly directs otherwise."[46]

One internal domestic matter that falls squarely within this zone of tribal sovereignty is the relationship between the living and the dead. Therefore, domestic relationships involving the dead may not be interfered with by federal or state government except "when Congress expressly or clearly directs otherwise."[47] . . .

5. Treaties

Indian treaty rights may also provide a legal theory for tribes to repatriate members or ancestors who have been exhumed from lands ceded by treaty.[48] A treaty is "not a grant of rights to the Indians, but a grant of rights from them—a reservation of those not granted."[49] Simply stated, if a treaty does not expressly delineate the reserved tribal powers or rights, it does not mean that they have been divested.[50] To the contrary, "when a tribe and the Government negotiate a treaty, the tribe retains all rights not expressly ceded to the Government in the treaty so long as the rights retained are consistent with the tribe's sovereign dependent status."[51]

Therefore, no treaty expressly granted the United States a right to disturb Indian graves, expropriate Indian dead from ceded lands, or divest a tribe of its pre-existing power to protect those dead.[52] If burials are removed from lands ceded by treaty, a strong argument exists that the signatory tribe implicitly retained or reserved the right to repatriate and rebury the remains.

An implied treaty right becomes apparent when applicable canons of Indian treaty construction are applied to most land cession treaties. The canons require a court to interpret the treaties as understood by the Indians, given their practices and customs as of the date that the treaty was consummated.[53] Thus, even though treaties ceded tribal lands to the United States, it cannot be implied that signatory tribes also relinquished their right to protect tribal dead buried in the ceded lands. Grave robbing was abhorrent to tribal religion.[54] Therefore, the intent to allow desecration cannot fairly be imputed to the Chiefs who signed the treaties. Similarly, it cannot be presumed that the United States intended to obtain Indian lands in order to desecrate Indian graves and obtain dead bodies—at least not until the 1868 Surgeon General's Order. This type of activity was a common-law felony, and the canons of treaty construction preclude imputing an illegal intent to the United States as the fiduciary for Indian tribes.

Although a bundle of legal rights is clearly secured to Indian tribes by the Bill of Rights, treaties, common law, and Federal Indian law, the court system is too costly, time consuming, uncertain, and erratic to adequately redress massive repatriation problems. This is especially true for small, impoverished tribes faced with the problem of having to repatriate large numbers of tribal dead from many different states. Instead, remedial human rights legislation is the superior alternative. . . .

CONCLUSION

After centuries of discriminatory treatment, the Native American Graves Protection and Repatriation Act finally recognizes that Native American human remains and cultural items are the remnants and products of living people, and that descendants have a cultural and spiritual relationship with the deceased. Human remains and cultural items can no longer be thought of as merely "scientific specimens" or "collectibles."

This article was . . . written to remind people that NAGPRA is a part of a larger historical tragedy: the failure of the United States Government, and other institutions, to understand and respect the spiritual and cultural beliefs and practices of Native people. Governmental policies that threaten Native American religions are not merely historical anachronisms, but continue to have a devastating impact upon contemporary Native Americans. Sites sacred to traditional Indian religious practitioners are currently threatened with destructive development. Centuries-old religious peyote use is threatened by ethnocentric court decisions. Native American prisoners are unable to practice their religions in a manner comparable to the respect accorded Judeo-Christian religious practice. . . .

NAGPRA is unique legislation because it is the first time that the Federal Government and non-Indian institutions must consider what is sacred from an Indian perspective. Future legislation must be imbued with this same heightened consciousness of the nature of Indian culture and spirituality. The authors hope that the understanding, sensitivity, and moral outrage that gave rise to and is reflected in NAGPRA will likewise result in across-the-board protection and respect for traditional Native American religions—which continue to be under assault in the last decade of the Twentieth Century.

NOTES

1. See generally Catherine Bergin Yalung and Laurel I. Wala, "Statutory Survey, Survey of State Repatriation and Burial Protection Statutes," 24 *Arizona State Law Journal* 419 (1992).

2. See, e.g., Hearings on S. 1021 and S. 1980 Before the Senate Select Comm. on Indian Affairs, 101st Cong., 2d Sess. (May 14, 1990) (exhibit 5 to statement of Walter R. Echo-Hawk) [hereinafter Senate Hearing on S. 1021 & S. 1980].

3. See, e.g., *Stastny v. Tachovsky*, 132 N.W.2d 317, 325 (Neb.1964).

4. E.g., Neb.Rev.Stat. s 71-605(5), (6) (1989) (specifying that disinterment may only be done by a licensed funeral director under a permit from the Bureau of Vital Statistics requested by next of kin; if more than one human body is concerned, the applicant must also obtain a court order that must specify the place for reinterment).

5. See generally Percival E. Jackson, *The Law of Cadavers and of Burial and Burial Places* 2d. ed. New York, N.Y.: Prentice-Hall, 1950.

6. No accurate national census of these dead has yet been done. Various estimates, however, are compiled in Harris, supra note 4, at 195 n. 3, including Haas (100,000–150,000), Moore (300,000–600,000 in the U.S. alone), National Congress of American Indians (more than 1.5 million), and Deloria (2 million). NAGPRA requires federal agencies and federally funded museums to inventory these dead within five years. 25 U.S.C.A. § 3003(b)(1)(B).

7. One historical study in particular was made widely available to Congress to provide a historical backdrop for NAGPRA: Robert E. Bieder, "A Brief Historical Survey of the Expropriation of American Indian Remains," Bloomington, Ind.: R.E. Bieder, 1990 [hereinafter Bieder Report], reprinted in Senate Hearing on S. 1021 & S. 1980, supra note 8, at 278–363; see also Robert E. Bieder, *Science Encounters the Indian, 1820–1880.* (1st ed.) Norman: University of Oklahoma Press, c.1986; Douglas Cole, *Captured Heritage: The Scramble for Northwest Coast Artifacts,* Seattle, Wash.: University of Washington, 1985; Stephen Jay Gould, *The Mismeasure of Man,* (1st ed.) New York, N.Y.: Norton, c. 1981; Orlan J. Svingen, *History of the Expropriation of Pawnee Indian Graves in the Control of the Nebraska State Historical Society,* Boulder, Colo. Native American Rights Fund, 1989; James T. Riding In, "Report Verifying the Identity of Six Pawnee Scout Crania at the Smithsonian and the National Museum of Health and Medicine" (1990), reprinted in Senate Hearing on S. 1021 & S. 1980, supra note 8, at 211–229.

8. Dwight B. Heath, *Mourt's Relation: A Journal of the Pilgrims at Plymouth* New York, N.Y.: Corinth Books. Distributed by Citadel Press, 1963, pp. 27–28.

9. Id.; see also Russel Thornton, *American Indian Holocaust and Survival: A Population History since 1492.* 1st ed. Norman, Okla.: University of Oklahoma Press, 1987.

10. The Surgeon General's Order is reproduced in full in Bieder Report, supra note 13, at 36–37.

11. Riding In, supra note 7, at 223.

12. See Entries in accession records for the Army Medical Museum, Anatomical Section: A.M.M. nos. 8–12 from W.H. Forwood, Assistant Surgeon, U.S. Army, Ft. Riley, Kansas, Jan. 20, 1867.

13. Bieder, supra note 7, at 325.

14. 16 U.S.C.§ § 431–433 (1988).

15. American common law has always held that a dead body is not "property." See, e.g., 88–73 Kan.Op.Att'y Gen. (1988); Jackson, supra note 5, at 129–31, 133–134; 22A Am.Jur.2d Dead Bodies s 2; 25A C.J.S. Dead Bodies s 2; R.F. Martin, Annotation, Corpse-Removal and Reinterment, 21 A.L.R.2d 472, 480, 486 (1950).

16. 16 U.S.C. s 432 (1988); see also Archaeological Resources Protection Act, 16 U.S.C. s 470bb(1), 470(b)(3) (1988).

17. Preliminary figures of a few federal agencies supplied to the Native American Rights Fund in 1990 show almost 14,500 deceased Natives in their possession:

National Park Service	3500 Dead Bodies
Tennessee Valley Authority	10,000 Dead Bodies
Bureau of Land Management	109 Dead Bodies
Fish and Wildlife Service	637 Dead Bodies
Air Force	146+ Dead Bodies
Navy	85+ Dead Bodies

(Survey responses in possession of the Native American Rights Fund)

18. For example, American property-law principles provide that no one may assert a claim to stolen or wrongfully acquired property; nonetheless, it took the Six Nations Confederacy seventy-five years to negotiate the return of its wampum belts, which are important communally owned patrimony of the Confederacy. See *Onondaga Nation v. Thatcher*, 61 N.Y.S. 1027, 1028, 1032 (Sup.Ct. Onondaga Co.1899) (failed judicial attempt to repatriate belts); see also Memorandum from Thomas Sobol, Commissioner of Education, State of New York, "Proposed Return of 12 Wampum Belts to the Onondaga Nation" (undated) (on file with author).

19. Cole, supra note 7, at 286–310.

20. ("AIRFA"), 42 U.S.C. § 1996 (1988).

21. See, e.g., *The Concept of Sacred Materials and Their Place in the World* (George P. Horse Capture ed. Cody, Wyo.: Plains Indian Museum, Buffalo Bill Historical Center, 1989; Bowen Blair, "American Indians v. American Museums, A Matter of Religious Freedom," 5 *American Indian Law Review* 13 (1979); Bruce Davis, "Indian Religious Artifacts: The Curator's Moral Dilemma," 2 *Indian Law Supp. Court Reporter* 1 (1980); Bowen Blair, Note, "Indian Rights: Native Americans versus American Museums—A Battle for Artifacts, 7 *American Indian Law Review* 125 (1979).

22. See, e.g., Walter R. Echo-Hawk, "Museum Rights vs. Indian Rights: Guidelines for Assessing Competing Legal Interests in Native Cultural Resources," 14 *New York University Review of Law & Social Change* 437 (1986).

23. See generally H.C. Yarrow, *North American Indian Burial Customs* V. LaMonte Smith, ed. (1st ed.) Ogden, Utah: Eagle's View Publishing Co. (1988); David Bushnell, Burial of the Algonquian, Siouan, and Caddoan Tribes West of the Mississippi," 83 *Bureau of American Ethnology Bulletin* (1927).

24. 180 Cal. Rptr. 423 (Ct.App.1982).

25. Id. at 425–427.

26. 273 N.E.2d 893 (Ohio Ct.App.1971).

27. Id. at 896–898.

28. 52 N.E. 126 (Ohio 1898).

29. Id. at 127.

30. See generally Yalung & Wala, supra note 1.

31. Hugh Dellios, "Town Fears Burial Mounds May Never Be the Same," *Chi.Trib.*, Oct. 13, 1991, at 1.

32. See supra note 15; see also *Charrier v. Bell*, 496 So.2d 601, 607 (La.Ct.App.), cert. denied, 498 So.2d 753 (La.1986) (funerary objects from 200-year-old Indian graves belong to descendent Indian tribe).

33. See, e.g., *Busler v. State*, 184 S.W.2d 24, 27 (Tenn.1944).

34. See id.

35. These grave objects are defined as "funerary objects" in NAGPRA. 25 U.S.C.A. s 3001(3)(A), (B).

36. See, e.g., *Maddox v. State*, 121 S.E. 251 (Ga.Ct.App.1924); *Ware v. State*, 121 S.E. 251 (Ga.Ct.App.1924); *Ternant v. Boudreau*, 6 Rob. 488 (La.1844); *Charrier*, 496 So.2d at 607; *State v. Doepke*, 68 Mo. 208 (1878); *Busler v. State*, 184 S.W.2d 24 (Tenn.1944).

37. See, e.g., *United States v. Unknown Heirs*, 152 F.Supp. 452 (W.D.Okla.1957); *Charrier*, 496 So.2d at 607; *Matter of Indian Cemetery, Queens County, N.Y.*, 169 Misc. 584 (N.Y.Sup.Ct.1938).

38. *Rice v. Sioux City Cemetery*, 349 U.S. 70, 80 (1955) (Black, J., dissenting) (a discrimination claim by next of kin to a deceased Winnebago Indian who was refused burial in an all white cemetery was moot by the time it reached the Supreme Court).

39. See, e.g., Hearing on S. 187 Before the Senate Select Comm. on Indian Affairs on Native American Museum Claims Commission Act, 100th Cong., 2d Sess., 282–307 (1988) [hereinafter Senate Hearing on S. 187] (testimony of Roger Echo-Hawk of Pawnee Mortuary Traditions).

40. American Indian Religious Freedom Act Report 64, supra note 20.

41. See, e.g., *Fuller v. Marx*, 724 F.2d 717 (8th Cir.1984).

42. 494 U.S. 872 (1990).

43. Id. at 883–888; see also *Intercommunity Ctr. for Justice and Peace v. I.N.S.*, 910 F.2d 42 (2d Cir.1990); *Salaam v. Lockhart*, 905 F.2d 1168 (8th Cir.1990); *Salvation Army v. New Jersey Dep't of Community Affairs*, (3rd Cir.1990); *South Ridge Baptist Church v. Industrial Comm'n of Ohio*, 911 F.2d 1203 (6th Cir.1990); *Cornerstone Bible Church v. City of Hastings*, 740 F.Supp. 654 (D.Mich.1990); *Montgomery v. County of Clinton*, 743 F.Supp. 1253 (W.D.Mich.1990); *Yang v. Sturner*, 750 F.Supp. 558 (D.R.I.1990). A full discussion of the impact of the *Smith* decision is beyond the scope of this Article.

44. See *United States v. Kagama*, 118 U.S. 375, 383–384 (1883); Ex Parte Crow Dog, 109 U.S. 556, 570 (1181). Indian Tribes have an inherent sovereign right to regulate internal social relations. See, e.g., *United States v. Antelope*, 430 U.S. 641, 645 (1977); *United States v. Mazurie*, 419 U.S. 544, 557 (1975); *McClanahan v. Arizona Tax Comm'n*, 411 U.S. 164, 173 (1973). Tribes have exercised this authority in a variety of contexts. See, e.g., *United States v. Wheeler*, 435 U.S. 313 (1978) (criminal jurisdiction to punish members for illegal activity); *Fisher v. District Court*, 424 U.S. 382 (1976) (divorce and child custody matters); *Jones v. Meehan*, 175 U.S. 1 (1899) (inheritance); *Johnson v. Chilkat Indian Village*, 457 F.Supp. 384, 388–89 (D.Alaska 1978) (regulating property rights); *Wear v. Sanger*, 2 S.W. 307 (Mo.1886) (regulating property rights).

45. 241 U.S. 602 (1916).

46. Id. at 605–606.

47. Id.

48. See Echo-Hawk, supra note 4, at 4.

49. *United States v. Winans*, 198 U.S. 371, 381 (1905).

50. *Babbitt Ford, Inc. v. Navajo Indian Tribe*, 710 F.2d 587 (9th Cir.), cert. denied, 466 U.S. 926 (1983).

51. *United States v. Adair*, 723 F.2d 1394, 1413 (9th Cir.1984); see also *Oregon Wildlife Dep't v. Klamath Tribe*, 473 U.S. 753, 764–74 (1985); *Oliphant v. Suquamish Indian Tribe*, 435 U.S. 191, 208 (1978); *United States v. Ahtanum Irrigation Dist.*, 236 F.2d 321, 326 (9th Cir.1956), cert. denied, 352 U.S. 988 (1957).

52. Felix Cohen's *Handbook of Federal Indian Law*, Rennard Strickland et al. eds. Charlotesville, Vir.: Michie/Bobbs-Merrill, 1982, pp. 485–608. [hereinafter Cohen].

53. See, e.g., *Washington v. State Commercial Fishing Vessel Ass'n*, 443 U.S. 658, 675–676 (1979); *Choctaw Nation v. Oklahoma*, 397 U.S. 620, 631 (1970); *United States v. Winans*, 198 U.S. 371, 381 (1905); *Worcester v. Georgia*, 31 U.S. (6 Pet.) 515, 551–554 (1832); *United States v. Adair*, 723 F.2d 1394, 1412–1413 (9th Cir.1984); *United States v. Top Sky*, 547 F.2d 486, 487 (9th Cir.1976).

54. See, e.g., Senate Hearing on S. 187, supra note 39.

Congressional Hearings

Statement of Hon. John McCain, U.S. Senator from Arizona, Vice Chairman, Select Committee on Indian Affairs

. . .

A . . . milestone was reached this past year when the President signed into law legislation which established a museum for the American Indian.* As part of this legislation, an agreement was reached with the Smithsonian to repatriate the Native American human remains and funerary objects currently contained in their collections. It is my hope that the hearing today will continue this dialog and that we will be able to have frank and open exchanges of ideas as to how to best address these issues. . . .

Statement of Jerry L. Rogers, Associate Director, Cultural Resources, National Park Service, Department of the Interior

Mr. ROGERS: . . . I think it is important to understand that each agency makes its own policy depending upon the direction of statutes, so that there is no single policy that guides all Federal agencies. However, it is true that Federal agencies frequently—in fact, I would say generally—adopt the basic guidelines in the Department of the Interior policy for dealing with cultural resources. The Secretary of the Interior's policy, I think, is more important than just some other agency head's policy would be.

The present policy states that we are prepared to repatriate human remains. However, I think that the wording of the policy is such that it implies a difficult

From *Native American Grave and Burial Protection Act (Repatriation)*, Hearing before the Select Committee on Indian Affairs, United States Senate, 101st Congress, 2d Session on S. 1021 and S. 1980, May 14, 1990.

* 20 U.S.C.A. §§80 7–15 (West 1990).

negotiation process. It is one that American Indians themselves have generally believed to be not conducive to repatriation. Actually, we are only undergoing a modification of that policy to make it clearer that we are willing to deal with this as a human rights issue, as the Chairman eloquently stated it.

The CHAIRMAN*: At the present time, is there a policy for the repatriation of Indian remains and a policy for the return of non-Indian remains?

Mr. ROGERS: There is not a separate policy . . . but I think that we would have to acknowledge that in some cases there have been two practices.

The CHAIRMAN: What have the two practices been? Could you describe them?

Mr. ROGERS: For example, I think of the archeological investigations that the National Park Service conducted at Custer Battlefield National Monument three years ago. Fragments of human bodies were recovered and these were almost all fragments of the bodies of soldiers who had been killed in the fight and had been hastily buried a few days after the fight and then their remains had been recovered and moved to their present resting places some time afterward. Some fragments of those bodies were missed in that last move.

We discovered several of those and we studied them, which is, frankly, what I think we should do. We should try to gain that information which it is possible to gain. Then after doing that, we reburied them with honors in the grave where the rest of the human remains from the soldiers killed in the battle are buried. That is one practice.

I do not believe that we generally follow that practice when we are dealing with prehistoric and sometimes even late historic sites dealing with American Indians. I believe that a resolution that treats all human remains the same regardless of ethnic derivation should be one that is satisfactory to all parties.

The CHAIRMAN: So at this battle ground, we returned the remains of the soldiers and buried them with honors. What happened to the remains of Indians that were discovered at the same battle site?

Mr. ROGERS: The remains of Indians were not discovered in this archeological investigation. Basically, this was an investigation to identify the remains that were left on the battlefield at the end of the fight. The Indian remains that were left on the battlefield in those circumstances would have been only a very few Indians who happened to be allied with the United States Army at the battle.

The Indians who were in the encampment that Custer attacked—those bodies were recovered by their families and friends and disposed of in their way right after the battle. We don't know where they are. . . .

Senator McCAIN: Mr. Rogers, you stated that there is no single policy in the Federal Government; that each department has a different policy. Is that correct?

Mr. ROGERS: There is no overall policy that every agency has to follow.

Senator McCAIN: So obviously, there is a need for one.

Mr. ROGERS: Senator McCain, I believe that there is a need. . . .

---

* Senator Daniel Inouye.

Statement of Paul Bender, Trustee, Heard Museum, Phoenix, Ari.

Mr. BENDER: I am Paul Bender. Thank you very much for the kind words about the Heard Museum and about the dialog panel.*

The dialog process was a very interesting one for me. At the beginning of the dialog, if you had asked the members of the panel whether they could reach agreement on most of the issues, I think the answer would have been no. They perceived that they had vastly differing views. Nevertheless, after some difficulty in getting started, when the members of the panel started talking to each other directly about the issues, it turned out that there was an amazing amount of agreement. . . .

[T]his panel represented the first time that these constituencies had really sat down and talked to each other. The main thing that has struck me about the repatriation issue in the United States in the recent and far past is that there had been a marked lack of communication among the various parties. . . .

The central substantive recommendation of the dialog panel is what you might characterize as a principle of tribal determination of the disposition of culturally affiliated materials. That is, the majority of the panel believes that the tribe should not only have a full partnership role in discussions, but also in the decision making. If the discussions do not result in agreement, then the views of the tribe which is culturally affiliated with the materials must be followed.

This recommendation flows from a principle that . . . this is a human rights issue. It is a human rights issue because museums only have this material as a result of human rights violations.

If the Native American population in this country had been treated equally, with full respect, over the past 100–150 years, then these materials would not have been collected in the way they were. For the museums to continue to keep them over the objections of tribes from which they were taken without the tribe's full, free, voluntary consent, is a continuing human rights violation. That was the view that a very strong consensus of the panel agreed upon. . . .

There are a lot of other kinds of solutions that can be talked about and that can be reached if the concerned parties get together to discuss things. For example, it might be possible to return materials to the tribes under conditions that would permit access to scientists in the future if the need should arise.

Some tribes may not want some materials returned. They may want to leave them with museums, but would perhaps like to have control over the way that the materials are handled in the museums, the way the materials are displayed, whether they are displayed or not, and what kinds of things are said about them when they are displayed.

I think that it would be better if the legislation could affirmatively recognize that it is this kind of cooperative working out of a mutually agreeable solution that is important and that the solutions do not have to be either repatriation or nothing. There are a lot of in between possibilities.

---

* "Report of the Panel for a National Dialogue on Museum/Native American Relations (Feb. 28, 1990). Hearing Before the Committee on Interior and Insular Affairs, House of Representatives, 101st Congress, 2d Sess. on H.R. 1614 and H.R. 5237 (7/17/90). See also, Margaret B. Bowman, "The Reburial of Native American Skeletal Remains: Approaches to the Resolution of a Conflict," 13 *Harvard Environmental Law Review* 147 (1989).

Second, the current draft seems to me to permit either Federal agencies and museums—or perhaps only museums and other non-Federal institutions—the right to retain materials over the objections or contrary to the wishes of an affiliated group, if the museum can prove legal title to the materials. The term "legal title" is not defined in the legislation.

That is a very troubling provision depending upon what "legal title" means. If "legal title" means that something was acquired from a tribal official or an individual who had authority to alienate the material and who alienated it voluntarily and with full knowledge of what he or she was doing, then I don't think the panel would have difficulty with the concept that museums should be able to keep that material over the current wishes of the tribe. Very little material was acquired in that way, however.

If you say, without providing a definition, that a museum showing "legal title" can keep material, probably what you are doing is remitting those materials to State law definitions of what "legal title" is. I don't think that is the right policy to have in a Federal statute. I think there should be a uniform policy on this issue throughout the country.

Some State definitions of title might be such that most repatriation requests would be frustrated or denied. I think that would be a shame.

No. 1; it is not an *ex post facto* situation. That concept only applies to criminal laws or penalties, and this is not that. No. 2; I think it is very, very unlikely that we have a concept in this country that you can acquire property in human remains or funerary objects or other inalienable items. I don't think, therefore, that there is a strong property interest in these materials in the museums. No. 3; the legislation that you are considering does not require museums to do anything. It simply conditions Federal funding on their doing that. If a museum feels that the title concepts of State law are more important to it than the policies of the Federal Government it can reject the Federal funding and keep the materials, and finally; in the present draft there is another exception for materials that are indispensable for the completion of a scientific study, the outcome of which would be of major benefit to the United States. That is a little troublesome also.

In the first place, I think it would be good to have a time limit on those studies. The way it is now, those studies could go on for 10, 15, 30, or 40 years. Academic studies tend to go on as long as they possibly can unless a time limit is imposed. Even then, they tend to go on beyond the time limit.

I think there ought to be a fairly short time limit. If the study needs more time, then there ought to be a provision for applying for an extension of time, which again would have to be brief.

Second, as far as process goes, the need for a scientific study should not be determined by the museum or the scientific community unilaterally. That is the very kind of issue that needs to be talked about with the Native American community. I think the current bill could make it clearer that there has to be that kind of discussion of that issue.

Finally, if it comes down to scientific needs versus the tribe's claim that it wants the materials back or that it does not want to have scientific work done on the materials, I find it hard to think that the scientific value should predominate over what is a very strong human rights concern. Science is important, but I think that human rights are even more important.

The most difficult issue for the dialog panel was the treatment of unaffiliated or unidentified remains. A majority of the panel finally concluded after a tremendous amount of discussion that the human rights principle there requires that those remains be given a decent burial within a finite period of time. . . .

I think that the passage of this legislation will create a new era in museum/ Native American relations by emphasizing a tradition of cooperation between the two communities, which is going to lead to much better museums and finally to putting to rest the tremendous resentment that has grown up because of the fact that affiliated groups have not been given control over the materials with which they are affiliated. . . .

Statement of Willard Boyd, President, Field Museum of Natural History, Chicago, Ill.

Mr. BOYD: . . . Where I . . . depart from my colleague—I, too, am a former professor of law—is that I think Paul overstates what museums have done to damage our country. I think that while there are certainly examples that should never have happened, on the other hand, we have these great collections because of the concern and respect that people have had for each other's culture.

Where I do depart from the majority of the panel is on the question of legal standards. I believe that all legal standards should be applicable, including the Native American customary law and also the important standards that apply to museum stewardship such as fiduciary duties and the like. . . .

We are looking at human remains. Where a group with cultural affinity requests human remains for reconsecration, [the Field Museum] will transmit them to that group without any question whatsoever.

We are also concerned with sacred objects needed for the practice of religion where we would proceed on a case by case decision basis. Should we not be able to reach agreement on this subject, we would be prepared under the law of Illinois, the State arbitration statute, to submit this to an impartial tribunal with the right to judicial review, which would be necessary and which we also feel would be essential to confirm the transfer of title, protecting ourselves, because on the one hand, while you could cut off the Federal funds, we still do have the problem of the de-accession which we feel we could handle by judicial approval of the action of the arbitrator. . . .

Where there is not a local museum policy, then I think there needs to be State and/or Federal legislation. . . .

I would like to conclude by simply reiterating and reinforcing a very powerful statement made by Walter Echohawk in 1986 when he said, "Since their inception, museums in the United States have had a relationship with Native Americans that has been both beneficial and antagonistic. Museums played a vital role in the preservation of Native American culture during crisis periods in which the Federal Government actively sought to assimilate the Indian into the mainstream of American Society. Today, these collections provide a means for all Americans to better understand, appreciate, and respect past and present-day Indians. Museums have played and continue to play a role as a bridge between cultures." And Mr. Echohawk correctly concludes that, "The relationship between museums and Indians has not always lived up to its fullest potential."

I believe that it is essential that we take this opportunity to assure that the relationship between museums and Native Americans will live up to its fullest potential. Furthermore, I do not think that we should view this debate as only one between Native Americans on the one hand and insensitive, faceless museums on the other. What is involved here is the enlightenment and understanding of millions of Americans who come each year to museums to be educated and to learn about each other. Indeed, the Native American collections in the museums provide the means of teaching today's citizens about our Native American past in ways that benefit everybody. . . .

We have had a long relationship . . .—sometimes love, sometimes hate—but we have been together a long time and I see great possibilities down the line.

The CHAIRMAN: . . . I noted that Mr. Bender, in his statement, suggested that there is no one solution—it is not just repatriation. I must say that my unscientific study seems to bear this out as highlighted by Mr. Echohawk.

In my meetings with tribal leaders throughout this land during the past 2 or 3 years, many have suggested that, "We don't seek a return of these goods, but we would want our sacred objects to be treated with respect. No. 2, we notice that many of these objects are never displayed."

In the Heye Collection there are over a million items and it would be physically impossible to display all of them in a century's time. We would be lucky if we could display 10 percent during the next century, so we are going to have 900,000 items hidden away in boxes and such. They said, "Can't we even borrow them?"

Third, if title can be somehow determined, they would like to have that noted on the collection if it is going to be displayed, that this belongs to the Shoshone; this belongs to the Chippewa, and the Chippewa out of their good graces are permitting you to display this. These are not major obstacles. . . .

As far as the technical matter of legal title, I suppose that as a lawyer I would say that we should abide by what the courts have declared to be legal and, maybe in the process, work out a set of rules and legal precedent that would apply to this type of activity. I concur with you that there is much work ahead of us, but that will not deter us from acting. . . .

In discussing this matter with anthropologist scientists, and museum directors, they seem to be very fearful that you will have an onslaught, an avalanche of demands . . .

I can assure you that if that onslaught or avalanche was going to happen, it would have happened a long time ago. For all of these years, the Indian community has made very few demands and I do not see why this new law would add a new impetus to all of this.

I think that what the Indian community is seeking is very simple. They want to be treated like people—as you said, like all other people.

When I have addressed this matter to other groups, I have said, "How would you feel if we had a collection of just Irish skulls or Chinese skulls or Japanese skulls or German or Dutch skulls. There would be an uproar in the United States.

We have not had an uproar because we maintain collections of Indian skulls. I think this sad chapter should be closed. . . .

Senator McCAIN: . . . Mr. Boyd, how many human remains and Native American objects are in the possession of the Field Museum, roughly?

Mr. BOYD: We have approximately 1,200 human remains of Native Americans in the Field Museum. We have roughly 100,000 ethnographic materials from about 100 groups in the country, and we have about 135,000 archeological objects from nearly every State in the Union. Most of those are largely in the field of remnants of pottery and things of that nature.

Senator McCAIN: And how many remains or objects have been repatriated under the museum's policy to date?

Mr. BOYD: The policy went into force this summer. We are now in the process of repatriating two of the first requests we have had. . . .

Senator McCAIN: Mr. Bender, in your view, how would this legislation impact current efforts in various State legislatures, for example, Arizona, to address the issue?*

Mr. BENDER: I think it would facilitate those efforts. I think there is a place for both Federal and State legislation. I think the passage of this legislation will accelerate the trend in the States to take this kind of legislation seriously and to work out procedures, on the local level for dealing with things in their State museums. They would need to be consistent with the Federal legislation but I think there can be specific procedures to deal with a local problem depending on where things are and what the relationships are in the community. . . .

Senator McCAIN: Briefly, Mr. Boyd—I agree with your statements concerning the excellent contributions that museums have made in the area of preserving Native American culture, objects; and artifacts, particularly during a time when forced assimilation; or termination policy was the Nation's policy. I do have to tell you though that there is another side to that coin. It was exemplified by what the Chairman saw at the Smithsonian some time ago, which frankly was one of the triggering mechanisms here—thousands of remains sitting in boxes or lying around unattended for years and years and years.

In all candor and in all deep respect for museums across America, including the Smithsonian, I have to say that those remains were not treated the way other remains would be treated. It's a fact. So at the same time as I agree with your plaudits that you justifiably extend to museums, I also have to say in all candor that the record is indeed checkered as far as the kind of respect that was accorded to these artifacts while they were entrusted to museums.

I also have to get back to the basic question: How much does the keeping of human remains contribute to the preservation of Native American culture: Artifacts, drawings, and all kinds of things can contribute to Americans' treasuring

---

* Ariz. Rev. Stat. Ann. §§41–844 to 866 (1992). See also Paul Bender, 1990 "Arizona Repatriation Legislation," 24 *Arizona State Law Journal* 391 (1992).

and preserving Native American cultures. I am not clear as to why this emphasis is on keeping human remains as a way of preserving Native American culture. . . .

Statement of Walter Echohawk, Esquire, Attorney, Native American Right Fund, Boulder, Colo.

Mr. ECHOHAWK: Good afternoon, Mr. Chairman and members of the Select Committee on Indian Affairs. I am Walter Echohawk, a staff attorney for the Native American Rights Fund. I want to thank you, sir, for the opportunity allowing NARF to participate in this important hearing this afternoon. . . .

First, I would like to say that NARF is generally in support of the proposed . . . bill. . . .

Mr. Chairman, in my opinion, this bill may well be the most important civil rights legislation and human rights legislation for Native people since the passage of the American Indian Religious Freedom Act in 1978.[*] The purposes of the bill are straightforward. It does three basic things.

First, it grants needed legal protections for Indian graves. Second, it allows Indians and Native people to bury their dead under specified repatriation guidelines and procedures. Third, it restores stolen or improperly acquired property to the rightful Native owners upon request.

These are basic human rights, Mr. Chairman, and property rights which most Americans commonly take for granted. Sadly, this has never been the case for Native people. . . .

Today, as we all know, Federal land managers and Indian tribes are beset with illicit grave looting and interstate trafficking of booty from Indian graves. Contemporary examples of these kinds of problems abound. Even today as we speak, ranchers in certain Southwestern States let people dig up Indian graves on their lands for profit. Hundreds of Native dead are on public display in museums and tourist attractions. . . .

It seems clear to me that society's debate over whether these dead are entitled to be reburied or whether Indian tribes are entitled to recover their property is over, and that the focus now is on implementation details. . . .

Statement of Norbert Hill, Executive Director, American Indian Science and Engineering Society, Boulder, Colo.

Mr. HILL: Good afternoon, Mr. Chairman and members of the committee. I am Norbert Hill, Jr., member of the Oneida Nation and executive director of the American Indian Science and Engineering Society (AISES).

As a national organization which supports Indian involvement in the sciences, AISES feels that it is important to register our view concerning the scientific investigation of Indian skeletal remains, mortuary offerings, and grave sites. The reburial and repatriation issues are simple questions of humanity and morality—

[*] ("AIRFA"), 42 U.S.C. §1996 (1988).

of reconciling western scientific ideology and Indian spirituality, and of religious freedom.

Based on this, AISES feels that the dead of all races and nations are entitled to protection from arbitrary disturbances and treatment which is offensive to the rights and sensibilities of living communities. . . .

In the 1930's, one of the worst Smithsonian-sanctioned grave robbings took place in a Native Alaskan village on Kodiak Island.* The skeletons of more than 800 Koniag people were excavated in a cemetery that was still in use at that time. These remains are still housed at the Smithsonian.

Whatever arguments may be made for the potential benefit of research to Indian tribes, scientists must acknowledge the actual, not potential or theoretical, harm which proceeds from the circumstances of clandestine expropriation of the dead, confiscation of funerary offerings, and the conduct of scientific studies without tribal knowledge or consent. Under such conditions, scientific investigation can hardly be termed objective or ethical no matter what benefits might materialize. . . .

AISES disagrees with the reasoning which serves to elevate scientific curiosity above human rights, and which is designed to undermine the authority of Indian governments to protect the disposition and treatment of Indian human remains and grave offerings. We recognize that the treatment of the dead by the American academic institutions affects Indian communities throughout the United States.

Stanford University [had] 550 human remains; Yale, Harvard, and the University of Oklahoma each reported close to 500. Arizona State and the University of Colorado have approximately 350. The University of Missouri curates some 1,500 Indian remains, which the Director of the Museum of Anthropology defined in 1989 as, "a non-renewable resource essential to research," declaring that he had "no intention of letting them go." . . .

The historical emphasis of American universities on building and maintaining collections of Indian skeletal remains must shift to the recruiting of living Indian students. The mission of AISES would be materially served if more Indians were brought in to the academic science studies as students rather than as specimens, as well as the development of relations based on mutual respect between Indians and science communities. . . .

The heart of Indian people lives in the spirit of the past, the past that wells within our hearts and reminds us of the heritage when our ancestors lived in tribes and were close to the Earth. . . .

The CHAIRMAN: Mr. Echohawk, as we proceeded in the evolution of this bill, one question popped up quite constantly. That was: is it appropriate for the Congress of the United States to define the word "sacred?" Put another way, how would you define "sacred"? We have the words "sacred objects."

Do you think it is appropriate for the Congress to place a definition on the word "sacred"?

Mr. ECHOHAWK: I think it is very difficult. I have heard that comment, too, in my various travels, that some of the traditional religious leaders and practitioners

* Mr. Hill is referring to the Larsen Bay repatriation case. For a detailed discussion of this case, see *Reckoning with the Dead: The Larsen Bay Repatriation and the Smithsonian Institution* (Tamara L. Bray and Thomas W. Killion ed.) Washington, D.C.: Smithsonian Institution Press. 1994.

have a great concern about anyone defining the sacred aspects of their religion. However, it does seem to me that because these same practitioners are also requesting the return in limited instance of sacred property that, somehow, we do have to grapple with some kind of definition.

All I can say, Senator, is that hopefully that will be done in a real sensitive manner in consultation with the representatives of these religious leaders, that they might be satisfied. . . .

The CHAIRMAN: Another matter of concern to museums has been the definition of property rights. Many have claimed that they leave rights to this property—property which has been with the museum for many decades. What is your view of the assertion that this law would, in essence, result in an *ex post facto* law that would redefine their property rights. What would your comment be to that?

Mr. ECHOHAWK: . . . I think they are concerns that need to be raised and looked at, but I think that if you do look at it, you will find that there is no legal basis for those concerns because the property that is the subject matter of this particular legislation is human remains, which is not property under the eyes of the common law. . . .

Second, funerary objects—under the common law, they can be property, but they are property that belongs under the common law to the person that furnished the grave to begin with or that person's descendants. Therefore, if you return it, as envisioned under the present statute, to them, then you are not interfering with anybody else's property right.

The same is true with regard to the cultural patrimony which is very narrowly defined in the statute to that rare category of Native property that is inalienable by definition. . . .

The CHAIRMAN: In one of my discussions, the museum official brought up the matter of Egyptian mummies. They are human remains. He said, "We are not required to return them," and in all likelihood, they were also stolen.

Mr. ECHOHAWK: I would presume, sir, that those who are in possession of Egyptian mummies have the lawful consent of the Egyptian people and government to retain them. That is fine. If Egypt or Europe or any other culture, under certain circumstances, determines that it is okay to dig up their dead, well, that's fine and we can respect that. But here in the United States, Native cultures have different viewpoints. . . .

The CHAIRMAN: Will this bill cover the following situation, which has been described to me by one of the witnesses here? I own a large tract of land. I have grazing on this land at the present time. On this land, we recently found a burial site. Who owns the artifacts in that burial site?

Mr. ECHOHAWK: Under the common law there is a legal fiction and a myth that the landowner owns everything embedded in the land. On further examination, that is simply a myth because there is an exception to that rule whereby a landowner does not in fact own dead bodies or funerary objects embedded in his soil. He has technical possession of them, but only in trust for the descendants of those materials.

As this legislation is presently drafted, [it] would make it unlawful to sell those kinds of materials on an interstate basis. Congress does have the authority to do that. It would not interfere with or impair any rights of any property owners.

Implementing the National Policy of Understanding, Preserving, and Safeguarding the Heritage of Indian Peoples and Native Hawaiians: Human Rights, Sacred Objects, and Cultural Patrimony

Rennard Strickland

> You whites assumed we were savages. You didn't understand our prayers. You didn't try to understand. When we sang our praises to the sun or moon or wind, you said we were worshipping idols. Without understanding, you condemned us as lost souls just because our form of worship was different from yours.
>
> We saw the Great Spirit's work in almost everything: sun, moon, trees, wind, and mountains. Sometimes we approached him through these things. Was that so bad? I think we have a true belief in the supreme being, a stronger faith than that of most of the whites who have called us pagans.
>
> . . . Indians living close to nature and nature's ruler are not living in darkness.
>
> —Walking Buffalo (1871–1967)[1]

INTRODUCTION

During the House debate on the Native American Graves Protection and Repatriation Act ("NAGPRA"),[2] Congresswoman Patsy Mink of Hawaii stated quite simply the basis of what has become our national policy: "Preserving native American and Hawaiian culture is in the interest of all Americans, for these unique cultures are a part of the history and heritage of our Nation."[3] The Act is important because it represents the new American consensus about sacred objects and cultural patrimony, a consensus not only of members of the Congress and of Native peoples, but also of very diverse groups of scientists, museum trustees, and art collectors.[4] That consensus is: The sacred culture of Native American and Native Hawaiians is a living heritage. This culture is a vital part of the ongoing lifeways of the United States, and as such, must be respected, protected, and treated as a living spiritual entity—not as a remnant museum specimen.

The primary purpose of this essay is to facilitate an understanding of Native American approaches to sacred objects and cultural patrimony, while suggesting an appropriate tribal context in which to reach decisions consistent with the intended purpose of NAGPRA. . . . The thesis is that Native Americans, through their own codes of law and Indian tribal courts, are the best prepared decision-makers to evaluate factual issues under NAGPRA. Therefore, Indian tribes have an obligation to adopt and enforce their own Native arts, religion, and cultural codes. By enacting such legislation, most factual and interpretative issues can be resolved at a tribal level, which will provide a historical and cultural record that can serve as the basis for potential action by NAGPRA's Review Committee and the courts.

THE NEW NATIONAL POLICY OF UNDERSTANDING, PRESERVING, AND SAFEGUARDING THE HERITAGE OF INDIAN PEOPLES AND NATIVE HAWAIIANS

The enactment of NAGPRA brought to an end almost five hundred years of conflict about culture.[5] The debate about European and Native American lifeways began with such questions as whether or not the original inhabitants of the Americas were a human or a sub-human species. . . . The debate continued in ecclesiastical and governmental circles and resulted in such absurd federal policies as "renaming" Indians; outlawing "heathenish practices," including medicine men, dances, and traditional burials; and such tragic episodes as removal and allotments of tribal lands designed to convert Indians into dirt farmers.[6]

Similarly, the collections of human remains gathered for the cranial studies at the Smithsonian are but one example of a relatively recent variant on the human or sub-human debate.[7] Certainly, the ironic desire to "Americanize the American Indian" reflects this ethnocentric concept of the "civilized" European versus the "savage" Native American.[8] In 1990, newly enacted policies on religious or sacred objects and patrimonial resources signaled a dramatic recognition of the vitality of Native peoples and mandated an effort to understand the Indian's own worldview.

Throughout much of American history, the question for Indian tribes has not been one of cultural understanding and interpretation, but one of actual physical survival. Starvation, massacre, plague, and military ambush dominated much of historic tribal life. Assaults on religion and culture were equally relentless, but less immediately threatening. The magnitude of this historic holocaust was summarized by Russell Thornton:

> [T]he European expansion throughout North America during the sixteenth, seventeenth, and eighteenth centuries produced a demographic collapse of American Indians, primarily because of disease, warfare and destruction of

Indian ways of life. The removal and relocation of Indians also contributed to the collapse. . . . The collapse was so severe by 1800 that the total United States Indian population had been reduced to 600,000 from 5+ million in three centuries. Meanwhile, the non-Indian population of the United States had increased to over 5 million![9]

The nineteenth century was even more devastating in terms of Native survival. Thornton recognized that "the already decimated American Indian population . . . declined . . . from about 600,000 in 1800 to a mere 250,000 between 1890 and 1900."[10] Yet, during this same time period, the non-Indian population blossomed from a mere five million in 1800 to more than seventy-five million in 1900. Is it any wonder that the Creek Chief Pleasant Porter called the Indian a people "on the road to disappearance"?[11]

Although NAGPRA officially draws this tribal culturecide to an end, the task of implementing the new policy, particularly with regard to sacred objects and cultural patrimony, will require much cross-cultural understanding. . . .[12]

The spotlight of conscience and the duty of advocacy has now shifted from Congress, museums, collectors, and the scientific community back to Native peoples and the Indian community. The human rights of Alaska Natives, Indian peoples, and Native Hawaiians are now, under the terms of NAGPRA, back in their own hands. The passage of the legislation, even in the compromised and modified consensus form, brought an end to a long, bitter debate and was a great victory.[13] With victory comes responsibility, and that responsibility is to construct a system of law within the structure of Native tribal governments, courts, and legislative powers that will help all citizens fulfill the mandate of NAGPRA. It would, indeed, be a tragedy if the Native community failed in its task. NAGPRA is not self-actuating, but mandates Native group action if its purposes are to be fulfilled. . . .

NAGPRA's language is quite clear about the role of Native legal concepts, particularly in the definition of "sacred objects . . . cultural patrimony," and "rights of possession."[14] "Sacred objects" includes specific ceremonial objects that are needed by traditional Native American religious leaders for the purpose of traditional Native American religions by their present-day adherents.[15] "Cultural patrimony" includes objects that have ongoing historical, traditional, or cultural importance central to the Native American group or culture itself, rather than property owned by an individual Native American, which cannot be alienated, appropriated, or conveyed, regardless of whether or not the individual is a member of the Indian tribe or Native Hawaiian organization.[16] Moreover, objects of cultural patrimony must have been considered inalienable by such Native American group at the time the object was separated from such group.[17]

The question of *ownership* or "right of possession" is also cast in terms of Native American legal culture, a tribe's own concept of property, and authority of alienation.[18] Right of possession is defined in NAGPRA as:

[P]ossession obtained with the voluntary consent of an individual or group that had authority of alienation. The original acquisition of a Native

American unassociated funerary object, sacred object, or object of cultural patrimony from an Indian tribe or Native Hawaiian organization with the voluntary consent of an individual or group with authority to alienate such object is deemed to give right of possession of that object. . . .[19]

Thus, the interpretation and enforcement of NAGPRA as it relates to sacred objects, objects of cultural patrimony, and unassociated funerary objects requires an understanding of the nature of traditional Native American life and lifeways, as well as the operation of traditional law and tribal courts among Native peoples. NAGPRA has placed the primary task of factual determination in the Native culture itself. This is consistent with the underlying principles of American jurisprudence because the Native American is, in fact, the only source of accurate and meaningful interpretation of the traditional aspects of Native culture. Furthermore, existing Indian tribal courts provide an effective mechanism through which these legal determinations can most accurately be adjudicated.

IMPLEMENTING THE NATIVE OBLIGATION THROUGH TRIBAL COURTS AND ENACTMENT OF INDIAN REPATRIATION AND CULTURAL CODES

NAGPRA has made traditional Native Americans' conceptions the controlling national standard; therefore, it is imperative that traditional Indian lifeways and attitudes be understood. The central task under NAGPRA will be the interpretation and meaning of a tribe's own cultural and legal standards. Furthermore, NAGPRA requires that requests for repatriation come from the Native community; thus, NAGPRA's provisions do not become effective without Indian initiative. Indeed, the Indian concept of property and the right to transfer title to property is a crucial ingredient of the law. Academicians, museum directors, art dealers, collectors, and all concerned with Native arts are compelled by NAGPRA to follow its definition of an object's historic Native creators, not the categorization of commercial art consumers or museum educators, no matter how well-motivated the non-Indian collector might be.

The Native community acting under NAGPRA has a compelling duty and a tremendous responsibility. The tribe is the only unit with the ability to obtain the historical facts and interpret their cultural meanings relating to the return of sacred objects, objects of cultural patrimony, and unassociated funerary objects. The two crucial questions under NAGPRA are: (1) is the item one that meets NAGPRA's definition of "sacred object," "cultural patrimony," or "unassociated funerary object,"[20] and (2) could the transfer of possession of the object occur under tribal law at the time of transfer. These are questions that the . . . courts will be compelled to address if a conflict occurs and litigation ensues. Furthermore, these are questions that the tribe must be prepared to answer before seeking repatriation of sacred objects and cultural patrimony under NAGPRA.

At the present time, tribal legislatures and courts possess the legal rights to undertake the task, but few are prepared to address these questions. . . . Whatever [the] system . . . adopted [by a tribe], it must be meticulously fair and recognize that the intended purpose of NAGPRA is to return only those crucial objects of religious and patrimonial significance—not all arts and crafts produced by the tribe.[21] . . .

CONCLUSION

In the introductory epigram, Walking Buffalo complained that the white man "didn't [try to] understand our prayers."[22] In 1990, with the enactment of the Native American Graves Protection and Repatriation Act, the United States made understanding and preserving Native ways the official national policy. Nonetheless, the task of appreciating and, indeed, protecting the traditional religion of others—the sacred objects and objects of cultural patrimony—is not easy. The burden of implementing NAGPRA rests primarily with Native peoples who through their use of sovereign powers in courts and codes can ensure, as Congresswoman Mink argued, that these unique cultures remain forever "a part of the history and heritage of our nation."[23]

NOTES

1. Grant MacEwan, *Tatanga Mani: Walking Buffalo of the Stonies*, Edmonton, Alta.: M.G. Hurtig, 1969, pp. 181–182 (quoting Chief Walking Buffalo).

2. 25 U.S.C.A. § § 3001–3013 (West. Supp. 1991) (reprinted in appendix).

3. 136 Cong. Rec. H10991 (daily ed. Oct. 22, 1990) (statement of Rep. Mink).

4. Among the groups involved in shaping this consensus or compromise bill were the Congress of American Indians, Antique Tribal Art Dealers Association, the American Association of Museums, the Society of American Archaeology, the Native American Rights Fund, the Friends Committee, and the Association of American Indian Affairs.

5. See generally Robert F. Berkhofer, J., *The White Man's Indian: Images of the American Indian from Columbus to the Present*, 1st ed., New York, N.Y.: Knopf, 1978. Angie Debo, *A History of the Indians of the United States*, 1st ed., Norman, Okla.: University of Oklahoma Press, 1970. Leslie Fiedler, *The Return of the Vanishing American*, New York, N.Y.: Stern and Day, 1968. Hugh Honour, *The New Golden Land: European Images of America from the Discoveries to the Present Time*, 1st ed., New York, N.Y.: Pantheon Books, 1975. Roy Harvey Pearce, *Savagism and Civilization: A Study of the Indian and the American Mind*, Baltimore, Md.: John Hopkins Press, 1967, c. 1965. Richard Slotkin, *Regeneration Through Violence: The Mythology of the American Frontier, 1600–1860*, 1st ed., Middletown: Wesleyan University Press, 1973. Henry Nash Smith, *Virgin Land: The American West as Symbol and Myth*, Cambridge: Harvard University Press, 1950; reprinted New York: Random House, 1970. Raymond Stedman, *Shadows of the Indian: Stereotypes in American Culture*, 1st ed., Norman, Okla.: University of Oklahoma Press, 1982.

6. *See* Rennard Strickland, *The Indians in Oklahoma* 1st ed. Norman, Okla.: University of Oklahoma Press, 1980, pp. 36–54. (discussing renaming of Indians and related federal policies); "Rules for Indian Courts," in *Documents of United States Indian Policy*, Francis

P. Prucha ed., 2d ed., Lincoln, Neb.: University of Nebraska Press, 1990. (reviewing restrictions on Indian cultural practices).

7. 136 Congressional Record S17174 (daily ed. Oct. 26, 1990) (statement of Sen. Inouye).

8. Strickland, *supra* note 6, at 53 (one is reminded of the ironic tone of Will Rogers' observation that "Indians were so cruel they were all killed by civilized white men").

9. Russell Thornton, *American Indian Holocaust and Survival: A Population History Since 1492*, 1st ed., Norman, Okla: University of Oklahoma Press, 1987, pp. 90, 133; *see also* Rennard Strickland, "Genocide-at-Law: A Historic and Contemporary View of the Native American Experience," 34 *Kansas Law Review* 713–55 (1986).

10. Thornton, *supra* note 9, at 133.

11. *See generally* Angie Debo, *The Road to Disappearance* Norman, Okla: University of Oklahoma Press, 1967 (the Pleasant Porter quotation provided the title for Debo's definitive history of the Creeks).

12. For an overview of the long-established debate, and the scholarly as well as popular literature see *American Indian Sacred Objects, Skeletal Remains, Repatriation and Reburial: A Resource List* (Rayna Green comp., 1989). For the treatment of these same issues in the broader context of international law see *Protection of Cultural Property and Archaeological Resources: A Comprehensive Bibliography of Law-related Materials: International Law Bibliography*. New York, N.Y.: Oceana Publications, 1988, Frank G. Houdek comp., 1988. [hereinafter Protection of Cultural Property]. For studies of the issue prior to NAGPRA's passage see Bowen Blair, "American Indians v. American Museums: A Matter of Religious Freedom," 5 *American Indian Journal* 13 (1979); Walter R. Echo-Hawk, "Museum Rights vs. Indian Rights: Guidelines for Assessing Competing Legal Interests in Native Cultural Resources," 14 *New York University Review of Law and Social Change* 437 (1986); C. Dean Higginbotham, "Native Americans Versus Archaeologists: The Legal Issues," 10 *American Indian Law Review* 91 (1982); Dean B. Suagee, "American Indian Religious Freedom and Cultural Resources Management: Protecting Mother Earth's Caretakers," 10 *American Indian Law Review* 1 (1982); Paul E. Wilson and Elaine Oser Lingg, "What Is America's Heritage? Historic Preservation and American Indian Culture," 22 *Kansas Law Review* 413 (1974); and Bowen Blair, Note, "Indian Rights. Native Americans Versus American Museums—A Battle for Artifacts," 7 *American Indian Law Review* 125 (1979).

13. For general development of the basis of American Indian law and the powers of tribal governments and courts see William Canby, Jr., *American Indian Law in a Nutshell*, 2d ed., St Paul, Minn.: West Publishing Co., 1988; Robert Clinton et al., *American Indian Law: Cases and Materials*, 3rd ed., Charlottesville: Michie Co., 1991; Vine Deloria, Jr., and Clifford M. Lyttle, *American Indians, American Justice*, 1st ed., Austin, Tex.: University of Texas Press, 1983; *Felix S. Cohen's Handbook of Federal Indian Law*, (Rennard Strickland et al., eds.) Charlottesville: Michie, 1982; David Getches and Charles Wilkinson, *Cases and Materials on Federal Indian Law*, 2d ed., St. Paul, Minn.: West Publishing Co., 1986; Francis P. Prucha, *The Great Father: The United States Government and the American Indians*, Lincoln, Neb.: University of Nebraska Press, 1984; Charles F. Wilkinson, *American Indians, Time and the Law: Native Societies in a Modern Constitutional Democracy*, New Haven, Conn.: Yale University Press, 1987; and Robert A. Williams, Jr., *The American Indian in Western Legal Thought: The Discourses of Conquest*, New York, N.Y.: Oxford University Press, 1990.

14. 25 U.S.C.A. § 3001(3)(C), (D), (13).

15. Id. § 3001(3)(C).

16. Id. § 3001 (3)(D).

17. Id.

18. Id. § 3001 (13).

19. Id.

20. See 25 U.S.C.A. § § 3001–3013.

21. As Congressman Ben Campbell noted:

This legislation does not include every basket, every pot and every blanket ever made by Indian hands. It refers to human remains, funerary objects, and only the most scared of religious items which were taken from a tribe without permission. It affords current day Indians the opportunity to determine the proper way that their ancestors be treated. 136 Cong. Rec. H10988 (daily ed. Oct. 22, 1990) (statement of Rep. Campbell).

22. MacEwan, supra note 1, at 181.

23. 36 Cong. Rec. H10991 (daily ed. Oct. 22, 1990) (statement of Rep. Mink).

CHAPTER 5

TRIBAL GOVERNANCE/GENDER

S cholars often write that federal Indian law is characterized by pendulum-like shifts in federal policy toward Native American peoples. What is not so often said is that these swings occur along a single trajectory, one that denies the value of indigenous ways as well as the possibility of the United States respecting tribal societies enough to co-create with them a pluralistic American government. Each of the major eras in federal Indian law illustrates this point. They show that at critical moments in history, the United States has consistently chosen oppression and dispossession over embrace or real understanding.

Metaphors have the power to transform belief, and the metaphor of pendulum-like shifts supports the inaccurate belief that the United States has encouraged tribal life within its boundaries during certain "open" or "tolerant" periods. This is not the case. The United States, though shifting in its relation to tribal peoples and their traditional governments, has stayed steady in its subordination of them. Qualifying the metaphor of pendulum-like shifts in federal policy puts federal Indian law where it belongs, which is in the broad context of a colonial history.

With this in mind, one ought to know that scholars typically refer to six major historical periods when describing federal Indian law policy. These periods take their names primarily from U.S. statutes, thus further erasing the importance of Native American names, sensibilities, and experience from the field of federal Indian law. The eras described are the Treaty Era (1789–1871); the Removal Era, which started in 1830 and continued through the nineteenth century; the Allotment and Assimilation Era (1871–1928); the Indian Reorganization Era (1928–1942); the Termination Era (1943–1961); and the era we are in now, which is called the Self-Determination Era (1961–present).[1]

In the treaty era, relationships between many Native American nations and the United States were based on negotiated land cessions. Although definitions for treaties abound, Vine Deloria offers a clarifying one. Deloria says treaties are "primarily documents of diplomacy in which two nations pledge their honor to regulate their future relations according to a set of mutually agreed-upon principles."[2] This definition highlights the fact that early on, the United States dealt with Native American nations as political equals, as indeed they were far more nuanced and developed political entities than was the nascent United States. Deloria's definition is also useful, though, because it counters the view that treaties were simply documents of surrender between a powerful guardian and its tribal wards.

Although some treaties were entered into with integrity by the United States, many more were not. Yet American courts comfortably engage in a legal fiction that the United States always acted in the best interests of the tribes in negotiating treaties.[3] Astonishingly, this theory presumes full tribal consent for every treaty, a presumption that is seriously flawed as a historical matter, especially in light of the U.S. history of fraud and misdealing. Still, as Deloria points out, regardless of the validity of the terms of the treaty, the presence of a treaty itself signifies a nation-to-nation negotiation, not a mere guardian-to-ward adjustment.

As documents of diplomacy, treaties delineated the particulars of how tribal nations ceded land to the United States while simultaneously reserving important rights of sovereignty for themselves. Treaty making overlapped and gradually gave way to "removal," a process by which entire communities were forcibly taken from ancestral lands to small, crowded geographic reserves where it took tremendous effort to re-establish even a subsistence economy. Obviously, removal was a major imposition on tribal sovereignty, despite the blatantly self-serving federal premise underlying the Removal Act of 1830, which was that stripping Native Americans of territorial sovereignty was somehow sharply distinguishable from stripping them of the power to self-govern.[4]

The removal policy was followed by the general allotment policy, another major imposition on tribal sovereignty by the United States and its settlers. In the allotment period, the United States ostensibly tried to make yeoman farmers out of tribal peoples so as to continue the process of tribal suppression. The principal provision of the Allotment Act of 1887 authorized the carving up of tribal land holdings by granting individualized parcels, often of 160 acres, to each "family head."[5] This Act changed tribal landholding patterns, but it also accomplished a far more subtle change. Relying as it did on the "family head" provision to distribute land parcels, the allotment legislation allowed the United States to insinuate itself into the tribal social fabric by systematically privileging tribal males over tribal females. This designation further destabilized tribal traditions, particularly female-centered ones, and it gradually allowed the pluralistic and gender-inclusive ways that many Native American peoples had used in their processes of self-government to slip from practice, if not memory. Allotment brought forced assimilation in terms of schools and missionaries, but it also brought change in the ordering of gender relations. On this latter point in particular, the trauma of allotment still continues.[6]

In 1934, the United States interposed itself into tribal life yet again, this time when it "reorganized" tribal governments along western liberal lines.[7] Reorganization was useful to the United States because it facilitated the continued transfer of tribal property, primarily mineral resources, into nontribal hands. It also offered institutional support to the ongoing shift in tribal gender relations ushered in by the policies of removal and allotment. Reorganized governments authorized tribal governmental leaders, mostly male, and usually by secret ballot, not traditional leaders whose authorization may have been more openly discussed among tribal persons, as in the case of the Muscogee Creek.[8] In addition, newly elected tribal leaders got power under the reorganization policy to lease or negotiate away tribal property. Some did so with the backing of their traditional constituents; many others did so without.

The post–World War II termination era followed, representing a major shift in U.S. policy. Under termination legislation the United States explicitly severed its political and jurisdictional relationship with certain tribes.[9] Often this came when tribes were perceived as being too successful, as in the Menominee case, or else it came after a tribe received a per capita distribution of an Indian Claims Commission award. Tribal America generally opposed termination; eventually, in response to a new wave of Native American radicalism, the U.S. government enacted legislation to end termination and facilitate tribal self-determination.[10]

By examining the way in which these conflicting eras come together, this chapter examines the role law and scholarship play in influencing gender relations within tribal societies. It also presents material on the role of women within indigenous societies past and present, as well as on the impact of law on gender roles and possibilities. In the *Santa Clara v. Martinez* case[11] Santa Clara Pueblo, for fear of allotment, enacted a tribal ordinance in 1939 that excluded from membership only the children of tribal women who married nontribal members, not the children of tribal men who married nontribal members.

Recall that the tribal membership rolls recognized by the federal government are primarily legal creations, not necessarily sociological, cultural, linguistic, or religious ones. The Santa Clara tribal ordinance could arguably have been justified as the Santa Clara tribal government's concern with formally representing the children of women who married nontribal members in political matters between the tribe and the United States, not a cultural, intratribal rejection of those same children, many of whom spoke the tribal language and participated in tribal religious matters. In other words, a tribe could have enacted a gender discriminatory rule to protect property, or (before 1924) to comport with the federal statute that granted tribal women who married nontribal men U.S. citizenship.[12] It could then have justified the rule by noting that its only *real* effect would be to sever Western style political ties between the children of female tribal members who married nonmembers and the tribe, not necessarily cultural, traditional, or theocratic ties.

We have seen how legal doctrine—when it considers nonlegal, experiential accounts—is more likely to listen to professionalized accounts *about* Native Americans than it is to personal ones *by* them. The situation in *Santa Clara v. Martinez* was no exception. American feminists used *Santa Clara* as a foil to argue the plausibility of a universal patriarchal oppression of a universal female culture.[13] Even those who distanced themselves from the premise of a universal female "culture" still used the case to argue that issues like these needed to be viewed in context.[14] None of these feminists spoke with Julia Martinez, the women who brought the lawsuit against her tribal government; they simply supported or condemned her action. But as Ms. Martinez's own attorney noted, "Julia was *not* suing her tribe for feminist reasons. She was participating in her tribal government in the ways that were available to her."[15]

With *Santa Clara v. Martinez* as a backdrop, this chapter begins with an overview of the literature about, and more recently by and about, Native American women. Rayna Green's bibliography is a classic work that summarizes the scholarship about Native American women over the last century and through the 1970s. Green connected her bibliographic essay to the analysis of tribal governments by pointing out that scholars, especially early on, tended to ignore instances of female tribal governance in order to focus instead on figures like Pocahontas—figures Green called "Myth(s) America." While this reliance on stereotype is now being addressed in other fields, it remains a particularly troublesome problem in the area of federal Indian law and in the related area of gender relations within Western-style tribal governments.

In the late 1970s, as Green suggested, focus on stereotype partly derived from scholars either deliberately choosing *not* to study female governance, or—more likely—not being aware of the central role that women play in tribal life. In any event, one of the primary points that Green and others (Vine Deloria, Jr.; Robert Williams, Jr.; Oren Lyons, Wilma Mankiller, Gloria Valencia-Weber, and Christine Zuni, to name just a few) have made and continue to make, even today, is that the role of women is one of the main aspects of tribal society that the dominant society refuses to take seriously. This criticism applies to scholars as well as to others—teachers, administrators, missionaries, lawyers, and so on. Green's critique charges nonnative scholars, including those in the field of Indian law, with preferring to relate to mythical, fictional, symbolic perceptions of native women than to listen to what actual Native American women say about their experiences under U.S. rule. Reformers then embrace these Myths America rather than face the decidedly more anxious concerns of real women from tribal backgrounds. Indeed, part of the reality of tribal life, says Green, despite the fact that it has been entirely overlooked, is that traditions are maintained by women who take it upon themselves to affect change in their communities in ways that have meaning to them.

Since Green's article appeared in 1980, more work by and about Native American women has appeared in print, as Jo Ann Woodsum's updated bibliographic essay shows. But much of this work is typically disregarded in law, especially by scholars who concern themselves primarily with legal doctrine. Further, dismissing work by Native American women as "mere narrative" means that many of the strong (often implicit) critiques the narratives make of the legal system, as well as of the scholarship that supports it, will also be ignored. One important critique that rarely gets addressed, for example, is that federal Indian law, which purports to be supportive of Native American interests, fails to take Native American experience, and particularly the centrality of female governance within that experience, into account in fashioning legal solutions to problems. Another is that the field of Indian law exists to commodify and transfer Native American assets, not to protect them or otherwise keep them incommensurable with market exchanges, as was promised by so many treaties, statutes, and other agreements.

In most fields, the idea that a field of study could exist without reference to the experience it claims to describe would be the subject of sharp criticism and debate. But here, partly because of the closed-system nature of much legal theory, and partly because of the disparities of power that too often exist between the (nonnative) studier and the (Native American) studied, the idea of "helping" Native Americans without first talking with (as opposed to *to*) them is, amazingly, seldom questioned. Hence, one timeless point that Green makes is that scholars should stop studying "Myths Americas" before it is too late, and start studying— within agenda set by tribal peoples themselves—how Native American women have and still do lead and contribute to tribal governance, as well as narrate their own experience of sovereignty.

Scant research exists on female tribal leaders in tribal governments reorganized under the 1934 Indian Reorganization Act. Melanie McCoy's survey study is one of the first, and, as McCoy herself notes, it is extremely preliminary both because of its methodology (survey research) and because of the low response rate. Nevertheless, McCoy's study investigates whether (white) women-in-politics research is applicable to the experience of minority women, and especially Native American women. McCoy is particularly interested in elected female tribal officials' experiences: their views, their aspirations, their challenges. Again based on preliminary data, McCoy concludes that the female leaders who responded to her survey felt that they had to fit into a male world of (nontraditional) tribal politics, not that that world had to conform to them. In addition, these respondents perceived themselves as solving problems differently than their male counterparts, often because they envisioned their political work as a form of public service as opposed to as a career opportunity. In addition, while the respondents reported that male tribal leaders seemed to focus on broad, national issues, McCoy's female tribal leaders saw themselves as working with local communities, to solve local problems, but *within* a national pan-tribal framework of preserving tribal sovereignty.

Following McCoy's study is an excerpt from Wilma Mankiller's autobiography. Mankiller was the first woman to serve as Principal Chief of the Cherokee Nation, which she governed from 1985 to 1995. She was also the first female Deputy Chief, under Principal Chief Ross Swimmer. Upon Chief Swimmer's appointment to the Bureau of Indian Affairs under President Reagan, Mankiller assumed the office of principal chief as provided for by the Cherokee Nation Constitution, as it had been ratified in 1976. Then, in 1991, Mankiller ran a successful bid for election to the office of principal chief.

The next excerpt by Genevieve Chato and Christine Conte, raises concerns about the changes that dominant culture, laws, and ideas can bring to tribal women's status. By focusing on the Navajo context, Chato and Conte discuss how the law of the dominant culture is, in a sense, imported into tribal communities. With more and more Native Americans attending law school, and more and more law schools setting up helping centers for tasks such as drafting codes, dominant culture ideals inevitably make their way onto the reservation. (For a description of a tribal law program, see Robert A. Williams, Jr., "Vampires Anonymous and Critical Race Practice," 95 *Michigan Law Review* 741 (1997).) In addition, reservations such as the Navajo Nation employ nonnatives, some of whom devote their lives to assisting the Navajo Nation articulate and manage its justice system. These people bring with them their own ideas about the role of law and the lawyer in society, specifically their own dominant culture society. They also develop distinct ideas about the re-invention of tradition or the re-setting of tradition into what is now widely referred to as tribal "common law."

Yet, as Chato and Conte point out so well, American reservations are colonial spaces within the United States, spaces and places that absorb the dominant culture's law ways both through direct and indirect means. Thus, when tribal legal processes adopt different dominant culture legal rules, the effect may be to divest or disempower women on the reservation in ways that the adopters may not have predicted, much less intended. For the sake of clarity, Chato and Conte are not criticizing the importation of dominant legal system rules, processes, or ideals in reservation spheres, though it is a topic in need of full and frank discussion. Rather, what they suggest is that tribal justice system workers be aware and cognizant of the fact that rules—even if apparently fair as written, or even if progressive as applied within the dominant culture context—can work to dispossess or subordinate women and children in tribal or reservation contexts.

Chato and Conte's article strongly urges tribal lawmakers to consider the ways in which the importation of outside "equalizing" rules—such as, for example, community property rules—can work with other colonial, social, economic, and cultural forces to actually render women unequal and thus disempowered, even within their own otherwise female-respecting societies. As for tribal courts, some say that they are operating more fully, more traditionally, and with more legitimacy than they have in the past.[16] But Chato and Conte raise the possibility that this greater legitimacy may be the result of adopting systemic mechanisms from the surrounding society, mechanisms that pull tribal societies into adopting dominant culture methods of framing and resolving disputes.

Chato and Conte conclude that those who innovate and manage tribal justice systems ought to be aware and watchful of the effects of adopting concepts, categories, even labels ("common law," "torts," etc.) from the dominant legal system. And, if tribal courts should adopt those ways, they ought to be aware that the adopted mechanisms can veer the host society in directions that could fundamentally alter its foundation. Chato and Conte list several ways in which Navajo women have been disempowered by the piecemeal importation of legal principles into local decision-making processes. But they also note ways in which the Navajo Nation has committed itself to gender equality as a formal policy matter. This commitment on the part of the Navajo Nation to its female members is, as all the writers in this chapter might agree, a tribute to the Navajo Nation's grandmothers.

But it is also an explicit vote to hold steady to a tribal-centered view of gender equality—one that recognizes the central role of women in Navajo society, and one that hopes to redefine gender equality for the future in a way perhaps not previously imagined by the dominant culture.

The last excerpt in this chapter surveys the legislation passed by tribal governments to address domestic violence. Violence against women and children is an increasingly noticeable problem in reservation and urban Native American communities. As Valencia-Weber, a law professor, and Zuni, a tribal judge–turned–law professor, write, tribal governments are addressing the problem through legislation as well as through social programs. Still, domestic violence is a near-intractable problem in many areas. To return for a moment to the Julia Martinez's case and the debate surrounding it, in a sense Native American women writing today—such as Green, Chato, Conte, Valencia-Weber, and Zuni—concur with Martinez's concerns as they were expressed in court. They understand the difficult social problems faced by tribal communities; they understand the ways in which policies such as allotment and reorganization have insinuated patriarchal gender patterns of distribution into tribal culture; and they are conconcered about the negative impact these intrusions have on the lives of tribal women and children. They also recognize that tribal governments need the direction and participation of all groups and members to stay the course of time, not just the participation of one (elite) class, or one (dominant) gender, or one (status quo holding) age group. The writers in these chapters implicitly recognize that sometimes their tribal governments need to be challenged, though always with an understanding, as Green says, "that sovereignty is best debated without special exception."[17]

RECOMMENDED READINGS

The United States Federal District Court (D. N.M.) opinion in *Martinez v. Santa Clara Pueblo*, written by Judge Mechem, explains in thick detail the various cultural forces behind both the Santa Clara ordinance, and Julia Martinez's reasons for challenging the ordinance, since that cultural evidence came in at trial. Judge Mechem's opinion can be found in the Federal Reporter Supplement series, at 402 F. Supp. 5 (1975), as can the full text of the 1939 Santa Clara ordinance that Julia Martinez challenged.

The controversial parts of the ordinance read:

> Be it ordained by the Council of the Pueblo of Santa Clara, New Mexico . . .
> that hereafter the following rules govern the admission to membership to the
> Santa Clara Pueblo: . . .
> (2) All children born of marriage between male members of the Santa Clara Pueblo
> and non-members shall be members of the Santa Clara Pueblo.
> (3) Children born of marriage between female members of the Santa Clara
> Pueblo and non-members shall not be members of the Santa Clara Pueblo. . . .

"Dependent Sovereigns: Indian Tribes, States and the Federal Courts," 56 *University of Chicago Law Review* 671 (1989), by Judith Resnick, and "Race and Essentialism in Feminist Legal Theory," 42 *Stanford Law Review* 581 (1991), by

Angela Harris both offer brief, though widely cited criticisms of feminist accounts that tried to decontextualize culturally *Martinez v. Santa Clara*. The full text of the Valencia-Weber and Zuni excerpt included in this chapter also offers a wide range of citations to law review articles that analyze *Martinez v. Santa Clara*. In addition, "Gendered Checks and Balances: Understanding the Legacy of White Patriarchy in an American Indian Cultural Context," 24 *Georgia Law Review* 1019 (1990)," by Robert A. Williams Jr., provides an important framing analysis for understanding tribal gender issues. William's article is an excellent supplement to this chapter, as is *Justice and Gender: Sex Discrimination and the Law* (1989), edited by Deborah L. Rhode. Finally, "A Quincentennial Essay on *Martinez v. Santa Clara Pueblo*," 28 *Idaho Law Review* 307, by Robert Laurence, sets out the procedural facts of *Martinez v. Santa Clara* in a clear fashion, and so gives beginning students a basic understanding of how the case wended its way through the court system. In the feminist literature, see Aida Hurtado, "Relating to Privilege: Seduction and Rejection in the Subordination of White Women and Women of Color," *Signs: Journal of Women in Culture and Society*, 14:41 (1989).

There is an entire literature on "narrative" in law. For a glimpse of literature critical of narrative, see "Telling Stories Out of School: An Essay on Legal Narratives," 45 *Stanford Law Review* 807 (1993), by Daniel A. Farber and Suzanna Sherry. For an argument in support of narrative, see "On Telling Stories in School: A Reply to Farber and Sherry," 46 *Vanderbilt Law Review* 665 (1993), by Richard Delgado.

"Changing and Diverse Roles of Women in American Indian Cultures," *Sex Roles* 22(7/8): 455–476 (1990) is a strong compliment to Green's excerpt. "Navajo Mothers and Daughters: Schools, Jobs, and the Family," in the *Anthropology and Education Quarterly* at 26(2): 135–167 (1995), by Deyhle and Margonis, is too, as is *Messengers of the Wind: Native American Women Tell Their Life Stories* (1995), edited by Jane Katz. Likewise, "A Silent Minority: Battered American Indian Women," by Norton and Manson, is a good complement to Valencia-Weber and Zuni excerpt; the Norton and Manson article is in the *Journal of Family Violence* 10(3):307–318 (1995).

The Zuni Man-Woman (1991) by Will Roscoe is about the fluidity of gender boundaries among one tribal society, the Zuni. Roscoe particularly concerns himself with the story of We'wha, a nineteenth-century Zuni person whom Roscoe identifies as a berdache, which is to say a man who would dress as a woman, perform women's work, and be sexually oriented toward men, or—alternatively—a woman, who would dress as a man, perform man's work and be sexually oriented toward women. *The Spirit and the Flesh: Sexual Diversity in American Indian Culture* (1986) by Walter L. Williams is another well-documented book on the berdache tradition in Native American societies. For an early article on this same topic, see Evelyn Blackwood's "Sexuality and Gender in Certain Native American Tribes: the Case of Cross-Gender Females," in *Signs: Journal of Women in Culture and Society* 10(11): 27–42 (1984).

With respect to the broader topic of tribal courts and tribal governance, the literature is growing by leaps and bounds. Gloria Valencia-Weber's "Tribal

Courts: Custom and Innovative Law," 24 *New Mexico Law Review* 225 (1994), provides a broad look at justifications for tribal courts; this article also cites many more particular, foundational sources that are of use to anyone trying to make their way in this area. John Borrow's article "With or Without You: First Nations Law (in Canada)," 41 *McGill Law Journal* 629 (1996), provides a powerful analysis of tribal stories as tribal common law. Indeed, I recommend all of Professor Borrow's work to anyone who is interested in tribal lawmaking in general, and First Nations lawmaking in Canada in particular. Tom Tso's "The Process of Decision Making in Tribal Courts," 31 *Arizona Law Review* 225 (1989), offers an important view of lawmaking from the perspective of one who sat as the Chief Justice of the Navajo Nation. Chief Justice Tso's article appears in the "Indian Law Symposium," a journal issue well worth reading in full. In the same vein is Robert Yazzie's, "Law School as a Journey," 46 *Arkansas Law Review* 271 (1993).

Also of note is "The Navajo Peacemaker Court: Deference to the Old and Accommodation to the New," 11 *American Indian Law Review* 89 (1983) by James W. Zion. Frank Pommersheim's work, particularly "A Path Near the Clearing: An Essay on Constitutional Adjudication in Tribal Courts," 27 *Gonzaga Law Review* 393 (1991/92), is worth reading, as is Pommersheim's *Braid of Feathers: American Indian Law and Contemporary Tribal Life* (1996). The *Navajo Reporter* series collects individual, reported Navajo judicial opinions. This series illustrates Chato and Conte's premises, and gives a glimpse of tribal courts in action.

There is a vast literature on tribal, state, and federal court jurisdiction. That literature tends to be doctrinally focused and technical. For an entré into this literature, see the Judith Resnick article cited above, the work of scholars such as Robert Laurence, Robert Clinton, and Frank Pommersheim, to name just a few, and *F. Cohen, Handbook of Federal Indian Law* (1982). For works about the nineteenth century that accessible to a general audience, see Blue Clark, *Lone Wolf v. Hitchcock: Treaty Rights and Indian Law at the End of the Nineteenth Century* (1994); Jeffrey Burton, *Indian Territory and the United States, 1866–1906: Courts, Government and the Movement for Oklahoma Statehood* (1995); and Sidney L. Harring, *Crow Dog's Case: American Indian Sovereignty, Tribal Law, and United States Law in the Nineteenth Century* (1994).

Wilma Mankiller's book, *Mankiller: a Chief and Her People,* (1993) ought to be required reading in any course on Native American governance or Native American women. Mary Brave Bird's two autobiographies, *Ohitika Woman* (with Richard Erdoes) (1993) and *Lakota Woman* (under Mary Crow Dog, the author's married name, and Richard Erdoes) (1990) discuss "informal" female leadership, with a particular emphasis on its strengths and weaknesses for bringing about change. See also Rayna Green's *Women in American Indian Society* (1992), as well as her *Native American Women a Contextual Bibliography* (1983), which is part of a bibliographic series sponsored by the Newberry Library Center for the History of the American Indian. The latter work includes references about Native American, Eskimo, and Aleut women. See also Haunani-Kay Trask, *From a Native Daughter: Colonialism and Sovereinty in Hawaii* (1993).

NOTES

1. This periodization is reflected in two standard sources: *F. Cohen, Handbook of Federal Indian Law* (1982 ed.), Charlottesville, Vir.: The Michie Co., 1982, pp. 47–206; and David H. Getches, Charles F. Wilkinson, and Robert A. Williams, Jr., *Federal Indian Law: Cases and Materials* (3rd ed.), St. Paul, Minn.: West Publishing Co., 1993, pp. 83–285.

2. Vine Deloria, Jr., "Reflections on the Black Hills Claim," *Wicazo sa Review*, vol. 4:33–38 (1988), p. 33.

3. See *Lone Wolf v. Hitchcock*, 187 U.S. 553 (1903) for the still relied upon articulation of this fictional principle.

4. *Indian Removal Act of 1830, U.S. Statutes at Large* vol. 4 (1830): 411–412.

5. *General Allotment Act (Dawes Act) of 1887, U.S. Statutes at Large* vol. 24 (1887): 388–391.

6. For a general article on allotment and its legal aftermath, see Judith Royster, "The Legacy of Allotment," 27 *Arizona State Law Journal* 1 (1995). See also Bethany Ruth Berger, "After Pocahontas: Indian Women and the Law, 1830 to 1934," 21 *American Indian Law Review* 1 (1997).

7. *Wheeler-Howard Act (Indian Reorganization Act) of 1934, U.S. Statutes at Large* vol. 48 (1934): 984–988.

8. See, e.g., Sharon O'Brien, *American Indian Tribal Governments* Norman, Okla.: University of Oklahoma Press, 1989, pp. 119–137.

9. See, e.g., *House Concurrent Resolution 108, U.S. Statutes at Large*, vol. 67 (1953): B132; and *Public Law 280, U.S. Statutes at Large* vol. 67 (1953): 588–590.

10. *Indian Self Determination and Education Assistance Act of 1975, U.S. Statutes at Large* vol. 88 (1975): 2203–2214.

11. 436 U.S. 49 (1978). At issue was the applicability of the *Indian Civil Rights Act of 1968, U.S. Statutes at Large* vol. 82 (1968): 77–81.

12. *Marriage Between White Men and Indian Women, U.S. Statutes at Large* vol. 25 (1888):392.

13. Catharine A. MacKinnon's speech about *Santa Clara Pueblo v. Martinez*, which appears in *Feminism Unmodified*, Cambridge, Mass.: Harvard University Press, 1987, p. 67, is most typically—and I think wrongly—cited as an illustration of this position, and hence offered as an example of essentialism. However, MacKinnon's speech resonates strongly with female tribal political leaders' views, as discussed in this chapter. Those views are that: (1) tribal sovereignty and gender equality are *not* incompatible principles, notwithstanding that they are often framed as such; (2) distributive problems can and should be considered within the broad framework of tribal sovereignty; and (3) tribal governments ought to be extremely wary of perhaps unwittingly adopting definitions of equality that ultimately require tribal societies to remake themselves in the image of the dominant society.

14. Angela P. Harris, "Race and Essentialism in Feminist Legal Theory," 42 *Stanford Law Review* 581 (1991).

15. Interview with Alan Taradash, Albuquerque, N.M., December 17, 1997.

16. Gloria Valencia-Weber, "Tribal Courts, Custom and Innovative Law," 24 *New Mexico Law Review* 225 (1994).

17. Rayna Green, "Native American Women," *Signs: A Journal of Women in Culture and Society* 6:2, reproduced herein at p. 215, (1980).

Native American Women

Rayna Green

. . . Native American women have neither been neglected nor forgotten. They have captured hearts and minds, but, as studies of other women have demonstrated, the level and substance of most passion for them has been selective, stereotyped, and damaging. From John Smith's initial creation of New World nobility in the person of Princess Pocahontas down to my own and other Native American women's formal repudiations of his "Myth America," Native American women have been studied to death or to distraction.[1] Most of the clichés seem to be irresistible. Yet, somewhere between John Smith's ploy of creating dead princesses and saints (Kateri Tekakwitha) in order to make live white male heroes and General Sheridan's preference for murdering "squaws" and their children ("nits make lice," said he), there has been a middle of the scholarly road. . . .

[In the nineteenth century literature], [u]nlike Native American men, Native American women were elusive for those who did not have personal relationships with them, while relationships with unbiased observers were few. For those trappers, "squaw men," and missionaries who did write about Native American women, truth neither served their best interests nor was available. Distant princesses and saints were acceptable, but matriarchal, matrifocal, and matrilineal societies were neither acceptable nor comprehensible to members of European patriarchies, who misunderstood Eastern tribes so profoundly that they sabotaged their own treaties in making them with men who did not have the right to make such decisions. Few early Native American women wrote their own words down,[2] and writers who chose to write of early figures generally had their own religious or political agendas to follow in telling of women like Kateri Tekakwitha, the "saint of the Mohawks." Even when Winnemucca and the LaFlesche sisters, Suzette and Suzanne, became well-known activists and lecturers, reformist women and men gave them a voice merely to further their own reforms—which had little relevance to Indian causes.[3] Most Native

From "Native American Women," *Signs: A Journal of Women in Culture and Society* 6, p. 248 (1980). © 1980 by the University of Chicago.

American women of note—Winnemucca, the LaFlesches, Molly Brant, Wi-ne-ma, Mme. Dorion, Mme. Montour, Nancy Ward, Mary Musgrove, Milly Francis—received little attention until the twentieth century. When scholars finally took an interest in Indian women, they limited the terms of that interest. For example, they discovered matriarchy among the Iroquois, spending sixty years in debates about that one instance while other versions of matriarchy went unstudied—eventually disappearing or changing dramatically.[4] . . .

The two decades before 1920 introduced new topics—the discovery of the Southwest, for example, and individual figures. Students of Plains life discovered women, and "custom" studies (menstrual, marital, and ceremonial) dominated the literature for years. The period also brought the opening shot in what was defined as Native American women's clinical pathologies and social problems.[5] . . .

The years after World War I . . . saw . . . [n]ew types of scholarly work [like], for example, Lowie's and Michelson's autobiographies of a Crow and a Fox woman, respectively, recorded as told to the author. Ruth Bunzel's landmark study on Pueblo potters began the study of individual, compelling figures which endured through the seventies in the affection for "star" artists like Maria Martinez, Pablita Velarde, and Pitseolak.[6] In this third decade, anthropologists, art historians, and collectors alike became smitten with commercially viable Navajo weavers, Pueblo potters, and Apache and Washoe basket makers. . . .

The forties offered the now familiar array of psychoanalytic literature, little of it relevant to Indian women. A scattering of biographical and customs/behavior work appeared, and the interest in psychiatric problems shifted (in unpublished theses) to a concern for social problems and physical health, as professional sociology inspired women to work on juvenile delinquency, unmarried mothers, alcohol abusers, and consumers of Western health-care systems.[7] . . . When the obstetric/gynecological literature converted to a focus on fertility and contraceptive behavior, Indians watched with suspicion. The increasing amount of work on female-centered symbolic systems in language and myth received decent treatment in the forties in anthropological and folkloric studies, though such useful work never attracted the attention that matriarchy and puberty ceremonies drew.[8] The most distinctive works of the war years, however, were in two obscure articles on the participation of Indian women in war work, one by a Mohawk woman, and a contextual interpretation of the Plains traditions for "war work." These treatments of "bravehearted" or "manly hearted" women as nonpathological, modern creatures brought to older stereotypes contradictions and additions which, regrettably, were rarely followed up in later years. Finally, through files begun in the thirties, John Collier, the anthropologist who became head of the Bureau of Indian Affairs, confirmed what we suspected of government attitudes toward Indian women. Architect of the Indian Reorganization Acts which supported tribal men and virtually disenfranchised Indian women, Collier failed to understand and interpret the true Native American nationalist leader, Alice Lee Jemison, in any but male and non-Native American terms. His misinterpretation of her as a neo-Nazi has remained uncorrected until recently by Laurence Hauptman's fine work.[9] . . .

The favored topics of anthropological writing in the fifties were sexuality, child rearing, warrior women, and puberty rites,[10] while the unresolved arguments on matriarchy, matriliny, and matrifocality continued but with unusual vigor.[11] . . .

It was in the sixties and seventies that significant changes in the literature begin to appear . . . [t]he decade included change for women, and the call for women's liberation heard in society as a whole was paralleled by consciousness raising among Indian women. Demand from Canadian Native American women produced the first governmentally mandated studies of status among Native American women. In the first of a series of conference reports sponsored by women's societies, Native American women defined their own problems and began to articulate their own Native American and female solutions. These women indicated the discriminatory practices which affect their lives—from governmental rules that rob women, but not men, of tribal status when they marry non-Indians to less overt forms of discrimination in education and work. Canada's women made public themes that were reiterated in Native American women's writing throughout the seventies.[12] Such efforts put Indian women squarely in a feminist context, though they remained out of contact with non-Indian feminists. Their actions continue to stir controversy internally in tribes and externally in governments. . . .

The seventies bore the fruit of previous generations' seeds. Representing the notion that the study of Indian women was an idea whose time has come was Beatrice Medicine's bibliography on the role of women in Native American societies. Developed out of one of the first university courses on Native American women, the bibliography called attention to the need for work in the area; however, it did not contain a fraction of the items then available and it suffered from a number of errors. A 1980 "update" (by Gretchen Bataille) contains new critical and literary citations, but is marred by an eccentric and unevaluated choice of items. A number of books on Native American women have been published on the impetus given by the women's movement, but none offers the depth of most literature produced by that movement. . . .

The tales of young, militant, urban children of the sixties and seventies—one murdered in the Wounded Knee action of the seventies— . . . are the grimmer women's stories that rarely push the "braids-and-shades" rhetoric of urban, militant Indian men off the newspaper page. Only missing here are the tales of the older women inevitably in the forefront of any reservation or urban militant action. Their lives marred by the realities of drugs, poverty, city Indian bars, jails, and violence, Bobbie Lee and Anna Mae Aquash offer us modern versions of the past's bravehearted women. More conventional but realistic portrayals of real tribal and cultural leaders fill out the biographical literature of the decade. Jane Holden Kelley's *Yaqui Women* brings a fine addition to life-history literature dealing with essentially Hispanic Native American women—who are very different from their romanticized, fictionalized male counterpart, Carlos Casteneda's Don Juan. The unornamented hard lives of these women serve as the backdrop for the wars and displacements of their people. . . . [Their] words are well worth looking at for their portrayal of tribal leaders, women who used their power to become agents of change for their communities.[13]

Anthropologists' contributions increase in the seventies with several interesting and useful items. In more general analyses than we have seen before, several authors write on Native American cross-sex relations and offer revisionist and welcome views of Native American women and men.[14] Discarding views of powerless slaves to warriors, children, and subsistence life, these authors portray the pervasiveness of powerful roles for women, ones complementary to those of men. Challenging feminist scholars' insistence on the pervasiveness of male dominance in Native American cultures, these writers insist on tribal rather than Western definitions of role and status. The literature on culture change is enhanced considerably by several fine works which offer nonconventional views of what happens to men and women during periods of great change. . . .

Another body of material which bulks large in the seventies concerns Native American women's physical and mental health. While the anthropological literature as definer of Native American people is a constant irritant to them, the growing body of medical and psychological studies concern Native Americans even more. Since the exposures, in the sixties, of sterilization and experimentation abuse on Native American women and men in Indian Health Service facilities, Native American people have been warier than ever of contraceptive technologies. Their sense of themselves as guinea pigs for physicians in need of clinical practice or experimental populations is fueled by an ever-increasing literature on fertility, family planning, and contraceptive behavior in Native American populations. At the same time, studies which might lead to better health care for women—of alcoholism, suicide, cancer, and environmental health, for example—either subsume the data for women into those for men or deal with women not at all. Given the rise in morbidity and mortality from alcoholism, suicide, and cervical cancer, and given counseling, intervention, and testing programs directed primarily toward males, Indian women might well wonder whether researchers and clinicians have their best interests at heart. In mental health programs, too, Native American women come increasingly to feel that alien cultural models govern both the understanding of clinical personnel and the therapies developed for them. While the Freudian psychopathological approach is on the wane, the "social problems/counseling" models developed for middle-class white majority women or a black minority clientele are still favored for Indian women.[15] As bad as the existence of culture-bound, sex-biased studies and therapies is the absence of literature which validates and uses traditional Native American practice in tandem with useful Western practices. Increasingly, Native American women have begun to insist on that interface, especially in the inclusion of traditional female healers and herbalists in clinical settings that affect their care.

The real flowering of work on Indian women is represented in disparate scholarly articles by modern Indian women and non-Indian anthropologists, by revisionist historical writing and modern autobiography, and by Native American women leaders and writers talking about their own lives. Most of these women are not scholars and will never produce classic revisionist scholarship or write for wide audiences. Yet their critique of the scholarship about them and of social action and policy affecting them and their interpretation of their own experiences and lives are there to examine if scholars and the public wish to do so.

Several women show how the popular images of princess and squaw affect their personal lives as well as delineating realities that affect them. Others deal with issues of status in relation to health; relationships between Indian and non-Indian women and men; federal and local governmental statutes that affect them; culture change; work, education, and economics; modern and traditional leadership; and political action and rights.[16] Some of these assessments, like those in the sixties, came from federally and tribally sponsored meetings to assess Native American women's status and recommend changes. What makes all these works different from those produced by non-Indian social scientists, historians, and health personnel is that their power lies in the persuasiveness of testimony rather than in statistical fact. I know of no Indian woman preparing systematic studies on puberty rites, for example. Women may participate in them. They do not, on the whole, document change; they make change. This singularly different perspective requires an effort on the part of scholars to understand, because the focus here is on strategies to get beyond problems, not to document them. For example, overcoming the barriers their dual female/Indian status places on them is a theme that runs throughout these women's words, but an equally strong theme is the advantages of that status. It might come as a surprise to some who view Indian, reservation, female life as burdensome, for instance, that Native Canadian women are trying to retain just that status when, simply by marrying a non-Indian, they can lose it. It might come as a surprise to many that most Native American women look forward to being old—an elder—when their words, actions, and leadership come to be respected. These nonscholarly, very Native American female views are expressed in the impressive work produced by Indian women poets. Corn Mother and Changing Woman—the symbolic referents of Indian female life—join the powwow princesses, grandmothers, and female doctors, lawyers, and Indian chiefs of the real Indian female world to create an often harsh, unromanticized, truthful version of Native American women's lives. It is here that one might look for the real experience of Indian women's lives.[17]

In all this political, artistic, and scholarly work by and about Native American women, where is the feminist stance, the acknowledgment of political categories of thought and action that everywhere move women scholars and activists? As I have pointed out with respect to work by Native American women in the sixties and seventies, that consciousness is there. Indian women and scholars recognize the concerns of Native American women as similar to many shared by other women. But beyond a rhetorical recognition of the similarities, their writing bears little resemblance to conventional feminist analyses of the status and circumstance of women's lives. Feminist rhetorical consciousness is used by them to be explanatory and activating only in part but not to encompass the sum total of interest or concern. Areas of debate such as Marxist/lesbian/socialist feminism are entirely missing, and I cannot imagine that such variants ever would either be a part of Indian feminist discussion or a welcome part of discussion between Indian and non-Indian women. In fact, given the hostile climate on reservations for discussion of any theory applied to Indians, I doubt feminist theory of any stripe would be well received.

For Indian feminists, every women's issue is framed in the larger context of Native American people. The concerns which characterize debate in Indian country, tribal sovereignty and self-determination, for example, put Native American tribes on a collision path with regulations like Title 9 and with Equal Opportunity and Affirmative Action. Tribes insist that treaty-based sovereignty supersedes any other federal mandate. While many Native American women have personal difficulty with the application of tribal sovereignty to affirmative action in tribal hiring, for example, most agree that sovereignty is best debated without special exception. Other discussions about issues important to Indian women—better health care or the need for professional training, for instance—are always rooted in debate over the issues most germane to Indian people—the land, natural resources, water rights, and treaty guarantees. The ironies multiply when, contrary to standard feminist calls for revolution and change, Indian women insist on taking their traditional places as healers, legal specialists, and tribal governors. Their call is for a return to Native American forms which, they insist, involve men and women in complementary, mutual roles. I underscore these differences because they may teach us more than analyses of Indian female "oppression." I am not suggesting that a return to tradition in all its forms is "correct" but that attention to the debate about the implications of such retraditionalization would mean healthier, culturally more appropriate scholarship on Indian women.

Most of the very good work [about Native American women] is by women. Yet, very little [is about] real Native American women or real Native American categories of significance. Disciplines have essentially followed their own cues from decade to decade with either "primitivism" or popularization as the moving force behind most of what has been written. The clichéd concerns that every discipline has with women—those stemming primarily from their biological functions as mothers, their social functions as wives or lovers, and their economic functions as producers or helpmates—are still the concerns every discipline has with Native American women. Women as defective beings, psychologically and physically, or as inferior beings, socially, intellectually, and politically, are yet the interpretive frameworks within which Native American women are cast along with their non-Native American counterparts. Even our "heroines" serve white males, and it is they, not those who fought white males, who are beloved. Little is written about the women who mattered to Native American people. For example, apart from the work on Native American women as commercial artists and tillers of the cornfield, little is written on them as economic entities. Though occasional pieces have appeared on medicine women, herbalists, and shamans, they have ignored the spiritual and medical leadership of these women in favor of "personal" narrative. If we know little about the ways matriarchy really functions in Iroquois daily life, we must suspect that female decision making, along with non-myth-chartered, nonceremonial life, is of no interest to scholars. Little wonder, then, that no one has written about the modern female leadership in tribes that have been female-governed for a long time—Colville, Yavapai, Seminole, Puyallup, Menominee—or about the women who [had] been the political leaders of the [1960s and 1970s], Lucy Covington, Ramona Bennett, Ada Deer, Annie Wauneka, and Pat McGee. Little wonder, again, that a fixation with traditionality evolved into studies of nonthreatening older women—artists and relatives of famous war chiefs—rather than into studies of women who tell male members of the American Indian Movement what to do in the next militant actions. Our picture of how Native American women live and function from the cradle to the grave lacks not only clarity but also a realistic basis.

The literature bulks large with studies of the Navajo, the Inuit (Eskimo), Pueblo, and Iroquoian groups, with occasional forays in to the cultures of California tribes and the many Ojibway groups. Where are the women of the Northwest Coast, the Siouan and Southeastern peoples whose male members fill the literature on American Indians? The choice of tribes and topics shows a distinct preference for those that already interest anthropologists rather than for those which might offer contradictions to older ideas. Preference has clearly been for people who are visibly traditional (read: old-fashioned) and amenable to being studied (read: easy to work with) and women who fit the models drawn up for female "primitive" behavior (read: artistic hunter/gatherers). Of course, since the late sixties, no tribe has been easy for social scientists to work with, and many tribes have refused right of study to anyone who will not work on their agenda. And the very tribes once so amenable to being research objects are joining those who were never particularly hospitable to such research in their rejection of scholars. Unless the scholarly agenda changes, we will learn less and less about Native American women.

We are blessed to be rid, in their former number and nature, of the deviance studies, rug/pot articles, and puberty-rite descriptions, but we long for work that might be particularly useful to Native American women as well as to scholars. For example, Indian women and men are not very worried about unmarried mothers and illegitimate children, and receptivity to family-planning services. They point with pride to the growing and high birthrate among Native American populations. Yet they are terribly concerned about non-Indian adoption of Indian children, child-placement programs, sterilization abuse, clinical experimentation using Indians, diabetes, cervical cancer, and missionary activity in the schools. And they also worry about the grim future of Indian men, about their education, employment, familial relationships, legal problems, and ability to survive as Indians in this world. Where are the scholars who will lend themselves and their skills to Indian solutions for these concerns? While most of the studies of Pocahontas and her sisters focus on the ways in which they helped non-Indians defeat their own people, where is the serious study of such women as cultural brokers, working to create, manage, and minimize the negative effects of change on their people—working for Native American people and with white men and women? I know of no such study, and I know of only one—a fine one—which deals with the roles and functions of ritual/social networks among Indian women themselves.[18] No study yet deals with the resilient intratribal and pan-Indian networks, formed largely by women on and off reservation, networks which keep migratory and urban Indians working, educated, and in touch with their Indian identities. If there are scholars who recognize the roles the black churches and the black women's sororities have played in enabling black women to survive and assist their people, where are the scholars who will give the modern versions of quilling and beading societies—the North American Indian Women's Association, the Alaskan and Canadian Native Sisterhoods, the Women of All Red Nations, and the International Women's Year-inspired American Indian/Alaskan Native Women's Caucus—the attention they ought to have? The absence of puberty rites in these modern Native American social contexts ought not to deter scholars from studying Native American people. In fact, the substitution of tribal chairwomen in blue jeans for puberty celebrants, dead princesses, and prostitutes should benefit Indian women and scholars by introducing Native American versions of success and failure. . . .

NOTES

1. Rayna Green, "The Pocahontas Perplex: The Image of Indian Women in American Culture," *Massachusetts Review* 16, no. 4 (1975): 698–714; see also Vine Deloria, Jr., *Custer Died for Your Sins*, New York, N.Y.: Avon Books, 1969, for a bitter and humorous discussion of scholarly images of Indians.

2. Rufus Anderson, *Memoirs of Catherine Brown, Christian Indian of the Cherokee Nation*, 2d ed., Boston, Mass.: Choker & Brewster, 1825; Sarah Winnemucca Hopkins, *Life among the Paiutes: Their Wrongs and Claims*, New York, N.Y.: G. P. Putnam's Sons, 1883; A. B. Meachem, *Wi-ne-ma the Woman-Chief and Her People* (1876; reprint ed.), Madison, Wis.: American Publishing Co., 1977.

3. Elisabeth Peabody, "Sarah Winnemucca's Practical Solution to the Indian Problem," pamphlet, Chicago, Ill.: Newberry Library, 1886; Lydia Maria Child, *A Brief History of the Condition of Women* (1854); Linda K. Kerber, "Abolitionists' Perception of the Indians," *Journal of American History*, vol. 42 (September 1975).

4. Lucien Carr, "On the Position of Women among the Huron-Iroquois Tribes," 16th Annual Report of the Peabody Museum of Archaeology and Ethnology, no. 3, Cambridge, Mass.: Harvard University Press, 1884–87, pp. 207–33; also see n. 18.

5. Elsie Clews Parsons, "Mothers and Children at Zuni, N.M.," *Man* 19 (1919): 168–73; Parsons, "Waiyautitsa of Zuni, N.M.," *Scientific Monthly* 9 (1919): 443–57; H. R. Voth, *Oraibi Natal Customs*, Field Columbian Museum Anthropology Serial, vol. 6, no. 2, Chicago, Ill.: Field Columbian Museum, 1905; George Bird Grinnell, "Cheyenne Women's Customs," *American Anthropologist*, n.s. 4 (1904): 127–30; Francis LaFlesche, "Osage Marriage Customs," *American Anthropologist*, n.s. 14 (1914): 127–30; A. A. Brill, "Piblotoq or Hysteria among Peary's Eskimos," *Journal of Nervous Mental Disorders* 40 (1913): 514–20.

6. Robert H. Lowie, "A Crow Woman's Tale," in *American Indian Life*, Elsie Clews Parsons, ed., (1922; reprint ed.), Lincoln, Neb.: University of Nebraska Press, 1967; Truman Michelson, *Autobiography of a Fox Woman*, Bureau of American Ethnology Annual Report no. 40, Washington, D.C.: Government Printing Office, 1925, pp. 295–349; Ruth Bunzel, *The Pueblo Potter* (1929; reprint ed.), New York, N.Y.: Columbia University Press, 1972; see also Susan Peterson, *The Living Tradition of Maria Martinez*, New York, N.Y., and Tokyo: Kodansha International, 1977.

7. George Devereaux, "Mohave Indian Obstetrics: A Psychoanalytic Study," *American Imago* 5 (July 1948): 95–139; Devereaux, "Mohave Orality: An Analysis of Nursing and Weaning Customs," *Psychoanalytic Quarterly* 16 (1947): 519–46; Victor Barnouw, "The Phantasy World of a Chippewa Woman," *Psychiatry* 12 (1949): 67–76; Erika Bourguignon, "Life History of an Ojibwa Young Woman," in *Primary Records in Culture and Personality*, vol. 1, Bert Kaplan, ed., Madison, Wis.: Microcard Foundation, 1949; M. Inez Hilger, "Notes

on Cheyenne Child Life," *American Anthropologist* 47 (1944–46): 60–69; Anauta with Heluizé Washburne, *Land of the Good Shadows: The Life Story of Anauta, an Eskimo Woman*, New York, N.Y.: John Daly, 1940.

8. Flora L. Bailey, "Suggested Techniques for Inducing Navajo Women to Accept Hospitalization during Childbirth and for Implementing Health Education," *American Journal of Public Health* 38 (October 1948): 1418–23; Alice Marriott, *The Ten Grandmothers*, Norman, Okla.: University of Oklahoma Press, 1948; C. A. Weslager, "The Delaware Indians as Women," *Journal of the Washington Academy of Science* 34, no. 12 (1944): 381–88.

9. Bertha M. Eckert, "An Unpublished Report on Indian Women in the War Industries," New York, N.Y.: YWCA, 1943; Florence Smith Hill, "Patriotic Work of the Six Nations Women in World Wars One and Two," in *Six Nations' Indians: Yesterday and Today, 1867–1942*, Onandaga, N.Y.: Six Nations Agricultural Society, 1942, pp. 52–53; Oscar Lewis, "Manly Hearted Women among the North Riegan," *American Anthropologist* 43 (1941): 173–87; John Collier, "Memorandum on Indian Women" (November 1, 1940), in Indian File American Civil Liberties Union Archives, Collier, "Alice Lee Jemison" (1943) Office File RG75, both at Princeton, N.J., Princeton University Library; see Laurence Hauptman, "Alice Jemison: Seneca Political Activist," *Indian Historian* 12, no. 2 (Summer 1979): 15–40.

10. Flora L. Bailey, *Some Sex Beliefs and Practices in a Navajo Community*, Papers of the Peabody Museum of American Archaeology and Ethnology, vol. 40, no. 2, Cambridge, Mass.: Harvard University Press, 1950; Esther Goldrank, "Observations on Sexuality of the Blood Indians of Alberta, Canada," *Psychoanalysis and the Social Sciences* 3 (1951): 71–98; M. Inez Hilger, *Chippewa Child Life and Its Cultural Background*, U.S. Bureau of American Ethnology Bulletins, serials 146 and 148, Washington, D.C.: U.S. Government Printing Office, 1952; Irma Honigmann and John Honigmann, *Child Rearing Patterns among the Great Whale Eskimo*, Anthropological papers of the University of Alaska, serial 2, Fairbanks, Ala.: University of Alaska Press, 1952, pp. 31–50; Robert Anderson, "The Northern Cheyenne War Mothers," *Anthropological Quarterly* 29, no. 3 (1956): 82–90; H. E. Driver and Saul Riesenberg, *Hoof Rattles and Girl's Puberty Rites in North and South America*, Indiana University Publications in Anthropology and Linguistics, no. 4, Bloomington, Ind.: Indiana University Press, 1950; Driver, *Girl's Puberty Roles in Western North America*, University of California Anthropological Records, Serial 6, Berkeley and Los Angeles, Calif.: University of California Press, 1950, pp. 21–90.

11. Eleanor Leacock, "Matrilocality in a Simple Hunting Economy (Montaignais Naskapi)," *Southwest Journal of Anthropology* 11 (1955): 31–47; Martha C. Randle, "Iroquois Women, Then and Now," in *Symposium on Local Diversity in Iroquois Culture*, William N. Fenton, ed., U.S. Bureau of Ethnology Bulletin, no. 148, Anthropology Papers, serial 8, Washington, D.C.: U.S. Government Printing Office, 1951, pp. 167–80; Cara E. Richards, "Matriarchy or Mistake: The Role of Iroquois Women through Time," in *Cultural Stability and Cultural Change*, Verne F. Ray, ed., Seattle, Wash.: University of Washington Press, 1957, pp. 30–40.

12. Alberta Native Women's Society Conference, First (March 1968) and Second (March 1969) Reports (unpublished, Edmonton); Royal Commission on the Status of Women, "Study and Field Research on Indian Women" (unpublished; Ottawa, Ontario, 1968); Mary Ann Lavallée, "Problems That Concern Indian Women: A Report from the Saskatchewan Indian Women's Conference," *Qu'appelle* 3 (November 7, 1967): 10–15.

13. Richard Simpson, *OOTI: A Maidu Legacy*, Millbrae, Calif.: Celestial Arts, 1979; Jean Speare, *The Days of Augusta*, Seattle, Wash.: Madrona Publishers, 1977; Florence Shipek, *The Autobiography of Delphina Cuẽro*, Morongo Indian Reservation, Calif.: Malki Museum Press, 1970; Elizabeth Polingaysi Oóyawayma, *No Turning Back*, Albuquerque, N.M.: University of New Mexico Press, 1977; Pitseolak, *Pictures out of My Life*, New York, N.Y.: Oxford University Press, 1971; Elsie Allen, *Pomo Basketmaking* Healdsburg, Calif.: Naturegraph Publishers, 1972; Susan Peterson, *The Living Tradition* (see n. 10), esp. her bibliography for all works on Martinez; Stan Steiner, *Spirit Woman: The Diaries of Bonita Wa Wa Calachaw Nunez, an American Indian*, New York, N.Y.: Harper & Row, 1979;

Katherine M. Weist, ed., *The Narrative of a Northern Cheyenne Woman, Belle Hiwalking* (Billings, Mont.: Montana Council for Indian Education, 1979; see also Margot Liberty and John Stands in Timber, *Cheyenne Memories*, New Haven, Conn.: Yale University Press, 1967, for Hiwalking's brother's tale; Bobbie Lee with Don Barnett and Rich Sterling, *Bobbie Lee, Indian Rebel: Struggles of a Native Canadian Woman*, Richmond, B.C.: LSM Press, 1975; Johanna Brand, *The Life and Death of Anna Mae Aquash*, Toronto: James Larimer & Co., 1978; Jane Holden Kelley, *Yaqui Women: Contemporary Life Histories*, Lincoln, Neb.: University of Nebraska Press, 1977; Trilokey Nath Pandey, "Flora Zuni, Zuni, 1897–," in *American Indian Intellectuals*, Margot Liberty, ed., St. Paul, Minn.: West Publishing Co., 1978; Catherine S. Fowler, "Sarah Winnemucca (Hopkins), Northern Paiute, 1844–1891," in Liberty, above; Elisabeth Colson, ed., *Autobiographies of Three Pomo Women*, Berkeley, Calif.: University of California, Department of Anthropology, 1974; Alice Marriott and Carol Rachlin, *Dance around the Sun: The Life of Mary Little Bear Inkanish, Cheyenne*, New York, N.Y.: Thomas Y. Crowell Co., 1977; Anna Moore Shaw, *A Pima Past*, Tucson, Ariz.: University of Arizona Press, 1974; James et al. (see n. 2); Hauptman (n. 16 above).

14. Nancy O. Lurie, "Indian Women: A Legacy of Freedom," in Lurie, *Look to the Mountaintop*, San Jose, Calif.: Gousha Publishers, 1972; Alice Schlegel, "The Adolescent Socialization of the Hopi Girl," *Ethnology* 12, no. 4 (October 1973): 449–62; Alice Schlegel, "Male and Female in Hopi Thought and Action," in *Sexual Stratification: A Cross-cultural View*, Alice Schlegel, ed., New York, N.Y.: Columbia University Press, 1978; Patricia A. McCormack, ed., "Cross-Sex Relations: Native Peoples," special issue of *Western Canadian Journal of Anthropology*, vol. 6, no. 3 (1976).

15. John C. Slocumb et al., "The Use-Effectiveness of Two Contraceptive Methods in a Navajo Population: The Problem of Program Dropouts," *American Journal of Obstetrics and Gynecology* 122, no. 6 (July, 1975): 717–26; Christopher M. Doran, "Attitudes of 30 American Indians toward Birth Control," *Health Service Reports* 87, no. 7 (1972): 658–64; Stephen J. Kunitz, "Navajo and Hopi Fertility, 1971–72," *Human Biology* 46, no. 3 (September 1974): 435–41; Charles W. Slemenda, "Sociocultural Factors Affecting Acceptance of Family Planning Services by Navajo Women," *Human Organization* 37, no. 2 (Summer 1978): 190–94; Terry L. Haynes, "Some Factors Related to Contraceptive Behavior among the Wind River Shoshone and Arapaho Females," *Human Organization* 36, no. 1 (Spring 1977): 72–76; Joseph D. Bloom, "Migration and Psychopathology of Eskimo Women," *American Journal of Psychiatry* 130, no. 4 (April 1973): 446–49; Lusita G. Johnson and Stephen J. Proskauer, "Hysterical Psychosis in a Prepubescent Navajo Girl," *Journal of the American Academy of Child Psychiatry* 13 (Winter 1974): 1–119; Lillian A. Ackerman, "Marital Instability and Juvenile Delinquency among the Nez Percés," *American Anthropologist* 73, no. 3 (June 1971): 595–603; Robert E. Kuttner and Albert Lorincz, "Promiscuity and Prostitution in Urbanized Indian Communities," *Mental Hygiene* 54, no. 1 (January 1970): 79–91; Lynn Oakland and Robert Kane, "The Working Mother and Child Neglect on the Navajo Reservation," *Pediatrics* 51 (May 1973): 849–53; W. H. Miller et al., "Vocational and Personal Effectiveness Training of a Developmentally Delayed Navajo Girl," *White Cloud Journal* 1, no. 1 (Spring 1978): 11–14; Eugene Peniston and William Burman, "Relaxation and Assertive Training as Treatment for a Psychosomatic American Indian Patient," *White Cloud Journal* 1, no. 1 (Spring 1978): 7–10; Thomas McDonald, "Group Psychotherapy with Native American Women," *International Journal of Group Psychotherapy* 24, no. 4 (October 1975): 410–20.

16. Green, "Pocahontas Perplex" (n. 3); Cheryl Metoyer-Duran, "The Native American Women," in *The Study of Women: Enlarging Perspectives of Social Reality*, Elaine Snyder, ed., New York, N.Y.: Harper & Row, 1979; Jean Cuthand Goodwill, "Squaw Is a Dirty Word," in *Issues for the Seventies: Canada's Indians*, ed. Norman Sheffe, ed., Toronto, Ontario: McGraw-Hill Book Co., 1970, pp. 50–52; Rosemary Christensen, "Indian Women: A Historical and Personal Perspective," *Pupil and Personnel Services Journal* 4, no. 5, (Minnesota Department of Education, 1975): 13–22; Clara Sue Kidwell, "American Indian Women: Problems of Communicating a Cultural and Sexual Identity," *Creative Woman* (Governor's State University, Ill.), no. 3 (Winter 1979); Rosemary Wood, "Health Problems Facing Native American Women," in National Institute of Education/Women's Division,

Conference Report for the Invitational Conference of American Indian Women, Washington, D.C.: National Institute of Education, 1976 (hereafter cited as *NIE Report*); Shirley Hill Witt, "Native Women Today: Sexism and the Indian Woman," *Civil Rights Digest* 6, no. 3 (Spring 1974): 29–35; Jeela Alilkatuktuk, "Canada: A Stranger in My Own Land," *Ms.* 2, no. 8 (February 1974): 8–10; Julie Cruikshank, "Native Women in the North: An Expanding Role," *North/Nord* 18, no. 6 (November–December 1971): 1–7; Jean Cuthand Goodwill, "A New Horizon for Native Women in Canada," in *Citizen Participation in Canada: A Book of Readings,* James A. Draper, ed., Toronto: New Press, 1971, pp. 362–70; Shirley Hill Witt, "Native Women in the World of Work," in U.S. Department of Labor/Women's Bureau, *Native American Women in Equal Opportunity,* Washington, D.C.: U.S. Government Printing Office, 1979 (hereafter cited as *Native American Women*); Mary E. F. Mathur, "Who Cares That a Woman's Work Is Never Done?" *Indian Historian* 4, no. 2 (Summer 1971): 11–16; Clara Sue Kidwell, "The Status of Native American Women in Higher Education," *NIE Report;* Dorothy I. Miller, "Native American Women: Leadership Images," *Integrated Education* (January–February 1978), pp. 37–39; Evelyn Lance Blanchard, "Organizing American Indian Women," *NIE Report;* Clara Sue Kidwell, "The Power of Women in Three American Indian Societies," *Journal of Ethnic Studies* 6, no. 3 (1979): 113–21; Rayna Green, "Native American Women: The Leadership Paradox," in *Women's Educational Equity Communications Network News and Notes* 1 (Spring 1980): 4; Shirley Hill Witt, "The Brave-hearted Women," *Akwesasne Notes,* vol. 8, no. 1 (1976); International Indian Treaty Council, *Native American Women* (New York: United Nations, 1975); Women of All Red Nations, *WARN,* Porcupine, S.D.: We Will Remember Group, 1978.

17. For a bibliographic guide to some major works by Native American women poets and writers as well as examples of their writing, see *The Third Woman: Minority Women Writers of the United States,* Dexter Fisher, ed., Boston, Mass.: Houghton Mifflin Co., 1979.

18. Ann Nelson, "Native Women's Ritual Sodalities," in McCormack, supra note 14.

Native American Women: An Update

Jo Ann Woodsum

Since the publication of Rayna Green's review essay of Native American women's studies in 1980, there has been a remarkable increase in scholarly work by and about native women.[1] Much of this work has benefited from the constructive criticism set forth by Professor Green. In particular, this new generation of scholarship is characterized by a concern for native women's lived experiences and often focuses on issues which native women themselves have identified as being important to native communities.

Historians now place native women at the center of historical narratives by examining: the role of native women in the fur trade,[2] native women's responses to colonization through religious conversions,[3] education,[4] and land allotments,[5] and the impact of colonization on native families.[6] The publication of *The Hidden Half: Studies of Plains Indian Women* in 1983 marked the first collection of ethnohistorical writings on native women.[7] Although limited in scope to Plains women, this anthology set the standard for strong analytical work which rejected stereotypical portrayals of native women in favor of more nuanced examinations of their lives. More than a decade later, Nancy Shoemaker's excellent collection, *Negotiators of Change: Historical Perspectives on Native American Women*, included articles which covered the colonial period through the present and women from several tribes including Cherokee, Mohawk, Seminole, and Pima-Maricopa.[8] However, much work remains to be done on native women's experiences in the colonial period and the twentieth century, two historical eras which have generally been neglected in Native American history in favor of the perennial favorite, the nineteenth century.[9] Native women now often collaborate with non-native anthropologists in order to publish their life stories in their own words.[10] Increasingly, native women are writing compelling histories of their own lives and families.[11]

Historical and anthropological interest in the question of Iroquois matriarchy has waned in the past several years.[12] Anthropologists, however, are still interested in the relationship between gender and power in native cultures[13] and with native women's own categories for defining themselves.[14]

Recent autobiographies by Wilma Mankiller, Mary Brave Bird (formerly Crow Dog), and Janet Hale, among others, provide a personal perspective on the challenges facing native women today.[15] Prominent themes in these works include identity, cultural displacement, political activism, alcoholism, poverty, resistance, and renewal. Many of these themes permeate recent fiction, drama, and poetry by native women.[16] Native women produce insightful criticism of this literature as well.[17] Native women's literature is now also garnering well-deserved critical attention from non-native scholars.[18]

Scholarship about native women's "traditional" arts, e.g., pottery, weaving, basketmaking, continues to flourish.[19] The recent blossoming of native women working in painting, sculpture, photography, installation, and video, however, has yet to produce much art historical scholarship.[20] The exceptions are the fine catalogs that accompanied two major exhibitions of contemporary native women's art. In 1985, Jaune Quick-to-See Smith and Harmony Hammond curated the first show of native women's contemporary art, *Women of Sweetgrass, Cedar and Sage: Contemporary Art by Native American Women*.[21] The Heard Museum recently hosted *Watchful Eyes: Native American Women Artists*, an exhibition of twentieth-century Native American women's art, which included such canonical figures as Pablita Velarde, Helen Cordero and Tonita Peña, established artists such as Nora Noranjo-Morse, Judith Lowry, and Hulleah Tsinhnahjinnie, as well as emerging artists Pamela Shields Carroll, Shelley Niro, and Carm Little Turtle.[22] Nora Noranjo-Morse has published a wonderful book of poetry in connection with her artwork. These poems address both the content of her art and the experience of being a native woman artist in the contemporary art market.[23] Native women are also making innovative contributions in music.[24]

Scholars are turning their attention to new areas of investigation. Luana Ross is exploring the cycles of violence that trap native women, often involving episodes of incarceration.[25] Others examine the rise of domestic violence in native communities.[26] Scholars are also investigating the experiences of native women in the urban context.[27] During the past two decades, native women have become increasingly active in tribal politics. Ramona Bennett and Wilma Mankiller, among many others, have both served as tribal chairpersons.[28] In Canada, native women organized to challenge section 12(1) (b) of the Indian Act, which denied Indian "status" to native women who married non-Indians. Through grassroots organizing and coalitions with white feminists, native women successfully lobbied to change the law, which was repealed in 1985.[29] Despite the success of the coalition of native women and white feminists in Canada in connection with the status issue, native women often find themselves at odds with white feminists. In particular, native women's political activism privileges community well-being over individual needs.[30] Native women continue to organize women's groups to cope with issues as diverse as environmental degradation[31] and domestic violence.[32] Groups such as the California Indian Basketweaver's Association and Pauktuutit (Inuit Women's Association of Canada) have organized to preserve and pass on traditional knowledge.[33] Many of these groups have taken advantage of new technologies and have created web pages to communicate their interests and concerns to a wider audience.[34] One of the most active areas of native women's political activism centers on health issues. An almost pathological concern with Indian health continues to pervade much of the medical literature on native women.[35] However, as increasing numbers of Indian women enter the medical professions at all levels, they are insisting that Western technology be harnessed through traditional understandings about healing. For example, Katsi Cook, a midwife and Mohawk healer, combines Mohawk traditional women's knowledge with Western prenatal practices.[36]

The scholarship on native sexuality and gender variance is still relatively sparse. Although the anthropological study of the "berdache" in traditional native cultures abounds, critical insight into gender variance from native perspectives has yet to be articulated in an academic setting.[37] Moreover, there is a tendency in the literature to conflate traditional third or fourth gender categories with contemporary gay or lesbian native identities. Traditional third or fourth gender persons combined elements of male and female behavior. Frequently, these persons fulfilled specific spiritual roles within their native culture. Some native people continue to adopt a third or fourth gender role in their culture. The scholarship on this issue is minimal, but it does suggest that these people rarely think of themselves as "gay" or "lesbian" in the Western sense. Many contemporary native gays and lesbians, on the other hand, blend traditional concepts of Indian identity with a Euro-American or Western and urban definition of gay/lesbian identity. Scholarship on contemporary native gays and lesbians and their relationship to traditional third or fourth gender categories is almost nonexistent, although numerous poets, short story writers, and novelists have been chronicling their experiences.[38]

Even as cultural critics analyze the ways in which images of native women function in U.S. popular culture,[39] we are still living in the age of Disney's *Pocahontas*.[40] These representations of native women as "princesses" continue the legacy of colonization in pernicious ways by romanticizing the process of colonization.[41]

NOTES

1. Rayna Green, *Native American Women: A Contextual Bibliography*, Bloomington, Ind.: Indiana University Press, 1983; Gretchen Bataille and Kathleen Sands, *American Indian Women: A Guide to Research*, New York, N.Y.: Garland Publishing, 1991. See also, Gretchen Bataille and Laurie Lariersa, *Native American Women: A Biographical Dictionary*, New York, N.Y.: Garland Publishing, 1993; Annette Reed Crum, "Bibliography: Native American Women" In *Unequal Sisters: A Multicultural Reader In U.S. Women's History*, Ellen DuBois and Vicki Ruiz, eds., New York, N.Y.: Routledge, 2nd ed. 1994: 599–605; "Bibliography: Native American Women" *Journal of Women's History* 4 (Winter 1993): 235–240; Jo Ann Woodsum, "Gender & Sexuality in Native American Societies: A Bibliography" *American Indian Quarterly* 19 (Fall 1995): 527–554.

2. See, e.g., Jennifer Brown, *Strangers in Blood: Fur Trade Company Families in Indian Country*, Vancouver, B.C.: University of British Columbia Press, 1980; Sylvia Van Kirk, *Many Tender Ties: Women in Fur-Trade Society in Western Canada, 1670–1870*, Winnipeg, Manitoba: Watson & Dwyer, 1980.

3. See, e.g., Karen Anderson, *Chain Her By One Foot: The Subjugation of Women in Seventeenth-Century New France*, New York, N.Y.: Routledge, 1991); Edward Castillo,

"Gender Status Decline, Resistance, and Accommodation among Female Neophytes in the Missions of California: A San Gabriel Case Study" *American Indian Culture and Research Journal* 18:1 (1994): 67–93; Carol Devens, *Countering Colonization: Native American Women and Great Lakes Missions, 1630–1900*, Berkeley, Calif.: University of California Press, 1992; Michael Harkin, "Engendering Discipline: Discourse and Counterdiscourse in the Methodist-Heiltsuk Dialogue" *Ethnohistory* (Fall 1996): 643–661; Sergei Kan, "Clan Mothers and Godmothers: Tlingit Women and Russian Orthodox Christianity, 1840–1940" *Ethnohistory* 43 (Fall 1996): 613–41; Diane Notarianni, "Making Mennonites: Hopi Gender Roles and Christian Transformations" *Ethnohistory* (Fall 1996): 593–611. For a useful overview of work in this field, see Pauline Turner Strong, "Feminist Theory and the 'Invasion of the Heart' in North America" *Ethnohistory* 43 (Fall 1996): 683–712.

4. Jean Barman, "Separate and Unequal: Indian and White Girls at All Hallows School, 1884–1920" In *Indian Education in Canada, Volume I: The Legacy*, Jean Barman, Yvonne Hébert, and Don McCaskill, eds., Vancouver, B.C.: University of British Columbia Press, 1986: 110–131; Brenda Child, "Homesickness, Illness and Death: Native-American Girls in Government Boarding Schools" In *Wings of Gauze: Women of Color and the Experience of Health and Illness*, Barbara Bair and Susan Cayleff, eds., Detroit, Mich.: Wayne State University Press, 1993: 169–179; Carol Devens, "'If We Get the Girls, We Get the Race': Missionary Education of Native American Girls" *Journal of World History* 3 (Fall 1992): 219–38; Jo-Ann Fiske, "Pocahontas's Granddaughters: Spiritual Transition and Tradition of Carrier Women of British Columbia" *Ethnohistory* 43 (Fall 1996): 663–681; K. Tsianina Lomawaima, *They Called It Prairie Light: The Story of Chilocco Indian School*, Lincoln, Neb.: University of Nebraska Press, 1994; Devon Mihesuah, *Cultivating the Rosebuds: The Education of Women at the Cherokee Female Seminary, 1851–1909*, Urbana, Ill.: University of Illinois Press, 1993). For a contemporary examination of native women and education, see Ardy Bowker, *Sisters in the Blood: The Education of Women in Native America*, Newton, Mass.: WEEA Publishing Center, Educational Development, Inc., 1993. For autobiographical accounts by native women about the challenges of attending college, see Andrew Garrod and Colleen Larimore, eds., *First Person, First Peoples: Native American College Graduates Tell Their Life Stories*, Ithaca, N.Y.: Cornell University Press, 1997.

5. See, e.g., Wendy Wall, "Gender and the 'Citizen Indian'" In *Writing the Range: Race, Class, and Culture in the Women's West*, Elizabeth Jameson and Susan Armitage, eds., Norman, Okla.: University of Oklahoma Press, 1997: 202–229.

6. Ruth McDonald Boyer and Narcissus Duffy Gayton, *Apache Mothers and Daughters: Four Generations of a Family*, Norman, Okla.: University of Oklahoma Press, 1992; Linda Lacey, "The White Man's Law and the American Indian Family in the Assimilation Era," *Arkansas Law Review* 40 (1986): 327–379; Nancy Shoemaker, "From Longhouse to Loghouse: Household Structure Among the Senecas in 1900" *American Indian Quarterly* 15 (Summer 1991): 329–38.

7. Patricia Albers and Beatrice Medicine, eds., *The Hidden Half: Studies of Plains Indian Women*, Washington, D.C.: University Press of America, 1983.

8. Nancy Shoemaker, ed., *Negotiators of Change: Historical Perspectives on Native American Women*, New York, N.Y.: Routledge, 1995. A recent excellent collection on Canadian native women is similarly broad in scope, see Christine Miller and Patricia Churchryk, with Marie Smallface Marule, Brenda Manyfingers, and Cheryl Deering, eds., *Women of the First Nations: Power, Wisdom, and Strength*, Winnipeg, Manitoba: University of Manitoba Press, 1996. For a critique of the current state of native women's history, see Devon Mihesuah, "American Indian Women and History" *American Indian Quarterly* 20 (Winter 1996): 15–27.

9. On the colonial period, see, e.g., Kathleen Bragdon, "Gender as a Social Category in Native Southern New England" *Ethnohistory* 43 (Fall 1996): 573–592; Kathleen Brown, "Brave New Worlds: Women's and Gender History" *William and Mary Quarterly* 50 (April 1993): 311–328; Jean O'Brien, "Divorced from the Land: Accommodation Strategies of Indian Women in Eighteenth-Century New England" In *Gender, Kinship, Power: A Comparative and Interdisciplinary History*, Mary Jo Maynes, Ann Waltner, Birgitte Soland,

and Ulrike Strasser, eds., New York, N.Y.: Routledge, 1996: 319–333. For recent work on the twentieth century, see, e.g., Grace Mary Gouveia, "'We Also Serve': American Indian Women's Role in World War II" *Michigan Historical Review* 20 (Fall 1994): 153–182; Caroline James, *Nez Perce Women in Transition, 1877–1990*, Moscow, Ida.: University of Idaho Press, 1996); Victoria Patterson, "Indian Life in the City: A Glimpse of the Urban Experience of Pomo Women in the 1930s" *California History* LXXI (Fall 1992): 402–431; Robert Trennert, "Victorian Morality and the Supervision of Indian Working Women in Phoenix, 1906–1930" *Journal of Social History* 22 (Fall 1988): 113–128.

10. Freda Ahenakew and H.C. Wolfart, eds., *Our Grandmothers' Lives as Told in Their Own Words*, Saskatoon, Saskatchewan: Fifth House Publishers, 1992; Julie Cruikshank, *Life Lived Like a Story: Life Stories of Three Yukon Native Elders*, Lincoln, Neb.: University of Nebraska Press, 1990; Jeanne Shutes and Jill Mellick, *The Worlds of P'otsunu: Geronima Cruz Montoya of San Juan Pueblo*, Albuquerque, N.M.: The University of New Mexico Press, 1997; Fred Voget, *They Call Me Agnes: A Crow Narrative Based on the Life of Agnes Yellowtail Deernose*, Norman, Okla.: University of Oklahoma Press, 1995.

11. See, e.g., Loree Boyd, *Spirit Moves: The Story of Six Generations of Native Women*, Novato, Calif.: New World Library, 1996; Virginia Driving Hawk Sneve, *Completing the Circle*, Lincoln, Neb.: University of Nebraska Press, 1995.

12. Martha Harroun Foster, "Lost Women of the Matriarchy: Iroquois Women in the Historical Literature" *American Indian Culture and Research Journal* 19:3 (1995): 121–140; Nancy Shoemaker, "The Rise or Fall of Iroquois Women" *Journal of Women's History* 2 (Winter 1991): 39–57; Elizabeth Tooker, "Women in Iroquois Society" In *Extending the Rafters: Interdisciplinary Approaches to Iroquoian Studies*, Michael Foster, Jack Campisi, and Marianne Mithun, eds., Albany, N.Y.: State University of New York Press, 1984: 109–123.

13. See, e.g., Ramona Ford, "Native American Women: Changing Statuses, Changing Interpretations" In *Writing the Range: Race, Class, and Culture in the Women's West*, Elizabeth Jameson and Susan Armitage, eds., Norman, Okla.: University of Oklahoma Press, 1997: 42–68; Laura Klein and Lillian Ackerman, eds., *Women and Power in Native North America*, Norman, Okla.: University of Oklahoma Press, 1995.

14. See, e.g., Gwen Reimer, "Female Consciousness: An Interpretation of Interviews with Inuit Women" *Inuit Studies* 20:2 (1996): 77–100.

15. Mary Crow Dog with Richard Erdoes, *Lakota Woman*, New York, N.Y.: G. Weidenfeld, 1990; Mary Brave Bird with Richard Erdoes, *Ohitika Woman*, New York, N.Y.: HarperPerennial, 1994; Janet C. Hale, *Bloodlines: Odyssey of A Native Daughter*, New York, N.Y.: HarperCollins, 1994; Wilma Mankiller and Michael Wallis, *Mankiller: A Chief and Her People*, New York, N.Y.: St. Martin's Press, 1993; Lee Maracle, *I am Woman: A Native Perspective on Sociology and Feminism*, 2nd ed., Vancouver, B.C.: Press Gang Publishers, 1996; Anna Lee Walters, *Talking Indian: Reflections on Survival and Writing*, Ithaca, N.Y.: Firebrand Books, 1992. See also, Gretchen Bataille and Kathleen Sands, *American Indian Women: Telling Their Lives* Lincoln, Neb.: University of Nebraska Press, 1984; Jane Katz, *Messengers of the Wind: Native American Women Tell their Life Stories*, New York, N.Y.: Ballantine Books, 1995). For a list of autobiographies published prior to 1991, see Bataille and Sands, *American Indian Women: A Guide to Research*, pp. 281–365. The Bread and Roses Cultural Project recently released a poster series and study guide on notable contemporary Native American women as part of their "Women of Hope" series. The photographs for the posters were taken by noted native photographer Hulleah Tsinhnahjinnie. The poster set and study guide is available by calling Bread and Roses at 1-800-666-1728. A preview of the set has been printed as Hulleah Tsinhnahjinnie, "Women of Hope" *Native Peoples* 10 (Spring 1997): 50–56.

16. See, e.g., Betty Louise Bell, *Faces in the Moon*, Norman, Okla.: University of Oklahoma Press, 1994; Susan Power, *The Grass Dancer*, New York, N.Y.: Putnam & Sons, 1994. Several anthologies provide excellent introductions to native women's writing, see Rayna Green, *That's What She Said: Contemporary Poetry and Fiction by Native American Women* (Bloomington, Ind.: Indiana University Press, 1984; Joy Harjo and Gloria Bird, *Reinventing the Enemy's Language: Contemporary Native Women's Writing of North*

America, New York, N.Y.: W.W. Norton, 1997; Connie Fife, ed., *The Colour of Resistance: A Contemporary Collection of Writing By Aboriginal Women*, Toronto, Ontario: Sister Vision Press, 1993; Jeanne Perreault and Sylvia Vance, eds., *Writing the Circle: Native Women of Western Canada*, Norman, Okla.: University of Oklahoma Press, 1993. See also the wonderful web sites, "Native American Women Playwrights Archive" maintained by Miami University at: http://www.lib.muohio.edu/-wortmawa/nawpa/NAWPA.html, and "Finding out about Native Canadian Women Writers Published in English" maintained by the National Library of Canada at: http://www.nlc-bnc.ca/services/enative.htm.

17. See, e.g., Janice Acoose, *Ishwewak—Kah' Ki Yaw Ni Wahkomakanak: Neither Indian Princesses Nor Easy Squaws* Toronto, Ontario: The Women's Press, 1995; Sylvia Bowerback and Dolores Nawagesic Wawia, "Literature and Criticism by Native and Metis Women in Canada: A Review Essay" *Feminist Studies* 20 (Fall 1994): 565–81; Janice Gould, "American Indian Women's Poetry: Strategies of Rage and Hope" *Signs: Journal of Culture and Society* 20 (Summer 1995): 797–817; Ines Hernandez-Avila, "Relocations upon Relocations: Home, Language, and Native American Women's Writings" *American Indian Quarterly* 19 (Fall 1995): 491–508.

18. See, e.g., Erika Aigner-Alvarez, "Artifact and Written History: Freeing the Terminal Indian in Anna Lee Walters' *Ghost Singer*" *Students in American Indian Literatures* 8 (Spring 1996): 45–59; Noel Elizabeth Currie, "Jeannette Armstrong and the Colonial Legacy" *Canadian Literature* 124/125 (Spring–Summer, 1990): 138–153; Theresa Delgadillo, "Gender at Work in Laguna Coyote Tales" *Studies in American Indian Literatures* 7 (Spring 1995): 3–24; Barbara Godard, "The Politics of Representation: Some Native Canadian Women Writers" *Canadian Literature*, 124/125 (Spring–Summer, 1990): 183–226; Roberta Makashay Hendrickson, "Victims and Survivors: Native American Women Writers, Violence Against Women, and Child Abuse" *Studies in American Indian Literatures* 8 (Spring 1996): 13–24; Kristine Holmes, "'This Woman Can Cross Any Line': Feminist Tricksters in the Works of Nora Noranjo-Morse and Joy Harjo" *Studies in American Indian Literatures* 7 (Spring 1995): 45–63.

19. Lillian Ackerman, *A Song to the Creator: Traditional Arts of Native American Women of the Plateau*, Norman, Okla.: University of Oklahoma Press, 1996; Mary Ellen Blair and Laurence Blair, *Margaret Tafoya: A Tewa Potter's Heritage and Legacy* (Schiffer, 1986); Judy Hall and Sally Quimmiunaaq Webster, *Sanatujut: Pride in Women's Work: Copper and Caribou Inuit Clothing Traditions*, Canadian Museum of Civilization, 1994; Barbara Kramer, *Nampeyo and Her Pottery* Albuquerque, N.M.: University of New Mexico Press, 1996; Odette Leroux, Marion Jackson, and Minnie Aodla Freeman, eds., *Inuit Women Artists: Voices from Cape Dorset*, Seattle, Wash.: University of Washington Press, 1994.

20. See, e.g., Erin Valentino, "Mistaken Identity: Between Death and Pleasure in the Art of Kay WalkingStick" *Third Text* no. 26 (Spring 1994): 61–73. For interviews with several native women artists, see Lawrence Abbott, *I Stand in the Center of the Good: Interviews with Contemporary Native American Artists*, Lincoln, Neb.: University of Nebraska Press, 1994 (interviews with Shan Goshorn, Carm Little Turtle, Linda Lomahaftewa, Jaune Quick-to-See Smith, Susan Stewart, Kay Walkingstick, Nora Noranjo-Morse, and Emmi Whitehorse). For additional bibliographic information on native women's art, see Lawrence Abbott, "Contemporary Native Art: A Bibliography" *American Indian Quarterly* 18 (Summer 1994): 383–403. A group of Canadian-based native women artists organized "Native Women in the Arts" in 1993. In addition to sponsoring a variety of arts workshops and conferences, Native Women in the Arts publishes an annual journal. For additional information, write Native Women in the Arts, 401 Richmond St. West, Suite 363, Toronto, Ontario M5V 1X3: Canada, or call 1-416-598-4078.

21. Harmony Hammond and Jaune Quick-to-See Smith, *Women of Sweetgrass, Cedar and Sage: Contemporary Art by Native American Women*, New York, N.Y.: Gallery of the American Indian Community House, 1985. An excerpt from the catalogue is reprinted as, Jaune Quick-to-See Smith, "Women of Sweetgrass, Cedar, and Sage" *Women's Studies Quarterly* XV (Spring/Summer 1987): 35–41.

22. Theresa Harlan, *Watchful Eyes: Native American Women Artists*, Phoenix, Ariz.: the Heard Museum, 1994, exhibition catalog (November 4, 1994–October 8, 1995).

23. Nora Noranjo-Morse, *Mudwoman: Poems from the Clay*, Tucson, Ariz.: University of Arizona Press, 1992.

24. See, e.g., Helen Jaskoski, "My Heart Will Go Out: Healing Songs of Native American Women" *International Journal of Women's Studies* 4 (March/April 1981): 118–134; Richard Keeling, ed., *Women in North American Indian Music*, Bloomington, Ind.: Society for Ethnomusicology, 1989. See also, the compact disc *HeartBeat: Voices of First Nations Women*, Smithsonian/Folkways, 1994.

25. Luana Ross, "Race, Gender, and Social Control: Voices of Imprisoned Native American and White Women" *Wicazo Sa Review* 10 (Fall 1994): 17–40; Luana Ross, *Inventing the Savage: The Social Construction of Native American Criminality*, Austin, Tex.: University of Texas Press, in press. See also, Carol Lujan, "Women Warriors: American Indian Women, Crime and Alcohol" *Women & Criminal Justice* 7 (1995): 9–33; Coll-Peter Thrush and Robert Keller, "'I See What I Have Done': The Life and Murder Trial of Xwelas, a S'Klallam Woman" *The Western Historical Quarterly* XXVI (Summer 1995): 169–183.

26. Ilena Norton and Spero Manson, "A Silent Minority: Battered American Indian Women" *Journal of Family Violence* (September 1995): 307–19.

27. Diana Meyers Bahr, *From Mission to Metropolis: Cupeño Indian Women in Los Angeles*, Norman, Okla.: University of Oklahoma Press, 1993; Christine Conte, "Changing Woman Meets Madonna: Navajo Women's Networks and Sex-Gender Values in Transition" In *Writing the Range: Race, Class, and Culture in the Women's West*, Elizabeth Jameson and Susan Armitage, eds., Norman, Okla.: University of Oklahoma Press, 1997: 533–552; Jennie Joe and Dorothy Lonewolf Miller, "Cultural Survival and Contemporary American Indian Women in the City" In *Women of Color in U.S. Society*, Maxine Baca Zinn and Bonnie Thornton Dill, eds., Philadelphia, Pa.: Temple University Press, 1994.

28. Jo-Anne Fiske, "Native Women in Reserve Politics: Strategies and Struggles" *Journal of Legal Pluralism and Unofficial Law* 30, 31 (1990) 121–37; Robert Lynch, "Women in Northern Paiute Politics" *Signs: Journal of Women in Culture and Society* 11 (Winter 1986): 352–66; Bruce Miller, "Contemporary Native Women: Role Flexibility and Politics" *Anthropologica* XXVI (1994): 57–72; Bruce Miller, "Contemporary Tribal Codes and Gender Issues" *American Indian Culture and Research Journal* 18:2 (1994): 43–74; Bruce Miller, "Women and Tribal Politics: Is There a Gender Gap in Indian Elections?" *American Indian Quarterly* 18 (Winter 1994): 25–41; Bruce Miller, "Women and Politics: Comparative Evidence from the Northwest Coast" *Ethnology* 31 (October 1992): 367–384; Andrea Bear Nicholas, "Colonialism and the Struggle for Liberation: the Experience of Maliseet Women" *University of New Brunswick Law Journal* 43 (1994): 223–39.

29. For first person accounts of organizing at the grassroots level, see Janet Silman, *Enough is Enough: Aboriginal Women Speak Out*, Toronto, Ontario: The Women's Press, 1987. For details of the inequities of the Indian Act regarding status and native women, see Kathleen Jamieson, "Sex Discrimination and the Indian Act" In *Arduous Journey: Canadian Indians and Decolonization*, J. Rick Pointing, ed., Toronto, Ontario: McClelland & Stewart, 1986: 112–136. For an analysis of the consequences of the repeal of the Indian Act, see JoAnne Fiske, "Political Status of Native Indian Women: Contradictory Implications of Canadian State Policy" *American Indian Culture and Research Journal* 19:2 (1995): 1–30; Joyce Green, "Sexual Equality and Indian Government: An Analysis of Bill C-31 Amendments to the Indian Act" *Native Studies Review* 1 (1985): 81–95; L.E. Krosenbrink-Gelissen, "Caring is Indian Women's Business, But Who Takes Care of Them? Canada's Indian Women, the Renewed Indian Act, and its Implications for Women's Family Responsibilities, Roles and Rights" *Law & Anthropology* 7 (1994): 107–130; Wendy Moss, "Indigenous Self-Government in Canada and Sexual Equality under the Indian Act: Resolving Conflicts Between Collective and Individual Rights" *Queen's Law Journal* 15 (Fall 1990): 279–305.

30. Janet Billson, "Keepers of the Culture: Attitudes Toward Women's Liberation and the Women's Movement in Canada (Scottish Women, Mennonite Women, Iroquois Women)" *Women & Politics* 14:1 (1994): 1–34; M. Annette Jaimes with Theresa Halsey, "American Indian Women: At the Center of Indigenous Resistance in Contemporary North America" In *The State of Native America: Genocide, Colonization, and Resistance*, M. Annette

Jaimes, ed., Boston, Mass.: South End Press, 1992: 311–344; Danyelle Means, "From a Long Line of Strong Women" *Turtle Quarterly* 6 (1994): 30–32; Audrey Shenandoah, "Women: Sustainers of Life" *Turtle Quarterly* 3 (Summer 1990): 4–10.

31. For more information on the Indigenous Women's Network write: Indigenous Women's Network, Rt. 1, Box 308, Ponsford, Minn. 56575. Their web site is at: http://www.honorearth.com/iwn.

32. A group of Lakota women from the Pine Ridge reservation organized the Sacred Shawl Society to cope with domestic violence. See Carolyn Reyer, ed., *Cante Ohitika Win (Brave Hearted Women): Images of Lakota Women From the Pine Ridge Reservation*, Vermillion, S.D.: University of South Dakota Press, 1991.

33. California Indian Basketweavers Association, 16894 China Flats Road, Nevada City, CA 95959; 916-292-0141 email: ciba@oro.net. "Pauktuutit (Inuit Women's Association of Canada)" *Canadian Women's Studies* 10 (Summer/Fall 1989): 137–140.

34. The web page for the California Indian Basketweavers Association is located at: http://www.hermeticsphere.com/CIBA.html. Pauktuutit's web page is located at http://www.nunavik.net/pauktuutit/index.html. The Indigenous Women's Environmental Network is a Saskatchewan-based native women's group dedicated to combating pollution and other forms of environmental degradation. Their web address is: http://conbio.rice .edu/nae/docs/iwen.html.

35. For an overview of this literature, see Denise Drevdahl, "Images of Health: Perceptions of Urban American-Indian Women" In *Wings of Gauze: Women of Color and the Experience of Health and Illness*, Barbara Bair and Susan Cayleff, eds., Detroit, Mich.: Wayne State University Press, 1993: 122–129; Jennie Joe, "The Health of American Indian and Alaska Native Women" *Journal of the American Medical Women's Association* 51 (August/October 1996): 141–145; Jo Ann Kauffman and Yvette Joseph-Fox, "American Indian and Alaska Native Women" In *Race, Gender, and Health*, Marcia Bayne-Smith, ed., Thousand Oaks, Calif.: Sage Publications, 1996: 68–93; Lillian Tom-Orme, "Native American Women's Health Concerns: Toward Restoration of Harmony" In *Health Issues for Women of Color: A Cultural Diversity Perspective*, Diane Adams, ed., Thousand Oaks, Calif.: Sage Publications, 1995: 27–41. For a bibliographic guide to recent developments in the field of Native American health, see Sharon Gray, *Health of Native People of North America: a Bibliography and Guide to Resources*, Lanham, Md.: Scarecrow Press, 1996.

36. Katsi Cook, "A Native American Response" In *Birth Control and Controlling Birth: Women-Centered Perspectives*, Helen Holmes, Betty Hoskins, and Michael Gross, eds., Clifton, N.J.: The Humana Press, 1980: 251–258. Charon Aestoyer helped found the first native-run health clinic for women on the Yankton Sioux reservation, see Charon Aestoyer, "From the Ground Up [Indian Health Clinic]" *Women's Review of Books* 11 (July 1994): 22.

37. However, native perspectives on these issues will be included in the eagerly-antici-pated new anthology to be published in the fall of 1997, Sue-Ellen Jacobs, Wesley Thomas, and Sabine Long, eds., *Two-Spirit People: Perspectives on the Intersection of Native American Gender Identity, Sexuality & Spirituality*, University of Illinois Press, in press. For a brief discussion of the efforts of native gays and lesbians to revise the academic treat-ment of native gender variance, see Sue-Ellen Jacobs and Wesley Thomas, "Native American Two-Spirits" *Anthropology Newsletter* 35 (November 1994): 7. Much of the lit-erature neglects cross-gender females, however, for one of the few exceptions, see Evelyn Blackwood, "Sexuality and Gender in Certain Native American Tribes: the Case of Cross-Gender Females" *Signs: Journal of Women in Culture and Society* 10 (Autumn 1984): 27–42. For a general introduction to the history of gender variance in native cultures (although Williams gives gender variance among women scant attention), see Walter Williams, *The Spirit and the Flesh: Sexual Diversity in American Indian Culture*, Boston, Mass.: Beacon Press, 1986.

38. See, e.g., Beth Brant, *Writing as Witness: Essays and Talk*, Toronto, Ontario: The Women's Press, 1994; Beth Brant, "Giveaway: Native Lesbian Writers" *Signs: Journal of Women in Culture and Society* 18 (Summer 1993): 944–7; Lester Brown, *Two Spirit People: American Indian Lesbian Women and Gay Men*, New York, N.Y.:Haworth Press, 1996; Janice Gould, "Disobedience in Texts by Lesbian Native Americans" *Ariel* 25 (January

1994): 32–44; Will Roscoe, ed., *Living in the Spirit: A Gay American Anthology*, New York, N.Y.: St. Martin's Press, 1988.

39. See Barbara Babcock, "'A New Mexican Rebecca': Imaging Pueblo Women" *Journal of the Southwest* 32:4 (1990): 400–437; Laurie Meijer Drees, "Aboriginal Women in the Canadian West" *Native Studies Review* 10 (1995): 61–73; M. Annette Jaimes, "Hollywood's Native American Women" *Turtle Quarterly* 5 (Spring–Summer 1993): 40–45; Jennifer Mclerran, "Trappers' Brides and Country Wives: Native American Women in the Paintings of Alfred Jacob Miller" *American Indian Culture and Research Journal* 18 (1994): 1–41; Lucy Maddox, "Bearing The Burden: Perceptions of Native Women at Work" *Women: A Cultural Review* 2 (Winter 1991): 228–237; David Smits, "The 'Squaw Drudge': A Prime Index of Savagism" *Ethnohistory* 29 (1982): 281–306.

40. The starting point for understanding representations of native women in American culture is Rayna Green, "The Pocahontas Perplex: The Image of Indian Women in American Culture" *Massachusetts Review* 16 (1975): 698–714. For native reactions to Disney's *Pocahontas*, see Martha Whelshula and Faith Spotted Eagle, "'Pocahontas' Rates an 'F' in Indian Country" *Indian Country Today* (July 6, 1995), Sec. D, pp. 1–2; Charlene Teters, "Challenging the Myth [Review of Disney's *Pocahontas*]" *Indian Artist* 1 (Fall 1995): 50–51. For an analysis of the uses of the Pocahontas myth in pre-Disney American literature, see Robert Tilton, *Pocahontas: the Evolution of an American Narrative*, New York, N.Y.: Cambridge University Press, 1994.

41. See, e.g., Ziauddin Sardar, "Walt Disney and the Double Victimisation of Pocahontas" *Third Text: Third World Perspectives on Contemporary Art and Culture* 37 (Winter 1996–1997): 17–26.

Gender or Ethnicity:
What Makes a Difference?
A Study of Women Tribal Leaders

Melanie McCoy

Gender and politics was largely ignored in political science research prior to 1970 but since that time the role of women in politics has emerged as an important theme (Githens 1983). When you elect certain groups of individuals (such as women) whose entry into politics was once improbable, you increase the likelihood that the group's perspectives and beliefs will be reflected in their policy decisions (Gertzog 1984). Social science theory suggests that women's socialization, roles and life experiences are different from those of men; therefore, it is likely that there are significant differences in policy interests, political goals and perceptions as a result of gender (Darcy, Welch and Clark 1987; Sapiro 1982). For example, much of the research on elected women done in the last twenty years concludes that women elected leaders tend to give more priority or emphasis to "traditional women's issues," that is, policies concerning children, nurturance, child welfare, reproduction and education than do men elected leaders (Deutchman 1986; Gilligan 1982; Gurin 1985; Saint-Germain 1989; Shapiro and Mahajan 1986).

The Center for American Women and Politics (1987) reports that the number of women serving in elective offices has nearly quadrupled in the last twenty years, as has the research on women in elected office. A recent study of women state legislators (Saint-Germain 1989) found that the research on women elected elites in the decade of the 1980s continued to find that women political elites have different political agendas than do men and that elected men and women continue to exhibit differences in political behavior (for example, Karnig and Welch 1980; Meier and England 1984; Saltzstein 1986).

Research on women and politics may have increased in recent years, but this research has predominantly involved Anglo women political elites. The study of minority women political elites is needed to ascertain whether study findings concerning Anglo women elites are applicable to minority women. One political minority about which little is known concerning modern political leadership consists of North American Indian tribes. A new and growing trend in tribal governance is the increasing number of women participating in elective tribal politics. Although Native American women have historically had significant influence in many different tribal political systems, few have held formal elected tribal offices. Today, increasing numbers are doing so (Berkhofer 1978). However, the role of Native American women in tribal politics is almost unknown and unresearched.

A review of the current studies on Anglo women political elites and the perceptions of activists and scholars in the field of tribal politics gives rise to five research questions:

1. Will ethnicity or gender have more effect on women tribal leaders' conceptions of politics? A number of Indian activists and scholars in the field of tribal politics were asked for their perceptions concerning women tribal leaders. The consensus of those interviewed was that research on Anglo women political elites is ethnocentric and that ethnicity will have more effect on women tribal leaders' political behavior than will their gender (Bird 1990; Jean Chaudhuri 1990; Joyotpaul Chaudhuri 1990; Lujan 1990; Saint-Germain 1990; Seavey 1990; Tijerina 1990).

2. Is the contention that Anglo women elected leaders are more likely to give priority to "traditional women's issues" applicable to women tribal leaders (Deutchman 1986; Gilligan 1982; Gurin 1985; Saint-Germain 1989; Shapiro and Mahajan 1986)?

3. Is the contention that Anglo women elected leaders exhibit significantly different political behavior than men leaders applicable to women tribal leaders (Darcy, Welch, and Clark 1987; Gertzog 1984; Sapiro 1982)?

4. Do tribal cultures or traditions discourage or encourage Native American women from participating in tribal politics? A number of Indian activists and scholars in the field of tribal politics think that it is Anglo culture that has more effect on tribal women choosing not to participate in tribal politics than do tribal cultures (Bird 1990; Jean Chaudhuri 1990; Joyotpaul Chaudhuri 1990; Lujan 1990; Saint-Germain 1990; Seavey 1990; Tijerina 1990).

5. Will this study's findings confirm or reject the contention that the current literature concerning Anglo women political elites is ethnocentric?

METHODOLOGY

For the purposes of this study, women elected to the highest tribal office (head chief, chairman, president) in federally recognized tribes in the lower 48 states were surveyed. Because of funding limitations, the study did not include Native

American women village leaders in Alaska. According to the U.S. Department of Interior's Bureau of Indian Affairs, there were 61 elected women tribal leaders in the lower 48 states in 1990. The entire population of 61 elected women tribal leaders was asked to participate in the study. Of the 61 tribal leaders, 8 had been replaced by male tribal leaders, giving a final study population of 53 women tribal leaders. Of this population, 19 women tribal leaders agreed to participate. This is a 36% response rate. An open-ended questionnaire was used to survey the 19 women tribal leaders. Survey items for research questions two and three are comparable to those used by Kirkpatrick in her 1974 study of women legislators to ascertain women leaders concept of politics and whether men and women leaders' exhibit differences in political behavior. Three interviews were done in person, 13 by telephone and three in writing. All questions were asked in the same way of all respondents. Funding limitations severely limited the number of in-person interviews. Past studies in the field of tribal politics by this researcher show that in-person interviews with tribal leaders are the best method for contacting and eliciting information. Respondents to this study are self-selected and the response rate is relatively low (36%). As a result, one must be very careful in generalizing from these data. This study is exploratory and is merely the first step in examining this small minority. A profile of the typical woman tribal leader participating in this study is as follows:

- an average age of 52 years of age (youngest 33 and oldest 79)
- college educated (37% college degrees, 26% one or more years of college and 37% high school diplomas)
- married (63% are married, 32% widowed or divorced, and 1% single)
- 0–2 children (the number of children ranged from none to 10)
- For these tribal leaders, a stepping-stone to political office was prior service on the tribal council and/or a position in tribal government.

DISCUSSION

The first three survey items solicited information on how these women tribal leaders conceptualize politics. The majority of respondents saw politics as an arena of competition where the leader attempts to "get something for the people." There was less agreement among the respondents on whether compromise is the key to political success or whether politics is a method of improving the quality of life of tribal members. A clear majority said that politics is not a method for solving social problems.

Survey item two attempted to find out whether women tribal leaders see politics as a way of enhancing their own self-interest and economic well being or whether they see politics as a public service and obligation of citizenship. The majority of the responses to survey item two clearly showed that women tribal leaders tend toward the concept of politics as a public service and obligation of citizenship.

Seven of 19 respondents saw themselves as reformers who wanted to get rid of the spoils system in tribal government and to stop the corruption and inequities they saw in tribal politics. Twelve of the 19 respondents said they ran for tribal office to "make things better," to "set the tribe on the road to self-determination," and to "find solutions to tribal problems."

Survey item three attempted to solicit information on women tribal leaders' leadership styles. Thirteen of the 19 women tribal leaders saw themselves as working for long-term goals and final solutions. However, they emphasized that their leadership style was most influenced by tribal size and resources. If the tribe is small and with limited resources, the leader is often forced into crises management with little time to work on long-term solutions to tribal problems. The respondents also said that tribal factionalism forces most tribal leaders (male and female) to be crisis managers. All 19 respondents stated that they most often used their own judgment in making policy decisions or that they make decisions jointly with the tribal council. Many respondents said that only chaos results when you try to "go to the people." They said that with tribal conflict and factionalism it becomes a question of to whom do you listen.

When the responses to survey items one through three are considered, some preliminary conclusions can be drawn. Early studies on Anglo women political elites (Kirkpatrick 1974) found that these women did not see conflict as an important dimension of politics. However, women tribal leaders seem to perceive of tribal politics as an arena of conflict where there are clear winners and losers. Even though they may perceive that realistically this is the way the game of tribal politics is played, their personal conception of politics is much closer to politics as public service and an obligation of citizenship. Kirkpatrick's 1974 study of Anglo women political elites had similar finding for Anglo women. Looking at the responses to all three survey items it seems that the respondents perceive the realities of tribal life (tribal size, resources, factionalism) as having the most significant impact on the leader's conception of politics and political leadership style, just as the Indian activists and scholars in this field asserted.

The second research question raised in the study dealt with whether women tribal leaders would give priority to traditional women's issues, as many studies of Anglo women political elites have found. The survey asked women tribal leaders to rank their most important political agenda items. A summary of the 19 responses shows which of these 5 agenda items were most important (with one being the most important agenda item):

1. tribal economic development,
2. health care,
3. education,
4. housing,
5. tribal/federal relations.

This agenda of women tribal leaders was compared to the political agenda of a group of men tribal leaders identified in a 1989 study of tribal politics (McCoy 1989).

The comparison of ranked agenda items by men and women tribal leaders in these two studies show no significant differences. A study of the legislative, executive, and judicial branches of the Chickasaw government (McCoy and Delashaw 1991) also shows no significant differences in tribal agendas, between men and women tribal leaders. Tribal leaders, regardless of gender, seem to give priority to issues which concern the survival of their people. Women tribal leaders rank the same issue first as do men leaders, tribal economic development. In all three studies, men and women tribal leaders emphasized that without the basics of life—health, education, shelter—economic development cannot become a reality. Without federal Indian programs to support the tribes, economic development cannot become a reality. "Traditional women's issues" are ranked equally high by both men and women tribal leaders. While some current studies concerning Anglo elected women still identify political agenda differences between men and women elected leaders, this study does not show a similar finding for men and women tribal leaders.

The third research question raised in this study concerned whether women tribal leaders would perceive that there were differences in political behavior between men and women tribal leaders. Seventeen of 19 respondents perceived that there were differences in political behavior. Some of their responses were as follows:

- A woman leader must be a "superwoman"—mother, wife, and tribal leader— while a man leader does not have to play all these different roles. This makes it difficult for women leaders to travel and to participate in tribal politics at the state and national levels.
- Women tribal leaders have to fit into the male world of tribal politics and not vice versa. Women leaders must "play the game" if they are to be effective. This "good old boy" network puts women tribal leaders at a disadvantage.
- Men and women leaders deal with people and solve problems differently. Women listen more, are more objective, and try harder to get everyone's viewpoint than do men.
- Women leaders see themselves as there to serve the people while men leaders see themselves as superior to the people.
- Women leaders try to be role models for the tribe, and men leaders do not.
- Men leaders tend to think of themselves as dealing with broad issues while women leaders tend to deal more with people's problems.
- Women leaders sit and talk and compromise while men leaders try to dominate and force their views on the group.

The two respondents who thought male leaders acted negatively toward women leaders commented that women tribal leaders have more problems with the negative attitudes of men tribal members than men tribal leaders. These respondents said that men tribal members often try to find something which will reflect badly on the woman leader to try to "bring her down."

The research findings in this study are similar to much of the research involving Anglo women political elites in that women tribal leaders perceive that there are gender differences in political behavior between men and women leaders.

The fourth research question raised by this study was whether women tribal leaders perceived that tribal cultures or traditions encouraged or discouraged women from becoming involved in tribal politics. Fifteen of the 19 women tribal leaders said their tribal traditions and culture did not discourage them from running for tribal office. Many women leaders said their tribes neither encourage nor discourage women's participation in politics because their tribes have no viable tribal traditions. Some of the respondents' comments were as follows:

- "We have no tribal traditions left. Our elders are all gone."
- "I don't speak the tribal language or know our tribal history."
- "Our culture has been lost. Only two of the elders speak our language and know the tribal dances."

Those respondents who thought tribal traditions did discourage participation (four of the 19), said tribal culture discourages both men and women. Competitive values are not instilled in either men or women in some tribes, making it difficult for either to compete for offices in a tribal government structure imposed by Anglos.

The final research question raised in this study was whether contemporary studies concerning Anglo women leaders are ethnocentric. The research findings in this study do not clearly show whether research findings concerning Anglo elected women are applicable to women tribal leaders. This study seems to show that Anglo and Native American women may have similar perceptions concerning their individual political role, and that they share perceptions that there are differences in the political behaviors of men and women elected leaders. However, it also seems that the realities of tribal size, tribal resources, tribal factionalism and the need for tribal survival are as, or more, important influences in women tribal leaders' leadership styles and political agendas as is their gender.

The study does not show that the finding that Anglo women elected leaders have political agendas which are different than men elected leaders is applicable to women tribal leaders. Both men and women tribal leaders have very similar political agendas. Male tribal leaders seem to share "traditional women's issues." It may be that the disadvantaged conditions of minority groups (whether the group is ethnicity- or gender-based) have more influence on agenda-setting than does either ethnicity or gender alone. It is also possible that there may be more significant differences between Anglo men and women elected leaders than there are between Native American men and women elected leaders. A number of women tribal leaders stated that it is the Anglo culture which draws such sharp distinctions between the proper roles of men and women in public life, and if tribal women do exhibit different political behaviors than men or do define their political roles differently than do men, it may be more as a result of the imposition of Anglo culture and Anglo government structure on the tribes than the tribal cultures themselves.

This preliminary research is valuable because it addresses the important but previously unasked question of whether the research findings on Anglo women political elites are applicable to minority women elites. It also gives rise to a number of important questions which need to be researched. Would a comparative study of Anglo women leaders, women tribal leaders, and men tribal leaders show that women tribal leaders are more like men tribal leaders or like female Anglo leaders? Would a larger sample of women tribal leaders identify differences in responses and findings for women leaders in tribes of different sizes, resources, and cultures?

REFERENCES

Berkhofer, Robert F., 1978. "Native Americans" in John Higham, ed., *Ethnic Leadership in America.* Baltimore, Md.: Johns Hopkins University Press.

Bird, Penny, 1990. Telephone interview by author with Assistant Director of the Office of Indian Education, State of New Mexico, July.

Center for American Women and Politics, 1987. *Women in State Legislatures.* Brunswick, N.J.: Eagleton Institute of Politics, Rutgers University.

Chaudhuri, Jean, 1990. Telephone interview by author with Indian activist, June.

Chaudhuri, Joyotpaul, 1990. Interview by author with Dean of Arts and Sciences, Arizona State University, March.

Darcy, Robert, Susan Welch, and Janet Clark, 1987. *Women, Elections and Representation.* New York, N.Y.: Longman.

Deutchman, Iva Ellen, 1986. "Socialization to Power: Questions about Women and Politics." *Women and Politics*, 5: 79–91.

Elazar, Daniel J., 1984. *American Federalism, A View from the States.* New York, N.Y.: Harper & Row.

Gertzog, Irwin N., 1984. *Congressional Women: Their Recruitment, Treatment and Behavior.* New York, N.Y.: Praeger.

Gilligan, Carol, 1982. *In a Different Voice.* Cambridge, Mass.: Harvard University Press.

Githens, Marianne, 1983. "The Elusive Paradigm, Gender, Politics and Political Behavior" in Finifter, ed., *Political Science, the State of Discipline.*

Gurin, Patricia, 1985. "Women's Gender Consciousness." *Public Opinion Quarterly*, 49: 143–63.

Karnig, Albert K., and Susan Welch, 1980. *Black Representation and Urban Policy.* Chicago, Ill.: University of Chicago Press.

Kirkpatrick, Jeane J., 1974. *Political Women.* New York, N.Y.: Basic Books.

Lujan, Lance, 1990. Telephone interview by author with Director of Indian Resource Development, New Mexico State University, June.

McCoy, Leila M., 1990. Agenda Setting by Minority Political Groups: A Case Study of Oklahoma Indian Tribes, presented at annual meeting of Southwest Social Sciences Association, Fort Worth, Texas.

McCoy, Leila M., 1991. Chickasaw Election Study, unpublished research.

Meier, Kenneth, and Robert E. England, 1984. "Black Representation and Education Policy: Are They Related?" *American Political Science Review*, 6: 485–97.

Saint-Germain, Michelle A., 1989. Telephone interview by author with political science professor, University of Arizona, May.

Saltzstein, Grace H., 1986. "Female Mayors and Women in Municipal Jobs." *American Journal of Political Science*, 30: 140–64.

Sapiro, Virginia, 1982. "When Are Interests Interesting? The Problem of Political Representation of Women." *American Political Science Review*, 75: 701–16.

Seavey, Pat, 1990. Telephone interview by author with Assistant Director of the Southwest Institute for Research on Women (SIROW), June.

Shapiro, Robert Y., and Harpreet Mahajan, 1986. "Gender Differences in Policy Preferences: A Summary of Trends from the 1960s to the 1980s." *Public Opinion Quarterly*, 50: 42–61.

Tijerina, Katherine, 1990. Telephone interview by author with President of the Institute of American Art, Santa Fe, and past director of Indian Resource Development, New Mexico State University, July.

Mankiller: A Chief and Her People

Wilma Mankiller

HOMEWARD BOUND

In the times before the Cherokees learned the ways of others, they paid extraordinary respect to women.

So when a man married, he took up residence with the clan of his wife. The women of each of the seven clans elected their own leaders. These leaders convened as the Women's Council, and sometimes raised their voices in judgment to override the authority of the chiefs when the women believed the welfare of the tribe demanded such an action. It was common custom among the ancient Cherokees that any important questions relating to war and peace were left to a vote of the women.

There were brave Cherokee women who followed their husbands and brothers into battle. These female warriors were called War Women or Pretty Women, and they were considered dignitaries of the tribe, many of them being as powerful in council as in battle.

The Cherokees also had a custom of assigning to a certain woman the task of declaring whether pardon or punishment should be inflicted on great offenders. This woman also was called the Pretty Woman, but she was sometimes known as Most Honored Woman or Beloved Woman.

It was the belief of the Cherokees that the Great Spirit sent messages through their Beloved Woman. So great was her power that she could commute the sentence of a person condemned to death by the council.

The Ghigau, known by her later name of Nancy Ward, is often called to the last Beloved Woman. She earned her title, the highest honor that a Cherokee woman could achieve, by rallying the Cherokees in a pitched battle against the Creeks in 1755. As a War Woman of the Wolf Clan, she accompanied her first husband, Kingfisher, into battle. In the field, she prepared food for him and chewed his bullets to cause fatal damage when they struck their marks.

When Kingfisher was killed in the heat of the fray, she raised his weapon and fought so valiantly that the Cherokees rose behind her leadership and defeated the Creeks.

In recognition of her courage in war, Nancy was given her prestigious title. She spent the remainder of her life as a devoted advocate of peace between the Cherokees and all others.

Those first few years in the early 1980s were some of the most pivotal in my life. Everything about [moving from the San Francisco Bay Area to Oklahoma] was positive. My daughters were doing well in their schoolwork, and were learning more each day about their Cherokee heritage. Many members of my family were living within easy reach. My work was very satisfying. I was beginning to feel complete.

After enduring two back-to-back assaults on my physical self, that period was comforting to my mind and soul. It was the best medicine. Serving as the principal organizer and enabler at the Bell community marked the first time I had been given any real power within the tribe. I enjoyed the tasks and eagerly asked for more. Chief Swimmer was generous in his response to my requests. I was able to use federal grants to finance my people's dreams.

Then in 1983, history was made when Ross Swimmer asked me to run as his deputy chief in the next election. Just the year before, he had been deserted by most of his closest political supporters, partly because he had been diagnosed with lymphatic cancer. Those supposed allies of Swimmer's had little courage or loyalty. One of the reasons they decided to challenge him as chief was because they considered that he was too ill to remain in office, since he was out much of the time taking chemotherapy treatments. They wrote him off as a dead man. So the following year when the time came for Swimmer to announce his bid for reelection for another four-year term, he remembered me. I suppose he trusted me, and was satisfied with my work and my allegiance to the tribe. He asked me if I would consider being on the ticket as his deputy. . . .

Unquestionably, Swimmer was taking a great chance by bypassing his male friends to select me as his running mate. I suppose he saw me as an effective leader and manager. He [a Republican] must have forgotten that I am also a liberal Democrat.

I was greatly flattered by Swimmer's selection of me, but I thought the whole idea was totally ludicrous. Because our tribe is so large, running for tribal office is much like running for Congress, or even a national political post. It is very much a mainstream process, complete with print and broadcast advertising, campaign billboards, rallies, and all that sort of thing. I honestly believed I could not possibly get elected. I realized that I had successfully developed and managed tribal programs and had much experience, including my years in California, but I simply could not picture myself in high tribal office. I told Chief Swimmer I was honored that he had chosen me, but my answer was a polite no. I had to decline.

But almost immediately after I gave him my answer, I started to think about what was transpiring around me. I then gave Chief Swimmer's offer more thought.

I went out among some of our rural communities in eastern Oklahoma where we were facilitating development projects. In one small community, I came upon three of our people living in an abandoned bus without any roof. Their few extra clothes were hanging on a line. They had few other possessions. It was a very sad scene. It burned into my mind.

I knew this was not an isolated situation. Many Cherokees were forced to put up with poor housing, rising medical costs, and educational deficits. I realized I was being given an opportunity to create change for Cherokee families such as those living in the old bus. I knew that if I did not act, I would no longer have any right to talk about or criticize the people who held tribal offices.

The visit to that small community had a major impact on me. I drove straight to Ross Swimmer's home. I told him I had reconsidered, and I would run for election as deputy chief in the 1983 election. I quit my job with the Cherokee Nation so there would be no conflict of interest, and I filed for office.

From the start, I figured most people would be bothered about my ideas on grass-roots democracy and the fact that I had a fairly extensive activist background. I adhered to a different political philosophy than many people living in the area. But I was wrong. No one challenged me on those issues, not once. Instead, I was challenged mostly because of one fact—I am female. The election became an issue of gender. It was one of the first times I had ever really encountered overt sexism. I recalled that my first real experience with sexism had occurred in California. I had once slugged a boss during a Christmas party in San Francisco when he came up behind me and tried to kiss me. He did not fire me, but I do believe he got the message that I did not want to be mauled. The memory of that time came back to me during the 1983 campaign.

I heard all sorts of things—some people claimed that my running for office was an affront to God. Others said having a female run our tribe would make the Cherokees the laughingstock of the tribal world. I heard it all. Every time I was given yet another silly reason why I should not help run our government, I was certain that I had made the correct decision.

The reaction to my candidacy stunned me. It was a very low time in my life, but I would not be swayed. I figured the best tactic was to ignore my opponents. I remembered a saying I had once read on the back of a tea box. It said something like this—if you argue with a fool, someone passing by will not be able to tell who is the fool and who is not. I did not wish to be taken for a fool.

I built my run for office on a positive and cheerful foundation to counter the incredible hostility and great opposition I encountered. To say that the campaign was heated would be the understatement of all times. Most of the negative acts did not originate with my opponents for office, but with those who did not want a woman in office. I even had foes *within* the Swimmer-Mankiller team. Toward the end of the campaign, some of them openly supported one of my opponents.

Occasionally, the actions of those who were out to stop my election were violent. I received hate mail, including several death threats. After one evening rally, I returned to my car and discovered that all four tires had been slashed. On other occasions, there were threatening messages over the telephone. Once I picked up my ringing telephone and heard the sound of a rifle bolt being slammed shut on the other end of the line.

I also had a chilling experience while riding in a parade. I was waving and laughing and smiling at the crowd along the street when I spied someone in the back of the crowd. I saw a young man, and he had his hand cocked and his fingers pointed at me as if he were holding a pistol, then he drew his hand back, firing an imaginary gun. I never even blinked. I just calmly looked away. The parade continued. No matter how disturbing those incidents were, the scare tactics did not work. One consolation was that the people in Bell and other rural Cherokee communities where I had worked were very supportive.

My two opponents for officer were J. B. Dreadfulwater, a popular gospel singer and former member of the tribal council, and Agnes Cowan, the first woman to serve on the tribal council. She was older than I was, and already established in our tribal government. They were worthy opponents who liked to criticize me for having no experience in tribal politics. In truth, I had a great deal of applicable experience, but I did have much to learn about political campaigning.

Some of the early experiences were painful. For example, we sent invitations for the first campaign event and made a lot of preparations. That particular evening arrived, and everything was laid out beautifully. Only five people, however, came to hear me speak, and three of them were related to me. But I smiled and realized it could only get better from there.

I think my opponents ignored the fact that I had a great deal of experience as a community organizer. I had learned a long time ago, at the Indian Center in San Francisco, how to reach large groups of people and bring them together. That is just what I did. I went door to door and campaigned. I attended every event and rally. I kept encountering opposition as a female candidate, but I did not use it as an issue in my campaign. Gradually, I saw some changes, but they were very few and far between.

Finally, election day arrived. When the ballots had been counted, Ross Swimmer was reelected, to his third term. I beat out Dreadfulwater in that first election, but had to face Cowan in a July runoff. In a tough battle, I defeated her and was able to claim ultimate victory. It was truly a moment to remember forever. The people of my tribe had selected me to serve as the first woman deputy chief in Cherokee history. I took office on August 14, 1983. As one of my supporters put it, at long last a daughter of the people had been chosen for high tribal office.

> Women can help turn the world right side up. We bring a more collaborative approach to government. And if we do not participate, then decisions will be made without us.
>
> —Wilma Mankiller, Denver, September 1984

My two years as deputy chief proved to be difficult—very difficult. I had inherited many people on Ross Swimmer's staff, and would not have my own people aboard for some time to come. Although Swimmer had chosen me as a deputy and had stuck with me through the tough campaign, there were major differences between us. He was a Republican banker with a very conservative viewpoint, and I was a Democratic social worker and community planner who had organized and worked for Indian civil and treaty rights. Also, I had been elected along with a fifteen-member tribal council that, for the most part, did not support me. In fact, they had mostly worked against my election. Suddenly they were confronted with this young idealist woman, this veteran of Alcatraz, who was not only the newly elected deputy chief of the tribe but also acted as president of the council. I was shocked by how petty and political some of them behaved, even after my election.

Serving as president of a council that, at the start, did not support me was an interesting experience. Several members were almost hostile, but what surprised me the most was the lack of support I received from the three women on the council. Of course, they had also opposed my election, but I had naively assumed that once I was in office, we would all work together. But the situation did not get any better. In the subsequent election, two of the women supported my opponent, and the third did not seek reelection. I suppose that throughout those first few months, I felt a real lack of personal power. I had all the responsibility with none of the authority. Mostly, I just coped.

Gradually, I learned to adjust, and so did many of the council members. Still, it took all of us a while to figure out individual styles and ways of doing business. I stayed very busy as deputy chief, helping to govern an Indian nation spread over fourteen counties in northeastern Oklahoma. Despite our differences, Swimmer and I shared an absolute commitment to the rebuilding and revitalizing of our rural communities. As deputy chief, I helped to supervise the daily operations of the tribe. Those included more than forty tribally operated programs ranging from health clinics to day care, elderly assistance to water projects, Head Start classes to housing construction.

Then in September of 1985—just a little more than two years after I took office—there was more sudden change to deal with. Chief Swimmer was asked to go to Washington to head the BIA when he was nominated by President Ronald Reagan to serve as assistant secretary of the interior for Indian affairs. To assume the top Indian affairs post in the federal government, with fourteen thousand employees and a $1 billion annual budget, was an offer that Swimmer, then forty-one, did not want to refuse. The offer came at about the time other tribal officials and I had just about gotten used to each other.

Although it had never been invoked before, Article Six of our Cherokee Nation Constitution, ratified in 1976, provided for the replacement of a principal chief who leaves before the expiration of a term of office. According to this constitutional provision, the deputy principal chief automatically replaced the resigning chief. Legislation passed by the Cherokee Nation tribal council called for that body then to elect, from within its ranks, a new deputy principal chief. Members of the council would then recommend a name to fill the vacancy on the council, after which the nominee would be confirmed by the full tribal council.

When I first learned about Swimmer's upcoming departure, I was somewhat concerned that I would go through the same ordeal as before, when I ran for deputy chief. I immediately began to prepare myself—spiritually and emotionally—for the onslaught. But remarkably, the transition was not that difficult. I suppose many people who were opposed to me thought they could live with the tribal laws and wait for two years until the next election, when they could clobber me at the polls. My problem seemed clear. I had to serve the balance of Ross Swimmer's term—from 1985 to 1987—without any real mandate from the people.

Swimmer's presidential nomination was ultimately confirmed by the United States Senate, and on December 5, 1985, I was sworn in as principal chief of the Cherokee Nation in a private ceremony. Formal ceremonies were held on December 14 at the tribal headquarters. Right before I took the oath of office, Ross Swimmer called me to offer his best.

Memories of my public inauguration will stay with me as long as I live. It was not the happiest of occasions. Swimmer had had little time to prepare me for all the complex issues we were facing. His staff members and many other people felt that the Cherokee Nation would crash and burn with a woman in charge. I was very wary. I knew full well what was ahead.

For the ceremony, I wore a dark suit and white blouse. There was snow on the ground, but the sky was clear and blue and cloudless. So many people came to me with hugs and smiles and good wishes. There were tears of happiness. I recall sitting behind the chief's desk for the first time for an official photo, and someone in the office said, "You look very natural sitting there. It's very becoming."

The council chamber was packed. There were many photographers, reporters, and guests. At the proper time, I stepped forward and placed my hand on a Bible. I raised my other hand to take the oath of office. It was a very straightforward pledge.

"I, Wilma P. Mankiller, do solemnly swear, or affirm, that I will faithfully execute the duties of Principal Chief of the Cherokee Nation. And will, to the best of my abilities, preserve, protect, and defend the Constitutions of the Cherokee Nation and the United States of America. I swear, or affirm, further that I will do everything within my power to promote the culture, heritage, and tradition of the Cherokee Nation."

Thunderous applause followed when I finished the oath and stepped up to the podium. As the crowd became still, the sound of camera shutters clicking continued until I spoke. I thanked everyone in attendance, and all of my friends, family, and supporters. I spoke of the deep honor of assuming the position of chief. I complimented Ross Swimmer for his leadership, and I talked of the many tasks before me.

> . . . I think there's a bit of nervousness in the Cherokee Nation. I think any time there's a change, people wonder what's going to happen, is there going to be some kind of major change. And my political adversaries like to spread around rumors that there's going to be a purge of employees. That's just not the case. I like what's going on at the Cherokee Nation. There will be very little that will change. The only thing that will change is that there will be more of an emphasis on the development of the economy.
>
> —Wilma Mankiller, inaugural speech, 1985

By the time I took the oath of office, my eldest daughter, Felicia, had married, and I had my first grandchild, Aaron Swake. I was a forty-year-old grandmother, as well as the first woman to serve as chief of a major tribe. I told the reporters, who seemed to materialize from out of nowhere, that the only people who were really worried about my serving as chief were members of my family. That was because all of them knew very well how much time I tended to devote to my job. My daughters were, of course, concerned about my health. But my little grandson thought it was great that his grandma was the chief. . . .

One thing that I never tried to become as chief was "one of the boys," nor am I a "good ol' girl." I never will be. That goes against my grain. I do know how to be political and to get the job done, but I do not believe that one must sacrifice one's principles. Gradually, I noticed changes within the tribe and especially within the council.

Rural development was, and still remains, a high priority on my list of goals. For me, the rewards came from attempting to break the circle of poverty. My feeling is that the Cherokee people, by and large, are incredibly tenacious. We have survived so many major political and social upheavals, yet we have kept the Cherokee government alive. I feel confident that we will march into the twenty-first century on our own terms.

We are staffed with professionals—educators, physicians, attorneys, business leaders. Already, in the 1800s, we fought many of our wars with lawsuits, and it was in the courts where many of our battles were won. Today, we are helping to erase the stereotypes created by media and by western films of the drunken Indian on a horse, chasing wagon trains across the prairie. I suppose some people still think that all native people live in tepees and wear tribal garb every day. They do not realize that many of us wear business suits and drive station wagons. The beauty of society today is that young Cherokee men and women can pursue any professional fields they want and remain true to traditional values. It all comes back to our heritage and our roots. It is so vital that we retain that sense of culture, history, and tribal identity.

We also are returning the balance to the role of women in our tribe. Prior to my becoming chief, young Cherokee girls never thought they might be able to grow up and become chief themselves. That has definitely changed. From the start of my administration, the impact on the younger women of the Cherokee Nation was noticeable. I feel certain that more women will assume leadership roles in tribal communities. . . .

In 1987, after I had fulfilled the balance of Ross Swimmer's term as chief, I made the decision to run on my own and to win a four-year term of office. It was not an easy decision. I knew the campaign would be most difficult. I talked to my family and to my people. I spent long hours discussing the issues with Charlie Soap, whom I had married in 1986. Charlie had contracted with private foundations to continue development work with low-income native community projects. His counsel to me was excellent. He encouraged me to run. So did many other people.

But there were others who were opposed to my continuing as chief. Even some of my friends and advisers told me they believed the Cherokee people would accept me only as deputy, not as an elected principal chief. Some of those people came to our home at Mankiller Flats. I would look out the window and see them coming down the dirt road to tell me that I should give up any idea of running for chief. Finally, I told Charlie that if one more family came down that road and told me not to run, I was going to run for sure. That is just what happened.

I made my official announcement in early 1987, calling for a "positive, forward-thinking campaign." I chose John A. Ketcher, a member of the tribal council since 1983, as my running mate for the June 20 election. In 1985, John had been elected by the council to succeed me as deputy chief when I became principal chief. An eleven-sixteenths bilingual Cherokee, John was born in southern Mayes County in 1922. A veteran of World War II and a graduate of Northeastern State University in Tahlequah, Ketcher, as I do, considered unity and economic development to be the two priorities for the Cherokee Nation. He still does. John has remained deputy chief to this day, and is a great asset to the Cherokee people.

> After we debate issues, we remain friends and support each other. We are all Cherokees. The same blood that flows in the full-bloods flows in the part-bloods. We all have things we would like to see happen, but if we argue over issues or candidates the four years between tribal elections, we wouldn't be able to get anything done for those who need it and those we serve—the Cherokee people.
>
> —Deputy Principal Chief John A. Ketcher

I drew three opponents in the race for principal chief. I had to face Dave Whitekiller, a postal assistant from the small community of Cookson and a former councilman; William McKee, deputy administrator at W. W. Hastings Indian Hospital, in Tahlequah; and Perry Wheeler, a former deputy chief and a funeral home director from Sallisaw, in Sequoyah County.

From the beginning, the best description of the campaign came from someone on the council, who said there was an "undercurrent of viciousness." I ignored things that were going on around me. I did the same thing I had always done—went out to the communities and talked to as many of the Cherokee people as possible about the issues. I tried to answer all their questions. My critics claimed that I had failed to properly manage and direct the Cherokee Nation, which was obviously false. Our revenue for 1986 was up $6 million, higher than it had ever been to that point. I was not about to lose focus by warring with my opponents.

The election eliminated all the candidates except for Perry Wheeler and me. None of us had received more than 50 percent of the votes. I had polled 45 percent to Wheeler's 29 percent. We had to face each other in a July runoff. My supporters worked very hard during those last few weeks. Charlie was one of my main champions. On my behalf, Charlie visited many rural homes where English is a second language to remind the people that prior to the intrusion of white men, women had played key roles in our government. He asked our people to not turn their backs on their past or their future.

Charlie's help was especially important because I was stricken with my old nemesis, kidney problems, during the final weeks of the campaign. Finally, just before the election, I had to be hospitalized in Tulsa, but the physicians never determined the exact location of the infection and could not bring it under control. The lengthy infection and hospitalization would nearly cost me not only the election but also my life, since it brought on extensive and irreversible kidney damage. From that point forward, I was repeatedly hospitalized for kidney and urinary-tract infections, until I underwent surgery and had a kidney transplant in 1990.

Wheeler, an unsuccessful candidate for the chief's job against Ross Swimmer in 1983, tried to make my hospitalization a major issue. He waged a vigorous and negative runoff campaign. He publicly stated that I had never been truthful about my health. It all reminded me of the way Swimmer had been attacked when he was battling cancer. Wheeler, whom I can best describe as an old-style politician, also made claims that I had not hired enough Cherokee people for what he called the higher-paying tribal posts.

> When she [Mankiller] came back here [to Oklahoma], she had a different philosophy. She grew up in a time when the hippie craze was going on.
>
> —Perry Wheeler, Tulsa Tribune, 1987

When all the ballots from thirty-four precincts plus the absentee votes were tallied, the woman who supposedly knew nothing about politics was declared the winner. The night of the runoff election, we went to the Tulsa Powwow, where my daughter Gina was being honored. In a photograph taken that evening, Charlie, Gina, Felicia, and I look very tired and worn, as if we had just been through a battle. Later that night, we returned to Tahlequah to check on the election results. When the votes of the local precincts were counted, it appeared that I had won easily. Everyone around me was celebrating, but I was concerned about the absentee votes. Once that vote was included, I allowed myself to celebrate.

At last, the Cherokee Nation had elected its first woman as principal chief—the first woman chief of a major Native American tribe. I had outpolled Wheeler, and John Ketcher had retained his post as deputy chief. Wheeler conceded victory to me shortly before midnight.

At long last, I had the mandate I had wanted. I had been chosen as principal chief of the Cherokee Nation by my own people. It was a sweet victory. Finally, I felt the question of gender had been put to rest. Today, if anyone asks members of our tribe if it really matters if the chief is male or female, the majority will reply that gender has no bearing on leadership.

Because I have risen to the office of chief, some people erroneously conclude that the role of native women has changed in *every* tribe. That is not so. People jump to that conclusion because they do not really understand native people. There is no universal "Indian language." All of us have our own distinct languages and cultures. . . . Because Native Americans have our own languages, cultures, art forms, and social systems, our tribes are radically different from one another. Many tribal groups do not have women in titled positions, but in the great majority of those groups, there is some degree of balance and harmony in the roles of men and women. Among the Lakota, there is a very well known saying that "a nation is not defeated until the hearts of the women are on the ground." I think in some ways Rigoberta Menchú, the Nobel Peace Prize winner—a Guatemalan human-rights activist—may be a good rallying force for all of us. She represents to me the very best of what native womanhood is about. I am awestruck by her life and accomplishments, as are many other native people in Central, South, and North America.

In the instance of the Cherokees, we are fortunate to have many strong women. I have attained a leadership position because I am willing to take risks, but at the same time, I am trying to teach other women, both Cherokees and others, to take risks also. I hope more women will gradually emerge in leadership positions. When I ran for deputy chief in 1983, I quit my job and spent every dollar of my personal savings and proceeds from the car-accident settlement* to pay for campaign expenses. Friends describe me as someone who likes to dance along the edge of the roof. I try to encourage young women to be willing to take risks, to stand up for the things they believe in, and to step up and accept the challenge of serving in leadership roles.

> True tribal tradition recognizes the importance of women. Contrary to what you've probably read in history books, not all tribes were controlled by men.
>
> —Wilma Mankiller, Harvard University, 1987

If I am to be remembered, I want it to be because I am fortunate enough to have become my tribe's first female chief. But I also want to be remembered for emphasizing the fact that we have indigenous solutions to our problems. Cherokee values, especially those of helping one another and of our interconnections with the land, can be used to address contemporary issues. . . .

---

*Mankiller was in a tragic car accident that had a major impact on her life. She describes the details of this accident in her book on pp. 222–229.

The Legal Rights of American Indian Women

Genevieve Chato and Christine Conte

American Indians derive their citizenship from three sources—tribal, state, and federal Governments. Most importantly, as members of tribes Indians have rights and responsibilities that derive from tribal citizenship status. Because of tribal sovereignty, or the right of the tribe to govern itself, the extent to which federal and state laws apply to them varies from situation to situation. The nature of tribal sovereignty has been defined by the United States government both in the federal Constitution and in various Supreme Court decisions. Treaties executed in the nineteenth century set forth laws relating to Indian tribes on reservations.[1] The tribes entered into a trust relationship with the government, similar to that of a minor child whose parents have died. Minors may inherit from their parents, but do not have the legal right to hold and dispose of their own property. In such cases the courts appoint an adult to whom legal title of the property is given and who then disperses it for the minor's benefit. The tribal trust relationship operates in similar fashion. The United States government has legal title to the tribal land and, in exchange, provides services that were bargained for through treaties with the Indian nations. The tribes function as semi-independent nations in that they run their own government within the confines of the reservation and the extent of tribal law is territorial. In a sense they are similar to a state within a state, though no tribe would refer to itself as a state; for legal purposes they always refer to themselves as nations. Tribes have their own laws in such areas as the determination of membership in the tribe and the distribution of property after death. They have the right to regulate marriage, divorce, child custody, and child guardianship. Tribes are separate and distinct from the states in which they are located.

Whether an Indian is subject to tribal, state or federal jurisdiction depends on the location of the individual. For example, a Navajo woman residing in the state of Arizona has rights under state law as an Arizona citizen. In addition, even though the Navajo Reservation is separate and distinct, the same Navajo woman is still a United States citizen. Finally, the Navajo woman, who is simultaneously a citizen of the United States and of the state of Arizona, is also subject to tribal law as long as she resides on the reservation. Once she leaves tribal boundaries, she is no longer under tribal jurisdiction. Some Arizona laws apply to life on the reservations, such as the right to vote in state elections, to be educated, and to be provided with various social services and health benefits. The constitution of the state of Arizona, however, protects the Navajo woman only when she is off the reservation.

In some cases, distinctions between state and tribal jurisdictions are not clear cut. For example, in 1978 in the case, *Oliphant v Suquamish Indian Tribe,* 435 U.S. 191, the United States Supreme Court ruled that tribes do not have power over non-Indians who commit crimes within the confines of the reservation. Only the state has that power. Arrangements for highway management provide a second example of complexities of legal jurisdictions. When the state of Arizona builds highways through the Navajo Reservation, it is stipulated that the state reserves the right to maintain and regulate the highway. To accommodate this stipulation, a cross-deputization agreement was reached by which Arizona can issue tribal citations to Indians within the reservation and tribal police can issue state citations to non-Indians on the state highway. In sum, the question of jurisdiction is sometimes hazy, even with respect to such relatively minor situations as traffic violations.

Confusions over jurisdiction are compounded because tribal law is more difficult to codify than laws of the United States or the various state governments. Each tribe governs itself differently. The Navajo tribe is unique among the Indian nations in that it has a written tribal code, codified in the 1960s and revised since that time. The written code was not, however, drafted by Navajos but by non-Navajo law students from both Arizona State University and the University of New Mexico. They attempted to codify as much of the Navajo law as had been written or practiced at that time. The code contains a tribal bill of rights prohibiting the tribe from abusing a Navajo's right to due process and equal protection under the law. It also lists various protections and criminal procedures to be followed, such as the need for probable cause for arrest and the right to bear arms. In many ways the Navajo tribal code is modeled after the United States Constitution.[2]

The situation becomes even more complex when the status and rights of women are examined. A Navajo woman residing in Arizona has rights under the Arizona state constitution and under the United States Constitution, but the U.S. Bill of Rights does not apply to Indian tribes. It does apply however, with respect to federal programs that affect Indians, and their administration. American Indian women are protected against discrimination by the federal government, but, unlike state governments, the tribe has the right to make exceptions to federal laws. For example, Title VII of the U.S. Civil Rights Act, which prohibits employment discrimination on the basis of race, sex, national origin, color, and religion, does not apply to Indian tribes. This means that within the reservation, sexual discrimination is legal. This situation arose because the tribal government, in an effort to promote Indian employment, decided to allow preference in employment in the Bureau of Indian Affairs and the Public Health Service, agencies that provide most of the governmental social and health services on the reservations.

American Indian women are also protected by the Indian Civil Rights Act (ICRA) 25 U.S.C. 1301 (1968), passed by Congress in 1968. This act is similar to the federal Bill of Rights and limits authority of tribal governments with one significant difference. Under the federal Constitution, the state cannot support religion, and church and state must remain separate. That provision was excluded from the ICRA because some tribes, notably the Pueblo in New Mexico, are essentially, theocratic. Pueblo government and religion are so intertwined that if it were specified that the two must remain separate tribal government would be virtually destroyed. Under tribal law a Tribe has the right to establish a tribal religion. It cannot prohibit other religions but it can support and maintain its own. Nevertheless, the ICRA places a limitation on tribal action by setting forth provisions that include the right to due process and the right to equal protection under the law.

A case initiated in the early 1970s and which was subsequently addressed under the ICRA illustrates the different protections to which American Indian women must make their claims. This case, *Santa Clara Pueblo v. Martinez* 436 U.S. 49 (1978), decided by the United States Supreme Court was particularly important for Indian women because it involved blatant sex discrimination. The Santa Clara Pueblo tribe enacted an ordinance to state that if a male member of the tribe married an outsider, whether or not she was an Indian, their children were entitled to tribal membership. If a woman member of Santa Clara married a non-Indian or an Indian who was a non-Santa Claran, however, her children were not to be entitled to tribal membership. This provision contrasted with the traditional kinship system which accorded equal inheritance rights to men and women. When Mrs. Martinez married a Navajo and tried to enroll her children in the tribe so that they could be eligible for housing under the tribal housing authority, they were denied membership. She took the case through all levels to the Supreme Court, which did not rule on the merits of the case, to establish whether or not the tribal action had violated equal protection as defined by the ICRA. Rather, the Court held that because of tribal sovereignty the tribe could decide on the meaning of equal protection. They declared that it was not within the rights of the federal government to decide such a question, and that under the ICRA they would review tribal action only in criminal cases, leaving civil proceedings under the tribal jurisdiction. The judgment, although legally sound and important because it upheld tribal sovereignty, represented a defeat for the rights of American Indian women. The Santa Clara tribe was accorded the right to maintain its blatantly discriminatory practice with regard to the issue of marriage and tribal membership qualifications.

The contradiction between tradition and tribal law, illustrated by the case of *Santa Clara Pueblo vs. Martinez* underlines the need to reevaluate American

Indian women's legal situation today in the context of culture change. Without this background, we cannot understand why a tribe such as the Santa Clara would uphold such a discriminatory law. . . .

The Navajo present a different situation. An abundant ethnographic literature describes the traditional high status of Navajo women with respect to such rights and duties as economic decision making, healing and other rituals, inheritance rights, and the right to initiate courtship and divorce.[3] A major mythical figure in Navajo cosmology is Changing Woman, a symbol of protection and the source of life. According to Louise Lamphere, in Navajo tradition:

> . . . most crucial decisions are taken within the domestic group rather than in the wider political arena. Authority within the domestic groups is egalitarian, with the emphasis on individual autonomy. Under these conditions, Navajo women have a great deal of control over their lives. They do not need to wrest power from others who hold positions of authority or attempt to influence decisions that are not theirs to make.[4]

As a matrilineal people who trace descent through the female line, Navajos derive a person's place within the culture as well as in the clan subunit from women. The traditional Navajo concept of the family places primary emphasis on the mother-child bond. Second in importance, and by extension through the mother, is the bond between siblings. The bonds between father and child and husband and wife respectively are weaker in this view.[5] On the reservation the Navajo concept of women as the hub of the family is reflected in the prevalence of women-centered domestic groups called camps and the traditions surrounding women's property rights within them.

In rural areas of the reservation a typical traditional camp consists of clusters of dwellings (usually from two to as many as eight) dispersed across the countryside. Most commonly the camp or groups of camps which share a land use area center on sisters and their husbands and children. As their children grow and marry, daughters rather than sons bring spouses to live in the camp. These junior households may then break off and establish new camps within the land use area of the parent camp. In this setting, Navajo women—mothers, sisters, daughters and sisters' daughters, and sometimes sisters—and daughters-in-law cooperate intensively and retain control over the land, viewed as the traditional source of livelihood, not as a saleable commodity. Navajo women are at the heart of economic activities as decision makers and producers, engaging in livestock raising, craft production, farming, and gathering wild foods for sale. Today, younger women with some formal education and English language skills may choose from a wider array of roles. They can periodically sally forth into the wage labor market centered in reservation administrative centers or urban centers off the reservation. In the traditional Navajo system, older women receive the most respect and have greatest authority over the allocation of the labor, products, and cash, not only of their juniors but of their husbands as well. Because the livelihood of the family centers on the home and the land surrounding it, these women are "homemakers" in the fullest sense of the term. For such Navajo women, who control land-use rights and livestock and pass them on to their daughters, home and workplace are one and the same. Household decisions are also economic and political decisions.

For Navajo women who control the land, property rights are easily protected, even in the case of divorce. Traditionally, when parties wanted to divorce, the woman simply placed the man's clothes, personal belongings, and saddle at the front door and no further action was required. He took nothing more when he went back to his parents' camp. Because the livelihood of the family depended on livestock raising and small scale farming, activities in which even young children could participate, children were also an economic asset rather than "just another mouth to feed," and usually remained with the mother.

In terms of the law, changes from traditional ways are most apparent in domestic cases, especially those involving divorce, child custody, and child support. Today, divorce settlement on the reservation is rarely as simple as in the traditional system. Traditional Navajo concepts of property are integrated with those of the larger society. The Navajo tribal code requires that in the absence of relevant traditional law the court will look to federal law. If no federal law applies, then state law will be considered. The Navajo tribal code now incorporates concepts of community property, a concept never previously applied in the Navajo cultural tradition. Today if divorcing parties have built a house during their marriage, the woman often must struggle to obtain an interest in the house, especially if the couple resides in the land use area of her in-laws rather than that of her own family.

One divorce case in which Chato served as legal counsel illustrates the differences between property settlement in the tribal courts and in the traditional system. In this case, the parties built a hogan (traditional dwelling) on the customary use area of the husband's family. The husband chased the woman and their two children out of the house. She did not want the house, because it would have been difficult for her to live with the former in-laws, but she wanted at least half of the value she had invested in the house. She had also reared the children by herself for five years. If traditional custom were applied, she would have received everything except her husband's personal belongings. But the judge said: "Now it's different. Nobody lives traditionally all the time, or their whole life is not governed by traditional customs." So the judge awarded the house to the husband and gave the wife no compensation. Ultimately, an appellate judge awarded the woman a monetary settlement of half the value of the house.

Enforcement of child support through the tribal courts also appears particularly difficult. Women must pay to ensure enforcement and often they spend more in legal fees than they secure for their children. Decisions on domestic issues, such as child custody awards, almost always favor the woman. Tribal judges presume that children belong with their mother. Although the decision to award sole custody to the mother is in keeping with the emphasis on the bond between mother and child in Navajo culture, it fails to consider alternatives which, in some cases, might better serve the interests of all family members.

Divorce, child support, and custody are not the only areas in which Navajo women have lost traditional means of restitution in the morass of overlapping tribal and federal jurisdictions. In traditional Navajo society with its strong kin-ship bonds, rape appears to have been uncommon. If it occurred, settlement involved both the family of the victim and that of the offender. Usually the vic-tim's family required and received payments in goods or cash from the offender's family. In recent years Shepardson reports that

> Navajo police arrest husbands for beating their wives, but rape is one of the
> 11 major crimes prosecuted under federal law. This is a grey area because
> many rape cases are declined by the U.S. Attorney and remanded to the trib-
> al courts . . .[6]

Although the 1977 tribal court code covers sexual assault (under Title 17 sec-tion 454), relatively few rape cases are heard in tribal court. Victims are generally ashamed to report rapes to the tribal police force, which mainly consists of men. These police, although they receive some crisis intervention training in both their initial orientation and in periodic workshops, lack the background to deal with such a sensitive issue. The availability of other forms of crisis intervention and support remains questionable on the reservation, though a battered women's shel-ter has recently been established in Shiprock, New Mexico, operated by the Navajo tribal office.[7]

Navajo women not only suffer because of inadequate legal protections they also seem to be losing their customary protections if these compete with the legal sys-tem. In 1981 a young woman from an isolated and traditional area of the reserva-tion claimed to have been raped and made pregnant by a man from another, less traditional, community. Following customary law, the young woman, her mother, and several other close relatives went to the man's family to negotiate compensa-tion in cash or livestock. To their dismay the man's family refused to recognize their customary rights. They told the victim's family they would have to "prove it in court first," probably well aware that the traditional family would not pros-ecute and would not be rewarded by the legal system if they did.

Why are traditional protections no longer adequate and why has the modern legal system failed to uphold the rights of Navajo women? Answers to these ques-tions are not simple, but we can approach an explanation by considering the his-tory of political and economic development in the region. The Navajo Reservation, like American Indian reservations across the country, has much in common with developing Third World nations. According to Ruffing:

> The Navajo nation as an internal colony differs little from that of the Third
> World as the external colony of advanced countries. The same transfers of
> value, distortions in the economy and the structural characteristics of under-
> development which exist in Third world countries are present in the Navajo
> Nation (1976:608).[8]

Klara Kelley has detailed the linkages of production and exchange between Navajo, Hopi, and Zuni reservations and the larger regional economy. She has demonstrated how a few reservation bordertowns have historically dominated commerce and drained the reservation of natural resources, population, and purchasing power.[9] Such economic underdevelopment and the status of the Navajo Reservation as a semicolonial nation-within-a-nation has most affected Navajo women, their rights, duties, and strategies for achieving equality under the law in the several interrelated ways.

First is the problem of demographic pressure on a fixed land base. The reservation lacks sufficient land to support the fast growing population through pastoralism and small scale agriculture—the way of life in which women play a central role. The Navajo population is estimated to have almost doubled since 1960, but the federal government has not added land to the reservation since 1934.[10] Although the tribe has purchased and leased additional acreage in the reservation borderlands in recent years, the amount of new land cannot come close to sustaining an economy based on herding and farming for the current population.[11]

As early as 1930, reservation land showed signs of serious overgrazing and loss of fertile topsoil. At that time the federal government mandated a drastic stock reduction program in an attempt to solve the problem, but this dealt a crippling blow to the Navajo pastoral economy a blow which fell particularly hard on women. Simultaneously with the loss of their major food source, Navajos also lost alternative sources of cash income. During the depression, the restricted market all but eliminated wool, mutton, and handicraft sales. The New Deal administration attempted to ease the transition from a pastoral economy to one based on wage labor by hiring Navajos as manual laborers for public works projects on the reservation. Most of the jobs were short-term, however, and gave preference to men. Under continuing stock maintenance programs, per capita ownership of sheep and goats declined from twenty in 1930, to four in 1951, a totally inadequate holding to support a typical Navajo family of five.[12]

In the late 1950s, agricultural development projects, such as the Fruitland Irrigation Project, further eroded women's economic roles in that community. Under this project ten-acre parcels of land, too small to support a nuclear family through farming or to permit women to contribute to the economy through herding, were allotted to male "heads of household." Women thus lost the power they had maintained through a land-based economy and were not in a position to create new sources of strength in the changed economy. Further, the male basis of the allotment policy dispersed female kin, weakening the women-centered kin networks.[13]

By the mid-1950s the U.S. Bureau of Indian Affairs had initiated programs to relocate Indians in urban areas on the mistaken assumption that they would assimilate into mainstream Anglo society. Other Indians have been pushed off their lands by multinational energy developments on the reservation and by enforced relocation programs such as that attendant upon the current Hopi-Navajo land dispute settlement. Many Navajo men and women have "voluntarily" migrated from rural areas on the reservation to urban centers off the reservation in search of jobs, so that by 1980 over half of all American Indians, including Navajos, lived in urban centers off the reservation. A large literature describes the hardships faced by these migrants and the special problems encountered by American Indian women.[14]

Today livestock raising and farming, the traditional bases of Navajo women's authority in the household, account for only an estimated four percent of the Navajo income. Instead, the Navajo economy, like that of other American Indian tribes, is heavily dependent upon welfare (in its various state, federal, and tribal forms), which provides an estimated 22 percent of community finance.[15] For women who still retain primary responsibility for childcare this means income comes mainly from Aid to Families with Dependent Children (AFDC) and emergency food relief.

In one rural community on Black Mesa fully 36 percent of the thirty-nine reservation households studied in 1981 depended totally upon welfare. Although wage labor accounted for over half over the annual income of this community, only a small elite benefited from this source. Among the thirty wage earners from these same households, two men from a single household employed by a coal mining company earned nearly 15 percent of the total annual wage income. Six households accounted for 85 percent of the wage income.[16] This type of socioeconomic stratification is typical of the reservation as a whole and of Third World nations. It tends to divide, rather than unite, Navajo women both in terms of their access to important resources and the emphasis they place on particular types of legal reforms.[17]

Compounding problems created by the breakdown of the traditional subsistence economy, underdevelopment on the reservation results in a lack of employment opportunities, which represents a second challenge for women's rights. Historically, capital has been drained from the reservation through mercantile channels rather than reinvested in local infrastructure and industry. In the private sector, job opportunities vary considerably from one reservation community to another because merchants are constrained to locate in areas where their transport costs to the bordertown wholesalers are minimized.[18] Because tribal administrative centers have grown up around trading centers, reservation employment opportunities in federal and tribal agencies also cluster in these areas. Outside these centers, however, it is not uncommon for 75 percent of the men to be unemployed and higher percentages of women. Because most jobs on the reservation involve construction and other types of manual labor, men are given preference in employment.

When Tribal Chairman Petersen Zah held a women's conference at Navajo Community College in 1983, a cursory examination of employment within the tribe (the foremost employer on the reservation) showed that two-thirds of the women employed by the tribe were in secretarial positions. Very few Navajo women are in management ranks, even though Shepardson found nearly twice as many Navajo women as men in higher education or having had some education beyond high school.[19] She noted that women are motivated to undertake college education because vocational or basic high school education is not as useful to women seeking employment as it is to men.

Both men and women interviewed by Conte valued education and associated higher education with financial success, but pregnancy and childbearing responsibilities constrain educational advancement for many Navajo women.[20] In one Reservation high school in 1985 nearly twenty-five percent of the women students dropped out because of pregnancy.[21] When job training becomes available, it is men who most often seek it, not women.

Ironically, Navajo women have achieved a greater measure of equality in employment in the federal agencies of the Bureau of Indian Affairs and the Indian Health Service than they seem to have achieved under the tribe. As Shephardson points out, by 1981 women in these federal agencies had all but closed the gap with men in their representation in the professional occupations on the reservation. She attributes this success to the federal officers or Equal Employment Opportunity whose purpose was to promote affirmative action, a resolution not adopted by the Navajo Nation until 1980.

Tied to women's status in the labor force is a third issue—their representation in the tribal government and judicial system. The Navajo Nation, like many other tribal governments, modeled its political and judicial system on the federal organization of the United States. This was a practical response providing parallel structures to negotiate sovereignty issues and resource royalties for the tribe. However, this model has also been extended into the realm of discrimination against women in the political and legal arenas. Navajo women are dismally underrepresented on the Navajo Tribal Council and in the judicial system. As of the summer of 1986, only one of the eighty-seven members of the Tribal Council was a woman. Even at community Chapter meetings, most of the officers are men and, at least at the public meetings, women do not often speak out on the issues. Only one of the five tribal district judges is a woman, though two of the three judges in the newly established juvenile division are women.

This brings us to the last, and probably most important way that the history of Navajo relations with the dominant Anglo society has affected Navajo women's status under the law—that of values about women's abilities and potential. As we have seen, Navajo women lag furthest behind men in the area of involvement in politics and the law—areas where they could have the most direct impact on improving their status. This situation has evolved because traditional Navajo beliefs against female leadership outside of the household have been reinforced by discriminatory Anglo notions. One Navajo legend in particular involves a rift between the men led by First Man and the women led by First Woman over which of the two sexes should lead the other. In this story the sexes separated and were reconciled only when women agreed never again to seek the highest leadership role. Women were not warned against leadership or political involvement but only against occupying the top position. When understood in the traditional context in which most important decisions were made in the household, the restriction on women's political involvement does not seem severe. When the myth is considered in the modern context, however, reinforced by and reinterpreted through the ideas of the dominant culture, especially the male-centered dogma of evangelical Christian and Mormon missionaries, the result is very different from that intended by the original legend. The traditional injunction against women occupying top positions in the political realm becomes generalized and more restrictive. According to one rural Reservation woman who had recently been converted to an evangelical missionary sect: "It probably wouldn't be good for a woman to be a community leader or anything like that. . . . I learned this from our traditions but I also learned it from the Bible. . . . The Bible says the woman should be behind the man."

Navajo women like this one, whose control over their own lives has been shaken by migration, relocation, loss of land and livestock, unemployment and a host of other traumas related to economic underdevelopment, are especially vulnerable to these kinds of patriarchal ideas. The dominant society has also had negative effects on women's rights in several other ways, for example, by requiring a woman to use her husband's last name to be eligible for state and tribal welfare benefits, and by applying conventions that arbitrarily assign the role of head of household to the male. All these practices are contrary to the Navajo tradition of egalitarian gender relations. Combined with factors already discussed, the alien perspectives governing these practices have played a role in undermining the positive value placed on women's roles by Navajo men and women. . . .

On a more positive note, the Navajo tribe took steps to redress the inadvertent legal discrimination against women allowed by the tribe's rejection of Title VII. In 1980 the tribal council passed the Navajo Equal Rights Amendment so that discrimination on the basis of sex is not legal under tribal law. Here the tribal law is more progressive than law in the surrounding state of Arizona. The Amendment reads much like the proposed federal Equal Rights Amendment: "Equality of rights under the law shall not be denied or abridged by the Navajo Nation on account of sex."

At a time when only one woman served on the Navajo tribal council, it is amazing that the provision was passed unanimously. The provision did not, of course, mean that Navajo women were immediately accorded equal rights in practice, but at least the provision is on the books.

The courts are beginning to shift to a more egalitarian position with regard to the domestic issues that most directly affect women. Navajo women have been fighting an uphill battle to get their tribal judges to understand that a homemaker's work has value. That a woman has not worked outside the home does not mean that she has not contributed to the household, even if the family no longer makes its living from livestock or farming. Some younger judges now interpret community property in divorce cases so as to include the contributions of the husband and wife—equal contributions are interpreted to be justification for equal distribution of property. It is in assessing the value of that contribution that tribal law is evolving. Even child custody settlements are gradually becoming more egalitarian. More men are seeking custody of their children in good faith, and in time they will be given equal consideration. Another indication that the tribal legal system is becoming more responsive to women's needs is a three-fold increase in the number of women lawyers since 1975. Women may have lost their traditionally high place within Navajo society, but now, at least in domestic cases such as those involving property division and child custody, they are fighting their way back to equality.

Another indication that Navajo women are gaining in their fight for equality was the establishment in 1984 of the Navajo Office for Women. Tribal Chairman Peterson Zah created the office as evidence of his commitment to affirmative action. As of mid-1985 the office was staffed by two elected representatives from each of the five agencies. Services included job placement, domestic counseling, family planning, and the development of programs to provide day care services for mothers who are high school students. . . .

The status of American Indians and the legal issues which affect them have undergone profound changes in recent decades, Economic development has created tremendous variation from community to community and even from individual to individual in all areas of American Indian life. For the Navajo as for other tribes, overlapping and often unclear jurisdiction and protections, uneven regional economic development, the transition from a pastoral and farming economy to one based on wage labor and welfare, and the penetration of alien ideas about men's and women's roles in society have all contributed to the diversity and flux which characterize the current status of Navajo women under the law. As the judge in the divorce settlement case noted above observed, so-called "traditional" customs do not guide the life of every Navajo today. Tradition is constantly recreated in response to changing circumstances. Navajo society and culture are changing, and traditional law is intermingling with state and federal law. The Navajo are taking parts from each and we cannot predict what the resultant product will be. Women are more than half of the Navajo population. Their potential political strength has yet to be fully exercised.

NOTES

1. A number of good general works exist with regard to treaty history and U.S. policy, including Vine Deloria, Jr. and Clifford M. Lyttle, *American Indians, American Justice,* Austin, Tex.: University of Texas Press, 1983, and their second work on this topic, *The Nations Within,* New York, N.Y.: Pantheon Books, 1984. See also Alvin M. Josephy, Jr., *The Indian Heritage of America,* New York, N.Y.: Knopf, 1968.

2. The Navajo Tribal Code, was originally codified in 1962, with supplement's and revisions in 1970, 1977 and 1980–81, Orford, N.H.: Equity Publishing Corporation.

3. For a classic ethnography of Navajo women, see Gladys A. Reichard, *Dezba: Woman of the Desert,* New York, N.Y.: T. J. Augustin Publisher, 1939. More recent scholarly works on Navajo women, include Louise Lamphere, *To Run After Them,* Tucson, Ariz.: University of Arizona Press, 1977, and Ruth Roessel, *Women in Navajo Society* Rough Rock, Ariz.: Navajo Resource Center, 1981.

4. Louise Lamphere, "Strategies, Cooperation and Conflict among Women in Domestic Groups," *Women, Culture and Society,* Michele Zimbalast Rosaldo, and Louise Lamphere, eds., Stanford, Calif.: Stanford University Press, 1974, 101–3.

5. Gary Witherspoon, *Language and Art in the Navajo Universe,* Ann Arbor, Mich.: University of Michigan Press, 1977, 109–10.

6. Mary Shepardson, "The Status of Navajo Women," *The American Indian Quarterly,* 6 (Spring, Summer 1982), 161.

7. These several conditions make it difficult to assess the incidence of rape on the reservation and reports have been contradictory. Chato is under the impression that most Navajo women around Window Rock who report sex crimes go to off-reservation police in Gallup,

New Mexico, both because of the attitudes and practices employed there and because they prefer to shield themselves and their families from the embarrassment of an investigation in the home community.

8. Lorraine T. Ruffing, "Navajo Economic Development Subject to Cultural Constraints," *Economic Development and Cultural Change*, 24 (April 1976), 608. Chicanos in the Southwest have also been described as members of an "internal colony." See Mario Barrera, *Race and Class in the Southwest*, Notre Dame, Ind.: University of Notre Dame Press, 1979.

9. Klara Bonsack Kelley, "Commercial Networks in the Navajo-Hopi-Zuni Region" (Ph.D. diss., University of New Mexico, Albuquerque, N.M., 1977).

10. U.S. Department of Commerce, Bureau of the Census, *1980 Census of the Population*, Washington, D.C.: U.S. Government Printing Office; U.S. Department of Interior, Bureau of Indian Affairs, *Navajo Yearbook*, Window Rock, Ariz.: The Navajo Agency, 1961.

11. Ronald Faich, personal communication, Navajo Community Development Office, Window Rock, Ariz., August 1986.

12. David Aberle, *The Peyote Religion Among the Navajo*, Viking Fund Publications #42, New York, N.Y.: Wenner-Gren Foundation for Anthropological Research, Inc., 1966.

13. Laila Shukry Hamamsey, "The Role of Women in a Changing Navajo Society," *American Anthropologist*, 59 (February 1957). The major factors undermining women's roles with respect to the Fruitland project are detailed in Shukry's dissertation (1954) and analyzed by Louise Lamphere, "Historical and Regional Variables in Women's Roles" (Paper prepared for Advanced Seminar on Variability and Change in Navajo Culture, School of American Research, October 7–11, 1985).

14. Ann Metcalf, "Navajo Women in the City: Lessons from a Quarter Century of Relocation," *The American Indian Quarterly*, 6 (Spring/Summer 1982), 72. Among other relevant studies are Joan Ablon, "Relocated American Indians in the San Francisco Bay Area," *Human Organization*, 23 (Winter 1964): 296–304; Joyce Griffen, "Life is Harder Here: The Case of Urban Navajo Women," *The American Indian Quarterly*, 6 (Spring/Summer 1982): 90–104; Ann Metcalf, "Indians in the San Francisco Bay Area" (Paper presented to the Newberry Library Center for the History of American Indians, Conference on Urban Indians. Chicago, Ill., 1980); and Native American Research Group, *American Indian Socialization to Urban Life*, San Francisco, Calif.: Institute for Scientific Research, 1975.

15. Rock Point Community School, *Between Sacred Mountains: Stories and Lessons From the Land*, Chinle, Ariz.: Rock Point Community School, 1982.

16. Christine Conte, *The Navajo Sex-Gender System: The Impact of Economic Development in Two Northern Arizona Communities*, Ann Arbor, Mich.: University Microfilms International, 1985, 88–89. The stratification within Indian communities affected by energy resource development and the inadequacies of such projects for community support are discussed in Lyn Robins, *The Impact of Power Developments on the Navajo Nation*, Lake Powell Research Project Bulletin No. 7, Los Angeles, Calif.: University of California Press, 1975. E.B. Henderson and J.E. Levy, *The Survey of Navajo Community Studies*, 1936–1974, Lake Powell Research Project Bulletin No. 7, Los Angeles, Calif.: University of California Press, 1975, also documents socioeconomic stratification and its sources.

17. Christine Conte, "Ladies, Livestock, Land and Lucre: Navajo Women's Resource Strategies on the Western Reservation," *The American Indian Quarterly*, 6 (Spring/Summer 1982), 105–24.

18. See Kelley, "Commercial Networks in the Navajo-Hopi-Zuni Region," supra note 9.

19. Navajo scholarship records cited in Shepardson, "The Status of Navajo Women," supra note 6 at p. 155.

20. See Conte, "Ladies, Livestock, Land and Lucre," supra note 17.

21. Rena Williams, personal communication, Navajo Office for Women, Window Rock, Ariz., September 1986.

Domestic Violence and Tribal Protection of Indigenous Women in the United States

Gloria Valencia-Weber and Christine P. Zuni

CUSTOM AND TRIBAL CODES, ORDERS, AND PROGRAMS TO PROTECT SCOPE OF REVIEW[1]

. . . This review presents a discussion of the legal treatment of domestic violence by fourteen United States tribes. It is not intended to be a description of the state of the law among all 537 tribes. Rather, this article is a general survey of existing tribal law on domestic violence. The selected tribal laws were not chosen to represent the way that all tribes should approach domestic violence. Instead, they serve as a starting point from which to analyze the issues that arise when tribal communities confront issues of domestic violence. The laws demonstrate the effort of tribes to ensure the physical security of women within their respective jurisdictions.

Of the tribes examined, almost all have specific laws which address domestic violence.[2] Many of these tribal codes have common provisions. The most frequently recurring provisions are those defining domestic violence and identifying the persons protected under the law.[3] While our focus is on the protection of women, these laws are framed in much broader terms. In this review, we look closely and consider these codes not only in terms of the protections they afford women, but also in terms of the protections afforded to all members of tribal society.[4] Additionally we also consider how the laws reflect and impact tribal society. . . .

We begin with an overview of the persons protected by tribal law and the behavior proscribed by these codes. All of the tribal codes reviewed identify the persons protected and set forth what constitutes domestic violence, domestic abuse, or spousal abuse. The tribal provisions vary in that some tribes ascribe protection to a broad group of persons, while others protect a narrow group of persons. Generally, women who are spouses and family and household members are protected persons. Tribes, however, vary in their provisions by further qualifying the definition of 'spouse' and 'family and household member' or by further expanding the protected class. A minority of tribes restrict the definition by age and marital status.[5]

Most tribes broaden the definition to include relationships without reference to marital status or age. The Navajo Nation clearly identifies the protected class and uses the identification to expand the class beyond that of several state family violence protection provisions in the United States.[6] Others protect a broad class through the use of a general term such as 'persons' when describing the individuals protected.[7] . . .

The extended family plays a significant role in tribal life. Evidence of this role may be noted in the statutory presence which the extended family has in most tribal laws regarding domestic abuse.[8] Many of the tribes clarify their intent to include members of the immediate and extended family by expressly listing children, the elderly, persons related by blood, and persons related by marriage within the protected class.[9] Additionally, some tribes even protect persons who fall outside the extended family.[10] These protections demonstrate the great emphasis certain tribes place on addressing group disharmony and maintaining proper relationships within tribal communities. . . .

BEHAVIOR PROSCRIBED

The behavior proscribed by the tribal codes varies from a broad range of behavior to certain criminal offenses against persons generally associated with domestic violence. The Oglala Sioux Domestic Abuse Code defines abuse as 'physical harm, bodily injury, assault or the infliction of fear of imminent physical harm, bodily injury or assault.'[11] The Crow provisions differ slightly from the Oglala Sioux code. In addition to the acts included in the Oglala code, abuse under Crow law includes bodily 'harm' or imminent bodily 'harm' to any family or household member.[12] Under the Salt River Policy, an officer can arrest a person for simple assault or battery,[13] aggravated assault and battery,[14] and a violation of an order of protection restraining the person or excluding the person from the residence.[15]

The Rosebud Sioux and the Menominee codes are similar in that they proscribe abuse acts committed with specific intent. The Rosebud Sioux define domestic abuse as a crime[16] and prohibit purposely or knowingly causing bodily injury or apprehension of bodily injury to a family member or household member.[17] Bodily injury includes physical pain, illness, or an impairment of one's physical condition.[18] Causing apprehension includes any physical act intended to cause another person to reasonably fear imminent serious bodily injury or death.[19] Under the Menominee Code domestic violence is defined as intentional infliction of physical pain, physical injury or illness, intentional impairment of physical condition, or a physical act that may cause the other person to reasonably fear imminent engagement in any of the above.[20]

The Zuni Pueblo, Jicarilla Apache, and Navajo tribes broaden the behavior which is categorized as domestic violence. This is accomplished by including other types of offenses proscribed under the tribe's general criminal code. Under Zuni law, domestic violence includes any act or incident which constitutes a crime under the Zuni Tribal Code resulting in physical harm, bodily injury, or assault, or a threat which places a person in reasonable fear of imminent physical harm or bodily injury.[21] The Jicarilla Apache Domestic Violence Code states that abuse includes, *but is not limited to*, assault and battery as defined in the Jicarilla Apache Tribal code.[22] Navajo law incorporates criminal offenses more liberally by proscribing 'domestic violence,' including any conduct that constitutes an offense under Navajo law.[23]

The Navajo domestic violence law includes the following acts upon a victim: assault, battery, threatening, coercion, confinement, damage to property, emotional abuse, and harassment.[24] In addition, any other conduct that constitutes a tort under Navajo law qualifies as domestic violence.[25] Navajo law also clearly provides that domestic abuse does not include a victim's reasonable act of self-defense.[26] Under the Rules for Domestic Violence Proceedings, when parties fall out of harmony, they must proceed in a cautious way in their relations with each other (*hozhogo*), and any definition of domestic violence must be interpreted in such a way as to identify any instances of disharmony.[27]

The Navajo, the Jicarilla Apache, and Cherokee Nation codes also specifically include sexual offenses in their definition of abuse.[28] The Cherokee Nation further defines domestic abuse as causing or attempting to cause serious physical harm or threatening another with imminent serious physical harm.[29] This definition includes, but is not limited to, assault, battery, and aggravated assault and battery against family or household members.[30]

The Pascua-Yaqui Tribal Code forbids behavior by specifying acts beyond assault, physical injury, and intimidation. The code defines domestic violence as any act which is a dangerous crime against children.[31] These acts range from murder to drug offenses.[32] Domestic violence also includes custodial interference, unlawful imprisonment, kidnapping, criminal trespass, and disorderly conduct.[33]

TRIBAL REMEDIES AND SANCTIONS

. . . The majority of the tribal codes reviewed provide greater or equal protection to victims of domestic violence when compared to the states in which these tribes are located.[34] This is accomplished by proscribing a wide range of acts and behavior, and by protecting the physical integrity of an expansive class. The effectiveness of these provisions obviously is contingent upon the enforcement and actual reporting of incidents, as well as the final action taken against perpetrators.

Some tribes blend methods of traditional dispute resolution into the formal judicial process. This practice is evident in the specific provisions of the Navajo Nation's Domestic Abuse Protection Act and Supreme Court Rules for Domestic Violence.[35] The judges of the Navajo Nation courts established the Peacemaking system in 1982.[36] Peacemakers work with people to help them take care of their problems on their own.[37] Peacemakers are community leaders who employ the traditional Navajo method of "talking things out" to resolve problems. The Peacemakers use traditional methods of mediation and arbitration, but it should be noted that Navajo mediation and arbitration is different from the American "mediation" and "arbitration" models.[38] Many counselors to victims of domestic violence feel that mediation is inappropriate between the victim and the abuser.[39] The Peacemakers are tied to each of the seven district courts of the Navajo Nation.[40]

Other tribes, such as the Pueblos, accomplish this blend through the general recognition of traditional methods of dispute resolution. One example is the Pueblo of Laguna. The tribe incorporates the traditional method of dispute resolution into its formal judicial system.[41] The Pueblo recognizes the traditional authority of village officials to assist village members in resolving disputes without resorting to the court. The person seeking relief, however, possesses the choice of utilizing the traditional method of dispute resolution or of going to court. In addition, the Pueblo has a special method of dispute resolution for married couples, involving sponsors of couples who marry in the traditional manner.[42] The sponsors assist married couples in resolving their disputes by reminding them of their marriage vows, counseling them, and bringing the extended family into the dispute resolution process.[43] This method is available to those couples who choose to use it. This practice is common to other New Mexico Pueblos.[44] Sponsors, however, have now assumed more of a ceremonial role in the traditional marriage ceremony. As a result, couples are less inclined to utilize this traditional method. The Pueblo of Laguna, like several other Pueblos and tribes, does not have a specific code on domestic violence.[45] . . .

Criminal

. . . Many tribal domestic abuse provisions include criminal sanctions and provide for arrest of those persons committing certain acts of domestic abuse.[46] Both mandatory and discretionary arrest provisions are common. Those tribes with mandatory arrest provisions for the commission of certain acts of domestic abuse or violation of orders of protection include: Oglala, Jicarilla, Crow, Fort Belknap, Salt River Pima-Maricopa, Pascua-Yaqui, Zuni, Standing Rock, Rosebud, and Menominee.[47] Even the Navajo Nation, which has a civil domestic abuse code, provides for the mandatory arrest of persons who violate domestic abuse protection orders.[48] . . .

Mandatory arrest is not without its unique problems in tribal communities. Incarceration has never been a traditional method of punishment in Indian societies.[49] In this respect, mandatory arrest and incarceration are serious measures as well as reminders of the loss or breakdown of traditional constraints on tribal societal behavior. In 1883, incarceration was introduced into tribal societies by the federal government with the advent of Courts of Indian Offenses and Indian police.[50] While incarceration has been present in some tribes for at least one hundred years, inadequate jail facilities pose problems.[51] Many tribes do not have jail facilities, and must utilize other tribal or state facilities, at high costs. The utilization of non-tribal jail facilities can also require distant trips for law enforcement and family members. . . .

Civil

Tribal codes also provide civil remedies and sanctions to curb domestic violence. The majority of tribal codes allow for the issuance of protective orders on an emergency basis, regardless of whether the codes permit only civil remedies or both criminal and civil remedies. The Jicarilla Code allows a court to issue a temporary order of protection as a condition of release of the defendant when the defendant is before the court after mandatory arrest.[52] This court can issue the temporary orders at its own discretion, without an application to the court for a civil protection order.[53] . . .

Most temporary protection orders grant limited relief to the victims of domestic violence. This relief includes: restraining the abusing party from acts of domestic abuse; excluding the abusing party from a shared residence; restraining contact with the victim; restricting proximity to the victim; awarding temporary custody; and establishing temporary visitation of minor children.[54] Upon award of a final restraining order, some tribes provide for counseling, give temporary use and possession of property to the victim, require an accounting for all transfers made after the order is entered, mandate payment of rent and child support, and allow any other relief necessary.[55] . . .

REPORTING

Four tribes have provisions in their codes requiring mandatory reporting of possible domestic violence.[56] All four require reporting by medical personnel, such as physicians, nurses, and community health workers.[57] Moreover, the Oglala and Crow Codes require physician assistants, hospital interns, residents, field health nurses, and dentists to file a report when they suspect domestic abuse.[58] Additionally, the Standing Rock and Jicarilla Codes require mental health workers to report domestic abuse.[59] Outside of the medical profession, the Jicarilla Code mandates that school teachers, social workers, and probation officers report domestic abuse. The Standing Rock Code requires social workers, counselors, and personnel of domestic violence programs and shelters to report suspected situations of domestic abuse.[60] The Oglala and Crow Codes additionally require social workers, parent aides, adult service workers, law enforcement officers, court workers, alcohol program workers, and domestic violence personnel to report domestic abuse.[61] [Under] Oglala, Jicarilla, and Crow Law, the failure to report domestic abuse is a criminal offense.[62]

CODES GENERALLY

. . . Mostly, the tribal codes evidence the incorporation and influence of western jurisprudence. Perhaps this is inevitable in light of the Indian Civil Rights Act (ICRA),[63] and the tendency of tribes to look at both state and other tribal codes for guidance when developing their particular code.[64] When tribes develop laws to deal with areas of such critical social concern as domestic abuse, careful deliberation is required when outside laws and procedures are considered.[65] Equal consideration should be given to indigenous concepts of law and to traditional methods of dispute resolution when developing tribal law.[66] ICRA standards notwithstanding, tribes can infuse their law with principles and methods which reflect their values, precepts, and approaches to dispute resolution in far greater ways than present codes currently reflect.[67] . . .

INDIANS OUTSIDE THE TRIBAL SYSTEM

We have focused on tribal laws and systems, but we must also consider the large urban Indian population.[68] Generally, a large part of the urban Indian population maintains ties with the reservation, by moving between the reservation and urban areas. The urban centers, however, are increasingly becoming permanent homes to a large number of Indian people.

For this reason, it is important to consider the needs of the urban population. For those who maintain close ties to the reservation, tribal resources remain available. Urban Indians are no less Indian than Indian people who reside on the reservation. Thus, state judges and service providers must be aware of the need for approaches to domestic violence which consider the cultural needs of Indian people. The need for approaches to domestic violence which take culture into consideration is just as great among urban Indian families as it is at the tribal level.

Indian women and other women of color confront the same cultural insensitivity and racism at urban domestic violence shelters as they do elsewhere.[69] These shelters can be unaware of the cultural resources which should be used to assist Indian victims of domestic violence.[70] Consequently, shelters which provide services specifically directed at Indian women in urban centers are greatly needed. The Eagle's Nest, in St. Paul, Minnesota, is such a program.[71] The program is the result of the work of the Women of Nations, an advocacy group for battered American Indian women. The program provides shelter to native victims and uses traditional teachings, resources, and practices to overcome the damage that results from the abuse. These practices range from burning sage and cedar to calm the spirit to teaching traditional craftwork and survival skills. Participation in spiritual ways familiar to Native women is also available.[72]

In urban centers with large Indian populations, statistics reveal the presence of native people at shelters and within the court system.[73] Just as tribes cannot successfully address tribal domestic violence by adopting the same approaches to domestic violence as the non-Indian society, neither can individual Indian people and their families be expected to completely benefit from programs operated for majority clients.[74]

The intertribal community is a resource which can be utilized to assist in dealing with domestic violence in the Indian urban community. Urban Indian centers, with the multi-tribal membership among service providers and recipients, are important in providing varied and culturally appropriate intervention services to

Indian victims and offenders. Tribal input from local reservations, from which the urban Indian community populations come, can assist in efforts to assess the needs of the urban population.

State courts have jurisdiction when domestic violence occurs outside tribal boundaries.[75] The state courts and human services allied in domestic law proceedings can work to cooperate with the urban Indian organizations and centers as well as with local tribes. This cooperation should also include state subsidies for services, like those subsidies provided to other entities. Financially limited urban Indian organizations and centers cannot be expected to relieve the state of its responsibilities for intervention and its costs. Agreements between states and tribes are essential so that the urban and reservation Indians can obtain culturally appropriate and effective assistance to remove domestic violence from their lives.[76]

NOTES

1. The tribes addressed include the Fort Belknap Indian Community, Navajo Nation, Zuni Pueblo, Jicarilla Apache, Standing Rock Sioux, Pascua-Yaqui, Cherokee Nation, Menominee, Oglala Sioux, Laguna Pueblo, Rosebud Sioux, Salt River Pima-Maricopa, Blackfeet, and Crow.

2. The Fort Belknap Indian Community, Navajo Nation, Zuni Pueblo, Jicarilla Apache, Standing Rock Sioux, Pascua-Yaqui, Cherokee Nation, Menominee, Oglala Sioux, Rosebud Sioux, and Crow have specific domestic violence code provisions. The Pueblo of Laguna and the Salt River Pima-Maricopa do not have specific code provisions which address domestic violence. Rather they utilize general criminal code provisions. These tribes will be examined as examples of how tribes without specific domestic violence provisions address the problem. The law of the Blackfeet tribe is not included in this survey of tribal law. This article only examines its domestic violence prevention program.

3. Other common provisions are those addressing reporting, arrests, holding offenders in custody, protections afforded, requirements for counseling and participation in domestic violence programs, access to property and support, and requirements for peace bonds.

4. Several tribes clearly state in their purpose sections that protections are not limited to family members and recognize domestic abuse as a serious crime against tribal society as a whole. See, e.g., Navajo Nation Domestic Abuse Protection Act, Navajo Trib. Code. tit. 9 ss 1602–1604 (1993) (recognizing that domestic abuse affects all members of Navajo society); Standing Rock Sioux Code of Justice, tit. XXV, s 25–101 (1990) (discussing purpose and intent of code); Jicarilla Apache Trib. Code, tit. 3, s (1992) (noting that domestic violence is 'a serious crime against society'); Standing Rock Sioux Code of Justice tit. XXV, s 25–101 (1990) (discussing purpose and intent of code); Rosebud Sioux Trib. Code Ch. 38 (1989) (indicating purpose section recognizes domestic abuse as 'serious crime against . . . society').

5. See, e.g., Rosebud Sioux Trib. Code, ch. 38, s 1 A (1989) (stating that "[f]amily member or household member shall mean a relative, spouse, former spouse, adult, or elderly person related by marriage"); Crow Tribe of Indians, Crow Law and Order Codes, Domestic Abuse Code, (1991).

6. Navajo Trib. Code tit. 9, s 1605(b) includes, for example, members and former members of an abuser's immediate residence area, clan members, and any person who interacts with the abuser in an employment, academic, recreational, religious, social, or other setting. None of the states in which the Navajo Nation is located (Arizona, New Mexico, or Utah), nor any of the states in which the other tribes lie, have comparable provisions which would clearly include these relationships. For example, the protected class under the New Mexico Family Violence Protection Act is household members. 'Household member' is defined as 'a spouse, former spouse, family member, including a relative, parent, present or

former stepparent, present or former in-law, child or co-parent of a child, or a person with whom the petitioner has had a continuing personal relationship.' Family Violence Protection Act, N.M. Stat. Ann. s 40- 13-2(D) (Michie Supp. 1995).

7. The Oglala Sioux tribal code and the Salt River Pima-Maricopa Dept. of Public Service Policy use the term "persons."

8. See, e.g., Rosebud Sioux Trib. Code ch. 38, s 1(A) (1989) (stating that family member includes any adult or elderly person who resides or formerly resided in same residence).

9. Jicarilla Apache Trib. Code tit. 3, ch. 5, ss 2(D), (E) (1992); Standing Rock Sioux Trib. Code of Justice tit. XXV, s 25–102(c) (1990); Fort Belknap Indian Reservation, Domestic Abuse, (Definitions) (c) (1989); Rosebud Sioux Trib. Code ch. 38, s 1(A) (1989).

10. See, e.g., Oglala Sioux Trib. Code sec. 99.2, s 3(c) (1982) (stating that officer can arrest any person who threatens another with dangerous weapons).

11. Oglala Sioux Trib. Code sec. 99.2, s 2(a) (1982). Both the Standing Rock Sioux and Fort Belknap Indian Community domestic violence laws proscribe the same acts as the Oglala. Fort Belknap Indian Reservation, Domestic Abuse (Definition) (a) (1989); Standing Rock Sioux Code of Justice tit. XXV, s 25- 102(A) (1990) (defining 'abuse' and 'domestic violence,' respectively, with same terms used to define 'abuse' by Oglala Sioux Tribal Code).

12. Crow Tribe of Indians, Crow Law and Order Code, Domestic Abuse Code s 3(a) (1991).

13. Salt River Pima-Maricopa, Dep't. of Pub. Safety, General Order No. 89-25, P 2 (citing to s 6.51 - Simple Assault or Battery).

14. Id. P 1 (citing to s 6.52—Aggravated Assault and Battery).

15. Id. P 3 (citing to s 6.42—Disobedience to Lawful Orders of Court).

16. Rosebud Sioux Trib. Code ch. 38, s 2 (1989).

17. Id. s 2(1) - (2).

18. Id. s 1(B).

19. Id. s 1(C).

20. Menominee Nation, Ordinance No. 93-21, Domestic Violence ss III(A)(1–3) (1993).

21. Zuni Tribe, Ordinance No. 52, Domestic Violence Code (Definitions) (1991).

22. Jicarilla Apache Trib. Code tit. 3, s 2(a) (1992).

23. Navajo Nation Domestic Abuse Protection Act, Navajo Trib. Code tit. 9, s 1605(a)(1) (1993).

24. Id.

25. Rules for Domestic Violence Proceedings, Courts of the Navajo Nation Rule 1.3 (b).

26. Navajo Trib. Code tit. 9, s 1605(a)(2) (1993).

27. Rules for Domestic Violence Proceedings, Courts of the Navajo Nation Rule 1.5.

28. The Jicarilla Apache Code includes sexual assault or the infliction of the fear of sexual assaults within its definition of abuse, in addition to the infliction of physical harm or bodily injury. Jicarilla Apache Trib. Code tit. 3, s 2(A) (1992). The Cherokee Code includes rape within its definition of domestic abuse. Protection from Domestic Abuse Act, Cherokee Nation Code tit. 22, s 60.1(1)(c) (1990). The Navajo Nation includes sexual abuse. Navajo Trib. Code tit. 9, s 1605(a)(1)(I)(1993).

29. Cherokee Nation Code tit. 22, s 60.1(1) (1990).

30. Id.

31. Pascua-Yaqui Trib. Code ch. 11., s 11–1102(A) (1992).

32. Id. s 11–1101(A)(1–13).

33. Id. s 11–1102(A) (citing ss 11–1101(H)–(L)).

34. See Family Violence Protection Act, N.M. Stat. Ann. Secs. 40-13-2 (C)(Michie Supp. 1995) (defining domestic abuse as any incident resulting in physical harm, severe emotional distress, bodily injury or assault, threat causing imminent fear of bodily injury, criminal trespass, criminal damage to property, repeatedly driving by a residence or workplace, telephone harassment, stalking, harassment, or harm or threatened harm to children).

35. Navajo Trib. Code tit. 9, s 1652 (1993); Rules for Domestic Violence Proceedings, Courts of the Navajo Nation Rule 2.3. The Supreme Court may allocate authority to the Navajo Peacemaker Court to address domestic abuse in cases in which the victim consents. Navajo Trib. Code tit. 9, s 1652 (1993). The victim does have the option of going before a peacemaker or the Family Court. Id. s 1652(a). Parties may initiate a proceeding in the

peacemaker court. Additionally, the district and family courts may refer all or part of a domestic violence matter to a peacemaker court. Rules for Domestic Violence Proceedings, Courts of the Navajo Nation Rule 2.3. The peacemaker courts of the Seneca Nation in New York also acted as traditional dispute resolution institutions and served as a model for the Quakers in America. See Oren Lyons, "Land of the Free, Home of the Brave," in *Indian Roots of American Democracy*, Jose Barriero, ed., Ithaca, N.Y.: Akweikon Press 1992) pp. 30, 33–34. Their jurisdiction was recognized since the mid-19th century and remains so under New York State Law, and their judgments are to be enforced by state courts. N.Y. Indian Law Art. 4, s 46 (McKinney 1950). New York law provides for the jurisdiction of the Seneca peacemaker courts over three Indian reservations: the Allegany, the Cattaraugus, and the Tonawanda. Id.

36. Zion, "The Navajo Nation Peacemaker Court: An Introduction 2" (July 7, 1992) (unpublished manuscript, on file with *St. John's Law Review*).

37. See id. at 1.

38. See Bluehouse and Zion, "*Hozhooji Naat' aanii*: The Navaho Justice and Harmony Ceremony," 10 *Mediation Q.* 327 (1993), at 327 (addressing differences between Navajo mediation and arbitration and general American models of mediation and arbitration); see also Zion and Zion, "'*Hozho' Sokee'*—Stay Together Nicely: Domestic Violence, Under Navajo Common Law," 25 *Arizona State Law Journal* 407 (1993), at 423–25 (noting that Navajo process of mediation and arbitration not only involves particular families, but also includes clan). . . .

39. See Zion and Zion, supra note 38, at 423; see also Family Violence Protection Act, N.M. Stat. Ann. s 40-13-3(D) (Michie Supp. 1995) ('If any other domestic action is pending between the petitioner and the respondent, the parties shall not be compelled to mediate any aspects of the case arising from the Family Violence Protection Act unless the court finds that appropriate safeguards exist to protect each of the parties and that both parties can fairly mediate with such safeguards.').

40. See Zion and Zion, supra note 38, at 423.

41. Pueblo of Laguna Const. art. V, s 5

42. See Eileen Lente-Kasero, "Laguna Tribal Court, Family Mediation—Focus on Family Disputes (marriage/divorce) in the Native American Community" 2 (Dec. 2, 1991) (unpublished manuscript, on file with the St. John's Law Review). Lente-Kasero reports that:

> [e]ach partner would have a set of sponsors/witnesses. The parents usually would make the selection because of the role which the sponsors play. They are charged with the responsibility as advisors and mediators for the newlyweds. The sponsors/witnesses are usually an older couple within the community or sometimes traditional leaders within the community.

Id.

43. Id. ('The sponsors/witnesses would be the responsible parties to bring the couple together along with their parents and elder family members.').

44. See generally Edward H. Spicer et al., *Perspectives in American Indian Culture Change*, Chicago, Ill.: University of Chicago Press, 1961 (discussing cultural practices among nineteen New Mexican pueblo including pueblos of Taos, Picuris, San Juan, Santa Clara, Nambe, Pojoaque, San Ildefonso, Tesuque, Santo Domingo, Cochiti, San Felipe, Santa Ana, Zia, Jemez, Sandia, Isleta, Laguna, Acoma, and Zuni).

45. Interview with the Honorable William Bluehouse Johnson, Laguna Tribal Court Judge (Mar. 24, 1994). A Suquamish appellate court decision documents the use of the Tribe's criminal code in an incident involving domestic violence, for which the defendant was charged and convicted of assault and battery by the Tribal Court. The defendant was jailed for fifteen days, fined $120, ordered to perform thirty days of supervised community service and ordered to anger-management counseling with the Suquamish Tribal Social Services Department for one year. Suquamish Indian Tribe v. Mills, Sr., 21 Indian L. Rep. 6053 (Suquamish Tribal Court of Appeals 1991).

46. See, e.g., Fort Belknap Indian Reservation, Domestic Abuse (Mandatory Arrest Provision) (1989). The U.S. government, however, has affected tribal criminal authority over

non-Indians, nonmember Indians, and member Indians. See *Oliphant v. Suquamish* Indian Tribe, 435 U.S. 191 (1978). The Supreme Court ruled that the tribe did not have criminal jurisdiction to prosecute a non-Indian for a criminal act committed within the tribe's jurisdiction absent congressional delegation. Id. at 210. In *Duro v. Reina*, 495 U.S. 676 (1990), the Supreme Court ruled that the tribal court could not prosecute a nonmember Indian for criminal acts committed on tribal land. Id. at 688 ('In the area of criminal enforcement, however, tribal power does not extend beyond internal relations among members.'). In addition, the Federal government has assumed exclusive jurisdiction over Indians involving fourteen crimes. See Indian Major Crimes Act, 18 U.S.C. s 1153 (1994); 18 U.S.C. s 3242 (1994). Whether this jurisdiction is exclusive to the federal government has not been decided; however, several tribes exercise concurrent jurisdiction over the criminal offenses listed in the Indian Major Crimes Act. Congress restored the tribes' ability to prosecute member Indians in October 1991. See 25 U.S.C. s 1301 (1994). Tribes, however, continue to be prohibited from prosecuting non-Indians by the Oliphant decision. See Oliphant, 435 U.S. at 191. Thus, tribal criminal provisions on domestic violence are unenforceable against non-Indian offenders. See Navajo Trib. Code tit. 9, s 151(a)(5) (1993) (stating that criminal penalties apply only to those persons over which Navajo Nation has criminal jurisdiction). But see Taylor, "Modern Practice in Indian Courts," 10 *University of Puget Sound Law Review* 231 (1987), at 247 n.80 (explaining that authority of Courts of Federal Regulations to exercise criminal jurisdiction over non-Indians is undecided issue). In addition, tribes are limited in the sanctions they may impose for criminal offenses as a result of the Indian Civil Rights Act. 25 U.S.C. s 1302 (1994). Tribes can only impose sentences of up to one year and/or a $5,000 fine for any one offense. Id. s 1302(7). However, the existence of both civil and criminal remedies for domestic abuse allows tribes to deal in some way with all the people in their jurisdiction.

47. Menominee Nation, Ordinance No. 93-21 Domestic Violence s IV (1993); Jicarilla Apache Trib. Code tit. 3, ch. 5, s 4 (1992); Pascua-Yaqui Trib. Code ch. 11 s 11-1102 (1992); Crow Tribe of Indians, Crow Law and Order Codes, Domestic Abuse Codes s 4 (1991); Zuni Tribe, Ordinance No. 52 Domestic Violence (Arrest Without Warrant) (1991); Standing Rock Sioux Trib. Code of Justice tit. XXV, s 25–104 (1990); Fort Belknap Indian Reservation, Domestic Abuse (Mandatory Arrest Provision) (1989); Rosebud Sioux Trib. Code ch. 38, s 3 (1989); Salt River Pima-Maricopa, Dep't of Pub. Safety, General Order No.89- 25 (Mar. 23, 1988); Oglala Sioux Trib. Code sec. 99.2, s 3 (1982).

48. Navajo Tribal Code title 9, sec. 1663(a)(2) (1993).

49. See generally Robert N. Clinton et al., *American Indian Law: Cases and Materials* (3d ed.), Charlottesville, Vir.: The Michie Co., 1991. 36–37 (regarding CIO/CRF Courts as response to Ex parte Crow Dog, 109 U.S. 556 (1883)). In Crow Dog, the Court denied authority to try and punish an Indian for the murder of another Indian because tribes retained their self-government power absent explicit renunciation by the tribe or removal of the power by Congress. Id. at 572.

50. See Indian Bureau, Regulations of the Indian Department 78–88 (1884) (stating regulations of Court of Indian Offenses).

51. See generally Tim Vollman, "Criminal Jurisdiction in Indian Country," 22 *Kansas Law Review* 387 (1974) (noting that tribal governments often lack resources to punish crimes over which they have jurisdiction).

52. Jicarilla Apache Trib. Code tit. 3, ch. 5, s 5(A) (1992).

53. Id.

54. See Navajo Trib. Code tit. 9, s 1660(a) (1993) (restraining aggressor from acts of domestic abuse, excluding aggressor from residence, restraining aggressor's contact with victim, awarding temporary custody of children, awarding possession of personal property, providing for nondisposition of property, ordering law enforcement supervision of return to residence, and granting other relief); Jicarilla Apache Trib. Code tit. 3, ch. 5, s 6(C) (1992) (providing court with power to exclude abusing party from dwelling, restrain contact with victim, restrain respondent from committing further acts of domestic violence, award temporary custody or establish temporary visitation rights, provide child support and temporary support, order temporary guardianship, award temporary use and possession of property of respondent, restrain party(ies) from affecting property, order payment of debts, supersede

prior orders of court relating to domestic matters, and provide any other lawful relief deemed necessary for protection of claimed or potential victims); Pascua-Yaqui Trib. Code ch. 11, s 11–1103 (1992) (restraining party from further acts of domestic violence, excluding one party from home, restricting party contact); Cherokee Nation Code tit. 22, s 60.3 (1990) (excluding abusing party from dwelling, restraining abusing party from further acts of violence or interference with victim, restraining abusing party from contact with victim); Standing Rock Sioux Trib. Code of Justice tit. XXV, s 25–109(B)(1)- (3) (1990) (restraining abusing party from acts of domestic abuse, excluding abusing party from residence, awarding temporary custody of children, restricting or supervising visitation of minor children).

55. In addition to the protections afforded under a standing order for protection, the Oglala domestic violence law provides temporary visitation with minor children, counseling and social services, treatment or counseling for the abusing party, temporary use of property, prevention of parties from disposing of property, and other relief necessary for protection of family and household members, including orders that direct the public safety division of the tribe. Oglala Sioux Tribe Code sec. 99.2, Sec 7 (1982). The Navajo Nation provides for counseling, temporary use and possession of property, prevention of both parties from affecting property, payment of rent and mortgages, payment for alternative housing, child support, court costs and other relief including those listed as available under temporary orders. Navajo Tribe Code tit. 9, sec 1660(a)(1993). The Cherokee court can award attorney's fees and court costs in a final protective order in addition to the protections available under an emergency ex parte order. Cherokee Nation Code tit. 22, sec. 60.4 (D)(1990); see also Standing Rock Sioux Tribe Code of Justice tit. XXV, sec. 25–108(D)(1990) (allowing court to recommend or require party(ies) to obtain counseling from domestic abuse program or another agency, order support, and award temporary use of property.

56. Jicarilla Apache Trib. Code tit. 3, ch. 5, s 12 (1992); Crow Trib. of Indians, Crow Law and Order Codes, Domestic Abuse Code ss 6–9 (1991); Standing Rock Sioux Trib. Code of Justice tit. XXV, s 25–111 (1990); Oglala Sioux Trib. Code sec. 99.2, ss 15–20 (1982).

57. Jicarilla Apache Trib. Code tit. 3, ch. 5, s 12(A) (1992); Crow Tribe of Indians, Crow Law and Order Codes, Domestic Abuse Code s 7 (1991); Standing Rock Sioux Trib. Code of Justice tit. XXV, s 25–110(A) (1990); Oglala Sioux Trib. Code Sec. 99.2, s 16 (1982).

58. Crow Tribe of Indians, Crow Law and Order Codes, Domestic Abuse Code s 6 (1991); Oglala Sioux Trib. Code sec. 99.2, s 15 (1982).

59. Jicarilla Apache Trib. Code tit. 3, ch. 5, s 12(A) (1992); Standing Rock Sioux Trib. Code of Justice tit. XXV, s 25–110(A) (1990).

60. Standing Rock Sioux Trib. Code of Justice tit. XXV, s 25–110 (1990).

61. Jicarilla Apache Trib. Code tit. 3, ch. 5, s 12 (1992); Crow Trib. of Indians, Crow Law and Order Codes, Domestic Abuse Code ss 6–9 (1991); Standing Rock Sioux Trib. Code of Justice tit. XXV, s 25–111 (1990); Oglala Sioux Trib. Code sec. 99.2, ss 15–20 (1982).

62. Jicarilla Apache Trib. Code tit. 3, ch. 5, s 12(E) (1992); Crow Trib. of Indians, Crow Law and Order Codes, Domestic Abuse Code s 6 (1991); Oglala Sioux Trib. Code sec. 99.2, s 15 (1982).

63. Indian Civil Rights Act, 25 U.S.C. Secs. 1301–1341 (1994) (imposing requirements upon tribal governments to meet minimum standards of due process as imposed on state and federal government by the U.S. Constitution's Bill of Rights).

64. See Zion & Zion, supra note 38, at 416 (stating that Navajo domestic violence court rules are based partially upon Anglo-American common law).

65. See id. at 415–16.

66. Id. at 423–24.

67. See Christine Zuni, "Strengthening What Remains," Conference Paper Presented to Indigenous Justice Conference: Justice Based on Indian Concepts (Dec. 8–9, 1993) (unpublished manuscript, on file with the *St. John's Law Review*).

68. The total population of American Indian, Eskimo, or Aleut persons is 2,015,143. Bureau of Census 1990 Census of Population, Social and Economic Characteristics, United States tbl. 1. 768,135 Native Americans live in urban areas. Id. at tbl. 4.

69. Pat Prince, "Vision Becomes Reality, Shelter for Battered Indian Women to Open in St. Paul," *Star Trib.*, June 1, 1991, at 1B: 'Women of color end up having to choose between

going to the white community to feel safe from battering and going to their own community to be safe from racism.' Id. (comments of Marsha Frey, director of Minnesota Coalition for Battered Women). Canadian Indian women experience problems in this area similar to those of urban Indian women in the United States. Many Indian women must leave the reservation (U.S.) or reserves (Canada) as victims of domestic violence. In the United States, some leave the reservation because their tribes do not address domestic violence, as do the tribes whose law we reviewed, or because no resources are available on the reservations. Others simply choose to leave.

70. Other women's shelters are unable to offer the access to traditional teachings, resources and practices that can play such a powerful role in helping Indian women in crisis "find their way home." Id. at 1B (comments of Ellie Favell, Cultural Programming Coordinator for Eagle's Nest, women's shelter for Indian victims of domestic violence in St. Paul, Minn.).

71. Id.

72. Id.

73. For a three-month period, July 1 through September 30, 1993, the Women's Community Association, which operates the Women's Shelter in Albuquerque, N.M., showed that it served 736 clients. Of those, 137 were Native American. San Juan County Domestic Violence Task Force figures for 1993 show that Native Americans made up 36% of the population, and comprised 29% of the family crisis clients, 40% of the victims, and 40% of the suspects. San Juan County has three towns—Aztec, Bloomfield, and Farmington—which border the nearby Navajo Nation. See Family Crisis Center, supra note 11, at 7.

74. See Kimberle Crenshaw, "Mapping the Margins: Intersectionality, Identity Politics, and Violence Against Women of Color," 43 *Stanford Law Review* 1241 (1991).

75. But see *Penobscot Nation v. Paul*, 20 Indian Law Reporter 6101 (Penobscot Nation Judicial System App. Div. 1993) (holding that Tribal court retains jurisdiction over violations of protective orders regardless of whether violations occur within court's territorial limits on Penobscot Indian Reservation).

76. The Navajo Nation Code provides that foreign court orders shall be recognized and accorded comity upon a determination of the foreign court's jurisdiction, Navajo Trib. Code tit. 9, s 1666 (1993); see also Cherokee Nation Code tit. 22, s 60.7 (1993) (providing statewide validity of tribal court orders); N.M. Stat. Ann. s 40-13-6(D) (Michie Supp. 1995) (stating 'state courts shall give full faith and credit to tribal court orders of protection').

CHAPTER **6**

RELIGIOUS EXPRESSION

Two obstacles discourage tribal peoples from using the courts to protect Native American religious expression. The first is comprised of risks inherent to the litigation process itself; the second of legal doctrines that categorizes indigenous religious expressions with the sort of minority (or fringe) nonindigenous religions that mainstream U.S. society tends to regard with the most skepticism. Litigation is an obstacle because taking a case to court means, most obviously, that one could lose. It also means that one must ride the waves of evidentiary proof from day to day in a decisionmaking forum—the courtroom—where the introduction of evidence is constrained by an opposing attorney, a watchful judge, a formal set of rules whose purpose is to decide which points of fact can legitimately be offered to prove discrete elements of law, and sometimes a jury. Indeed, presenting historical evidence thoroughly and skillfully is a major task lawyers undertake in Native American rights cases, as much of this book points out.

The second obstacle to litigating Native American rights cases, though related to the first, is particular to tribal religious freedom claims. In U.S. law and legal theory, Native American religious customs and expressions are presumptively categorized with what are euphemistically called "small, unfamiliar, and unpopular religions."[1] According to this categorization, Native American Church practices, for example, get linked in the literature to emerging drug-centered religions,[2] thereby increasing the risk that courts will confuse the sacramental use of peyote, which is a practice that predates the U.S. Constitution, with other nonindigenous minority religions that use street drugs in ways that are neither regulated nor regulatable by intergenerational cultural mores or customs. World Renewal expressions, such as those practiced by the indigenous group in *Lyng v.*

Northwest Indian Cemetery Association[3] regrettably get appropriated by new age environmental expressions, some of which have more rhyme than reason, as Robert Williams Jr.'s essay in Chapter 3 suggests. And indigenous religious customs that depend upon the ceremonial transmission of esoteric knowledge get mistaken for nonindigenous religions that run the gamut from fundamentalist Christian offshoots guided by literal readings of the Bible to groups whose messianic leaders engage in securities and land fraud.

In addition, judges, lawyers, and law enforcement officers are justifiably concerned about the activities of extreme religious-political groups in their midst. This concern also increases the chance that when a Native American religious expression case arises, it might immediately be categorized with cases arising from the activities of fringe, nonindigenous religions. In other words, the coupling of indigenous religions with fringe religions that occurs in the scholarly literature, occurs in law practice too. This tendency unfortunately ensures that people like Alfred Smith, the original plaintiff in *Employment Division v. Smith*, [4] become confused with the increasingly growing number of minority religion adherents who want to be exempted from fair housing laws, antidiscrimination laws, traffic laws, even property and insurance laws. The burden of linking Native American religions with these minority nonindigenous religions falls squarely on Native American communities, because they end up bearing the brunt of protecting the U.S. majority populations from a growing but still minority population that, in the name of religion, might not believe in taxes, courts, or indeed the U.S. Federal Government itself. Doctrinal treatments that equate Native American religions with these small, unfamiliar, and unpopular nonindigenous religions are harmful to Native American religious freedom because the two lines of belief are historically, ethnographically, ethnogeographically, and politically distinct.

One would think that the trust responsibility of the United States toward Native American nations and peoples discussed in Chapter 1 could help the courts carve out a legal difference between indigenous religious expressions and minority nonindigenous religions. Unfortunately the trust responsibility has not been explicitly invoked for this purpose. Instead Native American religious freedom cases have been treated like all other religious freedom cases insofar as they are litigated under the Constitution, federal statutes and case law. [5]

Chapter 6 leaves discussions of current legal doctrine aside to cover two broad types of indigenous religious expression: the sacramental use of peyote within the Native American Church, and sacred site practices such as those that gave rise to *Lyng v. Northwest Indian Cemetery Association*[6] and *U.S. v. Platt*.[7] The chapter starts with two descriptions of a peyote meeting as practiced by Native American Church members. The first description is a narrative by Professor Silvester J. Brito, a Native American folklorist; the second is titled "Appendix A," by Professor Omer C. Stewart, an ethnohistorian whose expertise was the Native American Church and the sacramental use of peyote. Stewart's Appendix A is included as it appears in the public record, where it is part of the legal brief filed before the U.S. Supreme Court by the Native American Rights Fund in *Smith*.[8]

Klara Bonsack Kelley and Francis Harris's excerpt about sacred site research in and around the Navajo Nation follows. Kelley and Harris are part of a Navajo

Nation-sponsored sacred sites mapping project. Maps generated by this project are not compiled to disclose the location of sacred sites to the general public, and indeed tribal peoples remain staunchly opposed to revealing or otherwise opening up sacred sites to tourists and experience seekers. Instead the maps will be used by the Navajo Tribal Government to better protect for future generations of Navajo (Diné) people the sites and, equally important, the stories that are told about those sites. Kelley and Harris's excerpt is important because it provides a sense of how government agencies and utility companies engaged scholars in sacred site research in order to comply with the Native American Religious Freedom Act, or AIRFA.[9] Once AIRFA was gutted by *Lyng* and *Smith*, government and industry sponsorship of sacred site research declined. Nevertheless, sacred site research and mapping projects are still critical to establishing land rights and minimizing the potential for damage from land development projects, which is why entities like the Navajo Tribal Government have taken up the responsibility of sponsoring such research.

The Theodoratus Cultural Report appears next. It too is a public record document; it is titled in that record as "Appendix K to Defendant's Exhibit G." The Theodoratus Report is probably similar to many of the studies Kelley and Harris describe in terms of ethnogeographic detail, description, and focus. It is different, however, because whereas many sacred sites research reports were confidential documents, the Theodoratus Report appears in the public record as an appendix to legal briefs filed on behalf of the Native American litigants in *Lyng*. Initially authorized by the U.S. Forest Service, the Theodoratus Report's purpose was to gather ethnogeographic information on the Yurok, Karok, and Tolowa peoples, and particularly on the ways in which they used public land for religious expression. This information was then to be made available to federal agencies engaged in forest planning. Eventually, the Theodoratus Report made its way into the litigation record, and by default into the public record.

The Theodoratus Report raises two issues about litigation strategy that all Native American litigants must face if they decide to take a case to court. Those issues are whether to disclose esoteric information, either in discovery or in open court, and if so, to what degree. By using the Theodoratus Report, the Native American litigants in *Lyng* elected to reveal place names as well as esoteric activities conducted in relation to those place names. Surely not all was revealed, but some important information made its way into the public record. In presenting this material, I have omitted place names and site locations. Curiosity seekers are not welcome at sacred sites. Indeed there are many rules of ceremony and etiquette that one ought to follow should one be invited to participate in an indigenous religious custom or ceremony. One must research and be aware of these rules before participating in the ceremony so as to avoid harming oneself or others.

From the Theodoratus Report, Chapter 6 moves into a study of the *U.S. v. Platt* case, starting with an excerpt from *U.S. v. Platt* and then closes with two selections from *Zuni and the Courts*, edited by E. Richard Hart (1995). These excerpts were written by two people who were actively involved in the litigation. Hank Meshorer, who helped litigate the case, explains why the Zuni elected to sever property issues from religious expression issues for trial purposes. Edmund

J. Ladd, a Zuni who served as a translator during the trial, explains some of the challenges and difficulties that faced him during the trial. Ladd, who was not entrusted with the esoteric knowledge at issue during the trial, also makes the critical point that not all members of a given community or cultural group attain access to tribal esoteric knowledge, a point that is extensively made in relation to more familiar majority religions in Rodger Kamenetz's 1994 book, *The Jew in the Lotus: A Poet's Rediscovery of Jewish Identity in Buddhist India*.

RECOMMENDED READINGS

There is a vast amount of literature on Native American religious expression. Some basic starting points are listed here. Vine Deloria's classic work *God Is Red: A Native View of Religion* (2d ed. 1992) is indispensable reading. *Handbook of American Indian Religious Freedom* (1991), edited by Christopher Vecsey has an extensive bibliography that includes references to scholarship, court cases, and statutes. For a more concise treatment of Native American religious freedom issues, see any of the following: Walter R. Echo-Hawk, "Native American Religious Liberty: Five Hundred Years After Columbus," *American Indian Culture and Research Journal* 17(3): 33 (1993); John D. Loftin, "Anglo-American Jurisprudence and the Native American Tribal Quest for Religious Freedom," *American Indian Culture and Research Journal* 13(1): 1 (1980); or John Rhodes, "An American Tradition: The Religious Persecution of Native Americans," 52 *Montana Law Review* 13 (1991) (discussing the Ghost Dance and the Wounded Knee Massacre, the sacramental use of Peyote, and sacred sites).

For an introduction to the vast ethnographic literature on the sacramental use of peyote within the Native American Church, see *Peyote Religion: A History*, by Omer C. Stewart. This work is required reading for anyone interested in the Native American Church in North America and the United States, or in contemporary Native American religions. Stewart's book was widely reviewed. Useful and comprehensive reviews are Carol M. Hampton's, *"Peyote Religion: A History* (Book Review)," *The Journal of American History* 75(3): 887 (1988), which criticizes Stewart for relying too heavily on the work of anthropologists and not enough on the thoughts of Native American Church adherents, and thus concludes that "a history of that unique American religion has yet to be written"; L.G. Moses' *"Peyote Religion: A History* (Book Review)," *The Western Historical Quarterly* 20(1): 58 (1989), which characterizes Stewart's work as a "singular achievement in ethnohistory"; and Herbert T. Hoover's *"Peyote Religion: A History* (Book Review)," *Plains Anthropologist* 39(148): 245 (1994), which says that Stewart's book "represents half a century of careful fieldwork and documentary research by the ranking academic authority on the subject." An important earlier historical work on the sacramental use of peyote is *The Peyote Cult* (5th ed., 1989) by Weston La Barre. Both Stewart and La Barre's works have extensive bibliographies; Stewart's bibliography in particular refers to scholarship, government documents, relevant statutes, and court cases.

For concise articles on the legal history of the sacramental use of peyote, see Paul E. Lawson and Jennifer Scholes, "Jurisprudence, Peyote and the Native American Church," *American Indian Culture and Research Journal* 10(1): 13 (1986), which discusses peyote court cases from a nondoctrinal perspective. Paul E. Lawson and C. Patrick Morris, "The Native American Church and the New Court: The *Smith* Case and Indian Religious Freedom," *American Indian Culture and Research Journal* 15(1): 79 (1986), which also discusses peyote cases, though it does so in relation to *Employment Division v. Smith*, supra. For works written by and for lawyers, see David Perry Babner, "The Religious Use of Peyote After Smith II," 28 *Idaho Law Review* 65 (1991–1992); Harry F. Tepker Jr., "Hallucinations of Neutrality in the Oregon Peyote Case," 16 *American Indian Law Review* 1 (1991); and Ann E. Beeson, "Comment: Dances With Justice: Peyotism in the Courts," 41 *Emory Law Journal* 1121 (1992). For a political scientist's view, see Roald Mykkeltvedt, "*Employment Division v. Smith*: Creating Anxiety by Relieving Tension," 58 *Tennesee Law Review* 603 (1991).

Native American Church expressions can vary in detail from community to community. For a discussion of the therapeutic particularities of Native American Church peyote meetings, see the following articles: Joseph D. Calabrese II, "Reflexivity and Transformation Symbolism in the Navajo Peyote Meeting," *Ethos* 22(4): 494–527 (1994); Gilbert A. Quintero, "Gender, Discord, and Illness: Navajo Philosophy and Healing in the Native American Church," *Journal of Anthropological Research* 51:69 (1995). For an article about early Native American Church practices at Taos Pueblo, see Omer C. Stewart, "Taos Factionalism," *American Indian Culture and Research Journal* 8(1): 37 (1984). Eduardo Durán's *Transforming the Soul Wound: A Theoretical/Clinical Approach to the American Indian Psychology*, (1990), addresses the importance of respecting Native American religious and cultural traditions in psychotherapeutic work and interventions.

For discussions of the ethnopharmacological aspects of peyote, as well as of a wide range of entheogens (altering plants used ceremonially) see the following sources: Richard Evans Schultes, "Antiquity of the Use of New World Hallucinogens," *Archeomaterials* 2(1): 59 (1987); Richard Evans Schultes and A. Hofmann, *Plants of the Gods: Origins of Hallucinogenic Use* (1979); Gordon Wasson et al., *Maria Sabina and the Mushroom Velada* (1974); Gordon Wasson, *The Wondrous Mushroom: Mycolatry in Mesoamerica* (1980) (defining the word entheogens, and distinguishing between entheogens, which are ceremonial substances, and hallucinogens, which are often used for recreational purposes); and *Flesh of the Gods: The Ritual Use of Hallucinogens*, edited by P.T. Furst (1972). For a concise description of the peyotero trade, see George Morgan, "Hispano-Indian Trade of an Indian Ceremonial Plant, Peyote (*Lophophohora Williamsii*), on the Mustang Plains of Texas," *Journal of Ethnopharmacology* 9: 319 (1983).

In addition to Vine Deloria's *God is Red: A Native View of Religion*, cited previously, a particularly accessible article on the legal issues concerning sacred sites is Barbara S. Falcone, "Legal Protections (Or The Lack Thereof) Of American Indian Sacred Religious Sites: The Need For Comprehensive Legislation," 41

Federal Bar News and Journal 568 (1994). For law review articles and comments on sacred sites, see Fred Unmack, "Equality Under the First Amendment: Protecting Native American Religious Practices on Public Lands," 8 *Public Land Law Review* 165 (1987); Donald Falk, "Note: *Lyng v. Northwest Indian Cemetery Protective Association*: Bulldozing First Amendment Protection of Indian Sacred Lands," (Note) 16 *Ecology Law Quarterly* 515 (1989); Celia Byler, "Comment: Indian Sacred Site Preservation," 22 *Connecticut Law Review* 397 (1990); and Robert Charles Ward, "The Spirits Will Leave: Preventing the Desecration and Destruction of Native American Sacred Sites on Federal Land," 19 *Ecology Law Quarterly* 795 (1992).

Pipe, Bible, and Peyote Among the Oglala Lakota: A Study in Religious Identity (1990), by Paul B. Steinmetz, is an outsider's account of religious expression among the Oglala Lakota of Pine Ridge, South Dakota. Steinmetz, a Catholic priest, covers what he calls "traditional Lakota religion," which includes the use of the Sacred Pipe and the Sweat Lodge, as well as the practice of the Yuwipi Ceremony and the Sun Dance. He covers other Oglala religious identities on Pine Ridge as well, including the American Indian Movement, the Body of Christ Independent Church, Ecumenist Groups, and the Native American Church (Cross Fire and Half Moon). As part of his coverage of the Ecumenist movement, Steinmetz describes his own efforts as a priest on the Pine Ridge Reservation to establish the Sacred Pipe Ceremony as a sacramental in the Catholic Mass.

Religion in Native North America (1990), edited by Christopher Vecsey is a collection of scholarly articles on the broader topic of indigenous religious expressions, past and present. Vecsey's collection concludes with Åke Hultkrantz's "A Decade of Progress: Works on North American Indian Religions in the 1980s." Hultkrantz, Professor Emeritus at the Institute of Comparative Religion, University of Stockholm, includes in his essay important bibliographic sources that one should consult for more specific information. For a bibliography and analysis of the influence of literary works about Native American spirituality— such as *Black Elk Speaks* (1932, 1961)—on the American middle-class, see Amanda Porterfield's "American Indian Spirituality as a Countercultural Movement," also in Vecsey's collection.

Specific, detailed, and crosscultural discussions of shamanism can be found in *Ancient Traditions: Shamanism in Central Asia and the Americas* (1994), edited by Gary Seaman and Jane S. Day. This collection of scholarly articles is based on the proceedings of Eastern European-American academic symposia that were presented in conjunction with museum exhibitions on shamanism. Also on this topic is the considerably more general but accessible *Shamanic Voices: A Survey of Visionary Narratives*, by Joan Halifax (1979).

For an engaging story of songs and stories as medicine, see *Eye Killers* (1995), by A. A. Carr.

NOTES

1. Douglas Laycock, "Peyote, Wine and the First Amendment," *The Christian Century: An Ecumenical Weekly* 106(28): 876 (1989), p. 877.

2. See ibid. at p. 879–880.

3. 485 U.S. 439 (1988).

4. 494 U.S. 872 (1990).

5. Both *Lyng*, supra note 3, and *Smith*, supra note 4, interpreted the American Indian Religious Freedom Act (AIRFA) as constituting no more than a sense of Congress, not an enforceable law that created a private cause of action on the part of tribal peoples seeking to protect their religious freedom. Thus after *Lyng* and *Smith*, AIRFA was gutted. Subsequent efforts to refashion it have all but failed. For the text of AIRFA, see *American Indian Religious Freedom, Joint Resolution (Public Law 95-341) of 1978, U.S. Statutes at Large* vol. 92: 469 (1978).

6. *Lyng*, supra note 3.

7. Civ. No. 85–1478 PCT-EHC, U.S. District Court, D. Arizona, Phoenix Division, Feb. 8, 1990.

8. *Smith*, supra note 5.

9. See AIRFA supra note 5.

The Peyote Religion: A Narrative Account

Silvester J. Brito

In studying the development of the peyote ceremony in the United States, it was important for me to understand the Indians' historical view of the peyote religion. Several old roadmen told me, "Peyote people, in general, believe that the creator of all things took pity upon his Indian people and gave them this holy herb—peyote—so that their time on this earth could be more pleasant and hopeful. He—that man up there—realized that although he gave man the power of reasoning, there would be those who would thirst for power and the wealth of other people." To translate, God (for lack of a more encompassing term) saw the injustice which his Indian people, through no fault of their own, were being exposed to by the oppressing hand of the conquering European invaders. Hence, what had happened in other parts of the Old World was now coming to pass in the New World, namely, the invasion and conquest of the native people by those of foreign lands. The possibility that the Indians of North America would someday be attacked and conquered by a foreign power was not a complete surprise to the ancient Indian people.

According to Herman White Rabbit, "In old legends it was recorded, as it is spoken of today: there were wise men from different tribes who foretold the coming of powerful invaders from the east."[1] Thus, it came to pass that in the latter part of the 19th century, the invading Euro-Americans dealt the final devastating blow which subdued the defending natives of the New World. God, therefore, once again saw the need to intervene as he had done on behalf of subjugated people in the Old World. This time, however, instead of sending a holy person, such as Jesus Christ, Mohammed, or Buddha, he sent his help to the Indians of North America in the form of a holy herb. "The creator chose this holy medicine—peyote—as a way to send his help. He knew that this was one of the things which the Indian knew best; the knowledge of the use of herbs for healing physical and mental complications. Hence, peyote people believe that the Creator sent them this holy

From *The Way of a Peyote Roadman*, by Silvester J. Brito, New York, N.Y.: Peter Lang Publishing, Inc. © 1989 by Peter Lang Publishing, Inc.

herb—peyote—so that they could gain his attention and help in their oppressed lives under the dominant hand of the Anglo-American culture."[2]

A peyote meeting, a ceremony in which peyote people can express their needs to the Creator, consists of an all-night ceremony. Members generally go into the Peyote Church—a tipi is preferred—shortly after dark, generally around eight or nine P.M., depending on the time of year. This religious ceremony centers around the ingestion of peyote. With the use of this holy sacrament, peyote people sing and pray to God throughout the ten or twelve hour ceremony. In accordance with prescribed procedure they pray first for the welfare of the person for whom the meeting is being sponsored and secondly, for their own needs. My teachers instructed me that with the use of this holy herb one can communicate directly with God, without the medium of a priest. The famous Comanche and peyote leader, Quanah Parker, eloquently stated that, "When the Indian Peyotist goes to church (a peyote ceremonial meeting) he talks to God, and not about what man has written in the scriptures about what God said." I believe in this way. From my own experience I know that in their everyday life, peyote people do their best to live according to the Peyote Way—much as the Christian abides by the dictates of the Old World's "Ten Commandments" of God. And in coordination with its God-given supernatural power, peyote is also used for medicinal purposes. Peyote people believe "that when nothing else will work, namely, the use of white man's medicine, this holy herb and Indian fireplace is their last and only recourse." In addition to hearing this proverb in many meetings, I know from my own experience and observation, that this belief and practice has proved to be true.

During the ceremony, peyote is eaten because it helps one attain a gratifying sense of ease and well-being. This holy herb induces a feeling of brotherhood towards one's fellow man. In some cases, members will also use peyote because of its psycho-therapeutic effects. In addition, by closing their eyes a few individuals will experience visual sensations, and thus, mentally see rich color schemes and patterns. It is known that a few people have had bad experiences with peyote. In my experience, participating members under the watchful eye of a good roadman in a carefully conducted peyote meeting do not experience bad hallucinations.

Most groups emphasize native beliefs and practices with regard to the religious use of peyote. Among some of the older adherents of this religion, however, emphasis is given to certain Christian beliefs and practices, equating peyote with the incarnation of the Holy Ghost. Passages may be read from the scriptures in the King James Version of the Christian Bible especially in the peyote meetings in the northern plains and western Great Lakes area.

Native American Church people generally believe in the supplication of the passion of Jesus Christ. In their own Indian way they believe he is the son of God, the Creator of all things. On the other hand, they do not follow the white man's form of Christianity, such as adhering to those dictates which are part of the dogmas of various Western Christian denominations. I have learned from my own experience that peyote people do believe that in conjunction with the aid of the holy herb peyote, they can communicate directly with God, without the aid of a priest or roadman. My teachers have also told me, "These people feel that the

Creator gave the Indian the holy medicine so that he might also know and understand him and his son Jesus Christ in the Indian way—by using and reinterpreting their traditional customs and practices." The main Christian syncretic element present in all Native American Church peyote ceremonies is the supplication of the passion of Jesus Christ. Other than this, the Peyote Ceremony of this Native American Church is basically Native American. Other Christian syncretic elements present in a particular peyote meeting are there because of the whims of smaller groups or branches of the intercontinental organization, the Native American Church of North America.

Several old peyote men have said to me that the European term, "Indian religion," did not exist in the traditional cultures of the older Native Americans. This particular usage of the term "Peyote Religion" has a tendency to obtrude itself when Indian people of the traditional religions criticize peyote people for their adoption of a new Indian religion. They contend that there is no such thing as an "Indian religion." Their point is well taken—the white man has coined this term, like others, in order for him to deal with a new phenomenon from a separate reality.

NOTES

1. This information was related to me in the summer of 1972 after a meeting which was held several miles west of Oklahoma City, Oklahoma; at the time Herman was 55 years old.
2. My paraphrase of a comment which Herman White Rabbit made on this particular subject .

Appendix A to a Brief Submitted by the Native American Rights Fund in the Case of *Employment Division, Department of Human Resources of the State of Oregon v. Smith*

Omer C. Stewart

Except for the changes described below, the ritual remains the same. It generally begins about nine o'clock on a Saturday night. Today the participants are both men and women, although men are usually the leaders. They come dressed in their best clothes, having clean shirts and dresses. Many men wear a silk handkerchief around the neck folded in a particular way and held together with a silver bola in the form of some peyote symbol—a button, a peyote bird, a cross. Some may wear read bead necklaces or other Indian jewelry, and some will have decorated cases which hold ceremonial feather fans handsomely beaded and tasseled with buckskin, to be used for incensing themselves with cedar smoke, and small gourd rattles similarly decorated. Some will wear blankets and shawls, for things Indian are the preferred dress. Some, especially women, will wear moccasins.

Even if the ceremony is held in a house, the peyotists sit on the floor in a circle, the roadman[1] facing east, the chief drummer to his right and the cedarman to his left. The ceremony begins when the roadman takes from a special case his ceremonial paraphernalia consisting of a staff, usually carved or ornamented with beads and dyed horsehair (it will be placed in front of him in a Half Moon ceremony, stood upright in a Cross Fire ceremony); a decorated rattle; a special fan, probably of eagle feathers; and an eagle bone or reed whistle. He also produces a large peyote button thought to be the Chief Peyote, which he places on the moon altar. He also brings forth a sack of peyote buttons and usually a container of peyote tea to be consumed during the night, and, in the case of a Half Moon ceremony, two sacks of Bull Durham tobacco and papers of corn husks for the prayer cigarettes.

Employment Division, Department of Human Resources of the State of Oregon vs. Smith, 494 U.S. 872 (1990). This excerpt is from the public record. It is also published in *Peyote Religion: A History*, by Omer C. Stewart. Norman, Okla.: University of Oklahoma Press. © 1987 by The University of Oklahoma Press.

The Cedarman throws a quantity of cedar on the fire, producing a dense aromatic smoke, and all the ritual objects, including the drum, are passed through this smoke in order to purify them. In the case of the Half Moon rite, the sacks of tobacco and papers are then circulated clockwise, and when all have prepared a cigarette, the roadman prays aloud and smokes his cigarette in concert with the others, who pray silently, all directing their smoke toward the fire and altar where rests the Chief Peyote. The sacks of peyote and tea are then passed clockwise around the circle, and each partakes either of tea or four buttons. The prayer and cigarettes finished and the first four peyote buttons eaten, the roadman, holding the staff and fan in one hand and vigorously shaking the rattle with the other, accompanied by the quick beat of the chief drummer, sings the ceremonial Opening Song, "Na he he he an yo witsi nai yo," syllables which go back to the Lipan Apache, to the songs of the first U.S. peyotists. He sings the hymn four times. He sings three more songs four times, and then the staff, fan, and rattle are passed clockwise to the next participant and the drum to that person's next neighbor. The person receiving the staff, fan and rattle then sings four songs four times, and passes it on the next participant, and so the staff, rattle, fan, and drum go around the circle, each participant singing four songs four times. Before midnight, the singing continues in this way only interrupted a few times when the peyote is circulated again.

At midnight, the roadman sings another ceremonially determined song, the Midnight Water Call. Then the fireman brings a pail of water, which the cedarman passes through cedar smoke and blesses while smoking a prayer cigarette. After pouring a little on the ground "for Mother Earth," the water is passed around the circle to all participants. Today, instead of a common dipper as was used in the past, paper cups are often used. Sometimes during the Midnight Ceremony, the roadman usually goes outside and blows his whistle to the four directions; this, however, is one of the more variable elements of the ceremony and may be dispensed with or changed. At the end of the Midnight Ceremony, there is a recess lasting ten to thirty minutes when everyone goes outside to relieve himself or to stretch. It is a quiet time with little talking.

When the meeting resumes, the singing begins again and continues. One-half to two-thirds of a peyote meeting is occupied in singing. Peyote may also be circulated. At this time the participants may take from their cases their own ceremonial rattles and fans for use during singing. Also, individuals may request a prayer cigarette from the roadman, and the singing will stop while all listen to the prayer. These prayers are sometimes testimonials, sometimes supplications for help and guidance. This is also the time for a special curing ceremony, if such has been planned.

As the first rays of sunrise appear, the roadman sings another special song, the Dawn Song. He may also blow his whistle again to the four directions. This is followed by the entrance of the peyote woman, usually the wife of the host, who brings in water which is again blessed and circulated. She also brings the ceremonial breakfast of corn, meat, and fruit, which is circulated, with each person taking a bit of each food. Following the ceremonial breakfast, the roadman may give a little talk. If this has been a Cross Fire service, the roadman may read a text from the Bible and interpret its meaning to the congregation. In full daylight the roadman sings the last of the ceremonially determined songs, the Quitting Song. Then he and the others carefully put away the ceremonial paraphernalia, wrapping the fans, rattles, and any other ceremonial objects in silk handkerchiefs and depositing them in their special boxes and cases. It is then that the meeting is over and all go outside to "welcome the sun."

Now the congregation begins to visit with one another, and the women begin preparation for breakfast. This will be the best meal that the host, assisted by his friends, can offer. There will be a good deal of talk concerning the feelings and experiences of the previous night. In the afternoon the peyotists will begin to leave for home, which for some could be a considerable distance. It is not unusual for peyotists to travel more than a hundred miles to attend a meeting.

Thus ends a typical ritual. Except for a few changes because of the circumstances of modern life and a few additions from Christian lore, the ceremony is the same as that observed by Mooney [in 1891].[2] It should be borne in mind that the roadman is expected to use his judgment in the conduct of each ceremony, and he may make some variations, such as dispensing with the eagle bone or reed whistle ceremony, or, for convenience, the fire and altar, if need be. But these are temporary, one-time variations, and all are aware of them. Anthropologists have recounted the ceremony many times, but peyotists themselves or the NAC [Native American Church] have never fully written down the ceremony in order to study it or establish its exact form. The ritual is always learned by one man from another and repeated attendance at many meetings for the purpose of learning how it should be done.

It should be pointed out that among peyotists their religion is more than a ritual to attend from time to time, generally about once a month. It is a part of everyday life. Peyote singing is enjoyed at home. Most peyote homes will have a peyote rattle hanging on the wall. It is easy to take it down, fashion a drum from a piece of inner tube stretched over a coffee can, and do some singing. Children use rattles and drums in play and try to imitate the peyote singing of their elders. Adults more formally practice hymns at night.[3]

NOTES

1. The term "roadman" or "road chief" refers to the spiritual leader of a Church ceremony, an elder who usually has a long association and intimate familiarity with the ritualistic aspects of the peyote ceremony. See, e.g., Paul Pascarosa, M.D., and Sanford Futterman, "Ethnopsychedelic Therapy for Alcoholics: Observations in the Peyote Ritual in the Native American Church," *Journal of Psychedelic Drugs* 8(3): 215–216 (1976).

2. James Mooney, "The Kiowa Mescal Rite." Report of speech to the Anthropological Society of Washington. Washington, D.C.: *Evening Star*, November 4, 1891, p. 6. Mooney was the ethnologist at the Smithsonian Institution's Bureau of American Ethnology, referred to *supra*.

3. Stewart, *Peyote Religion: A History*, Norman, Okla.: University of Oklahoma Press, 1987, pp. 328–30.

Other Studies [of Sacred Places]: What They Did and How They Did It

Klara Bonsack Kelley and Harris Francis

The purpose of [this essay] is to compare the results of our study of thirteen [local Navajo community governing] chapters with the results of similar field studies in Navajoland. Developers during the last fifteen years have sponsored most of these [latter] studies to meet federal and Navajo Nation legal requirements for rights-of-way, leases, and other land-use permits. A few other compilations of Navajo sacred and historical places exist (Van Valkenburgh 1941, Watson 1964, for example), but we have excluded them because they seem to be based on literature more than on interviews. We chose the studies discussed here for comparison with our thirteen-chapter study because only these studies both focused on "inventories" of large numbers of places important in Navajo culture and used interviews as the main method for getting these "inventories." When we started writing this book, these were all the studies like ours that we could identify (although a few have been completed since then, and are not covered here). Taken together, all these field studies illuminate one another. They also give one a more detailed understanding of the relationships between Navajo ways and the landscape, particularly the relationships that development threatens to disrupt. . . .

PURPOSES AND AREAS COVERED

Studies Connected with Land Claims

The earliest of these studies (Van Valkenburgh 1974), appropriately enough, covers the largest area. It was part of the documentation for the Navajo "aboriginal" (pre-conquest) land claim before the Indian Claims Commission, the area that the Navajo Nation claims to have used "exclusively" at the time of the Treaty of 1868. According to the principle of tribal sovereignty in federal Indian law, by signing that treaty, Navajo relinquished to the United States their clai~~~~o exclusive use of the pre-conquest area in exchange for a much smaller ~~~~ tion inside that area. Beginning in 1946, the Indian Claims Commissi~~~~ ed claims that Indian tribes made against the U.S. government f~~~~ compensation for aboriginal acreage that they gave up throu~~~~ ments as the 1868 Treaty. Van Valkenburgh, whose research d~~~~ b the 1930s and the early 1950s, gives information on 88 sacred places throughout the Navajo Land Claim, which extends from a few miles west of the Rio Grande in New Mexico westward beyond the Little Colorado River in Arizona, and from the Mogollon rim in Arizona northward past the San Juan River in Colorado and Utah.

Not until the 1970s were there more efforts to record many Navajo sacred places. Again, the purpose was related to land claims, this time in the 1882 Executive Order Reservation—a 55-by-70 mile rectangle in Arizona originally set aside, by executive order, for the Hopi Indians "and other such Indians as the Secretary of the Interior may see fit to settle thereon," at the request of an Indian agent who wanted authority over a large district to compel boarding school attendance (Indian Law Resource Center 1979:10–13; Kammer 1980:27). The south-central part encompasses the Hopi villages and surrounding lands that the Hopis use for farming and grazing, which the U.S. government has considered exclusively Hopi since 1936 (expanded in 1943) (Indian Law Resource Center 1979:56–64; Kammer 1980:38–41). Since before 1882, Navajos have inhabited the rest of the area, which is the object of the so-called Navajo-Hopi land dispute (Van Valkenburgh 1956:70–73; Stokes and Smiley 1964).

In 1974, forty years of efforts by oil and coal companies, the Bureau of Indian Affairs, and the Hopi tribal government (but with opposition from significant "traditionalist" segments of Hopi society who do not recognize the authority of the Hopi tribal government) paid off when Congress passed the Navajo-Hopi Land Settlement Act (U.S. Congress 1974). Among other things, this law eliminated the joint and undivided surface ownership (outside the exclusively Hopi area) established by a previous lawsuit of the Hopi government against the Navajo government, *Healing v. Jones* (1963). These interests evidently found joint, undivided surface ownership an obstacle to mineral leasing. Although Navajos occupied most of the land, the law divided the surface acreage equally between the two tribes, while keeping the mineral rights undivided. A federal mediator finished drawing the partition line in 1977 (Redhouse 1985a: 9–32; Indian Law Resource Center 1979:74–79; see Whitson 1985:377–78, 392–96, for a critical comment on the role of mineral development in this dispute). Anywhere from 2,500 to 4,000 Navajo families and about 30 Hopi families found themselves on the "wrong side" of the line and therefore were required to move, most (but not all) with federal assistance. An estimated third or more Navajo families are still on the land (Whitson 1985:372n; Colby, Aberle, and Clemmer 1991). According to the 1974 law, members of each tribe have sacred places on lands partitioned to the other and retain the right to use those places (*Attakai v. United States* 1991:9).

cause the court has needed to know the locations of sacred places, and
e Navajos who resist relocation have invoked those rights to justify their
move, several studies have been made. When the federal court asked the
identify sacred places in 1977, the Navajo Nation (1977) documented
ces. Two years later, when Navajos living on lands partitioned to
the Hopis (Partitioned Lands, or HPL) around Big Mountain refused to move,
the Navajo-Hopi Indian Relocation Commission (NHIRC), the federal agency
responsible for removing families from the "wrong" side of the line, sponsored a
study (Wood and Vannette 1979) about possible special religious significance of
the Big Mountain locality.

And finally, in 1990 and 1991, these and the other estimated third of all Navajo
families on HPL in 1977 who had still refused to move got two new chances to
plead their cause. One was an investigation by a federal-court-appointed mediator
who is to help the Navajo Nation and Hopi Tribal governments reach out-of-court
settlements in two lawsuits relating to Navajo use of HPL. The other was hearings by a U.S. Senate committee to oversee the recently reorganized NHIRC (now
Office of Navajo and Hopi Indian Relocation, ONHIR). In a report intended for
both of these initiatives (Kelley, Francis, and Scott 1991) we described 222 Navajo
sacred places in HPL.[1]

We know about one other inventory of Navajo sacred places connected with a
land claim: the study of Vannette and Tso (1988) of Navajo "religious uses" of the
Navajo Reservation in Arizona, the external boundary of which Congress con-
firmed in 1934. Forty years later, as part of the Navajo-Hopi Settlement Act (U.S.
Congress 1974), Congress allowed the Hopi Tribal government to file a claim
against the Navajo Nation for land within that area, excluding the 1882 Executive
Order Reservation (Whitson 1985:381). As part of the documentation of various
Navajo uses of that area for the resulting lawsuit (*Masayesva v. Zah* 1991), the
Navajo Nation engaged Vannette and Tso to record religious uses. They focused on
areas northwest and southeast of the 1882 Reservation rather than cover the entire
Arizona Navajo Reservation of 1934, probably because time didn't permit close cov-
erage of so huge an area. Even in the smaller areas they recorded 689 sacred places.

Studies in the Eastern Navajo Country

After the 1974 so-called Arab Oil Crisis, the Carter administration's energy policy threatened to make the San Juan River Basin of northwestern New Mexico a
"national sacrifice area" for the federally-owned coal it could contribute to the
domestic fuel supply (Radford 1986:43–44, 62–63, 137–63; York 1990:176–86;
Reno 1981:106–14; Kelley 1982:82–86). According to some (perhaps highly specu-
lative, in both senses of the word) estimates, the Basin holds 25% of U.S. coal and
17% of the world uranium supply (Holt 1981:46). Most of this area is called "the
checkerboard" because of the pattern of land ownership there. Navajos occupy
most of the land and have done so for centuries (Stokes and Smiley 1969; Kelley
and Whiteley 1989:5–30). Early twentieth-century federal efforts to place the land
in trust for the Navajo Nation as a whole failed because of opposition from the

non-Navajo ranchers and their influence in Congress. The federal government did, however, allot quarter-section tracts to individual Navajos in the early twentieth century (Brugge 1980:204–205 and ff.; Kelley 1982:49–63). The federal government administers most of the surrounding land through the Bureau of Land Management, and also asserts ownership of the coal under the Navajo allotments, although Navajos are contesting that ownership in court (Kelley and Whiteley 1989:147). The studies described here were done for energy development projects that the Carter and Reagan energy policies encouraged. The centerpiece was a power plant that Public Service Company of New Mexico (PNM) and a shifting group of partners proposed, and the coal mines to fuel the plant (Kelley and Whitely 1989:146–47; Radford 1986:137–63; York 1990:176–86).

As archaeologists swarmed over the San Juan Basin to study the famous prehistoric Anasazi "Chacoan" ruins that might be in the way of the new mines and power plants (Radford 1986: 59:61), Fransted (1979) tried to find out which large Anasazi pueblos have stories or other significance to Navajos (his report doesn't identify the sponsor). He found 44 such sites. PNM and related interests also sponsored several studies of overlapping areas in the general vicinity of the proposed power plant site near Bisti (Carroll 1982, 1983; York 1984; there were other, smaller studies not reviewed here because the work of Carroll and York incorporates their results) and the many widely scattered tracts of federal land that the U.S. Bureau of Land Management was considering leasing to supply coal, mainly to the PNM plant (York and Winter 1988; this study incorporates most information from an earlier inventory [York 1982 in Condie and Knudson, eds., 1982] which is therefore not covered here). The number of [sacred] places recorded by these studies ranges from 16 to 156.

The recently passed AIRFA apparently prompted these studies, although the federal government had not issued "implementing regulations." PNM and related interests reportedly expected that various federal agencies would soon make up their own internal procedures to do what AIRFA told them to do, namely try to avoid approving leases and rights-of-way and permits to mine and generate power that would prevent American Indians from freely practicing their religions (Carroll 1982). Compliance with the National Environmental Policy Act (U.S. Congress 1966 as amended) and the National Historic Preservation Act (U.S. Congress 1969 as amended) was also a factor.

Other Studies Sponsored by Federal Agencies with an Eye Toward AIRFA

AIRFA seems to have prompted federal agencies also to sponsor studies of how Navajos use lands under the agencies' jurisdiction for customary purposes, and how Navajos think agency plans might affect cultural resources important to Navajos. These studies were heavily weighted toward getting "inventories" of places on lands under agency jurisdiction. Perhaps the studies of the early 1980s, at least, were prompted by fears of a lawsuit like the one that Navajo medicine people, together with members of other tribes, brought against the U.S. Forest

Service for ignoring AIRFA in allowing a ski resort to expand on the San Francisco Peaks (*Wilson v. Block* 1983).

The first of these studies (Vannette and Feary 1981) covered the Coconino, Kaibab, and Apache-Sitgreaves National Forests (the San Francisco Peaks are in the Coconino). Through interviews, the authors identified 42 [sacred] places. The Bureau of Indian Affairs (BIA), as trustee, also sponsored similar studies about timber sales and a ten-year plan in the Navajo Forest on the Navajo Reservation (Kemrer and Lord 1984, incorporating information from earlier studies by Bartlett [1980] and Cleeland and Doyel [1982], which identified 15 [sacred] places (not counting a large number of homesites, grave sites, and sweathouses identified categorically but not individually as significant to Navajos). This flurry in the early years of AIRFA soon died down, however. Federal agencies quit sponsoring so many studies, probably because courts decided the dreaded lawsuits (again, including *Wilson v. Block*) in the agencies' favor. Also, perhaps seeing that neither Congress nor the courts would put the much noted missing teeth in AIRFA, the agencies' sense of urgency about developing their own procedures to follow their responsibility under AIRFA was eliminated.

No more sacred places inventories were done in the Navajo Forest until after 1989, when the Navajo Nation government invoked the American Indian Self-Determination Act (U.S. Congress 1975) to contract with the BIA for all that agency's cultural resource management responsibilities on the Navajo Reservation. By this time, the Navajo Nation had its own requirement that all developers make good-faith efforts to identify such [sacred and significant] places, and related Navajo concerns. The Navajo Nation furthermore insisted on such efforts under the National Historic Preservation Act. The result in the Navajo Forest was Mitchell's (1991) inventory of 27 sacred places (not counting homesites, grave sites, sweathouses, identified archaeologically but not by interviews as significant) in a proposed timber sale area. Many other similar inventories have been done on Navajo land since then but we don't include them here because all were in progress when we started writing this book and because most cover rather small areas.

The last study in this group is our own in Canyon de Chelly for the National Park Service [NPS] (Francis and Kelley 1990, 1992). This study was one result of a new "joint management plan" between the Navajo Nation, which owns the land, and the National Park Service, which has administered the Monument since Congress created it in 1931 (National Park Service and Navajo Nation 1990). Tourists of sixty years ago and more saw in this landscape a pristine, garden-of-Eden quality that non-Navajo entrepreneurs who have dominated Navajo Nation commerce since the nineteenth century were quick to exploit and thereby undermine. After 1931, the National Park Service licensed these early entrepreneurs to feed and lodge the tourists and haul them into the canyons (Brugge and Wilson 1976).

In recent years, local Navajos have tried to gain more direct benefits from the tourist trade besides low-paying jobs with the concessioner by forming an association of guides to take more tourists into the canyons. Monument staff have worked closely with the guides, but the non-Navajo concessioner still gets most of the business. As a result, in summer, tourists overrun the canyons, where about sixty Navajo families are living (Andrews 1991). The joint management plan is supposed to help the NPS and the Navajo Nation cope better with, among other things, these disruptions, including tourist intrusions on places important in Navajo culture, of which we recorded 154.

Place Name Studies

Finally, several studies have focused on places with names, regardless of whatever other significance they might have. Most of these studies have a more scholarly motivation than the others we have described. They include a collection of 170 place names by Fransted and Werner (n.d.) in a large region with Chaco Canyon at its center; a project of the Alamo Navajo School Board in which high school students collected 126 place names and stories about them (Walt et al. 1987); Christensen's (1990) list of 54 place names in and around Tsegi Canyon, which he collected as a sideline during archaeological field work there; and the collection of place names and stories that go with them by Jett, Neboyia, and Morgan (1992) in Canyon de Chelly, which started as an inventory of trails and has enumerated at least 153 places (not including Canyon del Muerto).

We include these studies because, as we learned from our work in the thirteen [Navajo tribal] chapters, place names are vehicles for older people to teach younger ones about the landscape. They are therefore a clue to which places people distinguish and link together into landscapes, and how those places function in the landscape. By analyzing the lists of names in these studies and the others covered here for patterns of association with landforms, stories, and so forth, we might learn what clues are in a place name.

Summary

All these studies have as their main purpose "inventories" of places with cultural significance to Navajos. Some studies aren't restricted to places with specific visible characteristics or reasons for significance, while others are—the studies limited to big Anasazi ruins, to places with names, and to sacred places. These studies also differ in the purposes of their inventories—most are either to establish land rights or to minimize potential damage from development. Except for the place name studies (and maybe the Anasazi ruins study), however, all (including our thirteen-chapter study) came about directly or indirectly at the behest of some governmental authority.

FIELD METHODS

The studies discussed here are like our thirteen-chapter study in focusing on "inventories" of culturally important places and seeking such information mainly through interviews. The studies differ mainly in what groups of people they focused on, how they chose people to interview from within the group, how structured were the interviews, and whether they verified the locations of places with maps, field visits with or without interviewees, and so forth. It is important to look at these methods because they account for many differences in the results.

Probably the main contrast in interview methods is between studies that defined the group to be consulted as all families living in or near the lands of interest, and studies that used what Vannette and Wood (1979:5) call "the snowballing, non-random technique"—start with a list of knowledgeable people, get them to refer you to others, interview the others, get more referrals, and so on until most of the referrals are to people you already know about.

Carroll's (1982, 1983) work for PNM electrical generation and transmission projects used the first approach. Carroll says that this type of survey should be analogous to archaeological inventory of 100 percent of the ground surface, "but what the investigator is attempting to sample 100 percent of is much harder to define . . ." (1983:45). The first step, he suggests, is "100 percentage coverage of Native American landholders to be directly affected or in close proximity to the proposed action." By coverage he means "opportunity for 100 percent of all primary landholders or their representatives to express their perceptions of significance or sensitive locations on the lands with which they were most familiar" and recommend other knowledgeable people (1983:5). Carroll's perception of his goal as making sure everybody has a chance to comment on how the proposed development might affect sacred places, rather than as getting an inventory of sacred places, shows a rare and welcome sophistication. Carroll's second step was to try to identify 100 percent of all significant places. For complex reasons, it is hard to tell how far he was from reaching this goal. Carroll wanted to visit medicine people and others whom land users recommended, no matter where they lived (1983:6) but apparently didn't succeed in this.

One of the most interesting things about Carroll's work is that it suggests the scope of knowledge of land users who are not religious specialists.

> even local grazing committee members [chapter-level officials] who have some direct knowledge of the land in question, claimed no knowledge of sensitive locations and deferred comment to the local residents. A similar inclination was found among residents at a short distance from study area lands. . . . It was found that at about three miles from the central study area, residents claimed only second-hand knowledge of major locations and no specific knowledge of lesser locations such as grave sites. (1983:64)

As Carroll interprets this pattern, "People have been told about significant locations in their own grazing areas by parents and kin but know only major locations in the surrounding region" (1983:64).

Because most residents knew about only limited geographical areas, even Carroll's attempts to ask all local residents for their opinions didn't guarantee that he would always have more than one opinion about every place, or prevent contradictory opinions from surfacing later.

The primary information [in the 1982 project] was questioned from several perspectives on the effect of the existing AF line and the proposed 500 kV line on these features [sacred cairns associated with rain requesting and other ceremonies]. He maintained that there was no effect from the existing line and he anticipated none from the proposed line—presumably so long as the actual sacred features [the cairns] are not disturbed. (1982:52)

Later, in connection with the 1983 project, Carroll (1983:78) reported the reaction of another local resident to construction in this same area: "Speaking as a medicine man for the Navajo people, this informant said he does not want . . . [the mesa] disturbed in any way."

Most of the other studies probably tried to approximate the second, "snowballing" approach, although few probably reached the point where most referrals were to people already known. Probably many studies (certainly our work in Canyon de Chelly) were more like the Big Mountain study of Vannette and Wood (1979): as time ran out, the researchers used their contacts from an earlier, large-scale land-use study (Wood, Vannette, and Andrews 1982)—or sought out chapter officials (Vannette and Feary 1981)—"to contact key informants"—people most likely to have the type of knowledge sought, and representing different parts of the geographical area and its social networks. At one extreme, Navajo Forest researchers (Bartlett 1980, Cleeland and Doyel 1982; information incorporated in Kemrer and Lord 1984) who relied on one "key informant" described the selection process (and the limits of confidence) this way:

> On behalf of the Navajo Medicine Men's Association, Mr. Eddie Tso of the Navajo Health Authority directed a letter to the [Navajo Nation government's] Cultural Resource Management Program expressing concern over planned timbering operations by Navajo Forest Products Industry. The association felt that such operations might damage sacred areas or objects in the project areas, and requested that an attempt be made to protect them. Accordingly, [BIA] Branch of Forestry specified that the services of a medicine man be acquired as part of the contract for a cultural resources inventory survey, and Mr. Tom Watson Sr. of Fort Defiance, Arizona was hired as consultant to the project. . . .
>
> The rapid economic development of the Navajo people, a high priority of the tribe, is juxtaposed with the traditional lifeway and the objects and places associated with it. The data gathered by the archaeologist and his recommendations, applied early in the planning process, can aid the continued economic growth while helping preserve elements of the traditional way of life. Thus, Navajo Forest Products Industry will be able to accommodate the concerns of the medicine men who in turn can cooperate with the logging industry.
>
> The drawback to the application of information provided by Mr. Watson is that it represents the viewpoint of only one medicine man. . . . (Bartlett 1980:33)

Mr. Watson also consulted on a later survey of an area overlapping Bartlett's, and the information he provided wasn't just "the viewpoint of one medicine man."

> Mr. Watson stated that his comments on these sites reflect the official policy of the Medicine Men's Association and not just his own opinion. Confirmation of his evaluations was sought from Mr. Eddie Tso, Director of the Native Healing Science program, who stated that while all of the medicine men agree that sacred shrines, graves, and ceremonial sites should be protected, they had not yet fully discussed other sites, such as habitations and herding camps. (Cleeland and Doyel 1982:237)

Mr. Watson's personal opinion, according to this source, was that homesites, herding camps, sweathouses, and the like are also likely to have absorbed some sorts of power from the ceremonial performances and other activities there, and therefore should be respected and avoided.

Trying to interview all residents in and near a project area is usually possible only when one is working in a rather small area, and even then may be hard with limited time and money. Also, one runs the risk of missing medicine people who have esoteric knowledge of the area but live elsewhere. The "snowballing non-random" technique to reach most of the knowledgeable people is better suited for large areas, and even then only researchers with the most time (Vannette and Feary 1981, Vannette and Tso 1988) seem to have come near the end of the snowballing referrals.

Virtually all researchers who describe how they structured their interviews say they were "open-ended." Only Fransted (1979) even mentions an interview schedule, which he says was a checklist to organize information, not a questionnaire used to structure the interview itself. We believe this testifies to the cultural sensitivity of these researchers. To use questionnaires gives the interviewer the superior, controlling role in the discourse and is therefore disrespectful of the elders and medicine people, as well as inconsistent with the way requesting the gift of valuable knowledge subordinates the interviewer.

Most studies are somewhat vague about how the researchers verified locations with the interviewees. Most evidently relied on a combination of visits to places with interviewees, having the interviewee point out locations visible from the homesite, and using place names already on maps. One variant is our study of sacred places on HPL, during which we met with local residents in several parts of the HPL to identify sacred places by having people point out their locations on maps (at the same time tape-recording any stories and other information about the places). This resulted in a very large number of places being identified by a relatively large number of people in a short time. We also believe the locations are accurate because most are places with names given on maps in English translation, and people who couldn't read the labeling on the maps nevertheless pinpointed places with Navajo names right where the map showed the same name in English. (Field verification is still desirable to validate the results for future reference, but it was not necessary for the essentially educational purposes of the report.) This approach only worked, however, because the interviewees were squarely behind the project and the meetings had been organized by community liaisons with the Navajo Nation government who had already been consulting the same people on related matters for years.

NOTE

1. At the time of this writing, mediation had stalled over several issues, including refusal of Navajos still living on HPL to accept 75-year leases from the Hopi government to live on what they consider their own lands.

CITED REFERENCES

Andrews, Tracy J. (1991) "Ecological and Historical Perspectives on Navajo Land Use and Settlement Patterns in Canyons de Chelly and del Muerto." *Journal of Anthropological Research* 47(1): 39–67.

  Attakai v. United States. (1990) CIV 88-964 PCT EHC, February 29.

Bartlett, Michael H. (1980). *Archaeological Resources in the Twin Buttes/Summit Pine Forests, Navajo Nation.* Navajo Nation Papers in Anthropology 2. Window Rock, Ariz.: Navajo Nation Cultural Resource Management Program.

Brugge, David M. (1980). *A History of Chaco Navajos.* Reports of the Chaco Center 4. Albuquerque, N.M.: National Park Service.

Carroll, Charles H. (1982). "An Ethnographic Investigation of Sites and Locations of Cultural Significance to the Navajo People to be Affected by PNM's Four Corners to Ambrosia to Pajarito 500 kV Transmission Project." Albuquerque, N.M.: Public Service Company of New Mexico.

_____. (1983) "Ute Mountain Land Exchange Ethnographic Study." Albuquerque, N.M.: Public Service Company of New Mexico.

Christenson, Andrew L. (1990). "Navajo Place Names—Tsegi Canyon Arizona." Ms. in Kelley and Harris's possession.

Cleeland, Teri A., and David E. Doyel. (1982) "Ethnic, Religious, and Scientific Significance of NFPI Compartment 9 Sites." In *Archaeological Survey of the Forest Highlands of the Defiance Plateau and Chuska Mountains, Navajo Nation,"* by Laurance D. Linford. Navajo Nation Papers in Anthropology 6. Window Rock, Ariz.: Navajo National Cultural Resource Management Program.

Colby, Benjamin N., David F. Aberle, and Richard Clemmer. (1991). "The Hopi Navajo Situation under the New Commission." *Anthropology Newsletter*, February.

Condie, Carol, and Ruthann Knudson, eds. (1982). *The Cultural Resources of the Proposed New Mexico Generating Station Study Area, San Juan Basin, New Mexico.* Albuquerque, N.M.: Quivira Research Center Publication 39.

Francis, Harris, and Klara Kelley. (1990). "Traditional Places in Canyons de Chelly and del Muerto." Confidential ms., National Park Service, Canyon de Chelly National Monument, Chinle, Ariz.: Southwest Regional Office, Santa Fe, N.M., and Navajo Nation Historic Preservation Department, Window Rock., Ariz.

_____. (1992). "Sacred Places in Canyons de Chelly and del Muerto, Phase II." Draft. Confidential ms. on file, Navajo Nation Historic Preservation Department, Window Rock, Ariz.

Fransted, Dennis. (1979). "An Introduction to the Navajo Oral History of Anasazi Sites in the San Juan Basin Area." Navajo Ageing Services, Fort Defiance, Ariz. Ms. in Kelley and Harris's possession.

Fransted, Dennis, and Oswald Werner. (N.d.). "The Ethnogeography of the Chaco Canyon Area Navajo." Ms. in Kelley and Harris's possession.

Healing v. Jones. (1963). 210 F. Supp. 125, 129 (D. Ariz. 1962), cert. Denied 373 U.S. 758 (1963).

Holt, H. Barry. (1981). "Navajo Sacred Areas." *Contract Abstracts and CRM Archaeology* 2(2): 45–53.

Indian Law Resource Center. (1979). "Report to the Hopi Kikmongwis and Other Traditional Hopi Leaders on Docket 196 and the Continuing Threat to Hopi Land and Sovereignty." Washington, D.C. Ms. in Kelley and Harris's possession.

Jett, Stephen C., Chauncey M. Neboyia, and William Morgan, Sr. (1992). "Navajo Placenames and Trails of the Canyon de Chelly System, Arizona." Draft. Ms. in Kelley and Harris's possession.

Kammer, Jerry. (1980) *The Second Long Walk.* Albuquerque, N.M.: University of New Mexico Press.

Kelley, Klara. (1977). *Commercial Networks in the Navajo-Hopi-Zuni Religion.* Ph.D. diss. in anthropology, University of New Mexico.

_____. (1982). *The Chaco Canyon Ranch: Ethnohistory and Ethnoarchaeology.* Navajo Nation Papers in Anthropology 8. Navajo Nation Cultural Resource Management Program, Window Rock, Ariz.

Kelley, Klara, Harris Francis, and Peggy F. Scott. (1991). "Navajo Sacred Places on Hopi Partitioned Lands." Confidential ms. on file, Navajo-Hopi Land Commission and Navajo Nation Historic Preservation Department, Window Rock, Ariz.

Kelley, Klara, and Peter M. Whiteley. (1989). *Navajoland: Family and Settlement Land Use.* Tsaile, Ariz.: Navajo Community College Press.

Kemrer, Meade F., and Kenneth J. Lord. (1984). *Cultural Resources Overview for the Navajo Forest.* Albuquerque, N.M.: Chambers Consultants and Planners.

Masayesva v. Zah, (1992). Federal District Court, Phoenix, Ariz., Final Judgment (as amended December 18, 1992) (Appealed 1993 U.S. Court of Appeals, Ninth Circuit, No. 93-15109).

Mitchell, Edward. (1991). Appendix B—Supplemental Ethnographic Reports. In A Cultural Resources Inventory of Compartments 34, 28, 45, and 50, Navajo Nation Forest, The Whiskey Creek/Ugly Valley Timber Sale, by Greg L. Bowen, Dennis Yazzie, Harold Yazzie, and Edward Mitchell. Report Number HPD-91-109. Ms. on file, Navajo Nation Historic Preservation Department, Window Rock, Ariz.

Radford, Jeff. (1986). *The Chaco Coal Scandal: The People's Victory Over James Watt.* Corrales, N.M.: Rhombus.

Redhouse, John. (1985a). *Geopolitics of the Navajo-Hopi Land Dispute.* Albuquerque, N.M.: Redhouse/Wright Productions.

Reno, Philip. (1981). *Mother Earth, Father Sky: Navajo Resources and Economic Development.* Albuquerque, N.M.: University of New Mexico Press.

Stokes, M.A., and T.L. Smiley. (1969). "Tree-ring Dates from the Navajo Land Claim: II. The Western Sector." *Tree-Ring Bulletin* 29: 13–27.

Stokes, M.A., and T.L. Smiley. (1964). "Tree-ring Dates from the Navajo Land Claim: IV The Eastern Sector." *Tree-Ring Bulletin* 26: 2–14.

Vannette, Walter M., and Alison Feary. (1981). "Navajo Sacred Places and Resource Use In and Near the Coconino, Kaibab, and Apache Sitgreaves National Forests." Confidential ms. on file, U.S. Department of Agriculture, Coconino National Forest, Flagstaff, Ariz.

Vannette, Walter M., and Reed Tso. (1988). "Navajo Religious Use of the 1934 Reservation Area." Expert Witness Report, Brown and Bain, P.A., Phoenix and the Navajo Nation Department of Justice, Window Rock, Ariz.

Van Valkenburgh, Richard F. (1940). "Sacred Places and Shrines of the Navajos: Navajo Rock and Twig Piles Called Tsenadjih." *Plateau* 13(1): 6–9.

_____. (1941). "Dine Bikeyah." Ms. U.S. Indian Service, Navajo Agency, Window Rock, Ariz.

_____. (1956). "Report of Archaeological Survey of the Navajo Hopi Contact Area." Prepared for Indian Claims Commission, Navajo Hopi Land Claim. Ms. on file, Laboratory of Tree-Ring Research, University of Arizona, Tucson, Ariz.

_____. (1974). "Navajo Sacred Places." In *Navajo Indians III*, David A. Horr, ed. New York, N.Y.: Garland.

Walt, Henry, Denny Apachito, Jr., George Apachito, Jackson Pino, Patsy Apachito, Betsy Brandt, Mike Marshall, and Chris Musello. (1987). "Alamo Navajo Place Names: Mapping Database." Ms. Alamo Navajo School District, Alamon, N.M.

Watson, Editha. (1964). *Navajo Sacred Places*. Window Rock, Ariz.: Navajo Tribal Museum.

Whitson, Hollis A. (1985). "A Policy Review of the Federal Government Relocation of Navajo Indians under P.L. 93-531." *Arizona Law Review* 17(2): 371–414.

Wilson v. Block. (1983). 708 F. 2d 735 (D.C. Cir.), Cert. Denied, 104 S. Ct. 371 (1983).

Wood, John J., and Walter M. Vannette. (1979). "A Preliminary Assessment of the Significance of Navajo Sacred Places in the Vicinity of Big Mountain, Arizona." Ms. U.S. Department of the Interior, Bureau of Indian Affairs, Navajo Area Office, Window Rock, Ariz.

York, Frederick F. (1982). "The Results of the Ethnographic Survey." In *The Cultural Resources of the Proposed New Mexico Generating Station Study Area, San Juan Basin, New Mexico*, Carol J. Condie and Ruthann Knudson, eds. Albuquerque, N.M.: Quivira Research Center Publication 39.

_____. (1984). "Historic Cultural Resources in the Arch Joint Venture Project Area Along the De-Na-Zin Wash." Office of Contract Archaeology, University of New Mexico, Albuquerque, N.M.

_____. (1990). *Capitalist Development and Land in Northeastern Navajo Country, 1880s to 1980s*. Ph.D. diss. In anthropology, State University of New York, Binghamton, N.Y.

York, Frederick F., and Joseph C. Winter. (1988). *Report of an Ethnographic Study and Archaeological Review of Proposed Coal Lease Tracts in Northwestern New Mexico*. Office of Contract Archaeology, University of New Mexico, Albuquerque, N.M.

Appendix K to Defendant's Exhibit G

Dorothea Theodoratus, "Cultural Resources of the Chimney Rock Section, Gasquet-Orleans" in *Lyng v. Northwest Indian Cemetary Protective Association*

RELIGIOUS BELIEFS AND PRACTICES

The most important aspect of the present study has been the examination of those beliefs and practices which may be subsumed, although inadequately, under the discrete classification "religion." The "religious" aspects of the lives of Native Americans can only be roughly categorized into separate considerations. Because of the particular nature of the Indian perceptual experience, as opposed to the particular nature of the predominant non-Indian Western perceptual experience, any division into "religious" or "sacred" is in reality an exercise which forces Indian concepts into non-Indian categories, and distorts the original conceptualization in the process. A statement made by a Hupa woman testifying in 1954 before a committee of the United States Senate gives partial insight into the Indian concepts:

> . . . To most people, hunting and fishing is [*sic*] a sport. To the American Indian it is a part of a religious custom. The American Indians are a very pious—I do not like the insinuation of 'pious'—but they are very religious people. We did not believe in a church just one day; we believed in a church every day of the week and in every act that we did. And we have continued with that belief. Therefore, even the taking of food was a religious sacrament in a way, particular [*sic*] in regard to the hunting of deer. We had a set custom that we followed in the conserving of it and the way we used the meat and our sharing it with others and so forth. [U.S. Congress, Hearings before the Joint Subcommittees on Indian Affairs of the 83rd Congress on H.R. 7322 and S. 2749, 1954:453].

It is also important to realize for the purposes of this study that descriptions which single out specific cultural sites as isolates . . . are distortions of Indian conceptualizations of these important cultural properties.

Lyng v. Northwest Indian Cemetery Protective Association, 485 U.S. 439 (1988), Docket No. 86–1013, "Joint Appendix," p. 110.

The emphasis of this report has thus far been the delineation of events and features of Native American life as these features relate to uses of the project area. In many cases, seemingly unrelated elements have been shown, in fact, to be closely interrelated. Nowhere is an awareness of such interrelationship more important than in the examination of the religious life of the peoples concerned and of the relationships of religious beliefs and practice to certain geographic zones and regions within the project area.

Included below are discussions of the major ceremonial events and of the philosophical precepts upon which these are based. Many of these events stress the quest for rejuvenation of the world, the community, and the individual. In the latter case, particularly prescribed training and preparation practices were and continue to be rigorously observed. Since such training is an integral aspect of the religious use of the high country, these training practices have been described at some length. . . .

MAJOR CEREMONIES AND MYTHS

Northwest California cultures possess a religious complex generally called World Renewal, whose purpose is the stabilization and preservation of the earth from catastrophe, and of mankind from disease. These goals are expressed through the great dances held at specified times and places in the region—at present the Karok and Hupa and, in the past, by the Yurok as well. . . .

It is believed that these ceremonies were initiated by the prehuman spirits who are said to have inhabited the world and to have brought all living things and culture to mankind. These figures are called *ixkareya* by the Karok, *woge* by the Yurok, and *kixunai* by the Hupa. . . . The Tolowa also spoke of similar beings.

Traditionally, myths concerning these supernaturals and the songs which accompanied each myth, were held to contain a spirit and were often "owned" by individuals of families. In these myths, origin stories are interwoven with events from daily life to explain how things came about, some of these myths are parts of the formulae recited at ceremonies performed by individuals or groups. . . .

Fire once played a part in these World Renewal ceremonies. On the last night of the Karok ritual, while the Deerskin Dance was being performed, [a certain] sacred mountain was fired. The mountain was believed to be an immortal woman whose "hair" was singed so that there would be neither widows nor widowers that year. In 1939, an older Karok woman, stated that since the White man's regulations prevented the Indians (Karok) from kindling the fire on [place name omitted] and the Deerskin Dance had stopped, food had become scarce and the Indians were dying off. At the Panamenik (Karok White Deerskin) ceremony, a fire was also set on the last night on the mountain facing [place name omitted].

Dancers danced to provide an abundance of food, universal good health and repair to the earth . . . These dances are performed at the sites where the prehuman figures are said to have first brought certain gifts to man. Dances are a reaffirmation of the gifts which the people had been given by the spirits and a technique for removing evil from the world by reestablishing balance to the earth. Wealth enables families to support these ceremonies, and the rituals allowed the wealthy to confirm their prestige through display. The exact relationship of wealth and display in Northwest California ceremonies has been open to various interpretations in the ethnographic literature, however. Local Theodoratus Cultural Research [TCR] consultants readily took exception to the analysis proposed by [researcher's name omitted] during his work in the area, in which he stated that Yurok dance regalia were "wholly unsymbolical and in no sense regarded as sacred" and that they "comprise the most valuable things in the world known to the Yurok." Consultants reiterated that these statements were in fact untrue or at best misinterpretations of information received by [researcher's name omitted]. In fact, consultants state, the regalia are highly sacred and are of extreme value to the Yurok because they are regarded by them as living spirits and sacred objects. In addition, consultants felt that such anthropological emphasis on material wealth has led to other misinterpretations or distortions of field information. One consultant stated, "Dances are our religion." Another said that when ceremonies are held, the people pray about everything, for the salmon to come, for the acorns to grow, for the presence of all kinds of game, and for children to grow up to be good.

Other ceremonies were also important in Northwest California life. The Yurok opened the Klamath River every year, using herbs brought from the high country. The Yurok, Hupa, and Karok had a "first salmon" ceremony. (The Hupa also performed a first eel and first acorn ceremony.) The Karok held that first salmon ceremony in the spring at Amaikiara.

> The Kareya [a religious man] Indian retires into the mountains and fasts the same length of time as in autumn. On his return the people flee, while he repairs to the river, takes the first salmon of the catch, eats portion [sic] of the same, and with the residue kindles the sacred smoke in the sudatory. No Indian may take a salmon before this dance is held, nor for ten days after it, even if his family are starving.

A TCR Yurok consultant stated that the first salmon ceremony was "wonderful;" all the people were out waiting for the first salmon to be speared. "The people fast during this time, and the children would be there and they would feed them. . . . They [children] don't need to fast—they don't know [about the meaning]." She stated that the older people prayed all day and everybody came, lining both sides of the river. "After the first salmon was caught everyone began to catch them. Then when they all looked up the mist started and this was the "tinkling" of the sky. The sky was weeping in sympathy. This is how the Indians felt about these things. These are stories that people still learn."

The privilege of giving dances was linked to blood inheritance, and owning regalia was not equivalent to having the right to give a dance. A consultant explained that not everyone can give dances, only those who have the right to do so. Those who inherit the privilege may be unable or unwilling to give the ceremony. Sometimes those with inherited rights can join with others who have the means and equipment to do so. Rights and privileges surrounding dancing and ceremony continue to be respected today. . . .

PEOPLE WITH POWER

In Northwestern California, two major social categories of people with "power" can be discussed. The first is that composed of "doctors" and includes those persons who have the ability to cure ill patients. The second category includes those who have acquired personal "medicine" for a particular purpose, exclusive of curing the sick. Today such individuals are often called "doctors," too. Both of these catgories include persons who have been trained in the high country, and only those who train in the mountains are said to achieve great power. This section contains a detailed discussion of these two categories of people with power, with a particular emphasis upon training. Emphasis is given to the role of high country training and experiences as they relate to the acquisition of power by these practitioners. . . .

The word "doctor" is a locally accepted term for any of the esoteric practitioners who have had high country training. For purposes of clarity the term "doctor" is used herein to refer to a spiritual specialist who achieves "power" through trance from an order other than the "natural" world. For the Yurok, these doctors were women. Other kinds of "doctors" are herein referred to with a modifier signifying type, such as "herb" or "mourning." The description may or may not signify the same order of "power" as "doctor." The term "medicine man" here refers to male individuals (commonly called formulists or priests) who are ceremonial practitioners. This category is different from that of persons who sought particular expressions of power, such as that for "good," "long life," or "strong." These latter persons are here considered as "medicine makers." Medicine makers also sought medicine in the high mountains. Making medicine is defined following [researcher's name omitted]:

> . . . as an homogenous constellation of physical, mental, and vocal actions, and experiential events, undertaken or sought in a religious manner and frame of mind, the purpose of which is to maximize the practitioner's potential (i.e., "power") to act in a desired direction, or to live in a desired way. It invariably involves . . . the practitioner's experiencing contact with supernatural forces, either generalized or specific. While medicine making may incorporate given ascetic acts, and prescribed rituals, prayers, or deals, it is, in the purest sense, an inwardly experienced moment of intense awareness and, in the more lofty (or "High") medicines, of transcendent understanding. A man or woman might, then, carry out all of the prescribed actions, and yet not "make medicine"; that is not experience the requisite inner state.

> . . . "Power is defined here as a particular expression of a universal energy.

CURING DOCTORS

There are several ways of obtaining "power," a particular expression of a universal energy. Every Yurok child is born with a "fire," which is a manifestation of the universal energy, or "spirit." Everyone has this "fire," or "spirit," and he/she also has a "soul," a more individuated spiritual element, as well as a body and a mind-element. However, the "fire," which is also the "spirit," is part of the "[C]reator," the universal energy, or "[S]pirit." Some people get an extra portion of this "fire" which can be thought of as a natural proclivity for power. Another method of acquiring extra "spirit" can occur after birth. Among the Yurok, it is believed that the "soul" enters the body ten days after birth, at which point the child is recognized as a human being. At this point a High Man or doctor can "shoot" the child with power, giving the child an added increment of spirit and, hence, added potential for power.

In addition to the potential for acquiring power at birth or soon thereafter, a person may inherit potential power: the ability to train for doctoring. Another way of acquiring this potential for power is through the possession of a natural gift or proclivity. These persons are said to be born with power, as opposed to those who have been selected for training on the basis of their inheritance. Persons who possess this natural calling always have rights to training over those who have simply inherited the gift for power.

Although doctors, usually women, often come from a family whose members had previously produced doctors, each individual must seek the realization of this power on her or his own. The regimen required of a person training for doctoring is too strict for many people, even though becoming a doctor is an avenue to wealth. One TCR Yurok consultant said, "I had to fight against being a doctor. I drank water so I couldn't be a doctor. I had foresight to see future events. I foresaw an automobile accident. It was terrible. I woke up in the night singing doctor songs. That's why I drank water, to keep from being a doctor."

Those who seek to be curing doctors must first experience a "vision" in a trance or dream state. During this state, the novice is given guidance by the appearance of person or animal and also the gift of a "pain." The "pain" is an animate object introduced into the novice's body during the vision. Training follows during which the novice learns to bring forth this pain and control it for use in curing patients. The doctor usually possesses pairs of "pains" which are used to draw illness out of the bodies of others. Some Indians state that no one actually volunteers or is appointed to become a doctor; "One is called." A TCR consultant said one should be humble and wait for one's power. He said "I believe it (Indian religion) is going to get stronger in the next ten years."

In the course of training for power acquisition, the aspiring doctor is to dance in a sweathouse for a period of ten days under the guidance of an older doctor. During the dance, the doctor learns to control her "pain," and she is herself considered ill until she does so. This is called "cooking the pains" to make them amenable to her control. The Kick Dance, used by the Yurok, Karok, Hupa, and Tolowa, is associated with this procedure.

In the summer following this dance, the novice goes to the mountains to a stone seat or enclosure where she spends the night in dancing, usually accompanied by another doctor or assistant who watches over her. Another Kick Dance follows her return from the mountains, and then she is ready to enter the profession of a doctor:

> A doctor's first pain may come to her unsought in a dream, but may also be acquired when she is dancing in solitude in order to obtain power. To get its mate she goes to one of the mountaintop half-enclosures of stone which the Yurok called [place name omitted] and which in English they often speak of as seats. There she dances again, still alone, but under guard and at night, until the guardian spirit having put the second of the pair into her body, she goes out of her senses again and has once more to be taken down to the 'cooking' remohpo dance in the sweathouse. A strong doctor may ultimately acquire many pairs of pains; but the foundation of her ability and her strongest pains are the first two pairs.

Strong Doctors, i.e., those of greatest power and highest prestige in the past, were sucking doctors.

Women doctors traditionally commanded high bride-wealth and usually accumulated wealth for the family. A doctor obtains the highest fee possible for his or her services, but cannot refuse to treat a patient. In the past, any death resulting from a doctor's refusal to treat a patient made the doctor liable for damages, and inability to effect a cure resulted in the fee being returned to the patient or family. A narrative about a woman from a house in [place name omitted] details her experiences in becoming and practicing as a doctor, and tells that upon her unhappy death, she returned as a spirit to [place name omitted] to live.

The connection between the acquisition of powers and spirits in the mountains is evident in many accounts of the experiences of doctors. There is a particular orientation towards the east, or inland toward the mountains. . . . The mountains are sacred, the locales of power upon which the doctor can draw.

One TCR Yurok consultant, when asked how a person learns to become a doctor, said that one went to [place name omitted]. He said that sometimes a young girl will dream, perhaps that she has swallowed a water dog or a snake. This makes the girl ill. In turn, the experience "makes you dance—and you dance all night. You just keep on dancing for ten days in the sweathouse and that way you get power in your head. You get enough power to go back to [place name omitted]." He said that one would stay at [place name omitted] for ten days, but he did not know how long it took to get there—perhaps two days. Consultants indicated that one started at lower elevations and "worked up" to the "high places" to achieve full power. . ..

The doctors draw their powers from the woge-spirits who went to the mountains with the coming of humans to the earth. In death, the doctors' souls follow the path of the woge-spirits to the mountains. The high places, then, are the focal source of curative power for those who live in Northwest California.

In the past, disease was thought to be caused in several interrelated ways: the presence of semianimate objects ("pains") in the body, unconfessed sin or breach of taboo, witchcraft, poisons placed in food, or by a doctor who wished to earn more money. Modern disease theory, while accepted, has not changed basic curing patterns. The doctor diagnoses the precise cause of an illness before beginning treatment. The patient is placed by a living-room fire with assembled family and friends gathered to sing and watch the cure. The doctor smokes tobacco in her pipe and dances until reaching a state where she can divine the cause of the illness. Breaking of a taboo has to be publicly confessed.

One Yurok consultant said that "When a person gets sick, it's something bad you've done. If the patient can't or won't tell he won't recover." This consultant told a story of a woman who was sick and called in [name omitted] who saw in a vision that the woman had hidden poison in the rafters of her house. After the woman confessed, she was cured and the deaths in her family stopped. It was remarked by another consultant, in discussing one family which had had an unusual number of deaths, that someone must have done something wrong in the family to have caused this series of deaths.

After public confession of breaches of taboos (those pertaining to death or sex, usually), the doctor would effect the cure. She removed the "pain" from the affected part of the patient's body with her mouth. The pain would then enter the doctor's body, and she would vomit it into her hand or into a basket, exhibit it to the people, and then dance until it disappeared. . . .

The general training and curing techniques used by the Yurok were the same for the Karok, Hupa, and Tolowa although less evidence exists for the practices of the latter groups. Doctors from one tribe are sometimes called on by another tribe as experts in special cases. Traditionally, those who could withstand the discipline for becoming a doctor could look forward to wealth and success, the basis for social prestige among the peoples of the study area. One story tells of a Tolowa man turning to doctoring when he was humiliated at a Yurok White Deerskin Dance because he was of low birth and of no social consequence. He went

> . . . into the mountains, back to the very highest mountains where the bear, panther, and wolves were plentiful. All alone he went to where there is a large rock which we call [place name omitted], and he remained there for three days singing and praying, then with nothing to eat he wandered on through the wild timber and brushy country, back to [place name omitted], . . . and proclaimed himself a doctor.

The Karok have a number of "medicine mountains" which doctors have traditionally used for validation of their powers. . . . Forest Service files . . . indicate that [one particular location], due to destructive action by Whites, can no longer be used as a medicine-making site, but local Karok TCR consultants stated that the site continues to be used for other purposes such as World Renewal. The Hupa also have their own sacred mountains, the most notable being [place name omitted] to the east, but there is another to the west of their valley which is used by doctors and luck seekers. . . .

PERSONAL MEDICINE POWER

A person might seek supernatural help through proper ritual behavior at certain spots which were reported to have specific types of power. Fasting and abstinence from sex and water were part of the ritual of gathering sweathouse wood in the hills. All tribes in the study area observed this practice. Crying while gathering sweathouse wood is a traditional part of the ritual. . . .

Any serious trip to the high country is preceded by a ten-day purification period of fasting and praying, traditionally in the sweathouse, under the instruction of a trainer. The person may be doctored at this time in order to "clean him up" in preparation for the trip. At this time the individual confesses his mistakes, rids himself of grudges and bad feelings, and gets back "in the middle" before starting the trip. A major purpose of working vigorously in the purification procedures is to allow the individual sufficient power to enter the high country. During this period the individual waits for acknowledgment of the spirits which can come in the form of a dream, a sign, or a vision. By such signs, the spirits recognize the sincerity of the quest of the individual and sanction that quest in the high country. The high country training is a long-term endeavor involving a great deal of preparation, both on the part of the initiate and of the trainer.

Such training/doctoring, which takes place prior to beginning the trip into the high country, involves what might be termed "a community support system." A person who makes medicine in the high country may be said to be achieving more than just personal medicine. He may also be achieving knowledge or a skill which is of benefit to the community. In addition, any achievement of medicine is viewed by the remainder of the community as adding to the total store of medicine/power within that community. In this manner, villages gain recognition through the amount of power-related knowledge and skill held by its membership. Communal interest is thus very important. Only a very few individuals ever make medicine, for instance, on [place name omitted]. However, it is important to understand that the entire community has a vested interest in the success of those few individuals, whether they be doctors making medicine at [place name omitted] or [place name omitted], or men making "high medicine." In either case, the community will benefit, and thus is supportive of the person seeking power when his or her quest is not secret. This relationship between medicine and the community is reflected in the recent statement by a Karok man who reports that since he is not in the best physical condition, he has disqualified himself from attempting the powerful Pikiavish medicine because "the condition I'm in might affect the people."

One enters the high country to make medicine at a walk or a run. The trainer sometimes follows the medicine-maker at a distance. Every step of the way is important: "every step of the way you learn something." A TCR consultant states that vehicles may not be used. Often the trip itself is full of difficulties and tests the individual's endurance. The person is tested by dangers along the trail, by bears, for example, or by tempting food. It is also important that the seeker take the appropriate trail, which depends upon the type of medicine sought as well as the seeker's abilities. . . .

It is particularly important that individuals on their first medicine quest in the high country be accompanied by their trainers. The reason given for the trainer's presence is that he may have to save the student from making a disastrous mistake: that of getting the wrong (negative) power, or one which could cost the student his life, or, possibly, his mind. (This, too, is why training must be very gradual.) A second reason is that the trainer may "shoot" his power into his student when the student is ready to make his medicine. This gives the student a "boost" for making the necessary connection with the spirits involved.

It is also important that the seeker not look into the eyes of passersby along the trail, in order to maintain his purity, to protect innocent persons from the medicine one has, and to maintain secrecy. If a person who has no medicine at the time is in contact with someone who is at the peak of power, the powerless person is put in grave danger. This contact also interferes with the person who is experiencing power.

Again, when a man leaves the seat or medicine area and descends to his camp he does not talk or notice anyone along the trail. For example, his eyes are kept down; he does not look into the eyes of anyone along the trail, and does not let anyone look into his eyes so as not to disturb concentration. Eye contact would spoil the effort by bringing the person too quickly into a world in which he does not yet care to be.

Privacy is emphasized in the high country. . . .

When in the high country the medicine maker uses a number of techniques to induce trance states. One of these is the use of "Rhythm Sticks" made of yew wood. These are beaten in constant rhythm to get the person into the mental framework which allows him to be receptive to the spirit from whom he is seeking inspiration. He might concentrate his mind on seeking a vision similar to someone else's past vision. This might be done at a ceremonial site to "pull the ceremony back," but is normally only done in the high country. . . .

SUMMARY AND CONCLUSIONS OF THE ETHNOGRAPHIC COMPONENT

The ethnographic component of this report has demonstrated the existence of an ongoing indigenous religious system, shared by contemporary Northwest California Indian people since before the time of Indian/non-Indian contact. This belief system has been shown to incorporate elements of daily life, ritual practice, geographic locale, and ideas of origin and World Renewal into a conceptualization of sacredness. This concept is foreign in many ways to western European categories of thought. Further, it has been demonstrated that the [place name omitted] (and the G–O Road project area within it) is significant as an integral and indispensable part of Indian religious conceptualization and practice. Specific sites within the project area are necessary to the training and ongoing religious experience of individuals using the area for personal medicine and growth, curing medicine, . . . and medicine affecting the wellbeing of local communities as well as (today) the broader world community. These sites are necessary both as specific sites for specific medicines and as integrated parts of a system of religious belief and practice which correlates ascending degrees of personal power with a geographic hierarchy of power. Individuals progressively use sites of increasing power and this progression is a necessary part of religious growth. Experience at the lower levels of medicine is a prerequisite for the attainment of power at the higher levels. Research has also shown that successful use of the high country is dependent upon and facilitated by certain qualities of the physical environment, the most important of which are privacy, silence, and an undisturbed natural setting. (That such qualities are also held as valuable by present day environmentalists does not in any way detract from the authenticity and strength of traditional Indian belief systems, as some have suggested.)

Ethnographic research has shown that not all contemporary Indian people subscribe to the traditional religious belief system. However, the majority of nonfollowers interviewed in the ethnographic survey felt that the high country should be preserved as a sacred area. The overall findings of the ethnographic survey indicate that a large majority (72.2%) of all those interviewed were against the construction of the Chimney Rock Section of the G–O Road.

Based on the ethnographic findings summarized previously, it is the conclusion of the ethnographic researchers that the construction of the Chimney Rock Section of the G–O Road along any of its alternative routes would cause serious and irreparable damage to the sacred areas which are an integral and necessary part of the belief systems and lifeway of Northwest California Indian peoples. It is, therefore, the recommendation of the ethnographic researchers that the Chimney Rock Section of the G–O Road, along any of its alternate routes (1–9), not be constructed. A more comprehensive presentation of conclusions, together with specific impact analysis and mitigation recommendations, is presented in the final section of the report.

United States on Behalf of the Zuni Tribe of New Mexico v. Earl Platt

ORDER

Carroll, District Judge

The Zuni Indians, as part of their religion, make a regular periodic pilgrimage at the time of the summer solstice, on foot or horseback, from their reservation in northwest New Mexico to the mountain area the tribe calls Kohlu/wala:wa which is located in northeast Arizona. It is believed by the Zuni Indians that Kohlu/wala:wa is their place of origin, the basis for their religious life, and the home of their dead.[1]

There is historical evidence that the Zuni pilgrimage was occurring as early as 1540 A.D. [Hammond, George P. and Agaptito Rey, *Narratives of the Coronado Expedition 1540-1542*, The University of New Mexico Press; Albuquerque; 1940.]

The pilgrimage has been largely uncontested until recent times.

In 1985 defendant, Earl Platt, declared his intention of preventing the Zuni Indians from crossing his land on their pilgrimage. Earl Platt and the estate of Buena Platt (defendant), own or lease from the United States or the state of Arizona land in Apache Country over which the Zuni Indians cross on their pilgrimage to Kohlu/wala:wa. On June 12, 1985, the United States on behalf of the Zuni Tribe instituted this action claiming a prescriptive easement by adverse possession across the Platt land.

The United States also sought a temporary restraining order, which was granted by Judge Copple on June 12, 1985, restraining the defendant from interfering with the Zuni pilgrimage.[2]

On March 3, 1988, the Zuni Tribe was allowed to intervene as plaintiff. The intervenor's complaint, like the original complaint, alleged a right to prescriptive easement but it also bases the Zuni Indians' claim of right-of-way across the land in question on "rights to protection of its property and its free exercise of religion

U.S. on Behalf of the Zuni Tribe v. Platt, 730 F. Supp. 318 (1990).

under the treaty of Guadalupe Hidalgo and upon Public Law 98-408 (98 Stat. 1533)." The issues of whether under international or federal constitutional law the Zuni Tribe have rights to the land crossed on their religious pilgrimage were severed, for purposes of this trial, from the issue of prescriptive rights.

The Plaintiff's claim for a prescriptive easement across the defendant's land was heard at trial on January 3–5, 1990.

FINDINGS OF FACT

The evidence presented at trial shows that the Zuni Indians have gone on their quadrennial pilgrimage, approximately every four years[3] since, at least, the early twentieth century. There was direct evidence presented at trial, in the form of motion picture documentation, of the pilgrimage occurring in 1924. Exhibit 147 "Motion Pictures at Zuni," Indian Notes, Volume One, Number One, January, 1924, The Museum of the American Indian (Heye Foundation). Furthermore, John Niiha, the Zuni Dance priest, testified that he has been on 11 pilgrimages since his first in approximately 1949. Another Zuni religious leader, Mecalite Wytsallaci, the Zuni Rain Priest of the North for the last 39 years, who is ninety-nine years old, testified that he went on a pilgrimage when he was a young man but has not participated in the pilgrimage since he has been the Rain Priest. Wytsallaci's testimony indicates that he participated in a pilgrimage sometime prior to 1940. Since 1976 the Apache County Sheriff's office has set up a road-block, north of St. Johns, on [the highway] at the request of the Zuni Tribe, so as to ensure the safety and privacy of the pilgrims as they cross the highway going to and coming from Kohlu/wala:wa on their pilgrimage.

Eighty Tribe members are selected to participate in the pilgrimage. However, due to age, health and other considerations not all actually go along. The pilgrimage part generally consists of forty to sixty Zuni Indians and twenty to forty horses. The pilgrims walk or ride horses, vehicles are not allowed in the pilgrimage procession. The Zuni pilgrimage begins at the Zuni Reservation, in Northwestern New Mexico, and follows a fairly direct path to Kohlu/wala:wa in Apache County, Arizona. The pilgrimage generally crosses the defendant's land. . . . At this point the pilgrimage splits. One religious clan of the Zuni pilgrims goes north . . . , proceeding off the defendant's land. The other religious clan involved in the pilgrimage proceeds south. . . , proceeding off Platt property.

The two religious groups meet at Kohlu/wala:wa and begin the journey back to the reservation. The return route re-enters the defendant's property. . . at which time the route of egress merges with the route of ingress to Kohlu/wala:wa.[4]

The total trek is 110 miles in length. It takes four days for the pilgrims to travel to Kohlu/wala:wa and return back to the reservation. The pilgrimage crosses approximately 18–20 miles of land owned or leased by the defendant Earl Platt.

The path or route used by the Zuni Indians, on their religious pilgrimage has been consistent and relatively unchanged.[5] The plaintiffs concede that topographical changes may necessarily alter the route. However, man-made obstacles will not cause the Zuni pilgrims to deviate from their customary path. This is evidenced by the fact the pilgrims cut or take down fences in their way.

The pathway used by the pilgrims is approximately fifty feet wide.[6] The Zuni Indians use of the route in question is limited to a path or a place crossed en route to Kohlu/wala:wa. Other than the path itself there are no points or landmarks of religious significance to the Zuni Indians on the defendant's land and the pilgrims do not camp on the defendant's land but they do stop for lunch on Platt land.[7]

The use of the property, by the Zuni Indians, along the pilgrimage route has been open, visible, and known to the community. Several witnesses who have been long-time residents of the St. Johns area, which is in close proximity to the land in question, testified that they knew of the Zuni pilgrimage and that it was generally known throughout the community.

The Zuni Tribe, and the people going on the pilgrimage, believed that they had a right to cross the lands traversed by their established route. There has been no showing that they sought to cross lands under permission or by authority of other persons.

Conclusions of Law

The Arizona statute defining adverse possession provides:

"Adverse possession" means an actual and visible appropriation of land, commenced and continued under a claim of right inconsistent with and hostile to the claim of another.

A.R.S. § 12–521. The Arizona statutes further provide that:

A. A person who has a cause of action for recovery of any lands, tenements or hereditaments from a person having peaceable and adverse possession thereof, cultivating, using and enjoying such property, shall commence an action therefor within ten years after the cause of action accrues, and not afterward.

A.R.S. § 12–526. The Arizona statutes follow the generally held rule that in order for one to acquire right to property purely by adverse possession, such possession must be actual, open and notorious, hostile, under a claim of right, continuous for the statutory period of 10 years, and exclusive. [citations omitted]

The Arizona Courts place the burden of proof on the party claiming the right to use another's land. Once the prima facie elements of prescription are met, the law presumes the use to be under a claim of right and not permissive. The burden of proving permissive use then falls upon the landowner.

The proof necessary to establish a prescriptive easement to use land is not the same as that to establish a claim of title by adverse possession. "[I]t is only the use to which the premises are put which must be shown to be adverse, open and notorious. To the extent that the use is established, it, of course, is hostile to the title of the servient [i.e., burdened] estate." Therefore, although the plaintiffs in this case must prove all the elements essential to title by prescription,[8] their burden of proof must be measured in terms of the right to the use they claim, i.e., a very limited periodic use.

The Zuni tribe has had actual possession of the route used for the religious pilgrimage for a short period of time every four years. They have had actual possession of the land in the sense that they have not recognized any other claim to the land at the time of the pilgrimage, as evidenced by their lack of deviation from the established route and disregard for fences or any other man-made obstacle that blocks their course of travel. This Court also finds that the Zuni Tribe continually used a portion of the defendant's land for a short period of time every four years at least since 1924 and very probably for a period of time spanning many hundreds of years prior to that year.

Therefore, the plaintiffs have established the "actual" and "continuous" possession elements of their claim for adverse possession. Furthermore this "actual" possession has been continuous for over ten years which is required for a claim of a prescriptive right. . . .

The Zuni Tribe has not attempted to hide their pilgrimage or the route they were taking, although they do regard it as a personal and private activity. It was known generally throughout the community that the Zuni Indians took a pilgrimage every few years. It was also common knowledge in the community, generally, what route or over which lands the pilgrimage took place. Mrs. Hinkson, a resident of the St. John's area since 1938 and an owner of a ranch which the Zuni Indians cross on their pilgrimage, testified it was generally understood that the Zuni Tribe had set a precedent of crossing the land of ranchers that could not be changed even if owners of the land objected to such crossings or use of their property. The Zuni tribe also cut, tore down or placed gates in, fences on the property owned or leased by defendant and others.

This court draws the reasonable inference, from all the facts and circumstances, that Earl Platt, the defendant in this case, was aware that a pilgrimage occurred, that it occurred approximately every four years and that the pilgrimage went across his property.[9]

Consequently, the Zuni Tribe's open and notorious use of Platt land and the inference that Earl Platt knew of such use satisfies and/or obviates the "open and notorious" element of an adverse possession.

It is contended by the plaintiffs that the Zuni's use of the Platt lands also fulfills the requirement of the "hostile" and "claim of right" elements of adverse possession. "Hostile" as applied to possession of realty does not connote ill will or evil intent, but merely a showing that the one in possession of the land claims exclusive rights thereto and denied by word or act the owner's title. Similarly a "claim of right" is:

> [N]othing more than the intention of the party in possession to appropriate and use the land as his own to the exclusion of others irrespective of any semblance or shadow of actual title or right.

The record reflects, as discussed earlier, the Zuni pilgrims, at the time of their pilgrimage, claim exclusive right to the path they cross to Kohlu/wala:wa. The claim of right to temporary and periodic use of the defendant's land is evidenced by the cutting or pulling down of fences and the lack of deviation from the route. In recent years the Zuni Indians, with the aid of the Bureau of Land Management, placed gates in fences which impeded the pilgrimage route of the Zuni Indians.[10] The use, by the pilgrims, of the defendant's land is "hostile" to Earl Platt's title. Also there was no evidence presented at trial which would indicate that the Zuni tribe sought permission to cross the land of Earl Platt. The evidence clearly illustrated that the Zuni Indians never sought permission to cross lands on their pilgrimage but rather it was believed said crossing was a matter of right.

The record leaves no doubt that the "hostile" and "claim of right" elements of adverse possession has been satisfied by the plaintiffs.

Insofar as the exclusivity of possession is required, in the context of the claim asserted here, it is reasonable to conclude that if people are occupying a tract of land at a particular time, another person or other people cannot simultaneously occupy the same space. Therefore, the Zunis participating in the quadrennial pilgrimage have exclusive possession of the land upon which they cross en route to Kohlu/wala:wa when they are crossing that land.

The Zuni Indians' use and possession of the Platt land has been actual, open and notorious, continuous and uninterrupted for at least 65 years and under a claim of right. Such use was known by the surrounding community.

It is clear from the record that the plaintiffs have established that the Zuni Indians meet the standards of adverse possession, set forth in A.R.S. ¶ 12–521 and the applicable case law for the purposes of the limited use sought. The Zuni Tribe is entitled to a prescriptive easement over the land of the defendant for the purposes of their quadrennial pilgrimage. The defendant presented no evidence and has not otherwise proven that the Zuni Indians' use of the land in question was permissive or otherwise. . . .

IT IS ORDERED that the Zuni Tribe is granted an easement over the land owned by Earl Platt and the estate of Buena Platt, for 25 feet in either direction, of the route established by the October 27, 1987 Bureau of Land Management Survey, Exhibit 307.3, for the purposes of ingress to and egress from Kohlu/wala:wa by no more than 60 persons on foot or horseback.

IT IS FURTHER ORDERED that the Zuni Tribe shall use gates along the pilgrimage route already in existence and shall not construct gates in or alter existing fence lines without first obtaining leave of this Court.

IT IS FURTHER ORDERED the easement granted by this Court is limited to a 2 day period (one day each direction), during the summer solstice, once every four years to commence in 1993 and to continue on at four year intervals.

IT IS FURTHER ORDERED that the rights granted by this easement do not include the right to use defendant's water sources, nor does it include the right to light fires on the lands of the defendant.

IT IS FURTHER ORDERED that the Zuni Indian Tribe will be liable for any damage that occurs on defendant's property that is a result of the pilgrimage.

IT IS FURTHER ORDERED that the Zuni Tribe notify the defendant when the pilgrimage is going to occur at least 14 days prior to its commencement.

NOTES

1. These lands were lost to the Zuni Tribe as a result of an executive order in 1877, however, 1984 legislation, Public Law 98-409 § 4 (98 Stat. 1533), allowed the Tribe to acquire lands in Arizona for religious purposes. The legislation also allowed the Zuni Indians to acquire a permanent right of ingress and egress to Kohlu/wala:wa for traditional religious pilgrimages and ceremonies. As a part of the purchase of Kohlu/wala:wa, from Seven Springs Ranch Inc. the Zuni Tribe was granted a right to ingress and egress to the mountain connecting with an existing roadway from Hunt, Arizona. Exhibit 430, paragraph 6 (d). This point of access is on the west side of the mountain and would not enable the pilgrimage to have access to the area in the traditional manner.

2. Another Temporary Restraining Order was entered on June 12, 1989 to restrain the defendant from interfering with the pilgrimage which was to take place on June 21–24, 1989.

3. In 1985 the pilgrimage was conducted in the fifth year instead of the fourth, 1984, because, as the testimony indicates, the Zunis did not want to jeopardize legislation pending in Congress whereby the Zuni Tribe could purchase Kohlu/wala:wa to be held in trust by the United States for the tribe.

4. The Route of the Zuni Pilgrimage is most accurately portrayed by exhibits 307.3 and 308.

5. Expert witness Dr. Hart testified that the BLM survey, exhibit 397.3, was the most accurate description of the Zuni pilgrimage route.

6. Mr. Niiha stated that the pathway used by the Zuni pilgrims was about the width of the courtroom which is approximately 50 feet wide.

7. There are a number of sites with religious significance to the Zuni Indians along the pilgrimage route east of the defendant's land.

8. LaRue, 66 Ariz. at 303, 187 P. 2d 642 (1947).

9. The record shows that Earl Platt has owned or leased the property in question since the early 1940s.

10. This was done without permission of the owners of the lands upon which these fences were located.

The Sacred Trail to Zuni Heaven: A Study in the Law of Prescriptive Easements

Hank Meshorer

Someone once said that all cases are truly unique. I don't know if that is true, but I am certain that the litigation that led to the recognition of the right of the Zuni Tribe to conduct its quadrennial pilgrimage from its reservation in New Mexico to *Kohlu/wala:wa*, commonly known as "Zuni Heaven," in Arizona and return was, all things considered, a truly special case. In the spirit of John Nichols's 1974 novel *The Milagro Beanfield War*,[1] the controversy was fraught with long-standing grudges based partly on history and a clash of cultures, but, if the truth is known, more on personality than anything else. Not that the controversy wasn't taken seriously because it was, and with deadly intensity. Quite simply, to the parties nothing less than a whole way of life was at stake. And with such high stakes no means of battle was considered inappropriate.

The United States Department of Justice initially heard of the matter in early June 1985, when the Secretary of the Interior first requested that the federal government, in its capacity as trustee for the Zuni Tribe, seek an immediate restraining order to prevent one Earl Platt, a large landowner in northeast Arizona, from interfering with a planned Zuni pilgrimage across his lands. Between 1876 and 1946 Zuni had lost control of that portion of their aboriginal territory on which Platt's ranch was located, and he had vowed to stop the Zunis from entering and "trespassing" on his property. The Zunis had expressed an equal intention of continuing their little-known but centuries-old quadrennial pilgrimage. To the Zunis, an interruption of their sacred trek was simply incomprehensible, a thought so foreign to their psyches that the possibility of it even occurring was beyond verbalization.

Nor were the Zunis particularly comfortable with asking the federal government for its assistance. Differences between the two had existed for several years. First, a long-standing suit brought by the Zunis against the United States,

Zuni Tribe of New Mexico v. United States,* alleging a taking of certain tribal ancestral lands was then currently under way. Although the Claims Court suit sought money damages for all of those lands allegedly taken from the Zunis, which claim geographically encompassed both Zuni Heaven as well as the sacred trail to and from the reservation, the tribe had fortuitously decided prior to the initiation of the Claims Court suit specifically to exclude from their claim the lands immediately surrounding Zuni Heaven as well as by inference the quadrennial access. To both the Zunis and the United States, then, a claim, consistent with both parties' positions in the Claims Court, could now be made together for the sacred trail to Zuni Heaven. Nevertheless, at the outset both the tribe and the United States remained wary not only of Earl Platt but also of each other.

Second, the Zunis were also undergoing the last, delicate stages in the final acquisition of both the fee title to Zuni Heaven and a permanent quadrennial easement for the sacred trail. Pursuant to an act of August 28, 1984, to convey certain lands to the Zuni for religious purposes, the Secretary of the Interior had been directed "to immediately acquire by voluntary agreement the permanent right of ingress and egress to (Zuni Heaven) for the limited purpose of allowing the Zuni Indians to continue to use said lands for traditional religious pilgrimages and ceremonials."[2] Now both the Zunis and the United States were faced with one large and angry landowner who was absolutely refusing even to allow the Zunis on his lands, let alone entertain a "voluntary" acquisition of the sacred trail. Moreover, and perhaps most significantly, the landowner was hinting darkly of a possible violation of his constitutional rights under the First Amendment to the Constitution,[3] which charge might well have put in jeopardy the entire congressional scheme for the Zuni reacquisition of Zuni Heaven and the sacred trail.

Third, more or less contemporaneous with these events, the federal courts were also considering whether the First Amendment's Free Exercise Clause allowed certain tribes to halt the construction of a government road through an admittedly sacred former Indian area.[4] Very much on the minds of both the Zunis and the United States were the sentiments later articulated by the Supreme Court when it stated, "[Even though] the road-building projects at issue . . . could have devastating effects on traditional Indian religious practices . . . [and] . . . would virtually destroy the Indians ability to practice their religion, . . . the Constitution simply does not provide a principle that could justify upholding" the tribe's claim of a "religious servitude" over the subject lands.[5]

Simply stated, a claim based on the purely religious right to use of the sacred trail seemed at best dubious and most certainly extremely problematic. Any claim based on a First Amendment basis was fraught with danger.[6] But to the Zunis, the whole idea of the pilgrimage was a fulfillment of a religious obligation. "Why," they asked, "could they not practice their religion free from interference on land they considered always to be their own?" "How," the landowner Earl Platt must have been asking at the same time, "can the government impose these Indian religious

---

**Zuni Tribe of New Mexico v. United States,* 12 Cl. Ct. 607 (1987).

practices on me by forcing me to accommodate their pilgrimage across my lands? Isn't that a violation of my First Amendment rights?" Much on the minds of the government prosecutors was the fact that most, if not all, of the evidence to be offered by the Zunis would by definition reflect the very essence of the pilgrimage as very much a religious endeavor. On the eve of filing suit against Earl Platt, the shadow of *Lyng** indeed hung heavy on the parties. Perhaps mercifully, the Justice Department was not given much time to consider these imponderables because the case was thrust suddenly on it on the eve of the quadrennial pilgrimage of 1985. But let me first back up and set the legal landscape.

STATEMENT OF FACTS

For centuries approximately sixty Zuni religious priests had been making a religious pilgrimage from their central village in New Mexico along a sacred path learned by memory to an equally sacred area in northeast Arizona known as *Kohlu/wala:wa*, or "Zuni Heaven." The trek occurred once every four years at the time of the summer solstice and covered approximately 110 miles over a period of four days. The pilgrims, traveling by foot and horseback, were first witnessed by Spanish conquistador Francisco Vásquez de Coronado in 1540.

In 1985, the defendant, Earl Platt, one of the intervening landowners, challenged the right of the Zunis to cross his lands. To avoid the chance of violence (in 1882 the Zunis had burned out the last rancher to challenge their quadrennial right of passage), the United States secured a temporary restraining order on June 12, 1985, enjoining the defendant from interfering with that pilgrimage. The government also brought suit (*United States v. Earl Platt*)[†] on that date seeking to establish a prescriptive easement under Arizona law that would afford the Zunis the right of ingress and egress on the subject lands once every four years for the limited purpose of traveling from their reservation to *Kohlu/wala:wa* and return.[7]

In what proved to be a most fortuitous strategic move, the government's pleadings were particularly drawn to avoid the obvious difficulties that would inure from any (favorable or otherwise) decision based on a First Amendment right either to support the Zunis in their claim or to support the defendant in his oppositions.[8] Specifically, the government's suit purposely sought only to establish that the Zunis had satisfied the requisite elements necessary to establish a prescriptive easement under Arizona law solely to allow the tribe to cross Earl Platt's lands once every four years. No mention was made of any First Amendment–based privilege the Zunis may have retained to cross such lands. Rather, the only legally cognizable right sought was the distinctly nonreligious claim under state property law for an easement to enter on, cross over, and return through certain lands once every four years. The admittedly religious use of the claimed easement was thus forever rendered irrelevant to the court's limited inquiry.

Lyng v. Northwest Indian Cemetery Protective Assocation, 485 U.S. 439 (1988).

†*U.S. v. Platt, supra* page XX.

For the next four years the defendant, a former state senator and county attorney and one of the largest landowners in Arizona (reportedly owning or controlling approximately 400,000 acres), tenaciously opposed the prosecution of this case. Virtually every motion, discovery request, or other matter was bitterly resisted by the defendant. Meanwhile, the next quadrennial pilgrimage was coming due, and a second temporary restraining order was granted on May 26, 1989, for the then-impending June quadrennial trek across Earl Platt's lands. During that pilgrimage, the defendant, in violation of the second restraining order, interfered with the pilgrimage by, among other things, driving his truck through the pilgrimage and allegedly (but not proven at trial) hitting a horse and rider, cursing the pilgrims, and denying them access to water. After an August 31, 1989, hearing, the court held the defendant in civil contempt of court and fined him $5,000.

Over the centuries the Zuni pilgrimage had never been curtailed. Even with the sanctions of a civil contempt order, the entire Zuni nation was in a state of shock and anger because of the defendant's desecration of its ancient ceremonial pilgrimage. Members of the Bow Priests, who are charged with securing the safety of the religious beliefs of the tribe, along with a large contingent of the Zunis, attended the entire trial. For his part, Earl Platt was equally intent on blocking the Zunis from crossing his lands. Accompanying Platt were several of his ranch hands as well as his two sons, both of whom are hardened Arizona trial attorneys. The U.S. Marshal's Office was alerted to the possibility of open hostilities. It was in this charged atmosphere that the trial began in Phoenix on January 3, 1990.

The presentation of the government's evidence was made doubly difficult by virtue of the fact that the quadrennial pilgrimage had hitherto been a secretive activity unknown to most of the Anglo community. During the trial, the extensive preparation by the government's expert witnesses led to an avalanche of archaeological, ethnohistorical, and contemporaneous testimony to support the contention that the Zunis had in fact traveled to *Kohlu/wala:wa* under a claim of right once every four years over the same route, which route had been memorized by rote and passed on from one generation to another through song and prayer. Although the Zunis themselves were extremely reluctant to discuss the pilgrimage with any outsiders, the United States, through the services of its main expert witness, E. Richard Hart, was able to elicit invaluable testimony through the use of an interpreter of several elderly Zunis who could remember participating in numerous pilgrimages over the years. In addition, and again through the use of Hart, the government prosecutor was able to find several non-Indian local inhabitants, including Stewart Udall, the former Secretary of the Interior, who stepped forward to testify on behalf of the Zunis.

LESSONS LEARNED

What have we learned? The first lesson is obvious: An aboriginal property right can be successfully established under state laws of prescription even when that usage is deemed at first blush rather minimal or even scarcely visible. Care should be taken, however, before expanding this rather particularized event into a generalized trend in Indian law. Three major factors unique to this case helped lead to its successful result.

The first distinguishing factor was the Zuni Tribe. An incredible sagacity of purpose, which remained crystallized throughout these proceedings despite a myriad of political, legal, and economic distractions, kept the tribe focused on maintaining its consistency of approach to the one true task at hand: to have recognized its unfettered title to Zuni Heaven and the sacred trail. Throughout the decade of proceedings at the Claims Court, during a similarly long period of congressional machinations, and throughout the five-year tumultuous litigation with Earl Platt, the Zunis were never distracted. I believe that a steadfast clarity of purpose derived from their cultural maturity uniquely guided the Zunis in their quest. How else can one explain the Zunis' near-clairvoyant approach in what for them was the easy decision to exclude, nearly ten years *before* the *Platt* litigation, both Zuni Heaven and the sacred trail from their Claims Court litigation? That is, to refuse consciously to accept monies for these lands being taken from them simply because in their psyche these lands had never left their possession. Or their courage and faith in our system of jurisprudence to reveal through statement and testimony certain aspects of their hitherto near-secret quadrennial pilgrimage in what to them was a foreign court of law? Or their resolve to stay the course despite Earl Platt's provocations in attempting to disrupt their quadrennial trek in both 1985 and 1989? . . .

Second, throughout these proceedings the Zunis had been supported extremely well by their experts. Unique to this case, I can safely say that in my twenty-five-odd years of litigation I have never seen a cadre of more knowledgeable and dedicated consultants as I had the pleasure of associating with in the Platt litigation. Their preparation, intensity, and integrity well-served the Zunis and their cause. With the secretive nature of the pilgrimage itself, let alone the natural reticence of the Zunis to testify in mind, the totality and clarity of evidence presented to me by these experts made my job infinitely easier. Without their help, this case may well have been decided otherwise. Indeed, the court as much agreed when it ruled in favor of virtually every major factual inference asserted by the tribe during the trial.

Third, let's face it: Earl Platt never got the point. Aside from other missed opportunities, Platt never fully realized the inherent weakness of the government's claim to a prescriptive easement based on such a minimal use of his vast and unenclosed land. Rather than focusing on a pointed demand that the Zunis first and foremost prove his "actual knowledge" of their quadrennial trek, he chose, for whatever reason, to avail himself of other less forceful legal arguments, including an attempt to stop single-handedly the pilgrimages of both 1985 and 1989, which led ultimately to the court finding him in contempt. Such tactics may appear to work in the movies, but they are not the most effective means to prevail in federal court. As noted earlier, if the defendant had steadfastly argued, despite the evidence offered by the government to the contrary, for a showing of "actual knowledge" on the part of the landowner, perhaps the court might have been more sympathetic to his cause.

Finally, a second lesson that can be taken from this case is the possibility that in other, similar situations where a long-standing native religious practice requires the crossing of non-Indian lands, a successful claim for a prescriptive easement narrowly drawn to conform to the actual Indian religious needs may be possible without regard to First Amendment problems. As in the Zuni situation, even though most, if not all, of the evidence would be of religious orientation, the specific activity, that is the actual physical *use* of the land (walking across, stopping and praying at certain shrines, camping overnight, lighting ceremonial fires, ritually bathing at designated locations, etc.) would not be presented to the court as a legally cognizable religious right but as mere indicia of the fulfillment of the requirements for a prescriptive easement. . . .

NOTES

1. John Nichols, *The Milagro Beanfield War* (New York, N.Y.: Random House, 1974).

2. 98 Stat. 1533 (1984), sec. 4; emphasis added.

3. The first clause of the First Amendment to the Constitution states that "Congress shall make no law respecting an establishment of religion." In essence, the landowner was arguing that by enactment of Public Law 98-408, which would provide the Zunis with a property right across his lands for a religious purpose, Congress had violated this portion of the First Amendment by, in effect, establishing a religion.

4. The Free Exercise Clause of the First Amendment to the Constitution provides that "Congress shall make no law . . . prohibiting the free exercise (of religion)." See *Northwest Indian Cemetery Ass'n v. Peterson*, 565 F. Supp 586 (1883), *aff'd* in part 795 F. 2d 688 (9th Cir. 1986) reversed *sub nom. Lyng v. Northwest Indian Cemetery Protective Ass'n*, 485 U.S. 439 (1988).

5. *Lyng*, 485 U.S. at p. 439.

6. See ibid.

7. Civ. No. 85-1478 USDC, Ariz. (1985). As noted earlier, in a previous suit, *Zuni Tribe v. United States*, the tribe itself had sued the United States for money damages based, in part, on the extinguishment of its aboriginal title to an area that included the lands on which the easement was located. During the Claims Court litigation, however, the tribe specifically excluded from its claim the present-day Zuni Reservation in New Mexico as well as the lands immediately surrounding Zuni Heaven. Access once every four years between the two parcels was also impliedly excluded, and the Zunis so acknowledged throughout both the Claims Court and the instant litigation. The Zunis simply had never asserted that their quadrennial right of access was ever taken from them. The position advanced by the United States on behalf of the Zunis in the Platt suit was based on the particular elements of a prescriptive easement under state law and was therefore not in conflict with the government's stance vis-à-vis the tribe in the claims suit.

8. See, e.g., *Lyng*, supra.

Achieving True Interpretation

Edmund J. Ladd

I was appointed interpreter by the Zuni Tribal Council, who consulted closely with Zuni's claims attorneys: Stephen G. Boyden, assisted by John Boyden and Richard Hill. They were having a problem getting an interpreter who was fluent both in English and the Zuni language, and the Boydens recommended that the council select me, subject to tribal law and tribal authentication by Governor Lewis. Then I had to be accepted by the Justice Department as well—I had to be acceptable to both sides. When the case finally went to court, I went through a process of qualification, and both sides and the judge had to agree that they thought I would do an objective and fair job.

I had already done some work for the tribe working to recover the Zuni war gods (*Ahayu:da*) from the Smithsonian and from other organizations. So it wasn't anything that was brand new as far as integrity was concerned, except that it was more strenuous because of the exactness of the terminology that had to be used to translate. I had to take all possible care in my interpreting and translating so that the court heard both sides of the story—objective and straight. With the war gods, the work was strictly interpreting and strictly translating what the tribal elders had to say to the Board of Trustees of the Denver Art Museum and the Board of Trustees of the Smithsonian Institution. So the land claim work wasn't anything that was brand new as far as the process was concerned, but it was a project that was more frightening and more strenuous simply because of the accuracy of terminology that was required. I had to be very careful not to inadvertently put words into the mouths of the elders.

The depositions were probably harder to translate and interpret, because the attorneys had to rephrase and reread questions that were difficult to understand. In translation I had to put the questions into the proper context and make sure that the elders were given enough time to answer the questions that were being asked. Interpretation of the phrasing was necessary so that the elders could understand

From "Achieving True Interpretation" by Edmund J. Ladd, in *Zuni and the Courts: A Struggle for Sovereign Land Rights*, edited by E. Richard Hart. Lawrence, Kan.: University of Kansas Press. © 1995 by the University of Kansas Press.

the questions being put them. Those depositions are some of the most remarkable ethnological documents about Zuni that have ever been created for any purpose.

There are a whole host of words in Zuni that really have no equivalency in English. So in those cases you have to dig for the answers, dig for the interpreting and translating with the proper phrasing. It was probably the most difficult thing that I've ever had to do. I have basic knowledge of the Zuni religion system, but I don't have much of the proprietary knowledge as far as the esoteric religious ceremonies are concerned. For instance, I wouldn't have access to special knowledge of the *Koyemshis* ("Mudheads"). The priests are concerned with the origin and archaic place—names and esoteric knowledge that's only privileged to them. There I was with my basic knowledge trying to interpret to the Anglo world and the lawyers the difference between the Zuni language and the pressures of knowing and not knowing what the esoteric knowledge really meant. It was a very difficult process.

So there were areas of, not complete secrecy, but guarded statements that were made for the sake of the lawyers and the sake of the law, but the religious leaders' statements were very carefully composed. They would tell me, in essence, "This is not really for their [the outside world's] knowledge, but we still want to make it clear that they understand what our position is going to be." So I was put in a very tenuous and very difficult position of trying to know what to say at that point to keep it from being my words instead of theirs. It was very difficult. It was no simple thing that I had to do there.

There is a difference between interpretation and translation. Straight translation can be very inaccurate. Interpretation involves understanding vernacular in two languages. Take the simple phrase, "Do you work?" or "Are you employed?" You have to be careful to interpret it correctly. By saying in the Zuni language, "Do you work?" the answer would more than likely be "No," because Zunis consider that phrase to refer to a "regular job," like an eight-to-five job. So that would be a mistranslation in terms of the interpretive aspect of the culture itself. So you have to say, "Are you employed?" or "How do you feed yourself and your children?" That's interpretive. So that's why the simple phrase of "Do you work?" becomes a problem of how you say it to the person so that he realizes the answer that is being requested, that is, "How do you make a living?" It's just like trying to juggle four balls instead of three balls. The three balls are relatively easy, but to get a fourth ball in it gets more complicated because there is more movement. The way the lawyer asks the question and the way you want to phrase it so that you get the response for the lawyer that he wants, you're looking for, and the way you feel he should be responding to in terms of the English that you know is right. When the lawyer said, "Do you work? Are you employed?" the response will be, "Well, no, I am not employed, but I have an income from my jewelry business."

We completed two depositions a day and did thirty of them with Zuni elders as a part of Docket 161-79L, a total of about two or three weeks. Some were easy to do, and some were most difficult because of the way the questions were phrased by the lawyers. The phrasing of the question was as important as eliciting the right response in terms of interpreting the request for information. I knew all of the deponents from past years, and they knew who I was, so I had talked to them before, and I knew what their positions were in the community and what kind of religious background they had. So it wasn't like we were strangers. Knowing who I was, they always greeted me as "younger brother." So it was a rather easy task in that regard, in that I knew most of them intimately and some of them distantly, but still I could speak with them on their terms.

The trial took more than two weeks, and it was pressurized. We had time to be with each other during the evenings and during the trial period, which was kind of difficult because I had to keep myself as much detached from them as I was detached for the opposing parties. Consequently, it was a strain, but knowing the situation, they were very helpful; they would try not to talk about the case, try and not talk about things they were going to discuss at the trial in front of the lawyers, in front of the judge. So it was a strain for the two weeks we were there, but once it was over it was a great relief and very relaxing.

As a Zuni I naturally wanted to see the Zunis win this case, but on the other hand I had to be a strictly impartial translator. It was probably one of the more difficult transitions that one could make. When the opposing lawyers were asking questions, I had to remember that they were asking their questions in just the same way as our lawyers were asking our opponents. I tried to completely neutralize myself to the point where I was just like a sieve, with information coming in one side and going out the other side and coming back from the tribe. The phrasing of the questions and the interpretation and the translation were most difficult because just through simple voice inflection I could get a different answer, different response. So it was one of the more strenuous exercises of self-control, not to over interpret, not to over translate.

There were many instances that provided special difficulties in translation. For example, I remember one episode when I couldn't get the point across of what the lawyer was trying to say. The question was something to the effect that, "When did the Zunis become less hostile?" There is no word for "hostile" and there is no word for "less." So I was trying to interpret around that concept of "When did the Zunis become less hostile?" It became very difficult, and the response was coming back in the wrong context because I would say something like, "When did the time of goodness and nonwarfare begin?" And the concept of time would become so important because Zunis don't recognize time in terms of years. They say in Zuni, "a long time ago." I would say in Zuni, "What year were you born?" It was difficult to say, "What year?" It was difficult to achieve phrasing that would elicit the right concepts in terms of time—but the time elements were so critical [to the litigation]. It was very difficult to get through because in Zuni there is "now," "today," "tomorrow," and past tense, "very far in the past," and "extremely far" in the past tense. All are recognized as time markers, but they're not years. They don't say, "In 1984, 1968, 1970...," so I had to interpolate around those figures. I would ask in Zuni, using a direct translation, "What year were you born?" And they would say, "Well, I don't know because it was springtime."

There were also moments with some humor. Governor Lewis gave his answers in English. He was asked what Kiva group he belonged to. He belongs to the *Muhekwe*, the "Manure Clan," but when asked for an English equivalent his response was (with a straight face, too) that he was a member of the "Soil Restoration Clan." At first I was perplexed, and then all of a sudden, just like a light bulb, it dawned on me what he was saying.

It has really been a great victory for Zuni to finally win the land claim case. I feel very satisfied. It's been one of the highlights of my career as an anthropologist and archaeologist. My work with the tribe to successfully obtain the *Kolhu/wala:wa* easement was also a highlight of my career as interpreter. It was the hardest thing to try to be neutral and not phrase anything in a favorable way or a nonfavorable way for either us or the opponents. For this reason, especially, I had a feeling of accomplishment that I was responsible for something very important.

When we finally got to the Zuni trial and the Zuni witnesses were ready to enter the Utah Supreme Court Chambers where the trial was held, three of the religious leaders went ahead of the rest, leading the way into the chambers for the first time. They were performing a War Ceremony of the Galaxy Society. No one was allowed to get ahead of them or cross their paths. The Zunis all stayed behind them, and it was done so tactfully that no non-Indians got in front of them either. And each of them was reciting all the appropriate prayers as they went along. There's a phrase that is used that hits the heart of the people that you are fighting against, and they used this phrase. It was used by the Zuni religious leaders to put themselves in an advantageous frame of mind, a frame of reference for what they were about to undergo. The prayers and ceremony provide stamina, perseverance, proficiency at what you're supposed to be doing, and bravery. So we all got behind him, and we walked very slowly up there, and nobody said anything. Nobody said a word until we got inside and then for a few more moments. That was one of the most awesome things because I'd only heard of these things before, and then I was actually a part of them.

BOOKS CITED

Alexie, Sherman. *The Lone Ranger and Tonto Fistfight in Heaven*. New York, N.Y.: Atlantic Monthly Press, 1993.

_____. *Reservation Blues*. New York, N.Y.: Atlantic Monthly Press, 1995.

American Indian and the Problem of History, The. Edited by Clavin Martin. New York, N.Y.: Oxford University Press, 1987.

Anaya, James S. *Indigenous Peoples in International Law*. New York, N.Y.: Oxford University Press, 1996.

Ancient Traditions: Shamanism in Central Asia and the Americas. Edited by Gary Seaman and Jane S. Day. Niwot, Colo.: University Press of Colorado; Denver, Colo.: Denver Museum of Natural History in Cooperation with Ethnographics Press, Center for Visual Anthropology, University of Southern California, 1994.

Bones, Bodies, Behavior: Essays on Biological Anthropology. Edited by George W. Stocking. Vol. 5 of *History of Anthropology*. Madison, Wis.: University of Wisconsin Press, 1988.

Borah, Woodrow. *Justice by Insurance: The General Indian Court of Mexico and the Legal Aides of the Half-Real*. Berkeley, Calif.: University of California Press, 1983.

Brave Bird, Mary (formerly Mary Crow Dog), and Richard Erdoes. *Ohitika Woman*. New York, N.Y.: Grove Press, 1993.

Brito, Silvester J. *The Way of a Peyote Roadman*. New York, N.Y.: Peter Lang., 1989.

Brodeur, Paul. *Resititution: The Land Claims of the Mashpee, Passamaquoddy, and Penobscot Indians of New England*. Boston, Mass.: Northeastern University Press, 1985.

Brown, Dee Alexander. *Bury My Heart at Wounded Knee: An Indian History of the American West*. New York, N.Y.: Bantam Books, 1972.

Burton, Jeffrey. *Indian Territory and the United States, 1866–1906: Courts, Government and the Movement for Oklahoma Statehood*. Norman, Okla.: University of Oklahoma Press, 1995.

Campisi, Jack. *The Mashpee Indians: Tribe on Trial*. Syracuse, N.Y.: Syracuse University Press, 1991.

Canby, William C. *American Indian Law in a Nutshell*. St. Paul, Minn.: West Publishing Co., 1981.

Carr, A. A. *Eye Killers*. Norman, Okla.: University of Oklahoma Press, 1995.

Clark, Blue. *Lone Wolf v. Hitchcock: Treaty Rights and Indian Law at the End of the Nineteenth Century*. Lincoln, Neb.: University of Nebraska Press, 1994.

Clifford, James. *The Predicament of Culture: Twentieth-Century Ethnography, Literature and Art*. Cambridge, Mass.: Harvard University Press, 1988.

Clinton, Robert N., Nell Jessup Newton, and Monroe E. Price. *American Indian Law*. 3rd ed. Charlottesville, Vir.: Michie/Bobbs-Merrill, 1991.

Combs, George. *A System of Phrenology*. Edinburgh, ed. New York, N.Y.: William H. Colyer, 1983.

Commissioners of Indian Affairs, 1824–1977, The. Edited by Robert M. Kvasnicka, and Herman J. Viola. Lincoln, Neb.: University of Nebraska Press, 1979.

Crow Dog, Mary, and Richard Erdoes. *Lakota Woman*. New York, N.Y.: Grove Weidenfeld, 1990.

Deloria, Vine, Jr., and Clifford M. Lytle. *American Indians, American Justice*. Austin, Tex.: University of Texas Press, 1983.

Deloria, Vine, Jr. *God Is Red: A Native View of Religion*. Updated 2nd ed. Golden, Colo.: Fulcrum Pub., 1994.

_____. *Custer Died For Your Sins: An Indian Manifesto*. Norman, Okla.: University of Oklahoma Press, 1988.

Destruction of California Indians: A Collection of Documents from the Period 1847 to 1865 in Which are Described Some of the Things That Happened to Some of the Indians of California, The. Edited by Robert Heizer. Lincoln, Neb.: University of Nebraska Press, 1993.

Documents of United States Indian Policy. Edited by Frances Paul Prucha. 2d ed, expanded. Lincoln, Neb.: University of Nebraska Press, 1990.

DuBoff, Leonard D., and Sally Holt Caplan. *The Deskbook of Art Law*. 2d ed. Dobbs Ferry, N.Y.: Oceana Publications, 1993.

Duran, Eduardo. *Transforming the Soul Wound: A Theoretical/Clinical Approach to the American Indian Psychology*. Berkeley, Calif.: Folklore Institute, 1990.

Felix S. Cohen's *Handbook of Federal Indian Law*. Edited by Rennard Strickland et al. Charlottesville, Vir.: Michie/Bobbs-Merrill, 1982.

Finnegan, Ruth H. *Oral Traditions and the Verbal Arts: A Guide to Research Practices*. New York, N.Y. : Routledge, 1992.

Flesh of the Gods: The Ritual Use of Hallucinogens. Edited by Peter T. Furst. New York, N.Y.: Praeger Publishers, 1972.

Gamwell, Lynn, and Nancy Tomes. *Madness in America: Cultural and Medical Perceptions of Mental Illness Before 1914*. Ithaca, N.Y.: Cornell University Press; Binghamton, N.Y.: Binghamton University Art Museum, 1995.

Great Documents in American Indian History. Edited by Wayne Moquin, and Charles Van Doren. New York, N.Y.: Da Capo Press, 1995.

Green, Rayna. *Native American Women: A Contextual Bibliography*. Bloomington, Ind.: Indiana University Press, 1983.

_____. *Women in American Indian Society*. New York, N.Y.: Chelsea House, 1992.

Hale, Janet Campbell. *The Jailing of Cecelia Capture*. Albuquerque, N.M.: University of New Mexico Press, 1985.

_____. *Bloodlines: Odyssey of a Native Daughter*. New York, N.Y.: Random House, 1993.

Halifax, Joan. *Shamanic Voices: A Survey of Visionary Narratives*. New York, N.Y.: Penguin Books, 1979.

Handbook of American Indian Religious Freedom. Edited by Christopher Vecsey. New York, N.Y.: Crossroad, 1991.

Harper, Kenn. *Give Me My Father's Body: The Life of Minik, The New York Eskimo*. Frobisher Bay, N.W.T.: Blacklead Books, 1986.

Harr, Jonathan. *A Civil Action*. New York, N.Y.: Random House, 1995.

Harring, Sidney L. *Crow Dog's Case: American Indian Sovereignty, Tribal Law, and United States Law in the Nineteenth Century*. New York, N.Y.: Cambridge University Press, 1994.

History of the Indians of Shasta County, The. Edited by Dottie Smith. Redding, Calif.: CT Publishing Company, 1995.

Hutchins, Francis G. *Mashpee: The Story of Cape Cod's Indian Town*. West Franklin, N.H.: Amarta Press, 1979.

Indian Tribal Claims, Decided in the Court of Claims of the United States, Briefed and Compiled to June 30, 1947. Compiled by Elbert B. Smith in 1947. Washington, D.C.: University Publications of America, 1976.

Invented Indian: Cultural Fictions and Government Policies, The. Edited by James Clifton. New Brunswick, N.J.: Transaction Publishers, 1990.

Ishi, the Last Yahi: A Documentary History. Edited by Robert F. Heizer, and Theodora Kroeber. Berkeley, Calif.: University of California Press, 1979.

Irredeemable America: The Indian's Estate and Land Claims. Edited by Imre Sutton et al. Albuquerque, N.M.: University of New Mexico Press, 1985.

Joe, Rita. *Song of Rita Joe: Autobiography of a Mi 'Kmaq Poet*. Lincoln, Neb.: University of Nebraska Press, 1996.

Josephy, Alvin M. *Now that the Buffalo's Gone: A Study of Today's American Indians*. New York, N.Y.: Knopf, 1982.

Kamenetz, Rodger. *The Jew in the Lotus: A Poet's Rediscovery of Jewish Identity in Buddhist India*. San Francisco, Calif.: Harper Collins, 1995.

Kelley, Klara Bonsack, and Harris Francis. *Navajo Sacred Places*. Bloomington, Ind.: Indiana University Press, 1994.

Kellogg, Susan. *Law and the Transformation of Aztec Culture, 1500–1700*. Norman, Okla.: University of Oklahoma Press, 1995.

Kittredge, William. *Who Owns the West*. San Francisco, Calif.: Mercury House, 1996.

Kroeber, Theodora. *Ishi: Last of His Tribe*. New York, N.Y.: Bantam Books, 1973.

La Barre, Weston. *The Ghost Dance*. New York, N.Y.: Dell, 1972.

_____. *The Peyote Cult*. 5th ed. enlarged. Norman, Okla.: University of Oklahoma Press, 1989.

Lazarus, Edward. *Black Hills/White Justice: The Sioux Nation Versus the United States, 1775 to Present*. New York, N.Y.: HarperCollins, 1991.

Llewellyn, Karl N., and E. Adamson Hoebel. *The Cheyenne Way: Conflict and Case Law in Primitive Jurisprudence*. Norman, Okla.: University of Oklahoma Press, 1941.

Mankiller, Wilma, and Michael Wallis. *Mankiller, A Chief and Her People*. New York, N.Y.: St. Martin's Press, 1993.

Means, Russell. *Where White Men Fear to Tread: The Autobiography of Russell Means*. New York, N.Y.: St. Martin's Press, 1995.

Mendoza, Vincent L. *Son of Two Bloods*. Lincoln, Neb.: University of Nebraska Press, 1996.

Messengers of the Wind: Native American Women Tell Their Life Stories. Edited by Jane Katz. New York, N.Y.: Ballantine Books, 1995.

Minow, Martha. *Making All the Difference: Inclusion, Exclusion and American Law*. Ithaca, N.Y.: Cornell University Press, 1990.

Momaday, N. Scott. *House Made of Dawn*. New York, N.Y.: Harper & Row, 1968.

Native American Testimony: A Chronicle of Indian White Relations from Prophecy to the Present: 1492–1992. Edited by Peter Nabokov. New York, N.Y.: Viking, 1991.

Nierhardt, John G. *Black Elk Speaks: Being the Life Story of a Holy Man of the Oglala Sioux*. Reprint edition. Lincoln, Neb.: University of Nebraska Press, 1961.

Norhaus, Robert J. *Tipi Rings: A Chronicle of the Jicarilla Apache Land Claim*. Albuquerque, N.M.: Bow-Arrow Press, 1995.

Ortiz, Simon J. *From Sand Creek*. New York, N.Y.: Thunder's Mouth Press, 1981.

_____. *Woven Stone*. Tucson, Ariz.: University of Arizona Press, 1992.

O'Brien, Sharon. *American Indian Tribal Governments*. Norman, Okla.: University of Oklahoma Press, 1989.

Pommershein, Frank. *Braid of Feathers: American Indian Law and Contemporary Tribal Life*. Berkeley, Calif.: University of California Press, 1995.

Pratt, Mary Louise. *Imperial Eyes: Travel Writing and Transculturation*. New York, N.Y.: Routledge, 1992.

Prucha, Francis Paul. *American Indian Treaties: The History of a Political Anomaly*. Berkeley, Calif.: University of California Press, 1994.

Reckoning with the Dead: The Larsen Bay Repatriation and the Smithsonian Institution. Edited by Tamara L. Bray and Thomas W. Killion. Washington D.C.: Smithsonian Institution Press, 1994.

Religion in Native North America. Edited by Christopher Vecsey. Moscow, Ida.: University of Idaho Press, 1990.

Rhode, Deborah L. *Justice and Gender: Sex Discrimination and the Law.* Cambridge, Mass.: Harvard University Press, 1989.

Roscoe, Will. *The Zuni Man-Woman.* 1st ed. Albuquerque, N.M.: University of New Mexico Press, 1991.

Rosenthal, Harvey D. *Their Day in Court: A History of the Indian Claims Commission.* New York, N.Y.: Garland., 1990.

Schultes, Richard Evans, and A. Hofmann. *Plants of the Gods: Origins of Hallucinogenic Use.* New York, N.Y.: McGraw-Hill, 1979.

Scott, James C. *Domination and the Arts of Resistance: Hidden Transcripts.* New Haven, Conn.: Yale University Press, 1990.

Silko, Leslie Marmon. *Ceremony.* New York, N.Y.: Viking Press, 1977.

Skogen, Larry C. *Indian Depredations Claims, 1796–1920.* Norman, Okla.: University of Oklahoma Press, 1996.

Smith, Paul Chaat, and Robert Allen Warrior. *Like a Hurricane: The Indian Movement from Alcatraz to Wounded Knee.* New York, N.Y.: New Press; Distributed by W.W. Norton, 1996.

Stanndard, David E. *American Holocaust: The Conquest of the New World.* New York, N.Y.: Oxford University Press, 1992.

State of Native America: Genocide, Colonization, and Resistance, The. Edited by M. Annette Jaimes. Boston, Mass.: South End Press, 1992.

Steinmetz, Paul B. *Pipe, Bible, and Peyote Among the Oglala Lakota: A Study in Religious Identity.* Knoxville, Tenn.: University of Tennessee Press, 1990.

Stewart, Omer C. *Peyote Religion: A History.* Norman, Okla.: University of Oklahoma Press, 1987.

Sutton, Imre. *Indian Land Tenure: Biographical Essays and a Guide to the Literature.* New York, N.Y.: Clearwater Publishing Co., 1975.

Trails: Toward a New Western History. Edited by Patricia Nelson Limerick, Clyde A. Milner II, and Charles E. Rankin. Lawrence, Kan.: University of Kansas Press, 1991.

Trask, Haunani-Kay. *From a Native Daughter: Colonialism and Sovereignty in Hawaii.* Monroe, Maine: Common Courage Press, 1993.

Unrau, William E. *White Man's Wicked Water: The Alcohol Trade and Prohibition in Indian Country, 1802–1892.* Laurence, Kan.: University Press of Kansas, 1996.

Utley, Robert Marshall. *The Lance and the Shield: The Life and Times of Sitting Bull.* New York, N.Y.: Henry Holt, 1993.

Walters, Anna Lee. *The Spirit of Native America: Beauty and Mysticism in American Indian Art.* Del Mar, Calif.: McQuiston & Partners, Inc., 1989.

Warrior, Robert Allen. *Tribal Secrets: Recovering American Indian Intellectual Traditions.* Minneapolis, Minn.: University of Minnesota Press, 1994.

Washburn, Wilcomb E. *Red Man's Land/White Man's Law: A Study of the Past and Present Status of the American Indian.* New York, N.Y.: Charles Scribner's Sons, 1971.

Wasson, Robert Gordon. *The Wondrous Mushroom: Mycolatry in Mesoamerica.* New York, N.Y.: McGraw-Hill Book Co., 1980.

Wasson, Robert Gordon, G. Cowan, F. Cowan, and W. Rhodes. *Maria Sabina and her Mazatec Mushroom Velada*. New York, N.Y.: Harcourt Brace Jovanovich, 1974.

Western Women: Their Land, Their Lives. Edited by Lillian Schlissel, Vicki L. Ruiz, and Janice Monk. Albuquerque, N.M.: University of New Mexico Press, 1988.

Wilkinson, Charles F. *American Indians, Time, and the Law: Native Societies in a Modern Constitutional Democracy*. New Haven, Conn.: Yale University Press, 1987.

Wilkinson, Charles F., David Getches, and Robert A. Williams, Jr. *Cases and Materials on Federal Indian Law*. 3rd ed. St. Paul, Minn.: West Publishing Co., 1993.

Williams, Robert A., Jr. *Linking Arms Together: American Indian Treaty Visions of Law and Peace, 1600–1800*. New York, N.Y.: Oxford University Press, 1997.

———. *The American Indian in Western Legal Thought: Discourses of Conquest*. New York, N.Y.: Oxford University Press, 1990.

Williams, Walter L. *The Spirit and the Flesh: Sexual Diversity in American Indian Culture*. Boston, Mass.: Beacon Press, 1986.

Zuni and the Courts: A Struggle for Sovereign Land Rights. Edited by E. Richard Hart. Lawrence, Kan.: University of Kansas Press, 1995.

ABOUT THE CONTRIBUTORS

SHERMAN ALEXIE is a member of the Spokane/Coeur d'Alene Tribe. Alexie, who has published extensively and won numerous national awards and prizes, was picked as one of *Granta* magazine's "Twenty Best American Novelists under the Age of Forty." His first collection of short stories, *The Lone Ranger and Tonto Fistfight in Heaven* (Atlantic Monthly Press, 1993) received the 1994 Great Lakes College Association Award for Best First Book of Fiction, and was a citation winner for the 1994 PEN/Hemingway Award for Best First Fiction. Alexie's first novel, *Reservation Blues* (Atlantic Monthly Press, 1995), was selected as a 1995 *Library Journal's* Best Fiction of the Year Finalist, a 1995 *Booklist* Editor's Choice Award for Fiction, and was also awarded a 1996 American Book Award from the Before Columbus Foundation.

ROBERT E. BIEDER is Visiting Associate Professor in the School of Public and Environmental Affairs, Indiana University, Bloomington. Bieder was a Fulbright Professor at the University of Tampere in Finland in 1997–1998, and he has also held Fulbrights to universities in Germany and Hungary. Bieder is the author of numerous books and articles on the repatriation issue and on American Indian history and cultures.

CHARLOTTE BLACK ELK is Oglala Lakota. She was the moving force behind the Chair of the Board for the Oglala Lakota Legal Rights Fund, the organization that in 1982 carried out the Lakota, Dakota, and Cheyenne oral history project, which is archived at the Oglala Lakota Community College.

SILVESTER J. BRITO is an associate professor in the English Department at the University of Wyoming, Laramie, where he is a poet and folklorist. Brito was the recipient of the prestigious Ford and Newberry Fellowships, and he was a Danforth Fellow. Brito is a direct descendent of Comanche and Tarascan Indians with ancestral roots in Mexico.

JACK CAMPISI testified as an expert witness in the *Mashpee Tribe v. New Seabury Corp.* land claims case.

JO CARRILLO is a professor of law at the University of California, Hastings College of the Law.

GENEVIEVE CHATO is a practicing attorney in Kayenta, Arizona.

JAMES CLIFFORD is a professor in the History of Consciousness Program, a founding director of the Center for Cultural Studies at the University of California, Santa Cruz, and author of *The Predicament of Culture: 20th Century Ethnography, Literature and Art* (Harvard University Press, 1988).

FELIX S. COHEN (d. 1953) was the principal drafter of the Indian Reorganizaton Act of 1934, a litigator, a Special Assistant to the Attorney General, and Associate Solicitor of the Department of the Interior. Cohen was a prodigious scholar in the field of federal Indian law. Cohen originally compiled the *Handbook of Federal Indian Law*, which had its genesis in a forty-six volume collection of federal laws and treaties and was first published in 1942 under the auspices of the United States Department of the Interior.

CHRISTINE CONTE worked at the Old Pueblo Museum in Tucson, Arizona, at the time her article was written.

VINE DELORIA, JR. (Standing Rock Sioux) is a professor of history at the University of Colorado at Boulder. His publications, awards, research grants, honors, and lectures are far too numerous and too longstanding to list. Without a doubt, Professor Deloria is one of the leading scholars in the fields of both federal Indian Law and Native American Studies. Deloria's most recent book is *Red Earth, White Lies* (Scribners, 1995).

WALTER R. ECHOHAWK is a Staff Attorney at the Native American Rights Fund in Boulder, Colorado.

WENDY ESPELAND is an Assistant Professor of Sociology at Northwestern University, specializing in Organizational Culture, Environmental Politics, and the Construction of Political, Legal, and Professional Identities.

HARRIS FRANCIS is a Navajo, Tachii'nii clan born for Tabaaha clan, who grew up on the Navajo Reservation speaking Navajo and observing traditions in daily use. He is an American Indian Cultural Rights Protection Consultant and is coauthor of several articles on Navajo cultural rights and sacred places.

RAYNA GREEN (Cherokee) is currently Director of the American Indian Program at the National Museum of American History, Smithsonian Institution. Green is the author of numerous books and essays, and is the director of three award-winning documentary films. She is well known for her work in museum exhibition, as well as for her performance art and media production.

KENN HARPER is an amateur historian. Harper owns and operates Blacklead Books in Iqaluit, Northwest Territories, Canada. Harper's book on Minik eventually resulted in the American Museum of Natural History sending the bones of four Eskimos back to Qaanaaq, Greenland, for burial.

FRANCIS G. HUTCHINS devoted the first half of his career to the study of South Asia, during which time he wrote two books on the history of India. He has spent the last 20 years researching Native American issues. He is currently working on a book entitled *The Constitution and the Tribes*.

KLARA BONSACK KELLEY is a consulting ethnologist who has lived and studied in Navajo communities since the mid-1970s. Kelley has coauthored numerous articles on ethnoarcheology.

WILLIAM KITTREDGE grew up on the MC Ranch in southeastern Oregon, where he lived until he was 35. His books include *Hole in the Sky*, *Owning it All*, and *We Are Not in This Together*. He now teaches at the University of Montana.

EDMUND J. LADD, a Shiwi (Zuni), works at the Museum of New Mexico, Laboratory of Anthropology in Santa Fe. Mr. Ladd grew up at the Pueblo of Zuni. He is of the Coyote Clan and a child of the Deer Clan. He is a member of the U/tsa na:que (Small Group Kiva).

ARVOL LOOKING HORSE was the Keeper of the Sacred Buffalo Calf Pipe for the Lakota people at the time his inteview was taken in 1982.

NANCY OESTREICH LURIE, an eminent anthropologist, is now retired from her second career as curator and head of the anthropology section of the Milwaukee Public Museum. Lurie's first career began in 1947 at the University of Wisconsin, and by 1954, she began work as an expert witness for Indian petitioners before the U.S. Indian Claims Commission, eventually testifying in seven different cases. Lurie later joined the University of Michigan faculty, and, while there, published *Mountain Wolf Woman*, an autobiography of a Winnebago woman's life (1961). Lurie has numerous publications and awards to her name, including having been elected to the presidency of the American Anthropological Association (AAA) in 1982.

WILMA MANKILLER is the former Principal Chief of the Cherokee Nation (acting, 1985 to 1987; elected 1987 to 1994).

MELANIE MCCOY is an assistant professor in the Political Science Department at Texas A&M University in Commerce, Texas.

HANK MESHORER is Special Litigation Counsel for the Department of Justice. He served as Chief of the Indian Resources Section and Natural Resources Division at the U.S. Department of Justice from 1982 to 1995. From 1970 to 1980, Mr. Meshorer served as a senior trial attorney for the Justice Department, where he litigated some of the most significant environmental cases of that decade.

NELL JESSUP NEWTON is a professor of law at American University. She has written numerous articles in the field of federal Indian law and has coauthored *American Indian Law*, one of the two casebooks available in federal Indian law. She is one of the editors-in-chief of a project to revise Felix Cohen's *Handbook of Federal Indian Law*.

OMER C. STEWART (d. 1991) was Professor Emeritus with the Anthropology Department at the University of Colorado, Boulder.

RENNARD STRICKLAND is Dean and Philip H. Knight Professor of Law at the University of Oregon. He teaches comparative law, Indian law, jurisprudence, law and anthropology, and legal history. Dean Strickland has taught at numerous law schools throughout the country, and has served as Dean at Southern Illinois and Oklahoma City University and as Acting Dean at the University of Tulsa. He was President of the Assocation of American Law Schools in 1994.

DOROTHEA THEODORATUS has been actively involved for 35 years in Native American concerns and issues and has developed a particular interest in sacred lands and traditional property rights of Native American peoples.

JACK F. TROPE is an attorney in the firm of Sant' Angelo & Trope, in Cranford, New Jersey. Trope has written numerous articles on Native American issues, and specifically on repatriation and sacred site protection issues and also litigates in these issues.

WILCOMB E. WASHBURN (d. 1997) was a historian and executive of the Smithsonian Institution in Washington D.C., where he was the director of its American Studies Program for 30 years. He was former president of the American Society of Ethnohistory, the American Studies Association, the Society for the History of Discoveries, and the Columbia Historical Society (now the Historical Society of Washington).

ROBERT A. WILLIAMS, JR., (Lumbee) is a Professor of Law and American Indian Studies at the University of Arizona. He is the author of the award-winning book, *The American Indian in Western Legal Thought: The Discourses of Conquest* (Oxford University Press, 1990), and many other leading works in the field of Indian law and policy. Williams' most recent book is *Linking Arms Together: American Indian Treaty Visions of Law & Peace, 1600–1800*.

JO ANN WOODSUM is an assistant professor of American Studies at the University of California, Santa Cruz, where she teaches courses on the social construction of race, federal Indian law, and native women. She is currently working on a study of representation of Pueblo peoples in U.S. law, anthropology, photography, and popular culture.

GLORIA VALENCIA-WEBER is a professor of law and director of the Indian Law Program at the University of New Mexico School of Law.

CHRISTINE P. ZUNI is a professor of law and director of the Southwest Clinic at the University of New Mexico School of Law.

INDEX